Modeling Archaeological Site Burial in Southern Michigan

Environmental Research Series, No. 1

David L. Ruggles, Series Editor

Modeling Archaeological Site Burial in Southern Michigan

A Geoarchaeological Synthesis

G. William Monaghan and William A. Lovis, with contributions by Michael J. Hambacher

Michigan State University Press
East Lansing

This research was funded through federal Enhancement Funds provided by
the Federal Highway Administration and a match provided by the
Michigan Department of Transportation.

♾ The paper used in this publication meets the minimum requirements of
ANSI/NISO Z39.48–1992 (R 1997) (Permanence of Paper).

Michigan State University Press
East Lansing, Michigan 48823–5245

Printed and bound in the United States of America.

11 10 09 08 07 06 05   1 2 3 4 5 6 7 8 9 10

LIBRARY OF CONGRESS CATALOGING-IN-PUBLICATION DATA

Monaghan, G. William.
    Exploration for buried archaeological sites in the Great Lakes Region :
modeling archaeological site burial in southern Michigan / G. William Monaghan
and William A. Lovis, with Michael J. Hambacher.
        p. cm.
    Includes bibliographical references and index.
    ISBN 0-87013-738-7 (pbk. : alk. paper)
    1. Paleo-Indians—Great Lakes Region. 2. Indians of North America—Great Lakes
Region—Antiquities. 3. Archaeological geology—Great Lakes Region. 4. Excavations
(Archaeology)—Geographic information systems—Great Lakes Region. 5. Great Lakes
Region—Antiquities. I. Lovis, William A. II. Hambacher, Michael J. III. Title.
    E78.G7M65 2005
    977'.01–dc22   2004016995

Enviornmental Research Series, vol. 1
David L. Ruggles, Series Editor

Michigan State University Press is a member of the Green Press Initiative and is
committed to developing and encouraging ecologically responsible publishing
practices. For more information about the Green Press Initiative and the use of
recycled paper in book publishing, please visit www.greenpressinitiative.org.

Cover design by Erin Kirk New
Book design by Em Studio Inc.
Cover image of Michigan courtesy of The Tropical Rain Forest Information Center,
a member of NASA's Federation of Earth Science Information Partners, at the
Center for Global Change and Earth Observations, Michigan State University.
Cover photo courtesy of William A. Lovis.

Visit Michigan State University Press on the World Wide Web at
www.msupress.msu.edu

Contents

Figures

TABLES

ACKNOWLEDGMENTS

Large research projects always benefit from the interaction, support, and advice of a variety of individuals and institutions. This project is no exception.

The authors wish to thank several groups and individuals for their assistance in providing funding and support during various portions of this research. First, we must acknowledge the Michigan Department of Transportation (MDOT) for not only funding this project through its Inter-State Transportation Enhancement Act (ISTEA) program but also for its ongoing support of numerous other transportation-related cultural resource management (CRM) projects during the past 20 years. In particular, their support of large corridor projects, such as the US-31 and US-23 expansion projects, has been invaluable. We especially acknowledge David Ruggles for his unflagging support for the routine incorporation of both geoarchaeology and other multidisciplinary approaches in MDOT archaeological compliance research. In addition, both the Office of the State Archaeologist and the State Historic Preservation Office of the Michigan Historical Center opened their files and libraries of published and unpublished documents and maps to us on numerous occasions. The cooperation of John Halsey, state archaeologist, has been central in this regard. Of particular note is the assistance of Barbara Mead, assistant state archaeologist, without whom we would have had substantial difficulty in compiling the necessary data for this project and bringing it to timely completion.

Several private CRM firms have assisted and encouraged our research over the years. Notable in this regard are Commonwealth Cultural Resources Group, Inc., and Great Lakes Research Associates, Inc. We particularly acknowledge Mark Branstner, James Robertson, Donald Weir, and Steven Demeter for their support and professional discussions concerning the location and discovery of buried archaeological resources. The late Earl Prahl of Caminos Associates, Inc. provided us with many stimulating late-night discussions about the roles of geology and geoarchaeology in archaeological research. Recognition of the importance of thorough research design and the incorporation of deep testing as a routine procedure in CRM surveys on the part of such forward-thinking, public-spirited corporations as Great Lakes Gas Pipeline Company, Vector Pipeline Company, and GM-environmental are greatly appreciated. The CRM work performed on projects sponsored by these and other companies has been central to providing the data for this research.

The majority of the research performed for this project was undertaken with the support, facilities, and personnel at Michigan State University, particularly through the Michigan State University Museum and the Department of Anthropology. Lynne Goldstein, chair of the Department of Anthropology, and

C. Kurt Dewhurst, museum director, are thanked for their assistance and support. Both computer support and project space were provided by the Michigan State University Consortium for Archaeological Research. As always, this research has benefited greatly from our many years of discussion with Margaret Holman and Professor Emeritus Charles Cleland.

This project could not have been brought to completion without the assistance of our research assistants. Brian Albright was responsible for all of the Geographic Information System (GIS) and data-management aspects of the project. Leah Merz had responsibility for compiling the primary data employed during our analysis. It is safe to say that without them, this report would not be as comprehensive. We thank them for their assistance.

In addition to Michigan State University and the private CRM firms previously mentioned, this work relied on information provided by several other educational institutions in Michigan. Of particular note are the University of Michigan Museum of Anthropology, Western Michigan University, and Grand Valley State University. We particularly thank Janet Brashler, Grand Valley State University, for allowing us access to unpublished manuscripts and data from the Prison Farm site.

Technical reading of the manuscript prior to publication was undertaken by Alan Arbogast, Michigan State University Department of Geography, whose detailed commentary has both enhanced the logic and substance of our discussion and made it more readable.

Given the many individuals and institutions to whom we are indebted, we trust that we have not inadvertently omitted any who assisted us with this research. As always, we accept responsibility for any errors of substance or interpretation that might arise.

Part One

Geological and Archaeological Background

CHAPTER ONE

Introduction

The State of Deep Testing in Michigan

Project Background, Rationale, and Goals

Over the past 10 to 15 years, geoarchaeological investigations have become generally accepted as an important component of cultural resource management (CRM) projects throughout the Great Lakes region. This is particularly true for the discovery of deeply buried and stratified archaeological sites during Phase I survey. Just what is meant by "deeply buried" archaeological deposits, however, is variable. In Michigan, deep testing for archaeological deposits refers to the discovery of any material that occurs below the surface and cannot be discovered by normal, ordinary methods usually employed for site discovery. Essentially, these are archaeological sites that lack surface expression and have been buried by either natural or cultural processes. In practice, such sites can be quite shallowly buried and often occur just below the normal plow zone or extend just beyond the limits of hand shovel testing (i.e., about 25–30 cm). The Weber I (Lovis ed. 1989), Bear Creek, and Shiawassee River (Branstner and Hambacher eds. 1994) sites all lie buried within 25–30 cm of ground surface within river valleys near Saginaw Bay. Sites can also be relatively deeply buried. For example, the Converse (Hambacher et al. 2003) and EPA-CERT (Demeter et al. 1994) sites both were discovered under nearly 2 m of historic urban fills. The process of discovering buried archaeological sites also refers to deeply buried components within a site, which even though deeply buried may have surface expression. In places, the Marquette Viaduct locale of the Fletcher site in Bay City extended to the surface but also included stratified components that lay nearly 2 m deep (Lovis et al. 1996; Lovis ed. 2002; Monaghan 2002).

Unfortunately, even though most archaeologists and regulators recognize the importance of deep site discovery, regulatory guidance in Michigan continues to lag behind guidelines in other studies. As yet, guidelines that outline where and when testing for buried sites is necessary have not been established in Michigan. In addition, neither acceptable methods nor professional standards and criteria have been specified. Sadly, for noninterstate projects in Michigan, the decisions about where and how to explore for buried cultural resources rest almost exclusively with CRM firms that bid on the project and not with the appropriate state agencies. Consequently, geoarchaeological methods have only been haphazardly applied to CRM projects in Michigan. Although many firms have been visionary and included geoarchaeological work in their projects, others have ignored deep testing, relying instead on "shovel testing a little bit deeper" along floodplains. This situation not only inadequately protects our shared cultural resources but also ultimately places those firms that desire to do a complete job at a competitive disadvantage. An important goal of this project, therefore, is to remedy this situation by aiding the Michigan Department of Transportation (MDOT) and the State Historic Preservation Office (SHPO) to establish guidelines, methods, and minimum reporting standards for deep testing in Michigan.

The overall goal referred to above will be accomplished by three main components, of which this component of the project is the first. As the first stage of the project, the main aim of Part I of this book will be to assemble the disparate pieces of preexisting deep-testing data accumulated throughout Michigan over the past few decades into an integrated monograph. It will not only serve as a single source that summarizes the results of more than two decades of deep testing but will also describe the background geological processes that control the burial and preservation of such sites. In addition, a Geographic Information System (GIS) has been developed as a companion to this volume. This GIS shows the relationship of deep-test location and associated or nearby archaeological sites with various geographical, geological, physiographical, and other natural and cultural spatial information deemed appropriate. Finally, a second part of this volume and related synthetic GIS overlay will be produced that integrates the information in this volume and the GIS mapping program to predict areas of high, moderate, and low potential for buried resources in the southern Lower Peninsula of Michigan.

The emphasis of this book and overall project is to integrate earth science information and methods with the more traditional North American anthropological focus of archaeology. This approach underlines the importance of a sound multidisciplinary approach to archaeological research. This emphasis is also reflected in the structure of the monograph. We will first present information regarding the geological and environmental history of the Great Lakes region. This will focus mainly on lake-level history for ancestral predecessors to the Great Lakes as well as related environmental and climate change during the past 12,000 to 13,000 years. This period encompasses the end of the last phase of glaciation, referred to as the late Wisconsinan, and the entire Holocene. It was chosen not only because it covers the main phase of human settlement in North America but also because deglaciation and the physiographic alteration in the region set the stage for the development of the modern environment of the Great Lakes region.

The geological and environmental background is important because it provides the context within which human settlement patterns must exist. Thus, using this background as a framework, an outline of the archaeological record of Native American occupation of the region will be presented. It will focus on the general sequence of changes in the cultural and settlement systems, particularly as they relate to the environmental history.

Finally, by integrating the environmental and archaeological backgrounds, we will describe the types of geological and sedimentological processes that promote archaeological site burial in certain preferred settings. We will also describe the aspects of Holocene climate history that enhance site burial during specific time periods and how these factors affect the human settlement systems in the region. Thus, by integrating the geological and environmental information into regional depositional models that describe processes, periods, and depositional environments that promote archaeological site burial, we can begin to model the buried archaeological sites as a predictable resource.

Although this study focuses on deep testing for archaeological resources in Michigan, it has wider relevance not only in the Great Lakes region but also throughout the northeastern and midwestern United States and most of eastern Canada, because much of this region shares a similar late Wisconsinan and Holocene history of environmental transformation as well as common, often related, archaeological traditions. They have experienced extensive continental glaciation and thus share the suite of landforms common to such regions. In addition, their environmental histories also share similar developmental, secular changes since deglaciation. They have experienced equivalent climatic cycles from the early-mid-Holocene mild hypsithermal and subsequent neo-glacial cooling to the more recent climatic alteration from the mild conditions of the Medieval Warm and succeeding harsh, cool, wet Little Ice Age. Moreover, the geological processes outlined for Michigan apply over most of the humid eastern half of North America. For example, the general fluvial processes that affect rivers in Michigan also affect those in Illinois and Ontario. From a CRM standpoint, the issues raised in this study and the solutions and recommendations proposed also generally apply throughout eastern North America. For example, the tendency of humans to focus settlement along fluvial systems, shorelines, and wetlands has meant that accelerated deposition during moister time periods commonly buried and preserved these settlements. The fact that such landforms generally remained the focus of settlement throughout the Holocene resulted in the preservation of stacked occupations that often span various cultures of the middle and late Holocene.

Historical Perspective on the Uses of Geoarchaeology and Deep Testing in Michigan

The use of geoarchaeology and archaeological geology (Rapp and Gifford eds. 1985) in Michigan has taken several forms of interaction between archaeology, geology, and geography over the last half century. Historically, this interaction has been a developmental process, which has been presented in other discussions of regional research design (Lovis, Holman, Monaghan, and Skowronek 1994; Lovis and O'Shea 1994; Monaghan and Hayes 1997, 1998). Perhaps the first and among the most overt of these interactions was the systematic application of macroregional geological models of postglacial lake-level adjustment, fluctuation, and lake terrace/strand formation to archaeological problems. These models have been keyed to two primary sets of causal processes: outlet downcutting and/or uplift and climatic control. Both approaches have been applied to further an understanding of the relationship between changing Great Lakes lacustrine and littoral environments, geochronology, and transformations in various aspects of prehistoric social systems, but they have been primarily keyed to issues of Paleo-Indian chronology (Greenman and Stanley 1940, 1941, 1943; Greenman 1943; Mason 1958; Quimby 1958, 1963; Farrand 1977).

Aspects of geochronological modeling in particular rapidly became an integral part of archaeological research design in Michigan and were soon applied to later Archaic and Woodland time periods (Mason 1965; Papworth 1967). Because of the success of the approach, it is often prominent in some of the most influential summary treatises on Great Lakes and Michigan prehistory, including George Quimby's *Indian Life in the Upper Great Lakes* (1960), James Fitting's *The Archaeology of Michigan* (1970, 1975b), Ronald Mason's *Great Lakes Archaeology* (1981), and contributions to John Halsey's *Retrieving Michigan's Buried Past* (ed. 1999; Larsen 1999a).

In large part, the macroregional perspective that earth sciences brought to archaeological research provided the wherewithal by which to interpret the sequential ages of sites situated on prominent landforms that were keyed to pro- and postglacial lake stages of different age and level in each of the Great Lakes' drainage basins (Superior, Michigan, Huron, Erie, and Ontario). This has historically also been a highly interactive exercise between geology and archaeology, as witnessed by the early collaborations of Greenman and Stanley (1940, 1941, 1943), and has energized both disciplines through the symbiosis. The process depended on geologists to identify landforms, such as lake terraces on a larger regional landscape, and then the archaeologists provided dated materials from human occupations on these landforms that assisted in development of the regional geochronology. These early studies largely focused on the period before 3000 B.P. The cumulative results then allowed for the sequencing of undated occupations on landforms of similar altitude, providing a *terminus ante quem* for the archaeological materials. Some would consider this last activity a minor but acceptable methodological and logical tautology, a topic that will not be further addressed here.

A second, and for our purposes highly significant, use of geoarchaeology began during the 1960s in the Great Lakes: the analysis and interpretation of sometimes deep and complex archaeological site stratigraphy in both eolian and alluvial contexts. While at times coupled with macroregional models of lake-level fluctuation and uplift, the goal of these inquiries was rather different, being keyed to an understanding of the changing depositional environments of occupation sites as they related to the formation of the features upon and/or in which the sites were situated. Thus, understanding the nature of site formation processes was central to this kind of analysis. Such studies varied greatly in quality because they were sometimes undertaken by archaeologists with very limited training in geology or geomorphology, while other studies were led by geoarchaeologists or archaeologists with extensive geological training. The better studies were not merely descriptive statements of site stratigraphy but analyses of process. Among the more influential of these early studies are the analyses of the Porte des Mort and Mero sites on the Door Peninsula of Wisconsin (Mason 1965), the study of site formation processes at the Juntunen site on Bois Blanc Island in the Straits of Mackinac (McPherron 1967), and Speth's reconstruction of the depositional sequences of the Schultz site at Green Point in Saginaw County (Speth 1972).

The outcome of the detailed use of site-level geoarchaeological reconstruction was that by the 1960s, Michigan archaeologists were fully aware that deeply buried archaeological deposits existed in the state. Moreover, these detailed studies showed that the location and burial of such sites could be systematically accounted for by multiple formation processes that involved both cultural and natural processes. These processes have been itemized by Lovis and O'Shea

(1994:109–110) as "regular and recognizable feature(s) of the archaeological landscape that warranted systematic attention." They include such factors as: alluviation in fluvial contexts, eolian activity in coastal contexts, transgressive lacustrine events in riverine and coastal contexts, and the direct and indirect effects of modern land use in a variety of different contexts. Despite this recognition, however, change was not readily evident in regional research designs, which viewed deeply buried archaeological sites as rare phenomena in contrast to the more visible components of the lake level sequences such as uplifted lake-front terraces.

It took almost 20 years for archaeologists in Michigan to systematize their knowledge of deep site potential and operationalize it as field research strategy. This perceptual transformation came with the sequential publication of two seminal works on the subject. Christopher Peebles (1978), who came to the University of Michigan with substantial experience in the southeastern United States, where deeply stratified floodplain site deposits were common, was among the first to recognize in print the potential of regional alluvial processes to preserve deeply stratified floodplain deposits in the Saginaw Valley of Michigan. Concurrent with Peebles's work, the Conference on Michigan Archaeology (COMA) received a National Register Matching Grant from the Michigan History Division, Michigan Department of State, to develop a planning document for Michigan archaeology. This was published as *Major Problem Orientations in Michigan Archaeology 1980–1984* (Mueller 1980), a completion report submitted by Commonwealth Associates, Inc. under contract with COMA. Other works soon followed. One of the most significant to the current discussion is the contribution of Curtis Larsen (1980), then of Commonwealth Associates, Inc., who reported on an early radiocarbon date and secondary archaeological deposits at the Kantzler site (20BY30) in Bay City (Larsen and Demeter 1979). This revealed that archaeological deposits in coastal environments were sometimes preserved on middle Holocene surfaces that were buried during the Nipissing transgression and that these deposits warranted systematic investigation.

While Peebles's and Larsen's work did not generate instant change in archaeological research designs, their successes lay in two other linked arenas. The first, and arguably more important of these, was to radically alter the vision of what geoarchaeology and geology could do for archaeology at a regional scale. Rather than view these specialties primarily as site-level applications, these discussions broadened the regional application of geoarchaeology to include site discovery and predicting the locations of buried surfaces that might preserve archaeological deposits.

Shortly after Peebles and Larsen expounded their views on buried site potential in the state, a major transformation occurred in the manner that compliance-related work, particularly site discovery or Phase I research, was conducted in alluvial settings. State Archaeologist John Halsey, of the Bureau of History, recognized that deep testing was essential to adequately assess the archaeological record and began to call for archaeological deep testing in those situations thought to possess deep site potential. "Deep" in this case referred to sites that were buried below the plow zone and generally exhibited little or no surface expression. Prompt payoffs from this altered strategy came with the discovery by the Saginaw Archaeological Commission of deep, stratified, alluvial deposits at the Dehmel Road Bridge Replacement in Frankenmuth (Brunett 1981a, 1981c). These buried deposits ranged in age from Middle Archaic through late nineteenth century (Lovis ed. 1989; see a more detailed discussion of the Weber I site in chapter 5). Significantly, there were no surface materials to reveal that these buried deposits existed, underscoring the fact that discovery methods for shallow sites would not have been successful at locating the site. This revelation underscored the need for systematic application of deep testing as a discovery device at the regional if not statewide level. Given the nature of funding for archaeological exploration, deep-testing strategies were eventually operationalized largely through compliance rather than through academically based research.

Large-scale implementation of such strategies at a macro regional level came with the proposal for a gas transmission pipeline running across the state from Duluth, Minnesota, to Port Huron, Michigan. The collective of state and federal bureaucracies, environmental planning firms, archaeologists, and the Great Lakes Gas Transmission Company all recognized that the site discovery phase of this project required deep testing in a variety of eolian and alluvial deposits along the proposed right of way. The research design for this project was developed by the present authors (Lovis 1990c; Monaghan 1990a) and implemented by Great Lakes Archaeological Research, Inc. Unlike prior research, the design for this work emphasized the reconstruction of regional processes such as depositional histories, alluviation rates, and the delineation of regionally pervasive buried soil horizons that might represent early stable surfaces potentially subject to human occupation. Additionally, based on the geological history, areas that were highly likely to contain archaeological deposits buried by alluvial and lacustrine events were delineated and tested.

The results of this field strategy firmly convinced both compliance agencies and researchers that deep-testing approaches were essential to an adequate understanding of the archaeological record in the state. Buried archaeological sites were discovered under as much as 2 m of sediments on the floodplain of the Saginaw basin (Branstner and Hambacher 1994; Dobbs and Murray 1993). Predictably, given the prior experience from the Kantzler and Weber I sites mentioned above, some of the sites dated to the mid-Holocene, which was the initial focus of the testing strategy. Unexpectedly, however, deposits of both earlier and later ages were also discovered. These included late Wisconsinan and early Holocene peat deposits underlying an eolian sequence associated with Archaic occupation materials, revealing the potential for material of very early age.

Perhaps even more significant, this work underscored the effects of historic flooding and sedimentation in the Saginaw River valley, a phenomenon recognized by Gary Wright almost 20 years earlier (Wright 1972). Several Late Woodland sites were recovered below up to 2 m of sediments, suggesting that land-use practices such as lumbering and agriculture since the mid-nineteenth century had altered the sediment load of the basin, allowing for the mantling of relatively recent sites. Sawed stumps along the Bad River, as well as a nineteenth-century horizon at the Weber I site, furthered this perspective to include the burial of historic Euro-American sites. These multiple revelations at least partially explained the lack of visible archaeological sites on the floodplains of the more evolved drainage systems of southern Lower Michigan, except in situations where raised eolian landforms were present.

In the past decade, deep testing at the project-specific and regional scale has become more commonplace as a discovery technique for locations with potential for buried soil surfaces. This phenomenon has resulted in the accumulation of vast amounts of information from locales producing archaeological deposits, as well as from locales that have proven culturally sterile but nonetheless yielded systematic geological and geomorphological information about depositional sequences, geochronology, and regional site formation processes. Given the project-specific and compliance-oriented aspects of such research, however, this has not resulted in a uniformly distributed set of data; rather, the information is skewed toward regions undergoing rapid redevelopment utilizing federal monies or requiring federal permits or licenses. Nonetheless, the cumulative effect is at a stage that allows for regional synthesis with varying degrees of precision.

While not the focus of this discussion, it would be remiss not to address the issue of deep testing for site discovery and reconstruction of depositional sequences in urban or developed environments. Here, human land use has resulted in the preservation of invisible and deeply buried surfaces, particularly in riverbank and floodplain context. This phenomenon was noted in the 1970s at the Kantzler site in Bay City by Larsen (Larsen and Demeter 1978) but only sporadically applied in the 1980s. In brief, multiple rebuilding episodes and the use of landfill to render otherwise unusable land suitable for occupation have resulted in the deep burial of both prehistoric and historic intact soil surfaces. In fact, archaeological testing in urban settings shows that in low areas adjacent to waterfronts, extensive filling was commonly the first modification made to the land surface by Euro-American settlers. Filling, rather than cutting, predominated. Moreover, foundation preparation for even multistory buildings was often minimal; trenching, because it was often done by hand, was as narrow and shallow as possible (Lovis 2004).

Because these notions had become increasingly accepted by the 1990s, agencies began to routinely include deep testing as part of archaeological explorations of urban environments. Not surprisingly, once begun, deep testing in urban settings has resulted in significant site discoveries. Key examples of the results of such strategies include the Center for Environmental Research Training (CERT) project in Bay City conducted by CCRG, Inc., which recovered intact precontact soil surfaces with late prehistoric occupation under better than 5 m of fill on the east bank of the Saginaw River in Bay City (Demeter et al. 1994); the Liberty Bridge Replacement Project in Bay City, undertaken by Michigan State University, which recovered Late Woodland materials on intact surfaces buried under 2 m of nineteenth- and twentieth-century fill (Lovis ed. 1993); and the Campau House in Detroit, another CCRG, Inc. project, which found intact prehistoric and early historic settler occupation under riverbank fills on the Detroit River (Demeter and Weir 1983). The most recent of these finds is the discovery of an intact "midden" associated with the Converse Mounds (20KT2) along the Grand River in downtown Grand Rapids (Hambacher et al. 2003).

Better than half a century of sometimes faltering steps have brought Michigan archaeology to the point where geoarchaeology and geoarchaeologists are routinely incorporated into site- and regional-level research designs. This process has resulted in the recognition of entirely new and unknown suites of information about the historic and prehistoric past, as well as the long-term and short-term geological processes responsible for the formation of the landforms past people utilized and occupied. The scope of such interdisciplinary research has likewise been transformed, from that of idiosyncratic descriptive applications in project-specific contexts to an increasing awareness of regional-level applications and an emphasis on formation and depositional processes.

The Current State of Deep Testing in Michigan

As the above discussion points out, most of the archaeological studies and surveys that involved deep testing in Michigan are related to compliance-oriented projects. This is a direct result of funding realities for modern archaeology. Moreover, only in the past two decades has deep testing been routinely incorporated in the scopes of work for these projects. Indeed, with the notable examples mentioned above, most of these studies have been local in scope and commonly focused on a single river crossing, such as bridge replacements or similar projects. In a few instances, some deep-test projects also targeted paleo-shorelines in addition to fluvial landforms. As a consequence of their small scope and often disappointing outcomes, the results of these studies have seldom been integrated into either regional archaeological settlement perspectives or even regional Holocene depositional histories. In fact, because the discovery of buried archaeological resources is relatively rare, the data (photographs, field notes, etc.) from reports and projects that did not find archaeological sites is often buried in limited-distribution, hard-to-find completion reports and not generally incorporated into regional summaries. This is unfortunate not only because negative information about buried archaeological sites can be just as significant as site discovery but also because a wealth of valuable information concerning Holocene depositional sequences, lake-level, and related environmental change is being squandered. Just as significant from a management perspective, however, this data constitutes the basis for development of a predictive buried site location model. Application of such a model could allow more rational, targeted, and productive deep testing.

All of this is not to say that deep testing has been generally wasteful, poorly implemented, or underreported. As mentioned above, many important sites have been discovered during Phase I deep testing of CRM surveys. For example, during the Great Lakes Gas Transmission Pipeline (GLGTP) study, whose design was mentioned above (Lovis 1990c; Monaghan 1990a), four buried archaeological sites were discovered along the seven rivers sampled in the southern Saginaw Bay region (Monaghan 1990a, 1990b, 1995a, 1995b; Monaghan and Schaetzl 1994). Each site was deemed significant enough to require Phase III data recovery. Given the relatively small amount of floodplain actually sampled during the GLGTP study, such a large number of discovered sites is significant. It not only suggests that buried archaeological components may be more common along many of the streams in Michigan than suspected, but it also demonstrates that traditional methods of locating sites (i.e., surface visibility coupled with shallow shovel testing) are probably inadequate to locate a whole population of sites. In addition to the GLGTP study, several other notable, well-designed, interdisciplinary CRM projects have been undertaken. These larger, regional-scale surveys, which were related to the construction of either interstate hydrocarbon transmission pipelines (i.e., GLGTP, Vector, Tristate) or statewide highway construction projects (i.e., US-31 in Allegan, Ottawa, and Muskegon counties and US-23 in Arenac and Iosco counties), are models of how sound deep testing can produce excellent results. Data collected during either the deep-test or data-recovery portions of these projects has led to several academic publications (e.g., Monaghan, Lovis, and Fay 1986; Lovis, Holman, Monaghan and Skowronek 1994; Lovis et al. 1996; Monaghan and Hayes 1997, 1998). Collectively, these studies provide the beginnings for an integrated picture of Holocene deposition and archaeological site burial in Michigan.

Because these large, interdisciplinary projects are multicounty or even statewide in scope, they commonly encompass multiple drainage basins. Consequently, they not only require a more formalized and systematic approach to deep testing but also a more regionally and chronologically integrated analysis. Fortunately, thanks to visionary managers and regulators, several large- and small-scale studies have a suite of ^{14}C age estimates. These, which were performed on buried soils and/or organic deposits, provided a chronology for the alluvial and archaeological sequences discovered and also allowed direct correlation of depositional sequences from other drainages. The deep test locations (DTLs) sampled in these studies were selected based on sound geomorphological grounds as well as on a detailed understanding of the Holocene depositional history in the area. This latter factor is important because a perusal of these studies shows that extensive alluvial deposition periods are not random but rather cluster during specific time intervals. This is significant because when combined with basic hydraulic and depositional processes, it permits the development of models that may be used to predict the occurrence and age of buried archaeological resources.

Deep Site Burial in Michigan: Processes and Models

Although the preservation of deeply buried archaeological sites in Michigan is complicated and may relate to many different depositional processes (Monaghan 1990a; Lovis, Holman, Monaghan, and Skowronek 1994; Lovis and O'Shea 1994), two important, obvious constraints apply within the Great Lakes region as well as the glaciated Northeast and Midwest. For humans to occupy a land area, it must be both ice-free and dry (i.e., not submerged). Ultimately, the burial of such sites hypothetically results from processes that deposit extensive sediment on the land surface. In Michigan, the most significant of these processes include burial under glacial sediment (till, outwash, etc.), burial under lacustrine sediments during lake-level transgressions, burial by shoreline processes (littoral and/or eolian), and burial along streams by channel alluviation.

The first two of these factors (burial under glacial and glaciolacustrine sediment) are not especially useful to predicting buried sites locales. Not only were humans relatively rare in the region prior to about 11,000 B.P., when most of Lower Michigan became ice-free, but also glacial depositional processes are mainly destructive. More important, despite the fact that glaciolacustrine and glacial sediments are spatially the most abundant throughout the Great Lakes region, specific locations or potentials for buried sites are nearly impossible to predict. Given the potential for either the reworking or destruction of sites in ice-marginal or subglacial environments, the probability of preserving valuable archaeological information in sites buried during glacial readvances (or even by ice-marginal processes) is very low. In fact, as far as we know, no sites buried by glacial readvances have been reported within the Great Lakes region.

Preservation of sites buried during lake-level transgressions, however, is not only more plausible but also has occurred. These are apparently limited to middle and late Holocene time and not related to the numerous late Wisconsinan fluctuations of the ancestral Great Lakes. For example, portions of the Weber I (20SA581; Lovis ed.1989), the Ebenhoff Dune (20SA596; Dobbs and Murray 1993), and Juntunen (McPherron 1967) sites were apparently stratified and preserved by rapid sedimentation following a rise in the Holocene upper Great Lakes levels. The absence of surficial morphological and environmental evidence for buried sites on the lake plain itself, however, dictates that such sampling would be most productive along or near the paleo-shoreline and is thus actually process three above. Because modeling the potential for site burial related to ice-marginal advances or lake transgressions would be both unprofitable and probably wasteful, they will be generally discounted for this discussion.

Depositional processes related to shoreline and stream channel environments (processes three and four above) offer the greatest potential for burial and preservation of archaeological sites. In fact, because they are appealing for human occupation as well, such environments are excellent places to find archaeological sites, buried or otherwise. Importantly, shoreline and alluvial environments also offer a high potential for accurately predicting buried site locations. The locations of abandoned shorelines, alluvial terraces, and floodplains are readily apparent, while paleo-environmental and depositional processes can be assumed in a uniformitarian framework based on analogy with modern processes. For example, shoreline sedimentation is dynamic and may include high-energy, littoral (foreshore) deposits formed along the shore margin; storm deposits developed along the back-berm of the beach; marsh deposits in swales behind beach berms; and eolian deposits. Even 1- or 2-m lake-level fluctuations may force significant shoreward or landward migration of these facies, which could allow burial and preservation of shoreline sites. Examples of such sites are the Woodland-period Juntunen and Portage sites (McPherron 1967; Lovis et al. 1998) in northern Michigan and the Archaic-period Weber I (Monaghan, Lovis, and Fay 1986; Lovis ed. 1989) and Ebenhoff Dune sites (Dobbs and Murray 1993) near Saginaw Bay. The high potential for archaeological site location and burial along shorelines requires that the effects of such shoreline processes be an important part of any predictive site burial model. Thus, a portion of this report will focus on outlining the complex history of lake-level phases that were ancestral to the Great Lakes from the end of the late Wisconsinan glacial stage through the Holocene.

Even more significant than shoreline sites, however, is site burial along rivers and streams. In fact, because alluvial settings are significant for human economic activities (such as food production and transportation), they are prime locations for archaeological sites. Such settings along streams are also relatively easy for prehistoric people to relocate and thus are commonly reoccupied, leaving a long-term record of cultural change. This reoccupation is important given that alluvial landforms are constructed by net sediment accretion related to active stream channel migration and episodic flooding. Variability in the hydraulic characteristics of streams results in soil formation on the floodplain during periods of stability or in the construction, partial erosion, and burial of successive terrace surfaces, along with any attending soil and archaeological deposits, during more dynamic periods. Taken over thousands of years, the stratigraphy of the sediment, soil, and archaeological deposits preserved in the resultant floodplain package indicates time-transgressive variation in the formation and utilization of alluvial terraces. By comparing and noting commonalities in the alluvial and occupational histories from adjacent as well as far-flung drainage basins, major, regionally significant intervals of environmental change can be constructed. This data represents the basis of a predictive model for alluvial and shoreline archaeological site burial and requires consideration of the variability of regional depositional sequences.

Regional Depositional Models and Archaeological Resources

The results of deep testing in several CRM corridor surveys from divergent areas in Michigan indicate that alluvial site development and preservation are regionally variable and complex. In some areas, buried sites and/or paleosols are commonly preserved, while in other areas, despite extensive deep testing, no or very few buried alluvial sites were discovered. A comparison of the differing depositional and settlement models proposed in these areas indicates why an understanding of alluvial and shoreline sedimentation and its relationship to climate change and drainage basin configuration is critical. It also shows that knowing the manner and probability of archaeological site preservation in alluvial settings is significant for reconstructing accurate human settlement patterns.

At least eight sites that were buried or stratified by alluvial or shoreline processes exist in the southern part of the Saginaw Bay region (i.e., "Shiawassee flats" area). Their formation and preservation in this region are apparently related to the interplay of topography, drainage basin configuration, Holocene climate change, and lake-level variation. For example, Monaghan and Schaetzl (1994) and Lovis et al. (1996) showed that variation in the Holocene level of Lake Huron resulted in extensive alluviation and site burial, and they have suggested a generalized model for site burial in similar settings. They propose that those drainage systems developed near the margins of the Great Lakes basins are generally graded to a specific base level controlled by the water-plane altitude of a specific lake in the basin. If the base level is lowered during a regressive event (or drop) of the lake, the stream will respond by incising its channel. During transgressions, however, base level rises, and the stream responds by "raising" its channel through alluviation (deposition of sediment). Sites that occur along the margin of streams may be buried during such an alluviation event. The rate and magnitude of such alluviation are controlled mainly by the rate and magnitude of the transgression and by the "upstream" distance of the site. In general, sites are most rapidly and deeply buried nearest to the lake margin and during a rapid rise of several or more meters in lake level. Importantly, even if the transgression does not actually flood the site, the site can be buried simply as a response to changes in regional base level associated with the transgression.

Monaghan and Hayes (1997, 1998, 2001) and Hayes and Monaghan (1997, 1998) have suggested a more generalized, less region-specific model for burial of sites in alluvial settings. While not disputing the "lake-level model" described above, they suggest that mid-to-late Holocene drainages in the eastern United States are characterized by variable, but generally short-term, periods of active net floodplain sedimentation. That is to say intervals of relatively more frequent and greater magnitude floods, which, consequently, allows for more rapid sediment accretion on the floodplain. Archaeological sites are buried during these alluviation events. These more active periods of alluviation are separated by generally longer intervals of relative fluvial quiescence, or even of actual active landform degradation, during which time relatively extensive soil and midden development occurs. These "high-flood"/"low-flood" intervals are believed to be driven by significant regional, or even worldwide, climatic events. Instead of alluvially buried sites confined only to the margins of the Great Lakes, this model suggests that site burial may occur in any fluvial basin where conditions are favorable to extensive floodplain accretion. The challenge is delineating the hydraulic factors and basin characteristics that dictate site burial and preservation. If they remain undiscovered, then a whole population of important sites will be ignored, which can only result in an incorrect understanding of prehistoric settlement patterns in the area.

In spite of the fact that the models described above are useful in understanding general factors controlling archaeological site burial, local basin-specific variables actually dictate patterns of sedimentation. For example, despite extensive deep-test excavations and close-interval shovel tests undertaken along the US-23 corridor on the north side of Saginaw Bay, no evidence of sites, buried or otherwise, was noted along any floodplain or valley bottom. Both large and small archaeological sites, however, were found in the uplands adjacent to rivers in the area (i.e., 20SA172 along the Pine River and 20SA173–176 along the Rifle River; Dunham et al. 1995). In the absence of deep testing or detailed geomorphologic analysis of the floodplain, the question of whether sites are absent because they were never there or because they were destroyed by fluvial processes remains unanswered. Clearly, these alternatives have important, but different, ramifications for the structure of regional archaeological settlement and subsistence models. The correct choice is important and can only be made when prehistoric human settlement systems are placed within the broader context of the depositional patterns revealed within drainage basins. Site distribution, particularly associated with site preservation, is linked to long-term patterns of sedimentation and cannot be fully understood isolated from local and regional drainage basin development. The articulation of this linkage, in the context of formulating a regional depositional model, is an important underlying objective of this study.

CHAPTER TWO

The Pre-Holocene Geological History

Geological Background and
the Formation of the Great Lakes

The Geological Background of Michigan

By far, the most important element controlling the physiography of Lower Michigan was the retreat of the Laurentide Ice Sheet between 15,000 and 10,000 B.P. It was during this time that morainal uplands, glacio-fluvial valleys, and lacustrine plains were formed. These were the principal predecessors to the modern drainage system and Great Lakes shoreline configuration. Because of their importance to understanding the evolution of both the modern drainage system and the ancestral Holocene Great Lakes, this chapter will focus mainly on the timing, connections, and relationships of glacial lakes formed in the Michigan, Huron, and Erie lake basins. In addition, processes controlling levels will be discussed in detail.

Although the physiography of Michigan is a direct result of Wisconsinan glaciation, the preglacial configuration of the state greatly influenced the configuration, flow direction, and depositional style of the Laurentide Ice Sheet. This is particularly true concerning the bedrock lithology and subcrop pattern. Geologically, Michigan is a sedimentary basin of Paleozoic age, with the oldest rocks outcropping along the rim of the state and progressively younger rocks forming concentrically smaller circles toward the center of the state. The western Upper Peninsula, north and west of a line from Gladstone to Marquette, is underlain chiefly by metamorphic rocks that are significantly older than the Paleozoic-age Michigan Basin. For example, banded-iron and quartzite formations near Marquette are greater than 2 billion years old, while bedrock within the Michigan Basin is generally between 350 and 500 million years old. The youngest formation within the basin (Pennsylvanian Saginaw Formation) underlies most of central Michigan between Jackson and Saginaw Bay, while the oldest rocks (Proto-Cambrian Munising and Jacobsville formations) occur along the south shore of Lake Superior.

The Michigan Basin was formed within a Paleozoic-age, shallow inland sea. As such, rocks within the basin are predominantly sequences of finer-grained clastic (shale, silt, and sandstone) or carbonate rocks (limestone and dolomite).

Because they are softer and more easily eroded, shale- and siltstone-rich formations underlie most of the Great Lakes. For example, Lake Michigan includes two deep basins. The northern basin is underlain by Devonian shale, while the southern is underlain by Mississippian shale. Initially, these basins probably formed as preglacial valleys eroded through softer bedrock. The valleys subsequently acted as conduits for glacial ice flow and were progressively deepened and broadened through the period. A similar configuration exists for Lake Huron. Conversely, because it is denser and resistant, carbonate bedrock probably formed uplands in the area that persisted through the Pleistocene. These bedrock uplands rim Lake Huron and form the Bruce Peninsula, Thumb of Michigan, and Manitoulin Island, as well as underlie the surface between Au Gres and Rogers City, Michigan. Lake Michigan is also rimmed by carbonate deposits. These are particularly obvious in the Door (Wisconsin) and Garden peninsulas and between Milwaukee, Wisconsin, and Gary, Indiana.

Even today, the carbonate bedrock formations commonly outcrop or are shallowly buried by glacial sediment throughout Michigan, particularly near the margin of the Great Lakes. This fact has had important consequences for site burial and preservation, as will be discussed later in this volume, but also probably influenced settlement and trade patterns throughout the state. This is suggested because carbonate bedrock commonly houses important prehistoric lithic raw materials. For example, chert and flint deposits are associated with carbonate outcrops around Saginaw Bay (Bayport chert from Mississippian Bayport Formation), northeastern Grand Traverse Bay (Norwood flint from Niagraian Traverse Formation), and near the Straits of Mackinac northwest of St. Ignace (Cordell chert from Ordovician limestone). These flints and cherts occur at archaeological sites throughout the upper Great Lakes, and their abundance is often used to indicate trade and/or kinship networks. Regardless, the modern and Holocene subcrop pattern for the chert and flint quarry sites was dictated by the rise and fall of the ancestral Great Lakes. Thus, the water-plane and altitude and timing for fluctuations in the water level, as well as isostatic adjustments of the land surface, are critical to determine when and where these materials can be quarried. This will be discussed below.

The present topography and configuration of Michigan were dictated mainly by depositional events associated with the Laurentide Ice Sheet, which spread over the state during the Wisconsinan (ca. 10,000–100,000 years ago). The surficial deposits in Lower and eastern Upper Michigan are associated mainly with glacial events related to the late Wisconsinan (ca. 10,000–20,000 years ago). These areas were covered by three major late Wisconsinan ice lobes: the Lake Michigan, Huron-Erie, and Saginaw lobes (Figure 2-1). In general, the Lake Michigan Lobe flowed south around western Lower Michigan through topographically low areas now occupied by Lake Michigan. It spread south and east into western Michigan as well as west and southward into eastern Wisconsin, northern Illinois, and northwestern Indiana. In Michigan, its margins are marked by sequences of mainly north-south-trending morainal highlands, which include the prominent Sturgis, Kalamazoo, Valparaiso, Lake Border, and Manistee moraine systems. The easternmost extent of the Lake Michigan Lobe in Michigan generally follows a line from South Bend, Indiana, through Kalamazoo, Grand Rapids, Cadillac, Grayling, and Cheboygan. On the other side of the state, the Huron-Erie Lobe generally occupied most of southeastern Michigan and flowed east and south from the Lakes Erie and Huron lowland. Within Michigan, limits of the Huron-Erie Lobe occur southeast of a line from Coldwater to Brighton, Lapeer, and Grind Stone City at the tip of the Thumb. Most of the area between the Lake Michigan and Huron-Erie lobes was occupied by the Saginaw Lobe, which flowed southwest from the Saginaw Bay lowland to the Indiana border near Sturgis. The extent of the Saginaw Lobe is marked by a series of arcuate moraines that generally parallel the present shore of Saginaw Bay. For example, these moraines trend southwest-northeast within the Thumb of Michigan and the area north of Bay and Midland counties; north-south north of the Maple, Grand, and Saginaw river systems; and generally east-west south of these rivers between Coldwater, Lansing, and Saginaw.

The configuration of the ice centers and moraines within the three late Wisconsinan ice lobes had a significant impact on the drainage patterns and style of deglaciation that developed as the Laurentide Ice Sheet retreated from Michigan. These factors also ultimately determined the general positions of the major modern river systems in the state as well as the configuration of the Great Lakes that we observe today. For example, early in the deglaciation of Michigan, when the three lobes were near their maximum extent in Michigan, drainage was generally south and west, away from the ice margin, into the Mississippi River. As the ice margins retreated back into the lake basins, however, meltwater was trapped between morainal uplands that rimmed the basins and isostatically depressed areas near the ice margin. As described below, this resulted in the

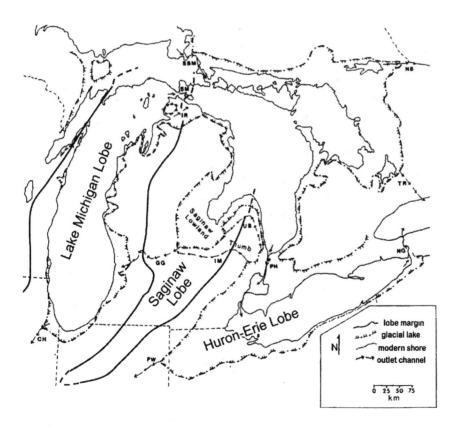

Figure 2-1. The Great Lakes region, showing the generalized extent of the highest lakes that occupied the Michigan, Huron, and Erie lake basins over the past 15,000 years. Maximum extent is indicated by hatched dash-dot line. Also shown are the locations of major outlet channels. CH = Chicago, FW = Fort Wayne, GG = Glacial Grand channel, IM = Imlay Channel, IR = Indian River lowlands, NB = North Bay, NG = Niagara, PH = Port Huron, SM = Straits of Mackinac, SSM = Sault Ste. Marie, TR = Trent River (Kirkfield-Fenelon Falls), UB = Ubly channel.

formation of the extensive proglacial lake system that is the hallmark of Michigan's Wisconsinan geological history. The lakes ultimately overflowed through sags in the rimming morainal uplands and drained generally north and west from one lake to the next (Erie to Saginaw to Michigan to Mississippi).

The purpose of this chapter is to describe the major lake phases that occupied the Great Lakes basin over the past 12,000–13,000 years. This information will provide critical background contexts within which to place changing prehistoric archaeological settlement systems. Based on an understanding of the geological events and processes controlling deposition in the region, areas can be demarcated that represent likely places for prehistoric archaeological site location. In addition, areas of high potential for deep burial of archaeological sites (burial greater than 1 or 2 m) can also be indicated.

Lake Phases in the Upper Great Lakes: Introduction and Background Summary

Data collected over the past 100 years within the Michigan, Huron, Erie, and Superior lake basins has resulted in a rich, complicated, and sometimes contradictory sequence of lake phases (Spencer 1888, 1891; Taylor 1894, 1897; Leverett 1897; Goldthwait 1908; Wright 1918; Leverett and Taylor 1915; Stanley 1936; Bretz 1951a, 1951b, 1953, 1955, 1959, 1964; Hough 1955, 1958, 1962, 1963; Dreimanis 1958, 1969; Lewis 1969, 1970; Dreimanis and Goldthwait 1973; Farrand and Drexler 1985; Fullerton 1980; Karrow et al. 1975; Karrow 1980; Hansel et al. 1985; Calkin and Feenstra 1985; Clark et al. 1985; Finamore 1985; Eschman and Karrow 1985; Kaszicki 1985; Larsen 1985a, 1985b, 1987; Monaghan, Lovis, and Fay 1986; Monaghan and Larson 1986; Thompson 1992; Thompson and Baedke 1995). The names of the lakes that occupied the Michigan and Huron lake basins, together with the stratigraphic periods in which they existed, are shown in Table 2-1. Also shown are the related cultural (archaeological) time stratigraphic periods defined in Michigan. A summary of the lake sequence, derived mainly from the references listed above, is given below, while a more detailed discussion is presented elsewhere in this chapter.

Table 2-2 presents a more detailed outline of lake-level history within the upper Great Lakes. It shows names, approximate ages, and probable correlations between major lake phases in the Michigan, Huron, and Erie lake basins (with reference to the Superior lake basin) over the past 15,000 years. Also shown are the channels that connected each basin, the ultimate outlet, and the direction of water flow between basins. Table 2-2 was constructed based on the most recent and generally accepted interpretation of the lake phases in the basins. In general, the level achieved by these lakes was controlled by the altitude of their outlets. The actual outlets that could be used over the past 15,000 years, however, were controlled mainly by the location of the Laurentide ice margin, the amount of isostatic depression and rebound within differing parts of the basin, and the amount of erosion possible for the outlet.

Today, Lakes Michigan and Huron are considered to be a single, hydraulic lake basin connected at the Straits of Mackinac, while Lake Superior exists as a separate lake basin and discharges southward, over a bedrock threshold near Sault Ste. Marie through the St. Mary's River into Lake Huron. The entire upper

Great Lakes system (Lakes Superior, Michigan, and Huron) ultimately discharges through the St. Clair River at Port Huron (Figure 2-1). Modern water levels for Lake Michigan-Huron (176.5 m) and Lake Superior (183 m) are controlled by a balance between the amount of water input to the basin and the amount that discharges through the outlet. Over the past 15,000 years, however, the lakes that occupied each basin had vastly different levels. These include both high-level (water-plane higher than modern level) and low-level (water-plane lower than modern) lakes that used several geographically diverse outlets at different times (Figure 2-1).

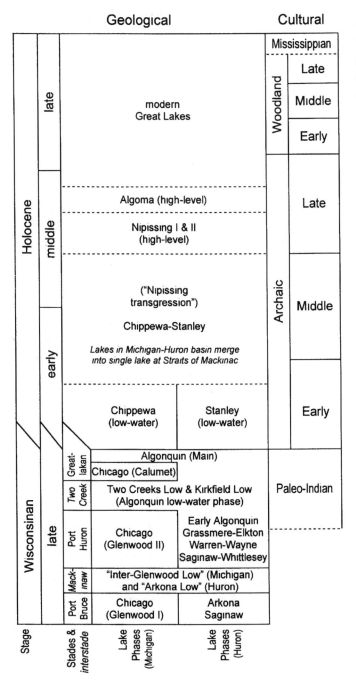

Table 2-1. Correlation and Temporal Relationships of Geological and Cultural Stratigraphy in the Upper Great Lakes Region.

Lake Chicago represents the only major glacial lake within the Michigan lake basin and existed from about 14,000 to 11,400 B.P. It has been divided into three high-level phases (Glenwood I and II and Calumet; Table 2-2) and two low-level phases (Intra-Glenwood low and Two Creeks low; Table 2-2). Unlike today, during high phases Lake Chicago existed as a separate lake basin and discharged to the Mississippi drainage via the Chicago outlet (Figure 2-1). Low phases of the lake drained east through the Straits of Mackinac region (Figure 2-1) into the Huron lake basin, much as Lake Michigan does today. Glacial lakes also occupied the Huron lake basin (including the Saginaw Bay region). These include (from oldest to youngest): Early Lake Saginaw; Lake Arkona, with three high phases (Arkona I, II, and III) and one low phase (Arkona low); Lake Saginaw; Lakes Warren and Wayne; Lakes Grassmere and Lundy; and Lake Algonquin, with two high-level phases (Early Algonquin and Main Algonquin) and two low-level phases (Kirkfield low and Post-Main Algonquin; Table 2-2). High-level phases associated with Lakes Saginaw, Arkona, and Warren were hydraulically

Table 2-2. Correlation and Time-Stratigraphic Relationships of Glacial and Postglacial Lakes in the Upper Great Lakes Region.

West Outlet	Lake Michigan[1,2,5]	Connecting Channel	Lake Huron[2,3]	Connecting Channel	Lake Erie[2,4]	East Outlet	Glacial and Other Events Controlling Lake Levels	Time kB P
	Michigan (176.5 m)	Straits of Mackinaw	Huron (175.6 m)				Holocene Port Huron sill eroded to modern level	3.0
	Algoma (181 m)[6]			Port Huron Outlet (St. Clair River)	"Modern" Lake Erie (rising to 173 m)	Niagara River	Port Huron outlet erodes below bedrock sill at Chicago Nipissing II phase initiated	3.5
Chicago Outlet	Nipissing I & II (184 m)[6,7] (used east & west outlets)						North Bay outlet rebounds above Port Huron and Chicago (all outlets briefly used)	5.0
	Chippewa (<107 m)	Straits of Mackinaw	Stanley (<80 m)	North Bay Outlet[8] (Erie bypassed)			Marquette Readvance in Superior Basin Minong outlet along St. Mary's River Ice margin retreats north of Ottawa River	9.9–10.3
	Post-Main Algonquin[6,9] ("Lower Group", <177 m)			Fossmill & South River (Erie Bypassed)		Ottawa River	Greatlakean Stade Huron Lobe retreats from Algonquin Highlands Drainage through Ottawa River to Ontario	10.9
	Main Algonquin[7,10] ("late Upper Group", 184 m)			Port Huron Outlet?	Early Erie (166 m)?	Niagara River	Kirkfield rebounds above Port Huron? Drainage may have transferred south	11.0
	Kirkfield-to-Main Algonquin transition (rising levels)						Michigan Lobe retreats north of Straits of Mackinaw Michigan & Huron basins confluent	11.2
Chicago Outlet	Calumet[11] (189 m)						Michigan Lobe advances to Two Rivers Moraine; Huron & Michigan basins separated	11.5
	Two Creek low (<177 m)	Straits of Mackinaw	Kirkfield Low of Algonquin (low and rising levels, <177 m)				Two Creeks Interstade Michigan Lobe retreats north of Straits of Mackinaw Michigan & Huron basins confluent	11.8
				Kirkfield/Fenelon Falls outlet (Erie bypassed, isostatic rebound of outlet controls level in Huron & Michigan basins)		Early Trent River	Huron Lobe retreats north of Trent River valley Drainage to Erie basin bypassed	12.2
			Early Lake Algonquin (184 m)	Port Huron outlet (Early Lake St. Clair and Lake Rouge)	Early Lake Erie (166 m?)	Niagara River? Mohawk Valley?	Port Huron Stade Ontario Lobe retreats to St. Lawrence Valley, lowers Ontario & Erie basin lakes Sill at Port Huron controls Huron basin lake level	12.2–12.4
				Grassmere & Lundy (Elkton) (195–189 m)		Mohawk Valley?	Erie/Ontario Lobe retreats from Niagara escarpment near Niagara Falls, N.Y.	12.6
				Warren & Wayne (210–205 m)			Huron/Saginaw Lobe retreats from Michigan "Thumb" Erie-Huron basin lakes confluent	12.8
Chicago outlet	Glenwood II (195 m)	Glacial Grand River	Saginaw (212 m)	Ubly Channel	Whittlesey (225 m)		Ice readvance to Port Huron Moraine throughout the Great Lakes region	13.0
	"Intra-Glenwood Low" (<177 m)	Straits of Mackinaw	"Arkona Low" (<177 m)	Buried channel of "Trent River"? / "Port Huron"?	Ypsilanti (166 m?)	Mohawk Valley? Niagara River?	Mackinaw Interstade Michigan Lobe retreats north of Straits of Mackinaw, Huron Lobe retreats north of Trent Valley, Michigan & Huron basins confluent, Erie Lobe retreats north of Niagara Falls	13.4
			Saginaw (215 m)	Arkona (216–121 m)			Port Bruce Stade Huron Lobe retreat north of Michigan "Thumb"	13.7
Chicago Outlet	Glenwood I (195 m)	Glacial Grand River		Imlay Channel	Maumee III (238 m)		Saginaw Lobe retreats north of Imlay Channel and then into Saginaw Lowland	14.0

Sources and Notes: [1]Hansel et al. (1985); [2]Fullerton (1980); [3]Eschman and Karrow (1985); [4]Calkin and Feenstra (1985). [5]Lake-phase water-plane elevation shown in parentheses under phase name. [6]Lake extended into Lake Superior basin. Lakes Algoma and Nipissing discharged through narrow straits formed along the St. Mary's River near Sault Ste. Marie. [7]Lake Nipissing also briefly used North Bay outlet during the earliest phases. [8]Level of Lake Minong was initially controlled by a "drift barrier" between Gros Cap, Ontario, and Nadoway Point. [9]Wyebridge, Penetang, Cedar Point, Payette, and Sheguiandah levels in the Lake Superior basin. [10]The 184-m level of Main Algonquin may not have been reached in the southern end of the basin and therefore may not have used the Port Huron outlet. [11]Calumet level may have been achieved before the Two Creeks Interstade.

separated from the Michigan lake basin but did drain into Lake Chicago via the Glacial Grand River (Figure 2-1). Low-level phases of Lakes Arkona and Algonquin were usually confluent with lakes in the Michigan lake basin and discharged eastward through either the Trent River valley near Kirkfield, Ontario, or the Ottawa River near and just south of North Bay, Ontario (Figure 2-1). Generally, as discussed below, the levels of these glacial lakes were controlled by ice-marginal fluctuations of the Lake Michigan, Huron-Erie, and Saginaw ice lobes.

The sequence of Holocene (post-10,000 B.P.) lakes within the Michigan and Huron lake basins includes Lakes Chippewa, Stanley, Nipissing, and Algoma as well as modern levels of Lakes Michigan and Huron (Table 2-2). Lakes Chippewa and Stanley existed as extremely low-level lakes, which, in their early stages, formed separate lakes in the Michigan and Huron lake basins. Younger stages of the lakes were probably confluent in both basins. They ultimately discharged east to the Ottawa River at North Bay, Ontario (Figure 2-1). Lakes Nipissing and Algoma (Table 2-2), the immediate predecessors to the modern lakes, existed as relatively high-level lakes and discharged mainly through the St. Clair River at Port Huron (Figure 2-1). The water level achieved by these Holocene lakes was controlled mainly either by isostatic rebound of the outlet at North Bay or by erosion (downcutting) of the outlet at Port Huron.

The sequence of lakes within the eastern Superior lake basin is younger than about 11,000 B.P. and includes relatively high glacial lake phases of Algonquin (Main Algonquin, Wyebridge, Penetang, Cedar Point, Payette, and Sheguiandah) and phases of Lake Minong (early, main, and post-Minong) as well as a low-level Lake Houghton. The Algonquin-phase lakes were confluent with various phases of Lake Algonquin in the Michigan and Huron lake basins, while Minong and Houghton were isolated from the southern basins and discharged into the Huron lake basin via a proto–St. Mary's River outlet. In addition, Lakes Nipissing and Algoma, whose lake-level altitude was above the bedrock sill in the St. Mary's River, extended into the Superior lake basin through a narrow strait near Sault Ste. Marie.

Controls for the Level of Glacial and Postglacial Lakes in the Great Lakes Region

Data compiled in Table 2-2 indicates that the level of glacial and postglacial lakes that occupied each basin within the Great Lakes region has fluctuated by nearly 100 m over the past 15,000 years. Changes in the water level for the sequence of lakes within each basin is apparently related to changes in the outlet utilized by each lake. In general, the water level achieved by a lake occupying the basin at a given time is controlled largely by the altitude of the outlet channel for that lake and to a lesser extent by the amount of water entering and leaving the basin (the water budget for the lake). The fluctuation in the water level through time for the sequence of lakes in each basin is controlled by at least four major processes, including: (1) fluctuations of the ice lobe margin that either uncovered lower outlets during retreats or blocked them during advances, (2) differential isostatic changes (postglacial rebound) in the altitudes of different parts of the lake basins or outlet channels themselves, (3) downcutting by erosion of outlet channels and sills, and (4) significant changes in the volume of water entering or leaving the basin by climatic changes and/or changes in the hydraulic configuration of the outlet channel (Hansel et al. 1985). Each of these processes probably played some role in determining the level of proglacial lakes that occupied the basin during the Pleistocene. Only the last three, however, influenced the level achieved by Holocene (nonglacial) lake phases.

The first of the above processes, ice-margin fluctuations that uncovered or blocked low-altitude outlets, is the most simple but also caused the most dramatic and probably catastrophic changes in lake level. For example, during both the Mackinaw and Two Creeks interstades, the Lake Michigan Lobe apparently retreated far enough north to uncover the Straits of Mackinac. Utilization of this lower, northern outlet caused the lake level within the basin to fall several tens of meters (Glenwood I to intra-Glenwood low and Glenwood II to Two Creeks low; Table 2-2) as drainage was shifted north and eastward from the Chicago outlet into the Huron lake basin. At the same time, the Huron-Erie Lobe retreated north to uncover a low outlet along the Trent River valley, which also resulted in similarly low-level lakes (Arkona low and Kirkfield low; Table 2-2). Subsequent southward readvances of the margin of these ice lobes during the Port Huron and Greatlakean stades again blocked and covered these outlets. This caused a rise in water levels in each basin, as drainage was transferred back to more southern outlets. Similarly, the final retreat of the Huron-Erie Lobe from the Great Lakes region uncovered the lowest outlet in the basin at North Bay, Ontario. This resulted in an extremely low-level lake in both the Michigan and Huron lake basins (Chippewa and Stanley). The rise in lake level subsequent to the Chippewa-Stanley low-level lakes (Lake Nipissing) illustrates the importance of the second process listed above, isostatic rebound of outlet channels.

Isostatic depression of the earth's crust during the late Wisconsinan resulted as the weight of the Laurentide Ice Sheet (as much as 2 km thick) displaced viscous mantle material from beneath the earth's crust that underlay the ice sheet. Because the greatest amount of depression occurs beneath the greatest ice thickness (i.e., the point of maximum load) and decreases closer to the ice margin, relatively greater crustal depression occurred generally northward from the ice margin. As the ice thinned during northward retreat, the load depressing the crust was removed, and displaced mantle material flowed back beneath the crust. This process results in a gradual rise, or "isostatic rebound," of the earth's surface. Within the Great Lakes region, the maximum amount of crustal depression, and consequently the maximum potential amount of isostatic rebound, occurs in the most north-northwestern part of the basin. The rate that rebound occurs varies through time by a factor of e^{-kt}, where e = base of natural logarithms, k = decay constant, and t = years since deglaciation (Andrews 1970; Fillon 1972). This relationship indicates first, that the rebound rate logarithmically decreases through time and, second, that the greatest rate of uplift occurred immediately following deglaciation (Farrand 1962; Broecker 1966; Andrews 1970; Walcott 1970). Data from lake-level gages collected from around the Great Lakes basin indicates that the region has not yet achieved isostatic equilibrium and that differential north-south rebound is still occurring throughout the basin (Figure 2-2; Clark and Persoage 1970; Larsen 1985b).

The process of isostatic rebound has had a profound and sometimes confusing effect on the study of glacial and postglacial lakes formed in the Great

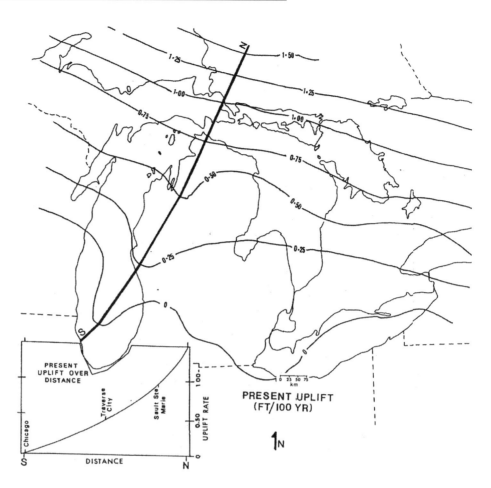

Figure 2-2. The current uplift rate throughout the Great Lakes region (modified from Clark and Persoage 1970 and Larsen 1985b). Insert shows profile of uplift along a north-south line normal to the trend in regional uplift.

Lakes basin. Differential rebound dictates that a beach formed at a specific time in the past will not occur today at the same altitude that it was originally formed. Importantly, the altitude that the beach is observed at today also will vary throughout the basin. For example, assuming that a water-plane is approximately horizontal throughout the lake basin, then a beach developed by the lake will originally also be horizontal and occur at the same altitude throughout the basin. However, because the amount of uplift increases northward, segments of the beach formed in the northern part of the basin will be raised relatively more than in the southern part. This differential uplift varies exponentially with distance and is approximately curvilinear (Larsen 1985b, 1987). This curvilinear relationship is illustrated in Figure 2-2. Because the rate of uplift decreases exponentially through time, beaches formed 10,000 years ago will be raised significantly more than those formed 5,000 years ago, even if the actual altitude of the outlet and consequently lake level remained the same.

Although at a specific time in the past the water level achieved in a lake was controlled largely by the altitude and hydrological properties of the outlet channel, differential isostatic rebound of the outlet compared to other parts of the lake basin affects both the preservation of beaches observed today and the rate of rise in lake level through time. Figure 2-3 diagrammatically shows how

23

differential rebound affects beach preservation as the outlet varies in geographic position. It illustrates the generally accepted model of lake-level change in the Huron lake basin for the Algonquin-Stanley-Nipissing sequence of lakes. Three hypothetical outlets—southern (Port Huron), middle (Kirkfield/Fenelon Falls), and northern (North Bay)—each have variable rates of rebound, with the greatest rate associated with the most northern. As the ice-marginal retreats to position A, it uncovers the middle outlet, and lake level falls to level A as drainage is transferred to this outlet. During retreat of the ice to positions B and C, the outlet rebounds, and lake level progressively rises from level A to levels B and C. When level C is achieved, the middle outlet has risen to the same altitude as the southern outlet, and drainage is transferred back to it. Although a simple transgressional sequence might be predicted as lake level rises from A to C, in fact isostatic rebound causes both "transgressional" and "regressional" beaches to form in different parts of the basin. This sequence of beaches, as they would appear today, is shown on the lower half of Figure 2-3. Because the rate of isostatic rebound increases northward in the basin and lake level is assumed to be controlled by the rate of uplift at the outlet, the rise in lake level would be greater than the rebound of the land surface south of the outlet. Beaches in this area would represent "transgressional" sequences as older beaches were reworked and submerged by younger, relatively higher-level lakes, and thus the youngest beach would occur at the highest altitude. North of the outlet, however, where the rate of isostatic rebound is greater than that at the outlet, the land surface would rise relatively faster than the level of the lake. The sequence of beaches formed in this region would appear "regressional," with the oldest beaches occurring at a greater altitude than younger beaches. The result of such an uplift-controlled lake level is that once discharge ceases through the outlet, a single beach would be preserved in the south, while to the north beaches would "split" and preserve a series of progressively younger and lower beaches. Many modern researchers (Larsen 1985b, 1987; Clark et al. 1985) believe this apparent splitting of beaches is actually the origin for the "hinge line" concept proposed by Goldthwait (1908). They suggest that this hinge line results from an incorrect correlation of differing age beaches.

Because the "stable" (i.e., least-warped) southern outlet controls lake level after level C (Figure 2-3), continued retreat of the ice margin to position D results in no actual change in water level within the lake. As a result of differential rebound in the northern part of the basin between levels C and D, however, the altitude observed today for the beach formed by level D will actually be less than that of level C. When the ice margin retreats to position E, the northern outlet is uncovered and consequently allows the lake level to drop again. Through time, lake level will rise at a rate controlled by the rebound of the outlet. Because the northern outlet rebounds fastest, however, the change in lake level will always be greater than the land surface south of the outlet. This results in a completely transgressional sequence and will continue until the altitude of the northern outlet reaches that of the southern (dashed line in lower part of Figure 2-3). At this point, drainage is again transferred south. Importantly, in the south end of the lake basin, this lake level will come close to the altitude of beach D and will create another apparent hinge line.

Uncovering or blocking outlets due to ice-margin fluctuations and isostatic rebound of outlets often result in dramatic changes in lake level of several tens of meters. Variation in water level of a few to several meters, however, generally results from either downcutting of outlet channels or changes in the basinwide water budget. Channel floor erosion, for example, has been suggested to account for the 6-m change in the level of Lake Chicago between the Glenwood II and Calumet phases, for the 2-m drop between Lakes Saginaw and Warren, and for the 8-m drop that occurred during Lake Warren (Table 2-2). Such erosion is probably relatively gradual and is controlled both by the lithology of the substrate comprising the channel floor and by the velocity of water discharging through the channel. For example, the channel floor of the Chicago outlet remained stable after the Calumet phase since by then it had been eroded to bedrock (Hansel et al. 1985). Although Lake Nipissing used both the Chicago and Port Huron outlets simultaneously because the Chicago outlet is floored by bedrock and more easily eroded, unconsolidated drift underlies the Port Huron outlet, the 7-m drop in lake level from Lake Nipissing to modern levels apparently resulted solely from erosion of the St. Clair River. The average rate of erosion for this drop was about 0.45 m/century. Bretz (1951b, 1953, 1964) suggested that variation in channel velocity related to minor fluctuations on the margin of the Saginaw Lobe is responsible for the episodic downcutting of the Glacial Grand channels observed during phases of Lake Warren and proposed a similar model to explain changes in the level of Lake Chicago.

Finally, changes in lake level for the Great Lakes were also affected by regional climate change. This was probably particularly significant during the middle and late Holocene (see chapter 3). Water level fluctuated related to basinwide variations in either precipitation or temperature (Fraser et al. 1975; Larsen 1985b). For example, reduced precipitation during relatively dry periods resulted in lower lake level because less water was input to the basin. Similarly,

Figure 2-3. Diagrammatic representation along a north-south line of shoreline uplift and lake-level change during ice-marginal retreat. Upper part of the diagram shows sequential ice-margin retreat and subsequent lake level achieved using three geographically different outlets. Lower part shows the variation observed today, accounting for uplift, in elevation over distance for beaches formed by each lake level.

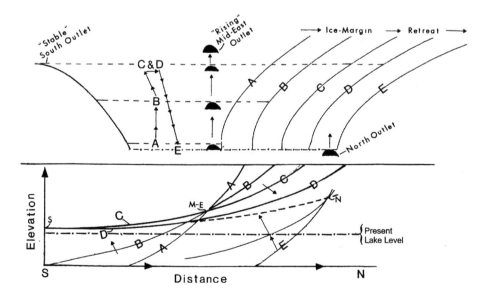

particularly wet intervals resulted in increased lake level because more water was input to the basin. Changes in temperature also affected lake level by increasing evaporation during warm periods or reducing evaporation during cool periods. Relatively long-term increases in evaporation will, of course, lower the lake level. Changes in water level due solely to variations in temperature and/or precipitation could only result in only a few meters difference in the level of the Great Lakes. In fact, the data from the Great Lakes region indicates that climate change, on the magnitude observed during the middle and late Holocene, probably caused only minor changes in lake level but is probably the main factor controlling the historic changes in lake level (Figure 2-4). Larsen (1985b) has applied this model of climate-controlled lake-level fluctuation to the middle and late Holocene lake sequence. He suggested that the level of Lakes Michigan and Huron varied about ±2 m from the mean lake level and that this variation occurred over a 200–300-year interval (Figure 2-4).

Chronology and Description of the Lake Phases

Port Bruce Stade and Mackinaw Interstade Lake Stages
This period, between about 13,000 and 15,000 years ago, includes glacial events associated with the end of the Erie Interstade (16,000–15,000 B.P.), the Port Bruce Stade (15,000–13,500 B.P.), Mackinaw Interstade (13,300–13,000 B.P.), and the beginning of the Port Huron Stade (13,000 B.P.; Dreimanis and Goldthwait 1973) and represents the beginning of the final retreat of late Wisconsinan ice from the Great Lakes region (Eschman and Karrow 1985). During the Erie Interstade (16,000–15,000 B.P.; Morner and Dreimanis 1973), which occurred prior to the Port Bruce Stade, the ice margin in the Great Lakes region had retreated northward some distance into each of the Great Lakes basins and apparently formed a series of glacial lakes within each lake basin (Dreimanis 1958; Morner and Dreimanis 1973; Johnson 1976; Monaghan and Larson 1986; Monaghan 1985a, 1989; Monaghan and Hansel 1990). The Port Bruce Stade was initiated at about 15,000 years ago when the ice margin of the Lake Michigan, Saginaw, and Huron-Erie lobes advanced southward across these glacial lakes to positions well south of and/or inland from each lake basin (Figure 2-5). These southern ice-margin positions are marked by a series of moraines, which include (from west to east): the Valparaiso-Kalamazoo moraine complex (Lake Michigan Lobe), the Kalamazoo Moraine (Saginaw Lobe), and the Mississineaw-Powell moraine complex (Huron-Erie Lobe). During the Port Bruce Stade, the ice margin began to retreat from these moraines back into the Michigan, Huron, and Erie lake basins and allowed water to pond in front of the ice. Within the Michigan lake basin, the Glenwood phase of Glacial Lake Chicago occurred; a series of glacial lakes, including Maumee, Arkona, Saginaw, and Whittlesey, occurred within the Huron and Erie lake basins. The altitude and direction of water flow through connecting channels for these lakes were controlled by opening and closing of major outlet channels due to fluctuations of the margins of the Lake Michigan, Saginaw, and Huron-Erie ice lobes related to the Mackinaw Interstade. The details of these lake levels and related ice-margin fluctuations within each lake basin are discussed below.

LAKE MICHIGAN BASIN. Recent summaries of the late Quaternary lake sequences for the Michigan lake basin by Fullerton (1980) and Hansel et al. (1985) indicate that the Glenwood phase of Glacial Lake Chicago occurred as a three-phase, high-low-high lake-level sequence related to fluctuations of the margin of the Lake Michigan Lobe just prior to and after the Mackinaw (Cary–Port Huron) Interstade. Glenwood I, represented by 195-m beaches (lake levels given as the lowest [least warped] beach altitude in m above mean sea level [m asl]) at the south end of the basin (Figure 2-5), was the oldest of these phases and was initiated at about 14,000 B.P., after the Lake Michigan Lobe ice margin had retreated from the Tinley Moraine (Hansel and Mickelson 1988). Drainage was through the southern outlet at Chicago (Figure 2-5). The Glenwood I phase ended when the level of Lake Chicago was lowered because the margin of the Lake Michigan Lobe had retreated far enough north during the Mackinaw Interstade to uncover a lower outlet in the isostatically depressed northern part of the basin, either the Straits of Mackinac or the Indian River lowlands (Figure 2-5). During this time, which is known as the "intra-Glenwood" (or Mackinaw) low-water phase, Lake Chicago drained north and eastward and probably had a water-plane below present lake level (ca. < 177 m). The Glenwood II phase was initiated between about 13,300 and 13,000 B.P. during the glacial readvance (Port Huron Stade) that followed the Mackinaw Interstade. Once the readvancing ice margin crossed the Straits of Mackinac and/or the Indian River lowlands, obstructing northward drainage, the level of Lake Chicago rose back to 195 m (Glenwood level), and the Chicago outlet was reactivated (Figure 2-5).

The possibility that the Straits of Mackinac were deglaciated during the Mackinaw Interstade, resulting in an "intra-Glenwood" low-water phase, was

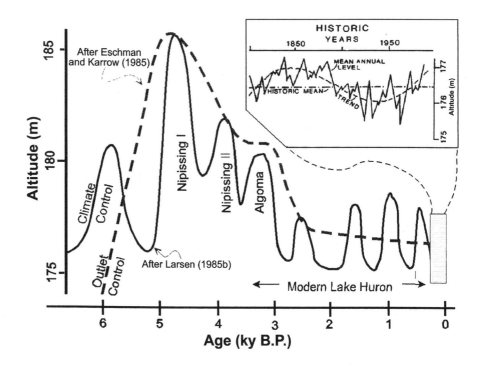

Figure 2-4. Middle and late Holocene variation in the levels of Lake Michigan-Huron; horizontal axis shows time in thousand years B.P. (ky B.P.); vertical axis shows altitude (in meters) of water plane. Insert is scatter plot showing fluctuations in the level of Lake Michigan-Huron from A.D. 1800 to 1986. Horizontal axis shows time (in calendar years); vertical axis shows observed average lake level (in meters) for each year. Datum is sea level. Dash line shows actual change in elevation; solid line shows three-component polynomial best fit line through the data.

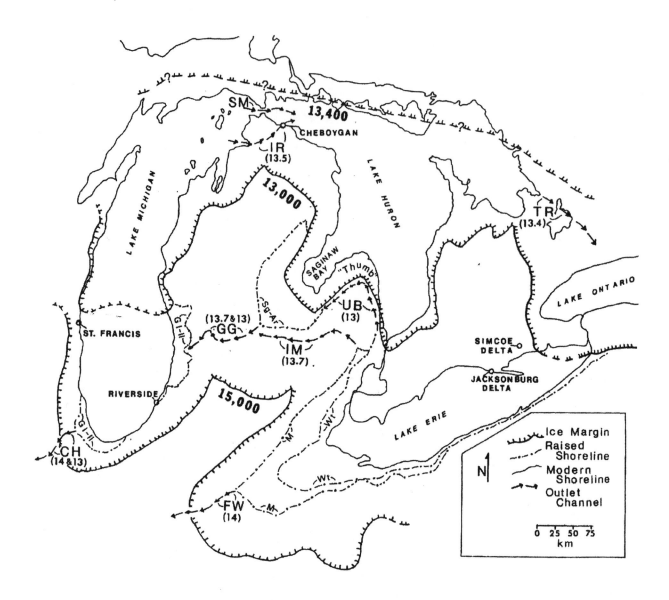

Figure 2-5. The ice-margin and shoreline positions, connecting channels, and location of sites discussed in text for the period 15,000–13,000 ^{14}C years B.P. Ice margins dashed where inferred or approximate; ages (B.P.) shown below ice margin. Ice margin at 15,000 B.P. after Monaghan, Larson, and Gephart (1986) and Monaghan and Larson (1986). Ice margin at 13,000 B.P. represents the Port Huron Moraine and its equivalent. Shoreline positions shown for high-level lake phases only; G I-II = Glenwood I and II, Sg = Lake Saginaw, Ar = Lake Arkona, M = Maumee III, Wt = Whittlesey. Low-level lakes assumed to lie within the boundaries of the modern lake margins. Positions of connecting channels and direction of water flow shown by arrows. Approximate time of activity of channels shown in parentheses below the name of each channel (in 1,000 years B.P.); CH = Chicago, SM = Straits of Mackinac, IR = Indian River lowlands, GG = Glacial Grand channel, IM = Imlay channel, UB = Ubly channel, TR = Trent River lowlands, FW = Fort Wayne Outlet.

first suggested by Hough (1963), partly on the basis of an unpublished thesis by Workman (1925). The first direct evidence for this event, however, was reported by Farrand et al. (1969), who described a bryophyte bed buried beneath red till at a site south of the Straits of Mackinac near Cheboygan, Michigan (Figure 2-5). Although ^{14}C age estimates from this bed range from 13,300 to 9,960 B.P. and average 11,790 B.P., only the oldest ages were selected by Farrand et al. (1969) and Farrand and Eschman (1974) as reliable. On this basis, they assumed a Mackinaw Interstade age for the bed and concluded that the Straits of Mackinac must have been free of ice during that time. More recently, Fullerton (1980) has questioned the reliability of these age estimates and has suggested that the bryophyte bed in fact may be related to the Two Creeks Interstade shoreline in southwestern Michigan (Riverside site; Figure 2-5). Here, a sequence of transgressive lake deposits related to Glenwood II occurs above dated detrital organic material. This organic material rests on an eroded till surface (Saugatuck till; Monaghan, Larson, and Gephart 1986) at an altitude of about 178 m and yielded a ^{14}C age estimate of 13,470±130 B.P. (ISGS-1378).

The age and altitude of this organic material confirm the occurrence of a low-water phase (<178m) during the Mackinaw Interstade. Other probable evidence for an "intra-Glenwood" low-water phase has been observed on the west side of Lake Michigan at the Saint Francis section (Figure 2-5) located south of Milwaukee (Monaghan and Hansel 1990). Here, a channel is cut in gray, clayey till and lacustrine sediment of the mid-Woodfordian (Cary) Oak Creek Formation. The channel is filled with sand and gravel and is overlaid by lacustrine sand and silt. The flat surface on the top of the exposure is mapped as part of the Glenwood lake plain (Alden 1918). The stratigraphy at the Saint Francis site suggests that a lower lake level existed sometime after the deposition of Oak Creek till (equivalent to Saugatuck till in Michigan; Monaghan 1985a) but before the "Glenwood" lake level was abandoned.

LAKES HURON AND ERIE BASINS. Lake Maumee, the oldest and highest major lake phase in the Lake Erie basin, is a multilevel lake with three stable phases defined at 244, 232, and 238 m (Maumee I, II, and III, respectively). Initially, Lake Maumee discharged southwest through the outlet at Fort Wayne, Indiana (Figure 2-5); however, sometime prior to about 13,800 years ago the Huron-Erie and Saginaw ice lobes had retreated far enough north to uncover an outlet across southeast Michigan near Imlay City. This allowed stabilization of the Lake Maumee level at 238 m and initiated the Maumee III phase. Drainage from Maumee III flowed west across Michigan through the Imlay Channel and glacial Grand River (Figure 2-5 and Table 2-2) and ultimately discharged into Lake Chicago during the Glenwood I phase (Fullerton 1980; Eschman and Karrow 1985). Continued retreat of the Huron-Erie and Saginaw lobes to north of the Thumb of Michigan just prior to the Mackinaw Interstade permitted confluence of the lakes occupying the Huron and Erie lake basins and allowed the level of Lake Maumee to drop below 238 m. The Imlay Channel outlet was abandoned, and Lake Arkona was initiated as a single lake in both the Huron and Erie lake basins. At least three Arkona levels (between 216 and 212 m) are recognized, each of which initially drained westward down the glacial Grand River into Lake Chicago (Fullerton 1980; Eschman and Karrow 1985). The minimum age for abandonment of the Maumee III drainage through the Imlay Channel, and consequently the time of retreat north of the Thumb of Michigan, is given by a ^{14}C age estimate of 13,770±210 B.P. (I-4899; Burgis 1970). A ^{14}C age estimate on organic material associated with the lowest of the three Arkona levels mentioned above indicates that Lake Arkona had lowered to the 212-m level by 13,600±500 B.P. (W-33; Goldthwait 1958).

Although little direct evidence exists, continued northward retreat of the Huron-Erie Lobe during the Mackinaw Interstade probably resulted in a waterplane ("Arkona" low) well below present-day lake level (176.5 m). Such a low-level lake is implied in the Michigan lake basin by the transgressive lake deposits overlying the eroded till surface at the Riverside site (Figure 2-5). Indirect evidence for similar low-level lakes in the Erie, Huron, and Ontario lake basins has also been presented by Kunkle (1963), Dreimanis (1969), and Barnett (1985). Based on bore-hole data obtained along the Huron River near Ann Arbor, Michigan, Kunkle (1963) proposed that an eastward-draining lake, named Lake Ypsilanti, occupied the Lake Erie basin during the Mackinaw Interstade and had a water-plane below 166 m. Barnett (1985) proposed that a series of progressively lower-level lakes existed in the Lake Erie basin between about 13,400 and 13,000 B.P. The altitudes and age of these lakes were determined based primarily on sedimentary structures associated with the Simcoe and Jacksonburg deltas in southern Ontario, as well as on a ^{14}C age estimate on detrital leaf material collected from the Jacksonburg delta (Figure 2-5). This data indicates that by 13,360±440 B.P. (BGS-929; Barnett 1985), water level in the Lake Erie basin was 26–37 m below the "lowest" (212 m) Arkona level. A stream channel eroded deeply into Simcoe delta bottom-set sediment, and later buried by Lake Whittlesey silt and clay, indicates that after the formation of the delta, water level in the basin fell to at least 161 m. This channel was apparently graded to Lake Ypsilanti (Barnett 1985).

Eschman and Karrow (1985) have postulated that if a low-level lake similar to Lake Ypsilanti also existed in the Huron lake basin, it may have drained eastward through an incipient "Trent River" channel (Figure 2-5) and had a level even lower than Lake Ypsilanti. Based on the altitude and age of the detrital organic material at Riverside in Michigan, the minimum level of Arkona in the Huron lake basin also must have been below 176.5 m sometime after about 13,400 B.P. This is suggested because a low-level lake in the Michigan lake basin (< 177 m) necessitates that drainage from the basin must have been through a low-level outlet, that is, an isostatically depressed northern outlet at or near the Straits of Mackinac. Such a drainage pattern requires confluence of the lakes and consequently a common lake level in both the Michigan and Huron lake basins. Importantly, a lake level below 176.5 m in the Michigan and Huron lake basins also requires that discharge from the basins must be eastward. This is indicated because the Chicago outlet is the lowest known outlet along the west margin of the Michigan lake basin and must have been well above the water-plane of any low-level lake in the basin. Drainage from the Huron lake basin probably discharged through the Trent River lowlands (Figure 2-5) into the Lake Ontario basin (Eschman and Karrow 1985). Alternatively, if the ice margin did not retreat sufficiently northward to uncover the Trent River lowlands, it may have discharged directly into Lake Ypsilanti (Fullerton 1980).

As the ice margin readvanced southward during the initial stages of the Port Huron Stade, blocking northward drainage of Lake Chicago through the Straits of Mackinac, separate lakes in the Michigan and Huron lake basins were formed. This initiated the Glenwood II phase within the Michigan lake basin as Lake Chicago rose back to the 195-m (Glenwood) level and reoccupied the Chicago outlet (Figure 2-5). During this readvance of the low-level outlet, the Huron and Erie lake basins were also apparently blocked, and the level of lakes within these basins rose. Continued southward advance of the ice margin in the Huron lake basin onto the Thumb of Michigan also resulted in the formation of separate lakes in the Huron and Erie basins (i.e., Lake Whittlesey in the Lake Erie basin and Lake Saginaw in the Huron lake basin; Figure 2-5). Lake Whittlesey rose to a maximum level of 225 m and discharged westward through the Ubly Channel into Lake Saginaw (Figure 2-5). Lake Saginaw rose back to the 212-m Arkona level and discharged westward through the Glacial Grand valley (Figure 2-5) into Lake Chicago (Fullerton 1980; Eschman and Karrow 1985). The age of Lake Whittlesey and consequently the end of the Arkona phase is given by two ^{14}C age estimates of 12,920±400 and 12,800±250 B.P. (W-430 and Y-240, respectively; Goldthwait 1958) on detrital wood buried beneath Whittlesey beaches in Ohio. These ages indicate that the ice margin of the Saginaw and Huron-Erie lobes must have readvanced back to the Thumb of Michigan by about 13,000 B.P. (Figure 2-5).

Port Huron Stade, Two Creeks Interstade, Greatlakean Stade Lake Stages
The period between about 10,500 and 13,000 years ago includes glacial events associated with the Port Huron Stade (13,000–12,200 B.P.), Two Creeks Interstade (12,200–11,500 B.P.), the Greatlakean Stade (< 11,500 B.P.; Dreimanis and Goldthwait 1973; Evenson et al. 1976), and the Marquette Stade, or readvance (9900–9500 B.P.; Farrand and Drexler 1985). It also includes lake levels related to the final retreat of late Wisconsinan ice from the upper Great Lakes region. As discussed above, by about 13,000 B.P. the margin of Laurentide ice had advanced to its greatest extent along the Port Huron and related moraines (Figure 2-6). This caused lakes in the Michigan, Huron, and Erie lake basins to transgress to the Glenwood (195 m), Saginaw (212 m), and Whittlesey (225 m) levels in each respective basin. The period after 13,000 B.P. represents one of the most complex and best-studied sequences of lake levels within the Great Lakes region. Within the Michigan lake basin, the Glenwood and Calumet phases of Glacial Lake Chicago as well as phases related to Lake Algonquin occurred (Table 2-2). Within the Huron and Erie lake basins, a series of glacial lakes—including Saginaw, Whittlesey, Warren, Wayne, Grassmere, and Lundy (Elkton)—and phases related to Lake Algonquin occurred (Table 2-2). The altitudes and direction of water flow through connecting channels for these lakes were controlled by several processes. These include the opening and closing of the Straits of Mackinac to fluctuations of the margin of Lake Michigan related to the Two Creeks Interstade, uncovering a series of progressively lower, northern outlets during a general retreat of the Saginaw and Huron-Erie ice lobes, and isostatic uplift of these outlets following deglaciation. The details of the formation of these lakes, their levels, and related ice-margin events within each lake basin are discussed below.

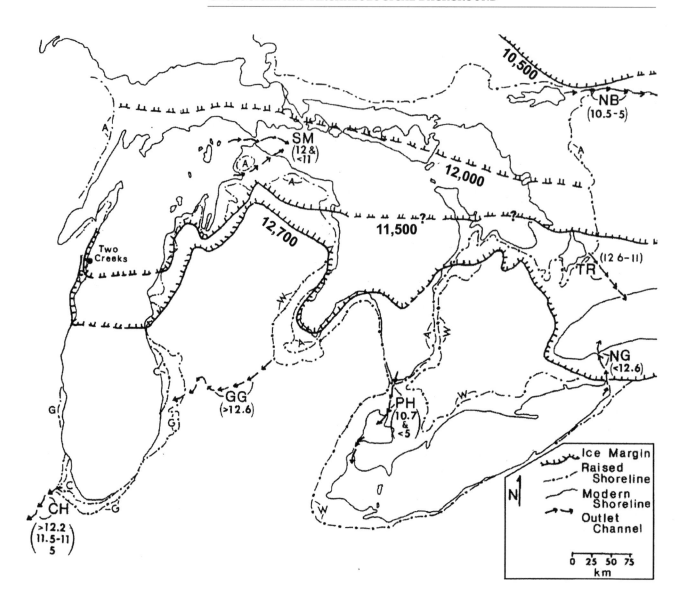

Figure 2-6. The ice-margin and shoreline positions, connecting channels, and location of sites discussed in text for the period 13,000-10,000 ^{14}C years B.P. Ice margins dashed where inferred or approximate; ages (B.P.) shown below ice margin. Shoreline positions shown for high-level lake phases only; G = Glenwood II, C = Calumet, W = Warren, A = Algonquin. Low-level lakes assumed to lie within the boundaries of the modern lake margins. Positions of connecting channels and direction of water flow shown by arrows. Approximate time of activity of channels shown in parentheses below the name of each channel (in 1,000 years B.P.); CH = Chicago, GG = Glacial Grand channel, NB = North Bay, NG = Niagara, PH = Port Huron, SM = Straits of Mackinac, TR = Trent River lowlands (Kirkfield and Fenelon Falls).

LAKE MICHIGAN BASIN. By about 13,000 years ago, during the initial advance of the Port Huron Stade, the margin of the Lake Michigan Lobe advanced south to the position of the Port Huron Moraine (Figure 2-6). This advance initiated the Glenwood II phase, as it blocked the isostatically depressed northern outlet used during the Mackinaw Interstade, forcing Lake Chicago to rise back to 195-m (Glenwood level) and transferring drainage to the southern Chicago outlet. The Glenwood II phase is recorded in the southern end of the basin by deposits at Dyer spit and the Glenwood II beach in its type area (Figure 2-6). [14]C age estimates of wood from these landforms indicate that they were formed by 12,660±140 to 12,400±300 B.P. (Schneider and Reshkin 1970).

Continued northward retreat of the Lake Michigan Lobe during the Port Huron Stade and early part of the Two Creeks Interstade ultimately uncovered a lower, northern outlet at either the Indian River lowlands or the Straits of Mackinac. As drainage was transferred from Chicago to these lower, northern outlets, Lake Chicago fell, and the Two Creeks low-water phase was initiated. Abandonment of the Chicago outlet requires that drainage through the northern outlets from the Michigan lake basin must have been eastward into the Huron lake basin and probably would have resulted in confluence of lakes formed in both basins. Lake Algonquin in the Huron Lake basin was contemporaneous with the Two Creeks low phase (Hansel et al. 1985) and ultimately drained eastward through the Trent River valley (Fenelon Falls outlet; Figure 2-6 and Table 2-2).

The Two Creeks low phase probably began before about 12,000 B.P. (Fullerton 1980; Hansel et al. 1985). Evidence for this low-level phase is provided by the occurrence of a forest bed a few meters above the present level of Lake Michigan at Two Creeks, Wisconsin (Figure 2-6). [14]C age estimates indicate that growth of this forest bed began before 11,950 B.P. (Broecker and Farrand 1963). The presence of Two Creeks–age wood associated with peat beneath sediments of a spit (Rose Hill spit; Figure 2-6) formed during the Calumet phase of Lake Chicago provides further evidence for a low-water phase related to the Two Creeks Interstade (Schneider and Reshkin 1970; Hansel et al. 1985). Importantly, the age and stratigraphic position of this peat deposit (i.e., below-shoreline features related to the Calumet phase of Lake Chicago) also indicate that the Two Creeks low phase must have antedated the inception of the Calumet phase in the basin.

During the initial advance of the Greatlakean Stade, the margin of the Lake Michigan Lobe advanced south to the position of the Two Rivers Moraine (Figure 2-6). This advance initiated the Calumet phase, as it blocked the isostatically depressed northern outlet used during the Two Creeks Interstade, forcing Lake Chicago to rise to 189 m (Calumet level) and transferring drainage back to the southern Chicago outlet. This post–Two Creeks transgression is recorded by the occurrence of lake sediments between the Two Creeks forest bed and overlying Two Rivers till at Two Creeks, Wisconsin (Figure 2-6), and by well-developed beaches at 189 m (Calumet level) in the southern end of basin. Hansel et al. (1985) show that detrital wood associated with beaches and other shoreline features related to the Calumet phase in the southern end of the basin is Two Creeks age and younger. They suggest that the Calumet phase of Glacial Lake Chicago ranges in age from 11,800 to 11,200 B.P.

The 11,200 B.P. lower age limit for the Calumet phase corresponds with the abandonment of southward drainage of Lake Chicago. As the margin of the Lake Michigan Lobe retreated north of the Straits of Mackinac during the Great-lakean Stade, it again uncovered a lower northern outlet, and water in both the Michigan and Huron lake basins became confluent. This latter event initiated Glacial Lake Algonquin in the Michigan lake basin. Drainage was eastward in the Huron lake basin, which discharged through the Trent River valley at Fenelon Falls (Figure 2-6).

LAKES HURON AND ERIE BASINS. As mentioned above, as the margins of the Huron-Erie and Saginaw ice lobes advanced southward after the Mackinaw Interstade, the levels in the Huron and Erie lake basins began to rise. Once ice had advanced to the Port Huron Moraine at about 13,000 B.P. (early part of the Port Huron Stade), separate high-level lakes were formed in each basin–Lake Whittlesey (225 m) in the Erie basin and Lake Saginaw (212 m) in the Huron (Saginaw) basin (Table 2-2). Lake Whittlesey drained westward through the Ubly channel into Lake Saginaw, which discharged through the Glacial Grand River into Lake Chicago. Lake Whittlesey was short-lived, with a duration probably fewer than 200 years (Eschman and Karrow 1985), and was abandoned in stages as the ice retreated from the Thumb of Michigan, uncovering progressively lower outlets (Eschman 1978; Drake 1980; Eschman and Karrow 1985). When the margins of the Huron-Erie and Saginaw ice lobes had retreated north of the Thumb, a confluent lake was formed in the Huron and Erie lake basins. This lake, called Lake Warren, drained westward through the Glacial Grand into Lake Chicago. By the time Lake Warren was initiated, the threshold of the Glacial Grand must have been lowered by about 2 m from the 212-m Saginaw level.

Lake Warren is represented by at least three levels (210, 206, and 203 m), each of which drained into Lake Chicago via the Glacial Grand. Based on mapping of terraces along the Glacial Grand River, Farrand and Eschman (1974) contend that highest Warren (210 m) drained into Lake Chicago when it had dropped to the Calumet level (189 m). This would necessitate that Lake Chicago fell from the Glenwood II level (195 m) to the Calumet level (189 m) by about 12,700 B.P., prior to the Two Creeks Interstade (Eschman and Karrow 1985). As mentioned above, however, ^{14}C age estimates of Lake Chicago sediments preclude this interpretation and indicate that the transition from Glenwood II to Calumet occurred after the Two Creeks Interstade.

According to most present-day interpretations, the Warren sequence was interrupted by a short-lived, eastward-draining, relatively low lake phase. This "intra-Warren" lake phase, called Lake Wayne, occurs at 201 m (about 2 m below the "lowest" Warren level) and is found in both the Huron and Erie lake basins. It was apparently formed during a minor fluctuation of the ice margin in western New York, which permitted drainage to open through incipient channels between the Genesee Valley and Syracuse (Fullerton 1980; Muller and Prest 1985; Calkin and Feenstra 1985). Westward drainage through the Glacial Grand was reestablished during the lowest and youngest Warren level as the ice margin in western New York advanced and again blocked these channels. Ice retreat from the Batavia Moraine, just west of Niagara Falls, reactivated these eastward-draining channels and caused the level of Lake Warren to fall. When the level of

Warren fell below 203 m, drainage through the Glacial Grand ceased. The age of the end of Warren is generally given as about 12,600 to 12,500 B.P., just prior to the Two Creeks Interstade and consequently before the Glenwood level (195 m) of Lake Chicago was abandoned.

The fall of Lake Warren initiated a series of very short-lived lakes in both the Huron and Erie lake basins (Table 2-2): Lake Grassmere (195 m), Lake Lundy (189 m), Lake Elkton (188 m), and Early Lake Algonquin (184 m). Because these lake stages are now represented by generally weak and discontinuous shore features, long-distance correlation of their strands is very tenuous. Neither the direction of water flow nor the outlets used by Lakes Grassmere and Lundy have been unequivocally determined (Table 2-2; Calkin and Feenstra 1985). In fact, some beaches associated with Lakes Grassmere and Lundy may have been either subaqueous bars formed in older lakes or eolian deposits (Eschman and Karrow 1985). This confusion of beach strands, and other correlation problems, probably results from the fact that this sequence of lakes occurred within only a few hundred years. An Early Lake Algonquin level within the Lake Erie basin has yet to be firmly established and is generally considered restricted to the Huron lake basin (Calkin and Feenstra 1985). The level of Early Lake Algonquin was probably controlled by a sill in the Port Huron area associated with the "ancestral" St. Clair River. The sequence of lakes (Grassmere to Early Lake Algonquin) was also probably isolated from the Michigan lake basin since the sill at the head of the Glacial Grand River at Maple Rapids, Michigan, was too high to carry drainage and the Straits of Mackinac were still covered by ice. However, several researchers have suggested that Early Lake Algonquin may have briefly occupied both the Michigan and Huron lake basins.

With retreat of the ice margin from the Batavia Moraine, a lower, eastward-flowing outlet channel was uncovered in the Niagara Falls area (Syracuse channel; Fullerton 1980). This channel caused the level of Warren to drop to 195 m and initiated Lake Grassmere. Lake Grassmere apparently had a congruent water-plane in both the Huron and Erie lake basins but was probably connected by a shallow, relatively narrow strait in the Port Huron area (Leverett and Taylor 1915). This level (195 m) was maintained for less than 100 years (Eschman and Karrow 1985).

Erosion of the outlet channel in northwestern New York and/or continued northward retreat of the ice margin in the Niagara Falls area caused the level of Lake Grassmere to fall 4 to 5 m. Lake Lundy and then Lake Elkton were initiated and apparently maintained congruent water-planes in both the Huron and Erie lake basins. In order for these lakes to maintain a concordant water level in both lake basins, the shallow, narrow strait at Port Huron that initially connected Lake Grassmere must have been incised. This marks the first stage in the development of the St. Clair River as an outlet channel for the Huron lake basin.

The final retreat of ice from the Niagara Escarpment at Niagara Falls removed the ice barrier separating the Erie and Ontario basins. This resulted in confluence of waters in both basins and lowered Lake Lundy as channels across the Buffalo–Fort Erie and Niagara Falls moraines were incised. This incipient Niagara River probably rapidly eroded to the Onondaga limestone surface and ultimately achieved a level about 40 m below modern Lake Erie (Calkin and Feenstra 1985). This initiated Early Lake Erie. When the water level in the Lake Erie basin was lowered below the sill at Port Huron, Lake Lundy became separated in the Huron basin and discharged southward through the ancestral St. Clair River. Water level within the Huron lake basin was lowered about 4 m to 184 m as the drift barrier underlying the river near Port Huron was eroded. This initiated Early Lake Algonquin, which represents the first of several phases of a complex glacial lake system collectively called Lake Algonquin.

Modern interpretations generally indicate that Lake Algonquin consists of a high-low-high-low sequence of four related phases (Table 2-2): (1) Early Algonquin—a high-level phase that drained south through the St. Clair River, (2) Kirkfield—a low-level phase that drained east through the Trent River valley into the Lake Ontario basin, (3) Main (or Late) Algonquin—a high-level phase that drained through the St. Clair River, and (4) Post-Main Algonquin—a transitional lowering phase that drained east through a series of progressively lower channels near North Bay, Ontario. Although this sequence is generally believed by most researchers, much controversy exists concerning the actual altitude of water-planes and the outlets used by each of these phases (Karrow et al. 1975; Eschman and Karrow 1985; Finamore 1985; Kaszicki 1985; Larsen 1987). The Lake Algonquin sequence of lake phases was initiated at about 12,400 B.P. with the inception of Early Lake Algonquin and ended just prior to 10,500 B.P., when retreat of the ice margin finally uncovered the North Bay outlet and initiated the low-level Chippewa-Stanley lakes. The water levels for phases of Lake Algonquin fluctuated because of the interaction between the rate that northward retreat of the ice margin uncovered isostatically depressed, low, northern outlets and the rate that previously uncovered outlets to the south isostatically rebounded.

Leverett and Taylor (1915) proposed that Early Lake Algonquin (184 m water level) occupied only the southern end of the Huron lake basin and discharged south and east through the St. Clair River in the Lake Erie Basin. They also suggested that northward retreat of the margin of the Huron-Erie Lobe soon uncovered an isostatically depressed low outlet near Kirkfield, Ontario, which caused the water level in the Huron lake basin to fall as discharge was transferred from Port Huron to the Trent River valley (Figure 2-6). The transference of drainage to the Trent River valley marks the inception of the Kirkfield phase of Lake Algonquin. Karrow et al. (1975) and Eschman and Karrow (1985) proposed that the beginning of the Kirkfield phase and consequently the time that the ice margin uncovered the Kirkfield outlet occurred sometime just prior to 12,000 B.P. This age is approximately the same as that suggested by Hansel et al. (1985) for the deglaciation of the Straits of Mackinac during the Two Creeks Interstade. In fact, Hough (1963, 1966) proposed that Early Lake Algonquin was actually confluent in both the Michigan and Huron lake basins and implied that the Straits region was deglaciated prior to the opening of the Kirkfield outlet. Although Hansel et al. (1985) have found no evidence to support this contention, based on the general imprecision of ^{14}C age determination as well as the similarity in age for deglaciation of the Straits and Kirkfield areas, it cannot be completely rejected.

Regardless of the exact temporal relationship of deglaciation between the Straits and Kirkfield areas, the Kirkfield phase was in existence during the Two Creeks Interstade. The Michigan and Huron lake basins must have been occupied by a congruent lake system that discharged eastward through the Trent River valley and shared a common water level controlled by the altitude of the sill near Kirkfield. Both basins shared a common, relatively low-level lake until the margin of the Lake Michigan Lobe readvanced southward to the Two Rivers Moraine during the Greatlakean Stade and blocked the outlet at the Straits of Mackinac. As mentioned previously, this occurred at about 11,500 B.P.

Once the Kirkfield outlet was deglaciated, the lake level was controlled by the local uplift rate at the outlet. This implies that the "lowest" Kirkfield level must have occurred just after deglaciation. Through time, as the outlet rose in altitude through isostatic rebound, lake level also rose. Such a rising lake apparently continued until the Kirkfield outlet was abandoned. Most researchers still espouse the model originally proposed by Leverett and Taylor (1915) that the Kirkfield outlet was abandoned because it rose above the outlet sill initially used by Early Lake Algonquin at Port Huron. Drainage was transferred south to the St. Clair River, and the lake level was stabilized at about 184 m. This initiated the Main Lake Algonquin phase. Although this model for transition from Kirkfield to Main Algonquin phases is generally accepted, many researchers have begun to question it (Kaszicki 1985; Larsen 1985b, 1987). They suggest that the Kirkfield outlet remained the sole outlet during the Main Algonquin phase and that lake level in the south end of the basin never rose above the sill at Port Huron. This difference in interpretation results both from the inability to trace Algonquin beaches near the Kirkfield outlet and from the splitting of beaches north of the outlet because of the geographic position of Kirkfield relative to the whole lake basin (see discussion concerning Figure 2-3). The apparent "splitting" of beaches at Kirkfield has in part frustrated all attempts to define the actual final altitude of the water level in the south end of Lake Huron during the waning stage of the Kirkfield phase and during the Main Algonquin phase. The definition and correlation of such water levels are complicated by the poor development of beaches just south of Kirkfield as well as by the fact that the younger Nipissing beaches apparently either reworked or obliterated them.

Regardless of whether it drained through Port Huron, the Main Algonquin phase continued until the ice margin had retreated far enough north to uncover still lower outlet channels at Fossmill and South River just south of North Bay, Ontario (Figure 2-6). When these channels were uncovered, the level of the lake began to fall, and the Algonquin-Stanley phase was initiated. Water level probably fell in stages as a series of progressively lower outlets were uncovered. This final phase of Lake Algonquin was probably relatively short-lived and ended when the ice margin uncovered the lowest of its outlets at North Bay (Figure 2-6) and initiated Lake Stanley in the Huron lake basin and Lake Chippewa in the Michigan lake basin (Table 2-2).

EASTERN LAKE SUPERIOR BASIN. As the Greatlakean ice margin retreated across the Upper Peninsula of Michigan and into the Superior lake basin, Lake Algonquin also expanded northward. By about 10,700 B.P., the lake had covered most of the eastern Upper Peninsula, as well as the Superior lake basin, and formed a confluent lake in the Superior, Michigan, and Huron lake basins (Farrand and Drexler 1985; Cowan 1985). This confluent lake was short-lived and, similar to the Algonquin phase in the Michigan and Huron lake basins, dropped in stages as the retreating ice margin uncovered a series of progressively lower outlets in the South River and North Bay region of Ontario (Figure 2-6). Several stages of falling water level during the Algonquin phase have been defined in the eastern Superior lake basin based mainly on raised beach and wave terrace features east of Sault Ste. Marie in the region around Whitefish Bay. These stages include (oldest to youngest) Wyebridge (165 m), Penetang (155 m), Cedar Point (150 m), Payette (142 m), and Sheguiandah (134 m; Stanley 1936; Hough 1958; Farrand and Drexler 1985; Cowan 1985).

When the level of Lake Algonquin in the Michigan and Huron lake basins fell to the Chippewa-Stanley low level, the Superior lake basin was isolated, and Lake Minong formed. Initially, Lake Minong probably covered much of the basin and discharged eastward through the St. Mary's River valley. Unlike modern Lake Superior, however, the level of Lake Minong (132 m) was controlled by the Nadoway Point sill, a "drift barrier" that extended from Gros Cap in Ontario to Nadoway Point in Michigan (Saarnisto 1975; Farrand and Drexler 1985). The Nadoway Point sill maintained the level of Lake Minong about 40 m above present lake level. Farrand and Drexler (1985) divided Lake Minong into three phases based on their relationship to the Marquette readvance: early Minong occurred before the advance, main Minong during the advance, and post-Minong during the retreat.

The Marquette readvance occurred at about 9900 B.P. (Farrand and Drexler 1985) and represents a fluctuation of the Laurentide ice margin restricted only to the Superior lake basin. The ice margin apparently advanced across early Lake Minong to the south shore of Lake Superior south of Marquette, Michigan. This resulted in the formation of separate lakes in the eastern and western parts of the basin. Lake Duluth formed in the western part and drained southwest into the Mississippi River; main Lake Minong formed in the east and was generally restricted to Whitefish Bay. Main Lake Minong continued to drain east into the Huron lake basin and probably maintained a similar level to that achieved during early Minong. As the ice margin retreated into Lake Superior, Lake Minong also expanded north and west and eventually became confluent with Lake Duluth in the west.

When the ice margin retreated north of the north shore of Lake Superior at about 9300 B.P., it uncovered a series of outlets for Lake Agassiz (located northwest of the Superior lake basin and covering most of southern Manitoba as well as parts of western Ontario and eastern Saskatchewan). This resulted in periodic catastrophic flooding of the Superior lake basin. The increased and catastrophic discharge from Lake Minong across the Nadoway Point sill accelerated the erosion of the drift barrier and initiated the post-Minong phase. As the sill was downcut, a series of progressively lower level lakes were formed in the basin. This continued until sometime just after 9000 B.P., when bedrock was reached in the St. Mary's River and controlled and stabilized water level in the Superior lake basin and initiated Lake Houghton.

Terminal Wisconsinan and Early Holocene Low-Water Lake Stages

EARLY HOLOCENE LOW-WATER PHASES: Chippewa-Stanley. The Holocene occurs after about 10,500–10,000 B.P. and includes several related lakes formed after the ice margin had completely retreated from the Lower Peninsula of Michigan. These include the low-level Lakes Chippewa (Michigan lake basin),

Stanley (Huron lake basin), and Houghton (Superior lake basin). This period is epitomized by a progressive, widespread transgression of the Lake Chippewa-Stanley (and Houghton) low to mid-Holocene Lake Nipissing high-water levels. The water level and the outlets used during this lake sequence were controlled mainly by the rate of uplift at North Bay. Basinwide variations in climate through time probably also affected, and continue to affect, the water-plane altitude sustained by these lakes.

When the outlet at North Bay was uncovered, water levels in the Michigan and Huron lake basins fell as drainage was transferred to this outlet. This initiated the Chippewa-Stanley phase. Initially, water level in the basin fell to an extremely low altitude and probably created a series of very low-level, connected lakes in both the Michigan and Huron lake basins. Two lakes were believed to have formed in the Huron lake basin, Lake Stanley in the main part of the basin and Lake Hough in the Georgian Bay region (Lewis 1969; Sly and Lewis 1972; Eschman and Karrow 1985). The lowest level achieved by these lakes was <80 m and may have been as low as 45 m (Sly and Lewis 1972). Lake Chippewa formed in the Michigan lake basin and was connected to Lake Stanley through a channel at the Straits of Mackinac (Figure 2-1). The lowest level of Lake Chippewa was at least 117 m and may have been as low as 107 m (Hough 1958; Hansel 1985; Buckley 1974). Early in its history, Lake Chippewa was actually two separate lakes, one that formed in a "southern" basin and another that formed in a "northern" basin. The southern basin existed south of a line from Ludington, Michigan, to Milwaukee, while the northern basin existed between this line and approximately Beaver Island, Michigan. The level of the southern basin was controlled by a relatively deep canyon through subcroppings of Paleozoic limestone located offshore from Milwaukee. Water level in the northern basin, on the other hand, was constrained by a deep bedrock canyon that forms the Straits of Mackinac.

The youngest ages from Lake Algonquin deposits and bogs on the Algonquin plain, as well as from stumps and peat deposits below the current level of Lakes Michigan and Huron, all indicate that the Chippewa-Stanley low phase began at about 10,000 B.P. This is supported by data presented by Lewis (1969), which indicates that the outlet at North Bay was deglaciated sometime prior to 9,820±200 B.P. As mentioned previously, Lake Houghton in the Superior lake basin was formed about 500–800 years later. During the next 5,000 years, isostatic uplift of the North Bay outlet progressively raised the water level in the basin. At some point, North Bay was raised higher than the Straits of Mackinac, and lakes in both the Michigan and Huron lake basins were again confluent. Somewhat later, North Bay was also raised above the St. Mary's River, and all three basins (Superior, Michigan, and Huron) were confluent. This probably occurred about 7500 to 7000 B.P. (Saarnisto 1975; Farrand and Drexler 1985). Although a whole series of lake levels and phases must have existed during this period, any record of them is now submerged below Lakes Michigan and Huron or was effectively destroyed around the periphery of the lakes by the later Nipissing transgression. Continued uplift of the North Bay outlet eventually raised it above the altitude of the previously abandoned southern outlets at Port Huron and Chicago, and drainage was transferred to these southern outlets. This initiated Lake Nipissing as a confluent lake in the Superior, Michigan, and Huron lake basins.

Middle-to-Late Holocene High-Water Lake Stages

MID-HOLOCENE LAKE NIPISSING AND ALGOMA. Initially, Lake Nipissing must have simultaneously drained through three outlets: North Bay, Chicago, and Port Huron (Lewis 1969; Hansel et al. 1985; Larsen 1985b). Lewis (1969) suggested two phases for Lake Nipissing based on the number of outlets used; Nipissing I was defined as the three-outlet phase, while Nipissing II was defined as the two-outlet phase (only Chicago and Port Huron). The maximum level of Lake Nipissing was achieved during the Nipissing I phase (Lewis 1969; Larsen 1985b). The age of the maximum level of Lake Nipissing (Nipissing I; 184 m) is generally placed at about 5000 B.P. (Eschman and Karrow 1985), but it may have occurred as early as about 5500 B.P. (Lewis 1969) or as late as about 4700–4500 B.P. (Dreimanis 1958; Larsen 1985b; Monaghan, Lovis, and Fay 1986). Larsen (1985b) has suggested that water level in the basin first rose above present-day lake level (176.5 m) prior to Nipissing I. He proposes that sometime just prior to about 6000 B.P., lake level in the southern end of Lake Michigan rose to an altitude of 179 m. It apparently again fell below 176.5 m before 5500 B.P. and finally rose to the Nipissing I maximum (184 m) at about 4500 B.P. The idea that the maximum Nipissing level was not achieved until after about 5000 B.P. is somewhat younger than suggested by Lewis (1969). The post-5000 B.P. age, however agrees with the 4800–4700 B.P. age suggested by Monaghan, Lovis and Fay (1986) and the 4700 B.P. age suggested by Lewis and Anderson (1989).

Originally, Lewis (1969) suggested that the level of Lake Nipissing remained stable at about 184 m between phase I and II. He further proposed that Nipissing II ended at about 4000 B.P., when progressive erosion at Port Huron began downcutting the outlet and eventually eroded it below the bedrock sill at Chicago. A short halt during the downcutting of the outlet was believed to have occurred at about 3500 B.P. This resulted in stabilization of lake level at about 181 m and initiated Lake Algoma in the Michigan, Huron, and Superior lake basins. Lewis (1969) indicated that Lake Algoma existed until 2500 B.P., when renewed erosion of the Port Huron outlet progressively lowered the water level to 176.5 m (modern level of Lake Michigan-Huron). As this level was achieved in the Michigan and Huron lake basins, Lake Superior was again isolated as a separate lake, with a level of about 184 m controlled by a bedrock sill in the St. Mary's River at Sault Ste. Marie.

LATE HOLOCENE CLIMATE CONTROLS FOR LAKE LEVELS. The model for periodic stabilization during a gradual fall in water level from Nipissing to Algoma to modern has been generally accepted by most researchers. It derives mainly from Hough (1958, 1963), who proposed that the level of middle and late Holocene lakes was controlled solely by the rate of erosion at Port Huron. This "outlet-controlled" model, however, has been questioned by Larsen (1974, 1985b, 1987). He proposed that although erosion at Port Huron was important, the actual level achieved by middle and late Holocene lakes was mainly controlled by periodic climatic fluctuations and may have varied as much as ±2 m from a "mean" level. For example, based on data collected from the southern end of Lake Michigan, Larsen (1985b) and Hansel et al. (1985) proposed that Nipissing I and II each attained different levels (184 m at 4500 B.P. and 182 m at 4000 B.P., respectively) and represented short-duration "spikes" in lake level. They further suggest that between phase I and II and after phase II, lake level dropped below 178 m. It rose again at about 3500 B.P. (Lake Algoma) and dropped below 176.5 m by 3000 B.P.

The "climate-controlled" model proposed by Larsen (1985b) derives partly from analogy with variation in lake level recorded over the past 200 years for Lakes Michigan and Huron (Figure 2-4). As discussed previously, the high-low fluctuation shown (Figure 2-4) apparently occurs as a response to variation in precipitation and/or temperature (Horton 1927; DeCooke 1967; Larsen 1985b). To some degree, similar variation and response probably also occurred during the Holocene. For example, the high-water levels associated with the Nipissing I and II and Algoma phases may represent periods of higher than normal precipitation, while the intervening low levels relate to lower than normal precipitation periods. The actual difference in water-plane altitude achieved during each of these high phases probably relates to a progressively lower "mean" lake level, which resulted during erosion of the Port Huron outlet.

The data presented above shows that Lake Algoma probably represents a very short duration (<300 years) transgression during a basinwide period of high precipitation. The most recent ^{14}C age estimates of Algoma and younger deposits indicate that the Algoma phase ended before 3000 B.P. and that modern lake levels were attained soon after (Larsen 1985b; Hansel et al. 1985; Monaghan 1985b). In fact, data reported by Miller and Kott (1989) indicates that lake level within the upper Great Lakes may have been substantially below 177 m by about 2800 B.P. They described a 2770±70 B.P. (Beta-17580) peat bed located along the Lake Michigan shoreline west of Traverse City, Michigan. The peat, which occurs at an altitude of about 177 m, is underlain by marl and overlain by nearshore sands. Accounting for uplift in the area over the past 2,800 years (Figure 2-2), the original altitude of this bed was no greater than 174 m and implies a lake level of <174 m. The fact that the peat is overlain by nearshore sand indicates that lake level subsequently rose. This is supported by data from the Bear Creek site (Branstner and Hambacher eds. 1994) that shows humans probably occupied the site, which was below the level of Algoma, by about 3500 B.P.

Based on data collected mainly from the southern end of Lake Michigan, Larsen (1974, 1985b) presented a similar but more detailed record of lake-level fluctuation. He proposed that over the past 2,000 years, lake level has regularly varied up to ±2 m from the mean historic level (176.5 m), and he suggested a 200–300-year period between highs and lows (Larsen 1985b). Transgressions of Lake Michigan-Huron to an altitude of between 178 and 179 m apparently occurred at about 2300, 1500, 1000, and 400 B.P. These high-water stages were interrupted by low stages at about 2000, 1200, and 600 B.P. Because of the vagaries of preservation, the imprecision of radiocarbon age estimates, and difficulties in sedimentologic interpretations, the Holocene lake-level curve presented by Larsen (1974, 1985b) remains at best preliminary. It is, however, conceptually useful and, as discussed in chapter 3, has an important impact on the location and potential for preservation of buried archaeological sites.

CHAPTER THREE

The Middle-to-Late Holocene Geological History

Geoarchaeology and Environmental Background
for Human Adaptation in Michigan

Holocene Lake-Level History and Depositional Processes

The previous chapter outlined the evolution of the upper Great Lakes. It focused on a simple classical "outlet-controlled" model for dictating lake levels within the basin. Although simplistic, this model adequately describes the general sequence of lakes in the region, particularly during the late Wisconsinan and the early Holocene, when fluctuations in the Laurentide ice margin alternatively exposed or covered outlets of differing altitudes and positions around the basins. These resulted in significant, sometimes catastrophic changes in lake level and configuration. Similarly, the outlet-controlled model broadly describes lake sequences during most of the early and middle Holocene. The levels of these lakes were controlled by outlet rebound at North Bay, Ontario, and subsequent erosion at Port Huron rather than by ice-margin fluctuations. The early Holocene is generally delineated by a regional transgression (Chippewa-Stanley to Nipissing), whose level was determined by the rate at which the North Bay outlet isostatically rose. The middle and late Holocene, on the other hand, witnessed a major regression of lake level (Nipissing-Algoma to modern), when North Bay finally rose above southern outlet at Port Huron, where erosion ultimately lowered lake level to the modern configuration (Figure 3-1). As pointed out in the previous chapter and detailed below, the outlet-controlled model does not adequately account for the sequence of minor, middle-to-late Holocene fluctuations in lake level. An additional model, the "climate-controlled" model, combined with the outlet-controlled model, more realistically depicts both the broad and the smaller-scale lake-level variations (Figure 3-1).

Even the simple, classic outlet-controlled model would have had profound effects not only on the actual locations of shorelines at any point in time but also on the rivers and streams draining into the lake (Lovis, Holman, Monaghan, and Skowronek 1994). During the early phases of Lake Stanley, for example, existing streams probably responded to low base levels by downcutting. As the lake transgressed, however, base level progressively rose, which resulted in lowered stream gradients and aggradation along the stream valleys. This aggradation culminated as the high-level Nipissing waters drowned and flooded the mouths and downstream portions of streams. Importantly, as stream gradients were lower during the Nipissing transgression, upstream portions were probably subjected to increased flooding and consequently increased rates of alluviation. Between 5000 and 3000 B.P., lake level fell, again lowering base level and thereby increasing stream gradients. During this time, stream channels in the area probably incised and partially eroded their valleys by downcutting through the veneer of "Nipissing" alluvium (Lovis, Holman, Monaghan, and Skowronek 1994).

Research undertaken during the past two decades in the Great Lakes region has resulted in an even more dynamic picture of lake-level change than suggested by the outlet-controlled model (Figure 3-1). This research suggests that even minor variations in climate may have affected water level within the Great Lakes region through basinwide variations in either precipitation or temperature (Fraser et al. 1975, 1990; Larsen 1985b). During the Holocene, periods of reduced precipitation result in a lowering of lake level because less water entered the basin. Similarly, wet conditions result in an increase in lake level mainly because more water is input into the basin. Long-term changes in temperature can also affect lake level by increasing evaporation during generally warm periods or reducing evaporation during more cool periods. Increased evaporation will lower the lake level (Fraser et al. 1975, 1990). Larsen (1985b) was one of the early proponents of this model of climate-controlled lake-level fluctuation for the middle and late Holocene lake sequence. He suggested that the level of Lakes Michigan and Huron varied about ±1–2 m from the mean and that this variation occurs in 200-to-300-year cycles (Figure 3-1).

The minor "transgressions and regressions" that resulted from the cyclical lake-level variation would have had a profound effect on rivers and streams

Figure 3-1. Holocene and historic variation of the level of Lakes Michigan and Huron based on different models and data sets. Insert shows historic variation based on historic records. Horizontal axis shows time (in calendar years); vertical axis shows observed average lake level (in meters) for each year. Datum is sea level. Dash line shows actual change in elevation; solid line shows three-component polynomial best fit line through the data.

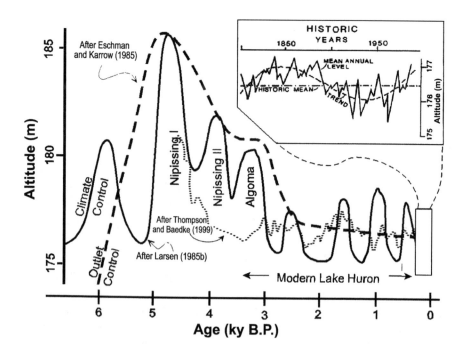

draining into the lake. They would result in generating a series of alluviation and incision events similar to those discussed above and ultimately have created a varied, thick, complex floodplain stratigraphy along stream channels (Lovis, Holman, Monaghan, and Skowronek 1994; Monaghan and Hayes 1998, 1999, 2001). In places rimming the Great Lakes region where broad, low-lying lacustrine plains exist just above modern lake level, these processes would have been greatly accentuated. One such area, informally called the "Shiawassee flats," includes one of the largest concentrations of Archaic-through-Woodland-period buried and stratified sites in Michigan. Here, a generally level ground surface lies only a few meters above present-day lake level and extends nearly 20 km inland (Figures 3-2, 3-3). Moreover, the rivers that drain the area flow

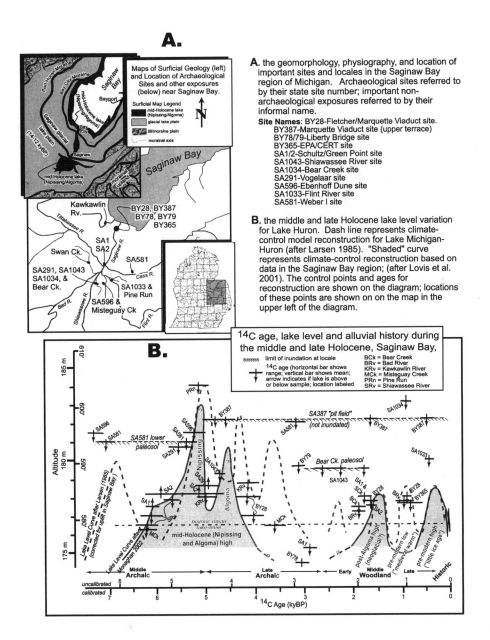

Figure 3-2. Middle and late Holocene lake-level curve in the Saginaw Bay region (after Monaghan 2002a).

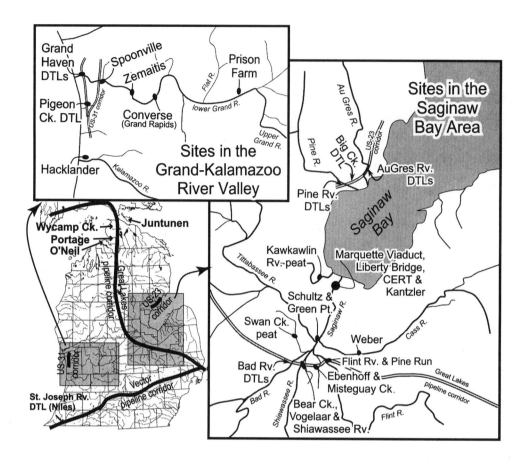

Figure 3-3. Michigan, with inserts of the lower Grand River valley and the Saginaw Bay region, showing the locations of sites and locales discussed in chapter 3.

from fine-textured moraine uplands that mark the margin of the flats and provide the source of fine sediments that ultimately mantle alluvial plains during episodic flood events. The great concentration of buried and stratified sites in the region is a direct result of the types of alluvial processes related to minor changes in base level discussed above (Lovis, Holman, Monaghan, and Skowronek 1994).

The kinds and magnitude of prehistoric lake-level variability discussed above are well documented by historic records. Beginning in the early nineteenth century, Euro-Americans residents in the region began keeping measurements of water levels in the Great Lakes basins. By 1860, the U.S. Army Corps of Engineers established and maintained a series of lake gages throughout the region. Data compiled from these records demonstrate that, at least during historic times, the mean annual level of Lakes Michigan and Huron has varied considerably (Figure 3-1). For example, in the mid-1830s the altitude of lake level was about 177.5 m (about 1 m above mean levels; Figure 3-1). High-water levels (above the historic mean altitude of 176.5 m) were generally sustained until about 1890, when lake level began to fall below the historic mean level. By 1930, lake level had fallen to about 176.5 m. With a few exceptions, below-mean levels were maintained until the mid-1970s and 1980s, when they rose nearly to the 1830s' high-water level.

Beginning with Larsen's (1985b) seminal work, many other researchers have also noted that minor but important cyclical lake-level fluctuations occurred throughout the Great Lakes region during the Holocene (Coakley 1999; Fraser et al. 1990; Larsen 1999b; Lewis 1999; Lovis, Holman, Monaghan, and Skowronek 1994; Lovis et al. 2001; Monaghan and Hayes 1997, 1998; Monaghan and Schaetzl 1994; Sellinger 1999; Thompson 1992; Thompson and Baedke 1995, 1997, 1999). Thompson (1992) and Thompson and Baedke (1995, 1997, 1999) are particularly relevant. Like Larsen (1985b), their work focuses on Lake Michigan during the past 4,000–5,000 years, but rather than relate lake-level fluctuations to climate alone, they suggest that natural, lacustrine evolutionary processes, coupled with climate change and isostatic rebound, controlled shoreline configurations. Others have come to accept the climate-controlled model as generally correct but have begun to look at the details of the Larsen (1985b) model. For example, although agreeing with the general tenor of Larsen's ideas, Monaghan (2002) has raised questions about some details of the model, particularly its timing. He has used data derived specifically from the Saginaw Bay region collected from various sources during the past 10–15 years but has particularly emphasized the most recent excavations at the Marquette Viaduct site (Lovis ed. 2002). This focus on the Saginaw Bay region is not coincidental but rather reflects the unique physiography of the area for enhancing floodplain aggradation during lake-level fluctuations. The area thus provides a long-term record that relates alluviation, climate, and lake level. Furthermore, because it provides a relatively large number of age-dated lake-level indicators from a geologically and geographically uniform area, the region also furnishes a unique window through which to compare the timing and levels for the middle Holocene Lakes Nipissing and Algoma. This is suggested because the area lies near the southern outlet at Port Huron and is subjected to only minimal north-south differential uplift.

Serious discrepancies in the timing of the mid-Holocene lakes (Nipissing and Algoma) become apparent when the age and altitude of lake-level indicators from archaeological sites and exposures in the Saginaw Bay region are superimposed on Larsen's curve (Figure 3-2). This is particularly obvious between 4,500 and 3,000 calendar years B.P. (cal B.P.). During this period, soils and archaeological features from several sites, including the Marquette Viaduct site (Lovis ed. 2002), ostensibly occur well below the lake level that existed during their formation. Such a relationship is unlikely. Similar inconsistencies, however, are also apparent during the late Holocene.

In order to accommodate this data with the sequence of Holocene lakes, Monaghan (2002a) developed a revised lake-level curve (shaded curve labeled Monaghan 2002; Figure 3-2). It indicates a much briefer interval for the mid-Holocene high-level Lakes Nipissing and Algoma than either the outlet-controlled or climate-controlled curves (lake-level curve by Larsen [1985b] shown in Figure 3-2 for comparison). It also shows a lower maximum level for the mid-Holocene high-level lakes more similar to that originally proposed by Leverett and Taylor (1915). Most important, this data suggests that modern lake level was achieved soon after about 4000 B.P., 1,000–1,500 years earlier than previously believed.

As implied by Larsen (1985b) and Monaghan and Schaetzl (1994), the new data (Figure 3-2 and Table 3-1; Monaghan 2002) also demonstrates that the "initial" level of Lake Huron formed prior to 3500 B.P. was typically lower than present. This low-level interval apparently lasted for 1,500–2,000 years (Figure 3-2). Beginning about 2000 B.P., however, lake level apparently rose above normal, which resulted in extensive flooding around the Great Lakes region (Larsen 1985b; Lovis et al. 1996; Monaghan and Schaetzl 1994; Monaghan and Hayes 1997, 1998, 2001; Thompson and Baedke 1997; Lovis, Holman, Monaghan, and Skowronek 1994). This event has been informally referred to as the "post-Algoma high" by Monaghan and Schaetzl (1994). It not only included an extended high-water level for Lake Huron but also apparently represented a period of relatively frequent flooding of streams, even away from the Great Lakes shoreline (Monaghan and Schaetzl 1994; Monaghan and Hayes 1997, 1998, 2001). The pattern of middle and late Holocene lake-level fluctuations and its significance for Archaic and Woodland settlement is discussed below.

Although secular variation in lake level and concomitant stream alluviation had an important impact on the burial and preservation of archaeological sites, historic land use, generally unrelated to the kinds of lake-level fluctuations discussed above, probably also resulted in increased alluviation along streams (Lovis, Holman, Monaghan, and Skowronek 1994). For example, after about 1850, much of the Grand and Kalamazoo river basins in western Michigan and the Saginaw Bay region in eastern Michigan were intensively logged. Once denuded of timber, these areas were settled and farmed by Euro-American immigrants. These agricultural activities generally removed permanent vegetation, resulting in increased runoff and erosion throughout the basin. As a consequence of increasing runoff and suspended-sediment load input to streams, flooding probably intensified (Wright 1972; Lovis, Holman, Monaghan, and Skowronek 1994). These processes ultimately resulted in deposition of a variably thick mantle of fine-textured sediment that effectively buried and "sealed" the presettlement floodplain surface (Lovis, Holman, Monaghan, and Skowronek 1994).

Several archaeological sites include components that were buried by flooding during this interval. Within the Bay City area, these include the Marquette Viaduct site (20BY28; Lovis et al. 1996 and Lovis ed. 2002) and the CERT site (20BY365; Demeter et al. 1994; Figure 3-2). Other sites in the region include the Green Point and Schultz sites (20SA1 and 20SA2; Demeter et al. 2000; Lovis et al. 2001) and the Bear Creek site (20BY1034; Monaghan and Schaetzl 1994). Water levels within the Great Lakes basin were again low after about 1500 B.P. and subsequently returned to high levels by about 800 B.P. (Monaghan and Hayes 1997, 1998).

The discussion of the two major models of the controls for Holocene lake level in the upper Great Lakes, the outlet-controlled and climate-controlled models, suggests that broad patterns of lake level fluctuation exist for the upper Great Lakes. This is particularly true for the Michigan-Huron lake basin and has important implications for the burial and preservation of archaeological sites. For example, the outlet-controlled model suggests that the first 5,000 years of the Holocene were dominated by a long-term, nearly 100-m transgression in the basin to the Nipissing high-water phase, followed by a shorter-duration regression of about 20 m to modern levels. The climate-controlled model, on the other hand, suggests that 1–2-m fluctuations of a few centuries duration were superimposed on these long-term changes. Based on data collected over the past

Table 3-1. Unpublished ^{14}C Age Estimates.

River Basin (location)	Material-Method	Lab #	^{14}C Age	^{14}C age 2-Sigma Calibration
Saginaw (Bay City)	wood-conventional	Beta-17545	3050+/-80	1495 B.C.–1046 (3445–2996 B.P.)
Swan Creek (Saginaw)	wood-conventional	Beta-17546	1870+/-110	95 B.C.–A.D. 414 (2045–1536 B.P.)
Deer Creek (St. Charles)	wood-conventional	Beta-18099	2720+/-70	1006–793 B.C. (2956–2743 B.P.)
Deer Creek (St. Charles)	wood-conventional	Beta-18100	2430+/-60	787–392 B.C. (2737–2342 B.P.)
Bear Creek	wood-conventional	Beta-40282	1900±60	38 B.C.–A.D. 243 (1988–1707 B.P.)
Bear Creek	wood-conventional	Beta-40283	5320±80	4338–3966 B.C. (6288–5916 B.P.)
Bear Creek	wood-conventional	Beta-40284	5030±70	3974–3656 B.C. (5924–5606 B.P.)
Bad River (N Fork)	wood-conventional	Beta-40285	2200±70	399–49 B.C. (2349–1999 B.P.)
Bad River (S Fork)	wood-conventional	Beta-40286	1060±60	A.D. 785–1152 (1165–798 B.P.)
Bad River (S Fork)	wood-conventional	Beta-40287	1940±50	44 B.C.–A.D. 212 (1993–1738 B.P.)
Straits (St. Ignace)	wood-conventional	Beta-40288	2630±70	915–547 B.C. (2865–2497 B.P.)
Straits (St. Ignace)	wood-conventional	Beta-40289	6550±80	5627–5325 B.C. (7577–7275 B.P.)
Straits (St. Ignace)	wood-conventional	Beta-40290	6430±70	5510–5297 B.C. (7460–7247 B.P.)
Crooked River	wood-conventional	Beta-40291	5440±70	4448–4048 B.C. (6398–5998 B.P.)
Crooked River	wood-conventional	Beta-40292	6450±80	5604–5297 B.C. (7554–7247 B.P.)
Ebenhoff Dune	peat-conventional	Beta-40293	12210±110	13483–11884 B.C. (15433–13834 B.P.)
Flint River	wood-conventional	Beta-40294	910±50	A.D. 1019–1245 (931–705 B.P.)
Fishdam River	wood-conventional	Beta-40295	5330±70	4336–3979 B.C. (6286–5929 B.P.)
Fishdam River	wood-conventional	Beta-40296	400±60	A.D. 1414–1642 (536–308 B.P.)
Fishdam River	wood-conventional	Beta-40297	7140±80	6203–5812 B.C. (8153–7762 B.P.)
Misteguay Creek	wood-conventional	Beta-40298	3410±70	1884–1521 B.C. (3834–3471 B.P.)
Misteguay Creek	wood-conventional	Beta-40299	5460±70	4453–4051 B.C. (6403–6001 B.P.)
Manisique River	wood-conventional	Beta-40300	4920±80	3940–3535 B.C. (5890–5485 B.P.)
Pine Run	wood-conventional	Beta-40301	4560±70	3515–3028 B.C. (5465–4978 B.P.)
Shiawassee River	wood-conventional	Beta-40302	5500±90	4516–4052 B.C. (6466–6002 B.P.)
Shiawassee River	wood-conventional	Beta-40302	1020±90	A.D. 782–1216 (1168–734 B.P.)
Sturgeon River	wood-conventional	Beta-40304	850±60	A.D. 1027–1283 (923–667 B.P.)
Saginaw (Saginaw)	wood-conventional	Beta-148249	5390+/-80	4030–4030 B.C. (6310–5980 B.P.)
Grand (Ionia)	charcoal-AMS	Beta-148250	4500+/-40	3060–3030 B.C. (5310–4980 B.P.)
Grand (Ionia)	wood-conventional	Beta-148251	6350+/-80	5480–5210 B.C. (7430–7150 B.P.)
Pine (S Br)	wood-conventional	Beta-148252	6750+/-90	5790–5500 B.C. (7740–7450 B.P.)
Pine (N. Branch)	woods-conventional	Beta-148254	550+/-50	A.D. 1300–1440 (650–510 B.P.)
Pine (N Branch)	wood-conventional	Beta-148255	5250+/-70	4240–3950 B.C. (6190–5900 B.P.)
Pine (N. Branch)	wood-conventional	Beta-148256	1810+/-70	A.D. 60–400 (1890–1550 B.P.)
Big Creek	wood-conventional	Beta-148257	9800+/-50	9340–9160 B.C. (11,290–11,110 B.P.)
Au Gres (North)	wood-conventional	Beta-148258	2060+/-50	190 B.C.–A.D. 50 (2140–1900 B.P.)
Au Gres (south)	wood-conventional	Beta-148259	350+/-80	A.D. 1420–1670 & 1780–1800 (530–280 & 170–150 B.P.)
Au Gres (south)	wood-conventional	Beta-148260	770+/-60	A.D. 1170–1300 (780–650 B.P.)
St. Joseph (Niles)	wood-conventional	Beta-148261	3700+/-70	2290–1900 B.C. (4240–3850 B.P.)
St. Joseph (Niles)	charcoal-AMS	Beta-148262	160+/-40	A.D. 1660–1950 (290–0 B.P.)
Saginaw (Saginaw)	squash seed- AMS	Beta-150203	2820+/-40	1060–880 B.C. (3000–2840 B.P.)
Saginaw (Saginaw)	charcoal AMS	Beta-150204	1810+/-40	A.D. 110–330 (1840–1620 B.P.)
Saginaw (Saginaw)	charcoal-AMS	Beta-150262	1830+/-40	A.D. 90–260 (1860–1690 B.P.)

two decades, we suggest that the Holocene can be characterized by five major cycles of stream alluviation. These are related to fluctuations in the level of the Great Lakes, which ultimately reflect broad episodes of secular variation in the regional climate. Informally, these are (1) the Early Holocene Chippewa-Stanley "Incision" (ca. 10,000–5000 B.P.), (2) the mid-Holocene Nipissing-Algoma "alluviation" (ca. 5000–3500 B.P.), (3) the late Holocene post-Algoma "low" (stabilization) and "high" (alluviation; ca. 3500–1500 B.P.), (4) the premodern "low" (stabilization) and "high" (alluviation; ca. 1500–200 B.P.), and (5) modern (post-settlement) alluviation.

Early Holocene Low-Level Lakes: Chippewa-Stanley Incision

The early Holocene in the Michigan-Huron lake basin drainage is generally characterized by stream incision related to the low-water Chippewa-Stanley phases. As mentioned above, during the early part of the Stanley phase, streams that existed in the region, particularly near the present shore of the Great Lakes, probably responded to lowered base and, consequently, groundwater, levels by downcutting. Evidence for such downcutting exists throughout the region. It is particularly clear near the present Great Lakes shorelines and was first noted in the nineteenth and early twentieth centuries (Leverett and Taylor 1915). In western Michigan, for example, the mouths of most of the major rivers, such as the Kalamazoo, St. Joseph, Grand, and Muskegon, are drowned. This is also true for the Au Sable and Saginaw rivers along the Lake Huron shoreline in eastern Michigan. The drowned mouths indicate that these rivers were previously graded to a lower lake level. They apparently downcut through the poorly consolidated glaciolacustrine deposits that underlay most of Michigan. Their now-drowned channels probably extended across what is now lake bottom and were progressively back-flooded as the Nipissing transgression continued during the early and mid-Holocene. In addition, several research projects in the lower Grand and Kalamazoo valleys in western Michigan as well as the Saginaw Bay region of east-central Michigan provide evidence for more deeply incised channels that were subsequently inundated during the Nipissing transgression.

The progressive rise of the Great Lakes during the early Holocene was probably periodically interrupted by smaller-scale climate-induced fluctuations similar to that of the modern Great Lakes. Evidence for this process, however, is generally absent because it either lies buried under the Great Lakes or was progressively destroyed by continually transgressing shoreline environments. Tantalizingly recent, more detailed bathymetric maps of the lake bottom in the more protected embayments, such as Grand Traverse and Saginaw Bay, reveal morphological evidence of complex, drowned "channel" networks that probably reflect early-to-mid-Holocene river systems. Along these lines, Lovis et al. (1994) have reconstructed the Nipissing transgression of the Saginaw Bay and have mapped the extension of the 8000–7000 B.P. Saginaw River out into Saginaw Bay. They have also provided a framework for recovering buried archaeological and ecological information from these drowned valleys.

Some of the most extensive testing of river valley and Holocene shorelines related to archaeological site excavations and cultural resource management (CRM) projects has occurred in the Saginaw Bay region. This is not surprising given the historic importance of the Schultz and Green Point sites (20SA2 and 20SA1, respectively) near Saginaw to the development of buried site models in Michigan. While most of the studies undertaken in the Saginaw Bay area focused on the post-Nipissing late Holocene in the hopes of finding another Schultz site, some included comprehensive suites of ^{14}C age estimates that shed light on the early-to-middle Holocene fluvial environment. For example, Larsen and Demeter (1979) reported an early radiocarbon date and secondary archaeological deposits at the Kantzler site (20BY30) in Bay City. This finding was important because it showed that archaeological deposits in coastal and/or early Holocene fluvial environments might be preserved on early-to-middle Holocene surfaces. Moreover, in places where conditions were right, such surfaces could be buried during the Nipissing transgression. Although no one has since found pre-Nipissing in situ archaeological deposits at Bay City, by taking Larsen's (1980) call for more systematic testing of concealed middle Holocene surfaces to heart, several researchers have since discovered and tested various Middle-to-Late Archaic archaeological sites that were buried and/or stratified during the Nipissing transgression around the Saginaw Bay region. Principal among these is the Weber I site (20SA581) along the Cass River in Saginaw County near Frankenmuth (Brunett 1981a, 1981c; Lovis ed. 1989; Monaghan and Fay 1989; Monaghan, Lovis, and Fay 1986;), the Ebenhoff site (20SA596) near St. Charles (Beaverson 1993; Beaverson and Mooers 1993; Branstner 1990a, 1991; Dobbs and Murray 1993), and the Bear Creek site, also near St. Charles (Branstner 1990a, 1991; Branstner and Hambacher eds.1994; Monaghan and Schaetzl 1994).

The Weber I site (Figure 3-3) is an excellent example of the type of interplay between a lake transgression and human settlement patterns discussed by Larsen (1980) for the middle Holocene. It also illustrates the fluvial and alluvial environments typical of the early to middle Holocene. Located in southeastern Saginaw County, the site was excavated by Lovis (ed. 1989) in the early 1980s soon after the work at the Kantzler site by Larsen and Demeter (1979). Because Lovis (ed. 1989) recognized the similarities in processes of site development outlined by Larsen (1980; Larsen and Demeter 1979) with Weber I, an interdisciplinary strategy that brought together specialists in archaeology, geology, and pedology was developed to decipher site sedimentology, stratigraphy, and formation history. The results of this work showed that, like the Kantzler site, Weber I includes mid-Holocene prehistoric artifacts that were buried during the Nipissing transgression. At Weber I, however, the buried mid-Holocene artifacts occur in an in situ Middle Archaic occupation horizon that includes cultural features as well as diagnostic artifacts that date between about 6200 and 4500 B.P. (Lovis ed. 1989; Monaghan, Lovis, and Fay 1986). The Middle Archaic horizon is overlain by Nipissing alluvial and lacustrine deposits, which are in turn overlain by stratified Late Archaic, Woodland, and nineteenth-century occupation horizons. The excavation at Weber I proved important not only because it supported the notion that streams in Michigan were undergoing downcutting and channel entrenchment during low-water stages in the upper Great Lakes but also that humans were apparently living along these rivers. Even more significantly, as lake level rose during the Nipissing transgression, the evidence for human occupation at Weber I was buried as Lake Nipissing back-flooded the Cass River valley.

The Ebenhoff site (Figure 3-3), also located in southern Saginaw County, is likewise illustrative not only of the mid-Holocene geological processes extant in Michigan but also of how the proper interdisciplinary research orientation can uncover important archaeological resources. The site occurs along the shoreline of the Shiawassee embayment portion of Lake Nipissing. It was first reported by Weir (1981), who, based on traditional surface reconnaissance survey techniques, concluded that it was probably not significant. He did note, however, that surface visibility was poor during the survey. The reason for poor surface visibility became clear about a decade later during Phase I testing along the proposed 1990 Great Lakes Gas Pipeline (GLGP) project. Because the research design for this project, which was developed by Lovis (1990c) and Monaghan (1990a), particularly emphasized testing stream channels and shoreline deposits related to the Nipissing transgression, several backhoe trenches were placed near the Ebenhoff site. The sediments observed during trenching (Branstner 1990a), as well as during Phase II archaeological testing (Branstner 1991), were shallow lacustrine and eolian sands that contained interstratified peat and prehistoric artifacts, which led Branstner (1991) to recommend the site for extensive data recovery. Samples of the peat yielded ^{14}C age estimates of between 12,210 B.P. (Beta-40293; Branstner 1991) and 4660 B.P. (Beta-47379; Dobbs and Murray 1993). Cultural material was also clearly interbedded within both eolian and shallow lacustrine (shoreline) sand beds (Dobbs and Murray 1993). By emphasizing landform development related to regional depositional processes and cultural settlement systems, the Ebenhoff site, which was earlier considered insignificant because of poor surface site expression, was tested and proved important to an understanding of Middle Archaic settlement. Moreover, like the excavations at Weber I (Lovis ed. 1989), it showed that Larsen and Demeter (1979) were correct that significant archaeological deposits are preserved in early-to-middle Holocene surfaces that were buried during the Nipissing transgression.

The GLGTP study, which focused on the southern margin of the Saginaw Valley within the Shiawassee embayment in east-central Michigan (Figure 3-3), was a landmark project because of its regional scope and multidisciplinary approach. As a result of this project, several buried sites were discovered in the area. The results of this work showed that streams in the area, particularly the Shiawassee and Flint rivers, apparently incised through their floodplains during the early to middle Holocene. Although no fluvial sediments related to this downcutting were observed, the fact that both valley bottoms extend below present lake level (ca. 176.5 m) and are partly filled with organic sediment of pre-Nipissing age (>5000 B.P.; Figure 3–4 and Table 3-1) certainly implies an eroded and incised stream channel. Channel sediments related to the Stanley phase streams may occur below these organic sediments (trenches Se1, PlTr, Be2, Be3, Be5; Figure 3-4). Just how far upstream and to what magnitude channel incision during the Stanley low-water phase may have extended is unclear. However, in the Bear Creek and Shiawassee River valleys, pre-Nipissing channels extended at least 3 m deeper than today and were significantly wider. Because the GLGTP study area occurs about 30 km from the present shoreline of Saginaw Bay, as well as near the mid-Holocene shore, early and mid-Holocene channel incision probably extended well inland.

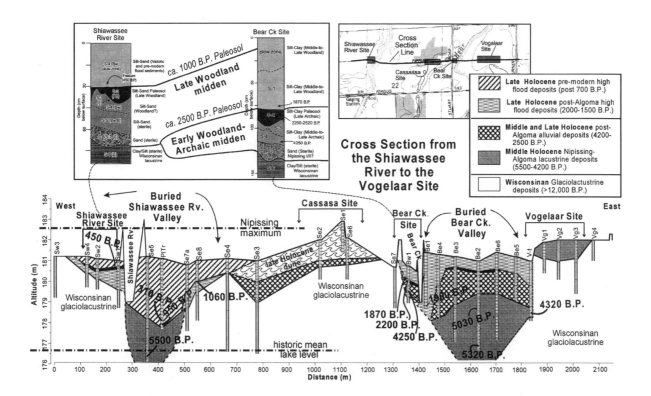

Figure 3-4. East-west cross section of the Shiawassee and Bear Creek valleys showing the stratigraphy of deposits discovered during the 1990–1992 GLGP Phase I, II, and III surveys. Inserts show details of the Bear Creek and Shiawassee River archaeological sites (after Monaghan and Schaetzl 1994).

The data from the GLGTP study also shows that the early-to-mid-Holocene drainage system in this area was different from today. Apparently, during this interval of downcutting most of the water presently flowing through the Shiawassee River probably drained through Bear Creek (Monaghan and Schaetzl 1994). This is suggested based on the fact that the pre-Nipissing Bear Creek valley is deeper and more extensive than that of the Shiawassee River valley (Figure 3-4) and would therefore have required a significantly greater flow than observed today. Some drainage must have also flowed through the Shiawassee River valley, although such drainage was probably much less than along Bear Creek. This drainage pattern is inferred because the valley was downcut during pre-Nipissing time (Figure 3-4). The relatively small, narrow, pre-Nipissing incision in the valley, however, suggests that the discharge of this stream was probably of relatively small magnitude.

Several of the more regionally oriented studies that shed some light on the early-to-middle Holocene fluvial environments of Michigan have been undertaken related to corridor studies in Michigan. These include the GLGTP studies mentioned above (Branstner 1990a, 1991; Monaghan and Schaetzl 1994; Monaghan 1995a, 1995b), the US-23 project between Standish and Tawas City north of Saginaw Bay (Dunham et al. 1995; Monaghan 1995c), and the US-31 project in Allegan and Ottawa counties (Dunham, Hambacher, Branstner and Branstner 1999; Monaghan 1999). The US-23 and US-31 projects occur on opposite sides of Michigan, but both show that the early and middle Holocene fluvial and alluvial systems can be characterized by generally eroding, downcutting streams. In addition to the evidence described for the Weber I and Ebenhoff sites mentioned above, this downcutting is indicated in the Saginaw Bay region by 5700–5200 B.P. and 9800 B.P. basal fluvial ages at the US-23 crossings north of Standish in Arenac County of the Pine River and Big Creek, respectively (Monaghan 1999 and ^{14}C chronology supplemented by this study; Table 3-1). Similar downcutting is suggested on the western side of Michigan by ages of 5200–5000 B.P. and 5600–5500 B.P. for basal fluvial deposits at the US-31 crossings of Pigeon Creek and the Grand River, respectively (Monaghan 1999), near Grand Haven. Additionally, studies of river valleys in these project areas also suggest that alluviation was probably minimal until the valleys were back-flooded as water level rose during the Nipissing transgression. This is indicated because the early mid-Holocene ages for most of the valleys derive from basal organic deposits, which suggests that lateral migration and continual reworking of floodplain sediments probably characterized rivers in the Saginaw and Grand valleys during most of the early Holocene. Once these valleys were back-flooded during the transgression of Lake Nipissing, vertical accretion began.

The model of widespread lateral stream migration and erosion during the early-to-mid-Holocene followed by extensive vertical accretion as Lake Nipissing rose above modern lake level has important ramifications for the distribution and preservation of archaeological sites in Michigan. Ultimately, only during the last stages of the Nipissing transgression, when vertical accretion rather than lateral channel migration processes predominated, were conditions right for alluvial site preservation. However, because flooding of valleys during the Holocene is time transgressive, floodplain sites located near river mouths and shoreline environments were selectively preserved, while more upstream, "interior" sites were more likely destroyed as the channel meandered across the valley bottom. Early Archaic sites located along now-drowned parts of river valleys, for example, were preserved but are now under water. Conversely, indicators for temporally correlative upstream sites were more likely destroyed because in these areas lateral migration rather than vertical accretion dominated the floodplain depositional environment. Similarly, during the later stages of the Nipissing transgression, when the lake rose above modern level and began flooding embayments such as the lower Grand and Saginaw river valleys, Middle Archaic sites located in more downstream positions were preserved while those from upstream locales were more likely destroyed. This model explains the general lack of Early Archaic sites from floodplain settings as well as the fact that buried and stratified Middle Archaic sites are more common in floodplains near the Nipissing shoreline and generally absent from more upstream locales. If this model is correct, Archaic settlement models should account for the potential missing parts of the systems.

Middle Holocene High-Level Lake Stages: Lakes Nipissing and Algoma

Lake Nipissing
As the North Bay outlet isostatically rebounded, the level of Lake Stanley rose and began the 5,000-year Nipissing transgression. During the later stages of the transgression, while the lake rose and began to flood various valleys, groundwater levels also increased in response to increased water level in the region. As a

result, swamp and other wetland deposits began to form in depressions on flood-plains. Some of the better examples of this occur along the Grand River (i.e., 5200–5000 B.P. peat associated with DTL-2, US-31; Monaghan 1995c; Table 3-1), along some of the rivers in the northern margins of Saginaw Bay (i.e., 9000–5000 B.P. peat along the branches of the Pine River and Big Creek; Monaghan 1995c [^{14}C chronology supplemented by this study] Table 3-1), and in the southern margins of the Shiawassee embayment (i.e., archaeological sites in the St. Charles area, southern Saginaw County; Figure 3-4; Monaghan and Schaetzl 1994).

In the Saginaw Valley, for example, Monaghan and Schaetzl (1994) show that old "channels" in the Bear and Shiawassee valley bottoms apparently formed wetlands at about 5500 B.P. These wetlands are represented by extensive mid-Holocene peat and organic silt-clay deposits (trenches Se1, PlTr, Be2, Be3, Be6; Figure 3-4). They occur at >3 m depths and apparently are of unknown thickness. The age of such buried organic deposits in both the Grand River valley and Saginaw Bay region (5500–5000 B.P.; Table 3-1) suggests that they must have been formed just before the inundation of the valleys by the Nipissing waters. The detailed work on buried wetlands in the Saginaw Bay region demonstrates that no beach or nearshore lacustrine deposits occur within the sequence (Monaghan and Schaetzl 1994). This implies that the maximum Nipissing level was not achieved until after about 5000 B.P., which agrees with the 4800–4700 B.P. age suggested by Monaghan, Lovis, and Fay (1986), the 4700 B.P. age suggested by Lewis and Anderson (1989), the 4500 B.P. age suggested by Larsen (1985b), as well as with data collected elsewhere in the Saginaw Bay region during this study.

Continued rebound at North Bay forced the lake to rise above the present-day level. Toward the end of the Nipissing transgression, Lake Nipissing began to flood the downstream portion of major river valleys and form embayments in low areas, such as the Shiawassee embayment in Saginaw County. The transgression has been recorded in several river valleys throughout Michigan. For example, deep testing associated with the Great Lakes Gas Transmission Pipeline (Branstner 1990a, 1991) in the Straits area of Michigan and the north shore of Lake Michigan records the rising Nipissing level along the Crooked River near Burt Lake, the Manistique River near Manistique, and between Brevort Lake and St. Ignace. Taken together, these data show that the Nipissing transgression reached within 6 m of maximum by 6540–6450 B.P., 4 m by 5440 B.P., and 1 m by 4920 B.P. (Beta-40289–40290–40292, Beta-40921, and Beta-40300, respectively; Table 3-1). Further south in the Saginaw Bay region, the Nipissing I water-plane ultimately reached an altitude of about 184.4 m. Accretion of fluvial sediments related to rising Nipissing water was observed in the several branches of the Pine River near Standish in the northern Saginaw Bay region (Monaghan 1995c, and ^{14}C chronology supplemented by this study; Table 3-1), along the Saginaw River near Bay City (Larsen and Demeter 1979) and Saginaw (Speth 1972; Demeter et al. 2000, and ^{14}C chronology supplemented by this study, Table 3-1), along the Cass River (Monaghan, Lovis, and Fay 1986), Bear Creek (Monaghan and Schaetzl 1994; Table 3-1), Misteguay Creek (Table 3-1), and Pine Run in southern Saginaw County (Table 3-1). Similarly, the beginning of alluviation related to the Nipissing I was noted along the Grand River near Grand Haven and Pigeon Creek between Grand Haven and Holland in western Michigan (Monaghan 1999).

A detailed study undertaken in the Shiawassee embayment within southern Saginaw County by Monaghan and Schaetzl (1994) describes the dramatic changes in the hydraulic configuration of the nearby rivers related to the Nipissing transgression. By mapping the approximate position of the shoreline formed by the maximum level of Lake Nipissing near St. Charles, they show the positions of the Shiawassee River, Casassa, Bear Creek, and Vogelaar sites (Figure 3-5) relative to controlling geomorphological features. The results of their work demonstrate that during Nipissing I (maximum), the Shiawassee River flowed into a small "embayment" of Lake Nipissing a few kilometers south (upstream) of the Bear Creek site and may have formed a "delta" or at least an "estuary-type" deposit at its mouth (Figure 3-5; Monaghan and Schaetzl 1994). This is indicated by several small "distributary" channels that occur at an altitude of 183 m (Figure 3-5). Evidence for such "delta" channels can be observed on the Chesaning East United States Geological Survey (USGS) quadrangle map between Deer Creek and Shiawassee River in Sections 28, 27, 33, and 34, T9N R3E.

Recent work in Bay City at the Marquette Viaduct site (20BY28 and 20BY387; Lovis ed. 2002) sheds important new light on the timing for Lake Nipissing. The site is located along the west bank of the Saginaw River. Although it is actually considered a locale of the Fletcher site (20BY28; Lovis ed. 2002), the site occurs on two different landforms: an "upper" (20BY387) and a "lower" terrace (20BY28; Monaghan 2002). The "upper" terrace is believed to have formed as a beach associated with Lake Algoma (Larsen and Demeter 1979; Monaghan 1991, 1993) and occurs at about 182–183 m. The "lower" terrace lies on the modern floodplain of the Saginaw River at an altitude of about 178 m (<2 m above Lake Huron). The age and altitude for cultural features on the two terraces constrain the timing of inception or abandonment of Lakes Nipissing and Algoma as well as for modern Lake Huron. For example, ^{14}C age estimates of cultural features on the upper terrace (20BY387) indicate that lake level must have fallen below 182 m by 4200 B.P. and, because no evidence of subsequent inundation was noted on the upper terrace, apparently never rose above that level again (Figure 3-2; Monaghan 2002). Moreover, other ^{14}C age estimates from cultural features on the lower terrace indicate that essentially modern levels of Lake Huron were achieved by 3800 B.P.

Monaghan and Schaetzl's (1994) detailed description of Nipissing deposits in the Shiawassee flats area allows the GLGTP archaeological sites to be placed in the regional chronology and depositional history of the Saginaw Bay region. Their work at the Bear Creek site shows that nearshore or beach sand and gravel containing detrital wood and snails directly overlie glaciolacustrine sediment and that the contact between these two deposits is erosional. The beach sediment grades upward into laminated silt and clay deposits that contain a few discontinuous interbeds of sand, which suggests a transgressive sequence. A large piece of detrital wood collected from the beach sand and gravel deposits just below the contact with the overlying lacustrine sediments (altitude ca. 178 m) yielded a ^{14}C age estimate of 4320 B.P. (Monaghan and Schaetzl 1994; Figure 3-4). This age demonstrates that the sand and gravel unit was deposited in a Lake Nipissing nearshore environment. Given their relatively young age (300–500 years younger than the Nipissing I maximum), the sand and gravel sediments probably represent beach deposits formed during the waning stage of Lake

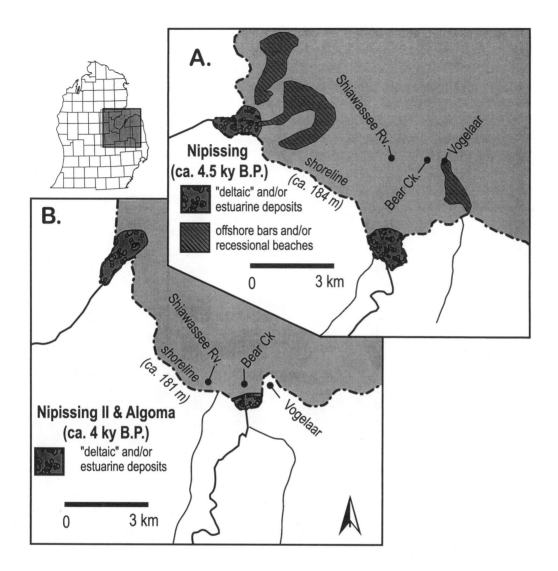

A.

**Nipissing
(ca. 4.5 ky B.P.)**

"deltaic" and/or
estuarine deposits

offshore bars and/or
recessional beaches

0   3 km

Shiawassee Rv.

shoreline
(ca. 184 m)

Bear Ck.

Vogelaar

B.

**Nipissing II & Algoma
(ca. 4 ky B.P.)**

"deltaic" and/or
estuarine deposits

0   3 km

Shiawassee Rv.

shoreline
(ca. 181 m)

Bear Ck

Vogelaar

Nipissing. The overlying laminated silt/clay deposit probably represents deeper nearshore sediments related to Lake Nipissing. The fact that the contact between the "beach" deposits and the overlying laminated silt and clay is gradational, however, implies that a minor transgression of Lake Nipissing occurred about 4300 B.P. and is probably equivalent to the Nipissing II stage (Monaghan and Schaetzl 1994).

Once the northern North Bay outlet isostatically rebounded above southern outlets at Chicago and Port Huron during the Nipissing maximum, drainage was transferred from the northern outlet back to the southern outlets. Erosion of the outlet channel at Port Huron allowed the water level in Lake Nipissing to fall below its maximum. As mentioned above, a brief transgression, Nipissing II, occurred at about 4300 B.P.

Monaghan and Schaetzl (1994) further suggest that, based on ^{14}C age estimates collected by them from the Saginaw Bay region, Nipissing II must have

Figure 3-5. Southern Saginaw County, showing drainage configuration and shoreline location related to the development of several important buried and stratified archaeological sites during the middle Holocene Nipissing I and II and Algoma phases (after Monaghan and Schaetzl 1994).

fallen below 180 m sometime just prior to 4000 B.P. The timing of this drop is based on the occurrence of archaeological material at the Bear Creek site. The altitude (ca. 180 m) and age of this material (4250 B.P.) (Monaghan and Schaetzl 1994; Figure 3-4) require that Nipissing II must have fallen below the Algoma level in order for humans to occupy the Bear Creek site at this time. Such a relationship suggests that the basal Holocene units in the Bear Creek site sequence probably were deposited during Nipissing II as its shoreline was forming near the site. If so, it is probably equivalent to the Nipissing II sand observed adjacent to the Vogelaar site discussed above (trench V-t; Figure 3-4). Alternatively, this unit may represent fluvial sediment related to early deposition along Bear Creek as Nipissing II waters fell. Evidence at the Bear Creek site also suggests that water level in the Huron lake basin may have subsequently risen and briefly flooded the site again sometime after 4000 B.P. This rise in lake level presumably represents Lake Algoma and is suggested based on the relative lack of archaeological material in the cultural zones that occur just above the 4250 B.P. horizon at the Bear Creek site. Cultural material occurs throughout the "Algoma" time interval at the site, which may indicate that Lake Algoma did not rise above 180–181 m for an extended period (Monaghan and Schaetzl 1994). The establishment of Lake Algoma just after 4000 B.P. occurs relatively early in the 4000–3500 B.P. age previously proposed for the Algoma phase. Importantly, it is also consistent with the ^{14}C age estimate of 3410 B.P. (Beta-40298; Table 3-1) for post-Algoma sedimentation along Misteguay Creek in the St. Charles area in southern Saginaw County discussed below.

Deposits related to Lake Nipissing occur at or near archaeological sites throughout the Saginaw Bay region. Deeper water, shallow lacustrine sediments were also observed at the Schultz and Green Point sites near Saginaw (Demeter et al. 2000; Speth 1972; Wright 1964). Shoreline sediments were noted by Larsen and Demeter (1979) at the Kantzler site near Bay City, by Monaghan and Schaetzl (1994) at the Bear Creek and Vogelaar sites in southern Saginaw County, and by Monaghan, Lovis, and Fay (1986) at the Weber I site along the Cass River near Frankenmuth. In addition, the Middle Archaic Ebenhoff site, which was formed on the Nipissing shoreline near the Bear Creek site, shows that Middle Archaic people lived along the Nipissing shoreline during fluctuations in the level of the lake. Here, discrete occupation layers that include artifacts, fire-cracked rock, and charcoal occur on or are reworked within beach cross-beds, nearshore, and/or eolian sand (Beaverson 1993; Beaverson and Moores 1993; Dobbs and Murray 1993). Middle Archaic occupation horizons also occur along the Cass River at the Weber I site. Unlike at Ebenhoff site, however, these occur below the Nipissing sediments and were not observed stratified within the lacustrine deposits (Lovis ed. 1989; Monaghan, Lovis, and Fay 1986).

Lake Algoma

The origin of Lake Algoma is uncertain. It may represent a minor transgression-regression during the general Nipissing "regression" (Larsen 1985b) or, alternatively, a short-lived lake stabilization formed during a brief "pause" in the otherwise progressive erosion of the outlet channel at Port Huron (Hough 1958, 1963, 1966). Data collected at several different places in the Saginaw Bay region suggests that Lake Algoma was formed as a short-lived transgression. In fact, the data from the Bear Creek site (Monaghan and Schaetzl 1994) implies that Lake

Algoma probably achieved the mapped, maximum level of about 181 m only briefly, if at all. If so, shoreline features that are commonly attributed to Algoma may be palimpsests on older features. They may have been formed mainly during the Nipissing II stage and, somewhat later, reoccupied by Lake Algoma. This is particularly apparent on the margins of Lake Algoma in southern Saginaw County.

The general shoreline of Lake Algoma (and/or the Nipissing II stage) in southern Saginaw County is shown in Figure 3-5. Also depicted are important archaeological sites from the area. During this time, while the Shiawassee flats were flooded, drainage from the Shiawassee River probably flowed into a small "embayment" in the Bear Creek valley just south of the Bear Creek site (Monaghan and Schaetzl 1994; Figure 3-5). The combined Shiawassee and Bear drainage system, informally referred to as the "Bear-Shiawassee River," formed during this time and is similar to the drainage configuration in the area suggested for pre-Nipissing time. The probable connection between the Bear and Shiawassee valleys is delineated by an abandoned "channel" that occurs in the Shiawassee River valley along the eastern side of the Nipissing "delta" area (Figure 3-5). This channel is conspicuous on the Chesaning East USGS Quadrangle in Section 27, T9N R3E, just east of the Shiawassee River. As was suggested for drainage during the Nipissing phase, the Bear-Shiawassee River probably formed a small "delta" or "estuary-type" deposit in this embayment (Monaghan and Schaetzl 1994). The suggestion that the Shiawassee River flowed into Lake Algoma/Nipissing II in the Bear Valley, which is east of its present course, is based mainly on the morphology and distribution of beach features in the Shiawassee Valley. Here, the "Algoma beach" occurs along Fergus Road (both to the north and south of the road), near the Sharon-Fergus road intersection. It then trends south and east, where it marks the embayment in Bear Creek valley. The fact that no similar "embayment" of this beach occurs in the Shiawassee Valley (Figure 3-5) indicates that the Shiawassee River did not flow along its present course while the beach was constructed.

Regardless of whether Lake Algoma represented a minor transgression or merely a pause in the downcutting of the Port Huron outlet, it was short-lived. Continued erosion at Port Huron allowed a further regression of lake level in the Saginaw Bay region. Data from the Kawkawlin River site, discussed above, indicates that Algoma fell below 179 m by 3800 B.P. This is supported by a ^{14}C age estimate from wood in fluvial gravel deposits sampled from a trench excavated along Misteguay Creek during the 1990–1991 GLGTP survey (Figure 3-3). These data indicate that by 3410 B.P. (Beta-40298; Table 3-1), lake level in the Saginaw Bay region fell below 177 m, the approximate modern level of Lake Huron. In order for these fluvial deposits to form, water in the Saginaw Bay region must have fallen to the modern level by 3400 B.P.

Early in the post-Algoma regression (between ca. 4000 and 3500 B.P.), as the Lake Algoma shoreline receded, rivers in the region began to entrench. This process was very significant in the Saginaw Bay region as the channels associated with the Cass, Flint, Bear-Shiawassee, and Bad rivers, as well as small drainages such as Misteguay Creek, began to extend their channels across the newly exposed lake plain within the Shiawassee flats area. Because the water level was still above present-day level and probably exhibited minor variations, Algoma and post-Algoma water may have also periodically back-flooded these valleys.

As a result, extensive, short-term alluviation may have occasionally occurred and caused periodic reorientation of the channel. Consequently, stream channels probably wandered through the flat areas between the abandoned Nipissing shoreline and Saginaw Bay. Thus, the locations of the channels today may only approximate their locations 3,000–3,500 years ago. From a site-prediction standpoint, archaeologists must recognize that Late Archaic sites could be found anywhere in this part of the Shiawassee flats. Importantly, the modern environment may only approximate that of the mid-Holocene paleoenvironment.

Climate Control for Peak Lake Levels and Inland Depositional Patterns
Larsen (1985a, 1985b) suggested that the "peak" levels of Nipissing I, II, and Algoma were only partly related to changes in outlet configurations. He proposed that climatic variation had a great impact on these levels. Based on the alluvial histories of valleys in the Great Lakes region (particularly, western New York State), Monaghan and Hayes (1997, 1998) further proposed that these high-level lakes suggested that wetter, possibly cooler, climatic conditions prevailed during the latter part of the middle Holocene. That climatic variation occurred during the middle Holocene is also supported by research at several locales in Lower Michigan. In western Michigan, for example, backhoe trenches across the Grand River valley at the Prison Farm site near Ionia indicate that alluvial accretion broadly characterized the middle Holocene between 5000 and 4000 B.P. (Figures 3-3, 3-6). The fact that this site is located in the upper reaches of the lower Grand River, nearly 100 km beyond the limits of the Nipissing I maximum near Grand Rapids, means that changes in alluviation or fluvial hydraulics were not caused by high lake levels. To account for increased alluviation along the Grand River, a wetter climate probably characterized the drainage during the middle Holocene.

Fluctuations in Nipissing and Algoma levels in the Saginaw Bay region are demonstrated at an exposure along the Kawkawlin River just downstream from the village of Kawkawlin in northern Bay County (NW1/4 of Sec. 6, T14N R4E; Figure 3-3). The site includes two components, an exposure along the south bank of the river that includes an organic-rich horizon that may represent an ephemeral paleosol and a pit on the north side of the river. The "paleosol" on the south bank is overlain by stratified sand and gravel, while the "pit" on the north bank contains laminated fine sand and silt overlain by organic (peat) deposits (Butterfield n.d.). Although it was a clear and distinct horizon, the south bank "paleosol" was not studied by professionals and may actually be more like a slightly weathered, organic-rich silt than a developed paleosol. Regardless, it formed in a discontinuous gravel lag that occurs on clay-rich, more erosionally resistant, late Wisconsinan glaciolacustrine deposits and occurs at an altitude of 178 m (about 1–1.5 m above modern lake level and 6.5 m below the maximum Nipissing level). It is overlain by about 3 m of stratified sands (Butterfield n.d.). A bulk peat sample from the paleosol yielded a ^{14}C age estimate of 4360 B.P. (Beta-31898; Table 3-1). The age and altitude of this paleosol, together with the erosional lag and overlying deposits, indicate that Nipissing I fell nearly to modern level prior to 4360 B.P., allowing drainage along the Kawkawlin River. Water level subsequently rose either to the Nipissing II or Algoma level and reflooded the site.

The north bank pit records a younger part of the Nipissing-Algoma sequence. It includes a basal unit of laminated, fine sand and silt that probably represents shallow lacustrine deposits of Lake Algoma. These are overlain by thin interbeds of peat and fine sand that grade upward into black, fine peat (Butterfield n.d.). A ^{14}C age estimate from the base of the peat (above the peat-sand interbeds), which occurs at an altitude of about 179 m, suggests that Lake Algoma must have fallen below 179 m to allow organic accumulation at the site prior to 3800 B.P. (Beta-38663). The "low-stage" between Nipissing I and II is apparently regional and was also noted at archaeological sites in the Saginaw Bay region.

Evidence for variation in the middle Holocene high-level lakes is also indicated at the Ebenhoff, Bear Creek, and Vogelaar sites in southern Saginaw County (Figure 3-3). Middle-to-Late Archaic occupation debris occurred associated with or reworked within Nipissing-to-Algoma phase deposits. Details concerning the archaeological results and significance of these sites are described in chapter 5. At the Bear Creek site, 4200 B.P. artifacts and related bone occur at an altitude of 180.5 m beneath probable Algoma deposits (Monaghan and Schaetzl 1994). This data suggests that prior to 4200 B.P., lake level fell far enough below 180 m to allow human occupation and, subsequently, after 4200 B.P. rose and back-flooded the site. A similar sequence indicating that sub-Algoma lake level occurred prior to about 4000 B.P. and subsequently transgressed occurs at the Vogelaar site (Monaghan 1995b). The sequence at the Ebenhoff site (Figure 3-3) also records numerous fluctuations during the Nipissing and Algoma phases. Archaic-age artifacts have been incorporated into 6200–4500 B.P. peat and shal-

Figure 3-6. North-south cross section across the northern Grand River floodplain at the Prison Farm site, Ionia, Michigan. Based on unpublished deep-testing results.

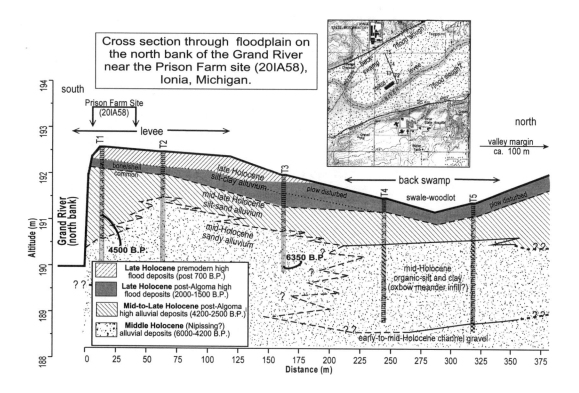

low lacustrine (littoral) sand units that occur at an altitude of 181 m and mark the base of the Ebenhoff cultural sequence (Dobbs and Murray 1993). These lie 2–3 m below the Nipissing I maximum level. The bulk of Archaic-age archaeological deposits at the site, however, occur within eolian sand that overlies these early Nipissing-age sediments. These deposits occur 1–2.5 m below the Nipissing maximum level and lie at or just above the level of Lake Algoma. Significantly, the eolian sand includes multiple, discontinuous, interstratified shallow lacustrine beds that indicate several transgressions and regressions during the Nipissing and Algoma phases (Beaverson and Mooers 1993; Dobbs and Murray 1993).

Taken together, the data from archaeological sites in southern Saginaw County indicate that water level fluctuated dramatically during the middle Holocene. Although a variety of explanations may account for this variation, including simple wind-setup in the shallow Shiawassee flats embayment, Larsen's (1980) contention that regional climatic changes caused the minor transgressions and regressions of Lakes Nipissing and Algoma seems most plausible. This explanation seems especially credible given the evidence of increased middle Holocene alluviation at the more inland Prison Farm site along the Grand River and given the fact that a regional low-level regression, nearly to modern level, occurred 4400–4200 B.P. Such dramatic regional changes in water level probably represent significant regional variation in precipitation.

Late Holocene: Post-Algoma Low- and High-Water Phases

The exposures and trenches along the Kawkawlin River and Misteguay Creek as well as the Marquette Viaduct site in Bay City, which have been discussed above, indicate that water level in Lakes Michigan and Huron had fallen to at least modern level by 3500 B.P. Several lines of evidence from throughout the Huron-Michigan lake basin, including several ^{14}C age estimates mentioned above, indicate that by 3000 B.P., water level had fallen at least 3 m below that of modern Lake Huron (Monaghan and Schaetzl 1994). This late Holocene low-water phase has been noted by Larsen (1986b) and Fraser et al. (1975, 1990). It is informally referred to by Monaghan and Schaetzl (1994) as the "post-Algoma low." Although the reason for a post-Algoma drop in lake level is not certain, as discussed below, it probably resulted from secular perturbation in regional climate from relatively cool and moist to warmer and dryer. It also marks the initiation of the modern configuration of the upper Great Lakes and the inception of millennial-scale climatic fluctuations (Monaghan and Hayes 1997, 1998).

As lake level lowered, streams throughout the region apparently incised through and partly eroded the Nipissing-Algoma sediments that mantled the downstream portions of the valleys. Evidence for this is particularly abundant in the Saginaw Bay region. In southern Saginaw County, Monaghan and Schaetzl (1994) suggested this downcutting by the presence of fluvial gravel at the base of several trenches near the Bear Creek site (Figures 3-3, 3-4). At Green Point in northern Saginaw County, fluvial deposits, which include a 2800 B.P. squash seed, also suggest erosion of middle Holocene lake sediments from the Saginaw River valley (Figures 3-3, 3-7). Similar age sequences occur elsewhere in the Saginaw Bay region and are implied by the occurrence of paleosols and archaeological middens at a few sites in the region. At the Bear Creek site, for example, most of the Early Woodland deposits occur near the Ab horizon of a 2500 B.P. paleosol (Branstner and Hambacher eds. 1994; Monaghan and Schaetzl 1994). The occurrence of this paleosol indicates that the floodplain underwent relatively little accumulation of sediment and therefore relatively limited flooding. This implies long-term stability of the floodplain as well as relatively dryer conditions and low water-level in Saginaw Bay. A similar stratigraphic sequence also occurred at the Schultz site in northern Saginaw County (Figure 3-3). Here, a channel was cut through Nipissing-Algoma deposits. It was then stabilized long enough to allow extensive Early Woodland occupation on the Saginaw River floodplain (Fitting ed. 1972; Lovis et al. 2001). The presence of a 2500 B.P. paleosol at the Zemaitis site in Ottawa County (Figure 3–3) indicates that fluvial stability also characterized the lower Grand River valley during this period.

The excavations associated with the 1990–1991 GLGTP survey along Bear Creek and Misteguay Creek show the process and results of channel entrenchment during the post-Algoma low-water stage. Channel gravel is evident under and adjacent to the Bear Creek site (Figure 3-4). Although the total amount of downcutting and erosion is unknown in this area because the base of channel gravel was not penetrated, downcutting is evident. It was obstructed, however, by the relatively resistant peat and organic silt/clay beds formed prior to the Nipissing transgression (Figure 3-4). Similar resistant beds were noted at the Kawkawlin River site and at locales along the Shiawassee, Flint, and Cass rivers (Figures 3-3, 3-4). Because of the resistant beds, lateral downcutting and erosion probably occurred. Along Bear Creek, it probably extended as far east as trench Be2 (Figure 3-4) but apparently did not significantly erode the floodplain west of the present channel (i.e., the Bear Creek site area; Figure 3-4; Monaghan and Schaetzl 1994).

Post-Nipissing or post-Algoma lateral channel migration is also indicated in western Michigan along the Grand and St. Joseph rivers. Both locales are inland and lie >15 m above the maximum Nipissing level. They were therefore not directly affected by changes in lake levels during the middle and late Holocene. A post-Nipissing shift in channel position apparently occurred at the Prison Farm site, which is located along the Grand River near Ionia and, as has been mentioned previously, dates probably sometime after 4500 B.P. (Figures 3-3, 3-6). This age is suggested because 4500 B.P. levee deposits were noted near the present channel rather than near the older, buried channel on the northern margin of the floodplain. Today, the northern channel is completely filled and acts as a back-swamp flood basin or flood chute (Figure 3-6). The St. Joseph River locale occurs just south of Niles, Michigan, and was excavated as part of the deep-test survey of the Vector Pipeline (Figure 3-3; Monaghan and Hayes 1999). These excavations show not only that the St. Joseph River entrenched >10 m during the early Holocene but also that at least two episodes of late Holocene alluviation occurred. The earlier of these episodes relates the organic infilling of a buried oxbow or channel meander that occurs below a younger sequence of channel and overbank deposition (Monaghan and Hayes 1999). Recently obtained ^{14}C age estimates of organic material from the buried channel indicate that infilling was ongoing at 3700 B.P. (Beta-14826; Table 3-1). This age is consistent with continued post-Algoma entrenchment and lateral channel migration.

Numerous ^{14}C age estimates from around the state indicate that the post-Algoma low continued until about 2000 B.P. These are particularly clear-cut

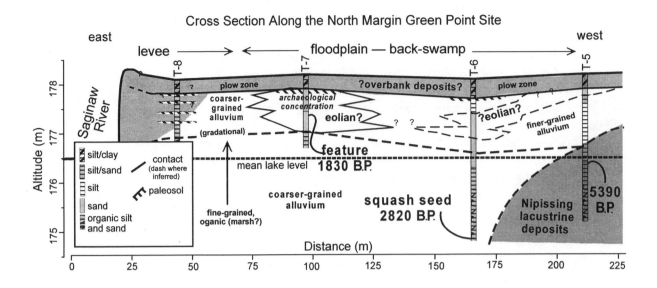

Figure 3-7. East-west cross section along northern margin of the Green Point site boundary. Based on deep-testing results from GM-Wetland Mitigation Survey (after Demeter et al. 2000).

at the Bear Creek, Schultz, and Zemaitis sites. Each of these sites included 2500–2200 B.P. paleosols that were buried by alluvium prior to 1800–1700 B.P. Thus, the levels of Lakes Michigan and Huron began to rise and transgressed above present-day level sometime after 2000 B.P. A rise in lake level just after 2000 B.P. has been suggested by Speth (1972) and by Larsen (1985b), who proposed that by about 1800 B.P., water level in the Michigan lake basin was nearly 3 m above present. Monaghan and Schaetzl (1994) informally referred to this high-level lake as the "post-Algoma high." Such a rise in lake level to an altitude of about 179 m would have resulted in back-flooding most of the large streams draining into the upper Great Lakes. Within the Saginaw Bay region, for example, most of northern Saginaw and southern Bay counties and the lower-lying areas of the Shiawassee flats must have been inundated. Similarly, a 3-m rise in lake level would have submerged parts of the floodplain of the lower Grand River valley nearly to Grand Rapids.

As lake level rose, back-flooded streams probably responded by increased flooding and alluviation, particularly in the downstream portions of their valleys near the Great Lakes shoreline. The results of these processes are especially apparent in the Saginaw Bay region, where several streams evidence a dramatic increase in alluviation during this post-Algoma high interval. For example, a sequence at Swan Creek, a tributary of the Shiawassee River in northern Saginaw County, shows that organic deposits, which lie near the present channel, are overlain by about 2 m of alluvial sand and silt (NE1/4 of SE1/4 of Sec. 9, T12N R3E; Figure 3-3). The organic debris, which includes wood and other detrital organic material as well as reworked shell, occurs at an altitude of 181.5 m, about 4 m above present lake level. A piece of wood from this deposit yielded a ^{14}C age estimate of 1870 B.P. (Beta-17546; Table 3-1). This data shows that 2 m of alluvium accumulated in Swan Creek beginning sometime after 1800 B.P. Similarly, evidence of alluviation after about 2000 B.P. can be noted along Bear Creek and the Au Gres River (Figure 3-3). This data shows that sand and gravel, probably related to channel deposition, accumulated and occurred about 2000 B.P. (Monaghan 1995c; Monaghan and Schaetzl 1994).

Major archaeological sites in the area, including the Schultz and Bear Creek sites in the Saginaw Bay region and the Zemaitis site in the lower Grand River valley, were affected. As the lake level in Saginaw Bay rose, base level for the Bear-Shiawassee and the Saginaw rivers also rose, which, particularly in the downstream portions, caused these rivers to flood regularly after 2000 B.P. At the Bear Creek site, the increased alluviation associated with the post-Algoma high resulted in deposition of the several centimeters of fine-textured sediment that overlies the ca. 2500 B.P. paleosol formed during the previous post-Algoma low. A ^{14}C age estimate of 1900 B.P. (Beta-40282; Figure 3-4 and Table 3-1) from the base of the channel gravel in a trench adjacent to the site suggests that alluviation along the Bear-Shiawassee River probably began about 2000 B.P. and continued for an unknown duration. Additionally, a ^{14}C age estimate of charcoal near the base of the alluvium overlying the Bear Creek paleosol indicates that flooding was probably most intensive after 1870 B.P. (Monaghan and Schaetzl 1994). A similar record is preserved at the Schultz site, where about 150 cm of alluvium was deposited between about 1800 and 1500 B.P. (Lovis et al. 2001). Peak flooding, however, apparently occurred between 1790 and 1640 B.P. (Beta-66989 and Beta-66990, respectively; Lovis et al. 1994; Lovis et al. 2001). Raised base level in the lower Grand River valley during the post-Algoma high probably also resulted in a similar interval of increased flooding at the Zemaitis site. As at the Bear Creek site, the 2500 B.P. paleosol at Zemaitis was buried by about 1 m of alluvium just prior to 1840 B.P. (Brashler and Kolb 1995).

Two partly stratified sites near the mouth of the Saginaw River in Bay City, Michigan, the Marquette Viaduct and CERT sites (Figure 3-3), also show evidence of extensive flooding after 1800 B.P. At the CERT site, for example, an eroded remnant of a Middle Woodland cultural horizon is overlain by fluvial gravel and by a Late Woodland cultural horizon. A ^{14}C age estimate from a composite of charcoal in the Late Woodland horizon suggests an average age of 1070 B.P. (Beta-69036; Demeter et al. 1994). This date suggests that sometime between about 2000 B.P., which is generally the earliest age for occupation of the lower Middle Woodland horizon, and 1000 B.P., flooding partly eroded the lower zone and deposited the intervening gravel. Excavations at the Marquette Viaduct site, a few kilometers downstream from the CERT site, show a similar record of flooding. Here, a lower, Middle Woodland cultural "midden" has also been partly eroded and in places is separated from a Middle-to-Late Woodland upper midden by a +20-cm-thick, discontinuous fluvial, cross-bedded gravel. A ^{14}C age estimate of charcoal from a remnant feature found in the lower midden yielded an age of 1740 B.P. (Beta-26380; Demeter et al. 1994). The age of this feature, together with the overlying gravel, suggests that extensive scouring and redeposition occurred at the site soon after about 1800 B.P. (Lovis et al. 1996).

Late Holocene: "Premodern Low" and "High" Water Phases

Relatively regular flooding and higher than normal lake levels associated with the post-Algoma high probably tapered off after about 1500–1400 B.P. Evidence from around the upper Great Lakes basin indicates that after this time, lake levels probably dropped below modern levels. Low water-level in the Great Lakes basins after 1500 B.P. was proposed by Larsen (1985b), Monaghan and Schaetzl (1994), and Monaghan and Hayes (1997, 1998). Monaghan and Schaetzl (1994) informally referred to this low-water period as the "premodern low." In the Saginaw Bay region, the premodern low is inferred from extensive downcutting of river channels as well as from the concomitant development of midden soils at several archaeological sites. Additionally, significant hydraulic changes that occurred in several valleys, particularly the Bear-Shiawassee River valley, indicate that major adjustments to drainage basin characteristics accompanied the falling Great Lakes levels. In fact, the absence of post-Algoma high and low sediments in the Shiawassee River valley indicates that the entire channel probably shifted about 1 km west from Bear Creek to its present course at this time (Monaghan and Schaetzl 1994).

Unlike the complex and rich record preserved in the Bear Creek valley discussed above, no direct evidence for significant deposition of sediment related to either the post-Algoma low or high was observed in the Shiawassee Valley. However, that such deposits are completely absent from the sequence shows that at least some erosion must have occurred. Although the precise timing of this erosion is unknown, the fact that a significant amount of sediments that are all younger than about 1000 B.P. occur directly above pre-Nipissing organic sediment in the Shiawassee Valley (trenches Se5 and PlTr in Figure 3-4; Monaghan and Schaetzl 1994) suggests that it probably occurred after the post-Algoma high. Although the downcutting could have been partly achieved during the post-Algoma low, if most of the Shiawassee drainage flowed through Bear Valley during the post-Algoma low, then drainage through the Shiawassee Valley must have been minor during this time. Such minor flow cannot account for the significant amount of erosion and subsequent infilling of the valley during the post-Algoma high interval. If correct, the major incision in the Shiawassee Valley must be related to a younger regression-transgression event distinct from the earlier post-Algoma low incision in Bear Valley.

The lack of post-Nipissing sediments older than about 1000 B.P. in the Shiawassee Valley (Figure 3-4) indicates that significant erosion, unrelated to the post-Algoma low, must have occurred prior to about 1000 B.P. As outlined above, such incision implies a drop in stream base level and, consequently, falling lake level. Although the age of the incision and erosion related to the premodern low is unknown, it probably occurred just prior to 1000 B.P. The 1000 B.P. limit is based on a ^{14}C age estimate of 950 B.P. (Beta-47876; Monaghan and Schaetzl 1994) on detrital wood from the base of channel gravel and by a similar ^{14}C age of 1020 B.P. (Beta-40320; Monaghan and Schaetzl 1994) on a piece of a charcoal "layer" in the alluvium just west of the Shiawassee River channel (Figure 3-4). The age of this charcoal layer also implies that at least some, albeit minor, alluviation occurred in the Shiawassee Valley prior to 1000 B.P. This is suggested because about 1 m of alluvium occurs below the dated charcoal layer. If so, the lower alluvium may be associated with a rise in lake level and may support a minor transgression just prior to 1000 B.P. as suggested by Larsen (1985b). Regardless of this minor rise in lake level, by 1000 B.P. water level in the basin fell below modern level (Larsen 1985b; Monaghan and Hayes 1997, 1998; Monaghan and Schaetzl 1994).

66

Major changes in the hydraulic characteristics of some channels also occurred during the premodern low. The Shiawassee River channel shifted from Bear Creek to its present course in the Shiawassee Valley during this interval (Monaghan and Schaetzl 1994). Such a shift in drainage is required to account not only for the relatively great amount of post–1000 B.P. vertical and lateral erosion in the Shiawassee Valley but also for the lack of widespread erosion along Bear Creek after about 1500 B.P. A shift in drainage to the Shiawassee Valley is also implied by significant post-1000 B.P. infilling of the valley (Figure 3-4). The magnitude of the drop in lake level during the premodern low is not known. Based on the altitude of the bottom of the channel gravels in several drainage basins, however, it probably fell to or below modern lake level. In the Shiawassee Valley, for example, fluvial deposits occur below an altitude of 176 m (Figure 3-4). Extensive vertical channel incision during the premodern low also occurred along the Flint, Pine, and Au Gres rivers (Figure 3-3). Deep testing along the Au Gres River associated with the US-23 project, for example, revealed a 3–4-m-thick sequence of fluvial and alluvial deposits (Monaghan 1999). Premodern low channel incision is supported at this locale by a recently obtained ^{14}C age estimate of 770 B.P. (Beta-148260; Table 3-1) on detrital wood collected from basal channel gravel within the deep-test trenches (Monaghan 1995c; Figure 3-8). The occurrence of this gravel, which is overlain by 250 cm of 350 B.P.-age (Beta-148259; Table 3-1) alluvium, indicates that another episode of accelerated deposition occurred prior to Euro-American settlement of the region.

The fact that vertically incised channels of the Shiawassee and Au Gres valleys were filled by more than 2 m of fluvial and alluvial sediment implies that the water level once again rose after downcutting occurred. Wood from channel gravel indicates that extensive fluvial deposition was ongoing along the Shiawassee River by 340 B.P. (Beta-47877; Figure 3-4). The fact that fluvial gravel and related alluvial sediments are more than 2 m thick and extend to within about 1 m of the present ground surface (trenches Se5 and PlTr; Figure 3-4) testifies to the amount of deposition along the river. The occurrence of a valley fill of this magnitude implies a significant change in base level for the river probably related to a major lake transgression. A regional transgression during this time was suggested by Larsen (1985b), Fraser et al. (1990), and Johnson et al. (1990). In fact, Larsen (1985b) proposed that in the southern Lake Michigan basin, lake level may have been as much as 3 m above present. Monaghan and Schaetzl (1994) informally referred to this transgression as the premodern "high."

Evidence for the premodern high is well recorded throughout the upper Great Lakes and is particularly apparent at two archaeological sites in the southern Saginaw Bay region, the Shiawassee River and Flint River sites (Figure 3-3). This data indicates that it apparently occurred after about 600–400 B.P. A ^{14}C age estimate of charcoal from a feature at the Shiawassee River site, for example, shows that the site was buried by about 50 cm of alluvium around 450 B.P. (Beta-56115; Figure 3-4). A similar timing for alluviation is indicated at the Flint River site, where features, which include 14 ^{14}C ages between 796 and 656 B.P. (Dobbs et al. 1993), were buried by >50 cm of sediment after occupation ceased.

Because the premodern low and high intervals occurred during more recent time when better, more comprehensive climatic records were maintained, the causes of variation in water levels in the Great Lakes region can be more completely understood. For example, Johnson et al. (1990) correlated high lake levels after about 500 B.P. with the Little Ice Age. Using data compiled from diverse sources, Larsen (1985b) showed that during this time, glaciers expanded worldwide and that cool, moist conditions dominated in the upper Great Lakes region. Monaghan and Schaetzl (1994) and Monaghan and Hayes (1997, 1998) have suggested that this interval is correlative with the Little Ice Age interval. The data we have presented here certainly supports that contention. If so, the premodern high water-level probably resulted from an interplay between elevated precipitation, which consequently increased stream runoff input into the lake, and decreased evaporation along the lake surface. Such environmental conditions would cause an increase in lake level. Conversely, the low water-levels indicated during the premodern low interval probably resulted from warmer and dryer conditions. Monaghan and Schaetzl (1994) and Monaghan and Hayes (1997, 1998, 2001) have suggested that this interval is correlative with climatically mild Medieval Warm interval. A more detailed discussion concerning the implications of cyclical climate change, prehistoric settlement and subsistence patterns, and buried site predictive models is presented in Part II of this volume.

Modern Drainage and Lake Conditions

Larsen (1985b) showed that at about 250 B.P., water levels in Lakes Michigan and Huron began to fall. The historic record of lake level (Figure 3-1) demonstrates that the premodern high water levels probably continued until the end of the nineteenth century. The fact that such high water-levels continued into the historic period, coupled with the historic hydraulic alteration of streams and the land-use pattern established by European immigrants in the region, has greatly affected sedimentation along streams throughout Michigan. For example, mid-nineteenth-century farming and logging activities, which removed permanent vegetation and increased runoff and erosion in the area, probably resulted in increased alluviation along streams (Lovis et al. 1991). The construction of dams to "shoot" logs during the heyday of logging in the northern Saginaw Bay and western Michigan regions greatly enhanced both deposition and erosion along all of the major streams draining into the upper Great Lakes.

Although separating the relative contribution of historic alluvium from that deposited during late prehistoric times is difficult, data collected during deep testing around the state suggests that in some places, historic deposition was significant. Such indications as overthickened plow zones at floodplain archaeological sites as well as buried historic features attest to the results of this process. For example, along the North Fork of the Bad River (a few kilometers east of the village of St. Charles), sawed stumps occur below about 2 m of silt-clay alluvium. Because the stumps are sawed, the overlying sediment must have been deposited during the past 150 years. Similar, albeit thinner, fine-grained alluvium commonly caps many of the floodplains in the Shiawassee flats. As was suggested for the Bad River alluvium, it probably represents sediment related to the "historic denudation" in the region. Importantly, the "silt cap" has effectively "sealed" the presettlement floodplain surface and, as demonstrated by the discovery of several undisturbed archaeological sites under the "cap," has preserved a wealth of archaeological resources (Lovis, Holman, Monaghan, and Skowronek 1994).

CHAPTER FOUR

The Archaeological Perspective
and Background

A Problem-Oriented Archaeological Perspective
on Michigan Prior to European Contact

Michigan Archaeology within a Temporal and Geographic Framework

Because of the tremendous physical diversity of Michigan, it is not possible to uniformly characterize its prehistory in a single chronological or interpretive framework. Rather, this summary, and indeed any larger view of the prehistory of the state, must account for the differing adaptations that developed in changing environmental contexts through time. To facilitate discussion, the conventional divisions of prehistoric archaeological periods within eastern North America—Paleo-Indian, Archaic, and Woodland—will be used. The names, subdivisions, and chronology for these periods, along with key geological events in Michigan, are shown in Table 4-1.

For purposes of this summary, the discussion area will be subdivided into regional segments: the western south shore of the Upper Peninsula; the eastern south shore of the Upper Peninsula, including the Straits of Mackinac and Sault Ste. Marie; the central Lower Peninsula; southwestern Michigan; the Saginaw Valley; and southeastern Michigan. The general distribution of important archaeological sites from these regions is shown in Figure 4-1. Discussion of the prehistoric adaptations and current problem orientations will be arranged chronologically by period within subregions.

Paleo-Indian Period

The Paleo-Indian period in Michigan is characterized by environmental readjustment from the effects of deglaciation. Tundra/spruce vegetation habitats prevailed, and the configuration of proglacial water bodies ancestral to the Great Lakes was markedly different from that of the present. Some areas of the state—for example, the Upper Peninsula-were deglaciated later and during this period were probably periglacial environments. Such conditions likely lasted longer in the Upper Peninsula than in the more southern reaches of the Lower Peninsula. Some have argued that barren ground caribou provided some of the protein to this big game-hunting, narrow-spectrum economy (Cleland 1965),

Table 4-1. Michigan Prehistory: Time Periods, Ages, and Key Events.

Cultural Periods		Inception of Cultural Phases Calendar / 14C Age		Key Cultural Events	Key Geological Events and Time Stratigraphy	
European Contact		A.D. 1640	0.36 kyB.P.	Europeans arrive in Michigan	High levels of Great Lakes; "premodern" flood phase (<0.8 kyB.P.–Little Ice Age)	Holocene
Upper Mississippian/ Late Woodland		A.D. 1200	0.8 kyB.P.	Upper Mississippian in southwest Michigan	Low levels of Great Lakes; few floods (1.0–0.8 kyB.P.– "Medieval Warm")	Holocene
Woodland	Late	A.D. 500	1.5 kyB.P.	Complex egalitarian social systems	Low levels of Great Lakes; few floods (1.0–0.8 kyB.P.– "Medieval Warm")	Holocene
Woodland	Middle	0 A.D./B.C.	2.0 kyB.P.	Complex mound burial; use of tropical and indigenous cultigens	High levels of Great Lakes; Post-Algoma flood phase 2–1.5 kyB.P.)	Holocene
Woodland	Early	550 B.C.	2.55 kyB.P.	Initial mound/earthwork construction First ceramics introduced	Low levels of Great Lakes; "Low" flood interval (3.0–2.0 kyB.P.)	Holocene
Archaic	Late	3000 B.C.	5.0 kyB.P.	First cultigens (squash)	Nipissing-Algoma high-water phase; flooding common (3.5–5.0 kyB.P.)	Holocene
Archaic	Middle	6000– 5000 B.C.	7-8 kyB.P.	First extensive regional exchange	Nipissing transgression Chippewa-Stanley Phase initiated Michigan-Huron basins ice-free	Holocene
Archaic	Early	8000 B.C.	10 kyB.P.	Early and Middle Archaic occupations now submerged under Great Lakes	Nipissing transgression Chippewa-Stanley Phase initiated Michigan-Huron basins ice-free	Holocene
Paleo-Indian		10,000– 9000 B.C.	11-12 kyB.P.	Earliest Paleo-Indian penetration in Michigan	Algonquin phase initiated Greatlakean Advance High-level lake in Lake Michigan basin Early Algonquin in Lake Huron basin	late Wisconsinan
Glaciated		11,000 B.C.	13 kyB.P.	Port Huron Advance; much of southern Lower Michigan ice-free High-level glacial lakes in all basins (low-level lakes between 13.5 and 13 kyB.P.)		late Wisconsinan

while others (e.g., Fisher 1984) have made the case that mastodons may also have contributed greatly to the seasonal subsistence round. Ecological arguments have figured prominently in these discussions, focusing on the structure of newly emergent biomes (Brown and Cleland 1968), the spatial relationships of Paleo-Indian sites and resources relative to these biomes (Mason 1958; Quimby 1958), and the dynamics of this relationship over time (Cleland et al. 1998).

The Upper Peninsula, Sault Ste. Marie, and Straits of Mackinac regions are currently devoid of known early Paleo-Indian–age fluted-point sites. Perhaps the most compelling argument for the potential presence of sites of the late Paleo-Indian period is based on the work of Buckmaster (Buckmaster and Paquette 1989, 1996) and Clark (1989) on the south shore of Lake Superior, where they recorded a series of Plano-related late Paleo-Indian sites on outwash features of the Marquette readvance. These sites are typified by Scottsbluff, Eden, Agate Basin, and collaterally flaked side-notched point styles, which are often found in dense concentrations, suggesting cremations or restricted activity areas. Salzer's (1974) Minoqua and Squirrel River phases from Wisconsin clearly relate to this time period, and the distribution of these phases may extend across the north shore of Lake Michigan into the western Upper Peninsula. These were clearly periglacial adaptations that extended eastward across the northern and eastern shores of Lake Huron into southern Ontario.

70

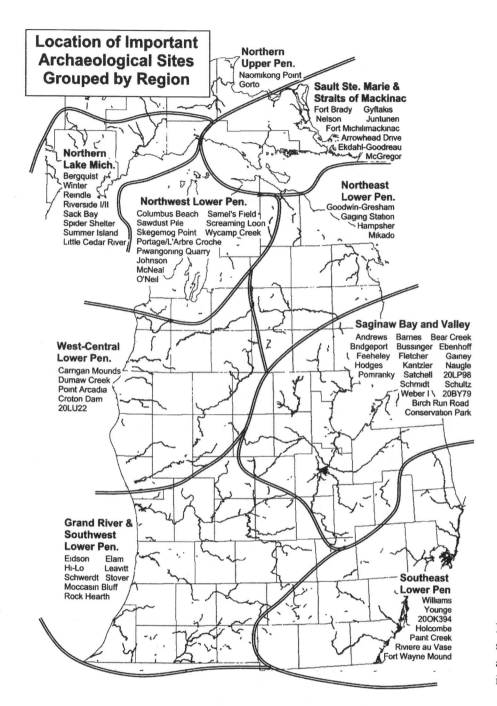

Location of Important Archaeological Sites Grouped by Region

Northern Upper Pen.
Naomikong Point
Gorto

Sault Ste. Marie & Straits of Mackinac
Fort Brady   Gyftakis
Nelson   Juntunen
Fort Michilimackinac
Arrowhead Drive
Ekdahl-Goodreau
McGregor

Northern Lake Mich.
Bergquist
Winter
Reindle
Riverside I/II
Sack Bay
Spider Shelter
Summer Island
Little Cedar River

Northwest Lower Pen.
Columbus Beach   Samel's Field
Sawdust Pile   Screaming Loon
Skegemog Point   Wycamp Creek
Portage/L'Arbre Croche
Piwangoning Quarry
Johnson
McNeal
O'Neil

Northeast Lower Pen.
Goodwin-Gresham
Gaging Station
Hampsher
Mikado

West-Central Lower Pen.
Carrigan Mounds
Dumaw Creek
Point Arcadia
Croton Dam
20LU22

Saginaw Bay and Valley
Andrews   Barnes   Bear Creek
Bridgeport Bussinger Ebenhoff
Feeheley   Fletcher   Gainey
Hodges   Kantzler   Naugle
Pomranky   Satchell   20LP98
                Schmidt   Schultz
            Weber I   20BY79
            Birch Run Road
            Conservation Park

Grand River & Southwest Lower Pen.
Eidson   Elam
Hi-Lo   Leavitt
Schwerdt   Stover
Moccasin Bluff
Rock Hearth

Southeast Lower Pen
Williams
Younge
20OK394
Holcombe
Paint Creek
Riviere au Vase
Fort Wayne Mound

Figure 4-1. Lower Michigan, showing general regions and archaeological sites discussed in chapter 4.

A major site of such periglacial adaptation is the Samel's Field site in Grand Traverse County, Michigan (Cleland and Ruggles 1996). Situated on a post-Algonquian upper group beach, the Samel's Field site postdates ca. 10,000 B.P. The lithic assemblage consists of collaterally flaked Agate Basin–style projectiles, large scrapers, and leaf-shaped bifaces. A mix of Norwood chert from northwestern Lower Michigan and Bayport chert from the Saginaw Bay region may reflect a high degree of mobility for these late Paleo-Indian peoples. A single fluted point has also been recovered from the Samel's Field site (Dekin 1966). Very few other sites have been described from this time period. Leaf-shaped bifaces similar to those from Samel's Field occasionally are present in collections from multicomponent sites. Despite small site samples for the region, however, recent stylistic analysis of late Paleo-Indian projectile points suggests that social boundaries may have been present and are recognizable during this period and also may have subtly shifted over time (Ruggles 2001).

Few major Paleo-Indian sites are found in the southern Lower Peninsula of Michigan, and the majority of these are earlier fluted-point tradition sites. These include the Barnes site in Midland County (Wright and Roosa 1966; Voss 1977), the Hi-Lo (Fitting 1965) and Holcombe sites in Macomb County (Fitting et al. 1966), the Gainey site in Genesee County (Simons et al. 1984), and the Leavitt site in Clinton County (Shott 1986). More recent nonfluted-point late Paleo-Indian sites include one chronological component (Lovis and Robertson 1989) of the Satchell complex initially described by Peske (1963).

The southern Lower Michigan Paleo-Indian sites noted above have been arranged into a relative chronology by Simons et al. (1984). Moving from earliest to latest, Gainey is placed at the earlier end, followed by Barnes and Leavitt, Holcombe, and finally Hi-Lo. These temporal trends are evident in both fluting technology and choice and/or access to different raw materials. For example, Gainey has a preponderance of Upper Mercer and Flint Ridge cherts from Ohio and a minority of more local, Saginaw Bay region Bay Port chert. The later period sites are dominated by Bay Port chert. Analysis of the late Paleo-Indian Leavitt site by Shott (1993) has brought attention to issues of assemblage formation and composition as they relate to Paleo-Indian mobility and the consequent structure of early settlement in the region. In some respects, Krist's (2001) simulation of Paleo-Indian period paleoenvironments and resultant locational decision-making analysis are complementary and result in an interpretation that suggests both logistic and residential strategies might have operated during this time period.

It is also instructive to review certain interpretations made for this period in southwestern Michigan. Lovis (1988), basing his interpretations of point distributions on the work of Meltzer and Smith (1986), has made the case that Paleo-Indian people in this region were foragers who keyed on a broad range of more widely distributed resources rather than a small range of resources with restricted distributions. This resulted in a less "visible" archaeological record (i.e., there are few sites displaying repetitive, multiseasonal occupations). Importantly, this is consistent with evidence derived from the Gainey site in Genesee County (Simons et al. 1984) and, if correct, suggests that due to their low visibility few major Paleo-Indian locales are likely to be discovered.

The Archaic Period

The Archaic period spans a time during which major readjustments of postglacial lake levels and forest distributions took place. During this period, changes from post-Algonquin, proglacial lake phases gave way to greatly reduced water levels during the Chippewa and Stanley stages in the Michigan and Huron basins, respectively. As mentioned in chapter 3, the water levels of these lakes were substantially below those at present (see Table 2-2; Butterfield 1986). However, by 5000–4500 B.P. these lowered levels transgressed to and exceeded their former altitudes of >184 m asl (Monaghan, Lovis, and Fay 1986). Although the base altitudes for Nipissing water levels may have fluctuated somewhat around this high (Larsen 1985b), they progressively receded to modern levels by at least 3500 B.P. Thus, marked changes in coastal environment characterize the entire Archaic period. Combined with the effects of crustal rebound, Late Archaic sites may be found at altitudes well above mid-Holocene or modern lake level and far removed from modern lakeshores. Moreover, the outcome of the substantial rise in lake level between the Chippewa-Stanley low and the Nipissing high stages reduced available land area dramatically, probably resulting in increased packing of populations into smaller spaces and consequently higher densities per unit area. Hypsithermal warming also wrought major changes in postglacial vegetation patterns. Spruce-and-fir-dominated contexts had shifted in southern Michigan to mixed-deciduous contexts by the onset of Lake Nipissing. Thus, Archaic adaptations in the region probably responded to major environmental changes.

An Archaic-stage chronology for the western Upper Peninsula is lacking due to insufficient data. This is true despite the fact that several sites dating to this period have been explored (see Robertson et al. 1999). Significantly, the Archaic period may actually extend until ca. A.D. 0 in this region. This is because in some places within the Upper Peninsula, ceramics, which by definition are the major time marker for the Archaic to Woodland transition, were not introduced until that time. Two prominent sites of this period include the Bergquist and Sack Bay sites in Delta County, Michigan. These are riverine and lakeshore sites, respectively. Their occurrence attests to the fact that sites of this time can occur both on stable terraces and in active eolian dune contexts. Interestingly, both sites are attributed to the Archaic period based on a lack of ceramics rather than actual ^{14}C age estimates. Although the lack of fauna and flora from these sites makes subsistence statements speculative, Fitting (1975b) argued that the tool assemblages and locations indicate that Bergquist was a fishing base camp and that Sack's Bay was a hunting camp. Franzen's (1986) summary of western Upper Peninsula settlement systems likewise reveals the low density of Archaic-age nonceramic sites in the region.

A third major site from this region is the Riverside site (Hruska 1967). This is an Old Copper site and contains both burial and occupation components. If the artifact variability and ^{14}C age estimates are any indication, the site probably has been repetitively reoccupied during several episodes spanning the Terminal Archaic through the subsequent Initial/Early Woodland periods, although Pleger (2000) would argue for a more restricted Late Archaic use of the site between 1000 and 400 B.C. However, three ^{14}C age estimates from the site range from 510 B.C. to A.D. 1, perhaps suggesting continued site use. These dates, combined with an abundance of stemmed and expanding stemmed projectile point styles reminiscent of more southern-tier Late Archaic complexes, reveal a substantial Terminal Archaic/Early Woodland occupation. Notably, Pleger (2000) employs analysis of the mortuary program at Riverside to suggest the presence of a nonegalitarian society by the Late Archaic; this needs to be viewed as a working hypothesis. The Middle Archaic period is not yet represented by any Upper Peninsula sites, which raises the question of whether they occur in contexts not readily identifiable by standard surface survey methods. Sites of this age correspond to relatively low-water lake stages and may be buried within littoral sediments in coastal contexts or are submerged within deeper water lacustrine deposits well offshore.

The eastern Upper Peninsula, Sault Ste. Marie, and Straits of Mackinac area has several sites of reputed Archaic age, although no absolute chronology has been reported (see Robertson et al. 1999). Conway (1980), for example, described small lithic assemblages from the St. Mary's River area, none of which include ^{14}C age estimates. The Nelson site in St. Ignace (Fitting 1974) contains both copper items and small notched projectiles that are clearly Late Archaic in age. In the northern Lower Peninsula of Michigan, several surveys of the Sleeping Bear Dunes area (Lovis, Mainfort, and Noble 1976), Fisherman's Island State Park (Lovis ed. 1976), and the Inland Waterway (Lovis 1976), have revealed a series of small Archaic sites, some of which have ^{14}C age estimates (Lovis 1990a).

Prominent among these northern Lower Michigan sites is the Screaming Loon site (Lovis 1990a) on the Crooked River in Emmet County. This site includes fauna indicating spring occupation and a ^{14}C age estimate calibrated to between 3637 and 3591 B.P. This site is clearly part of a Straits of Mackinac/northwest Lower Peninsula settlement system but also has ties to the Upper Peninsula and northern Lake Huron region. Based on the range of activities associated with the assemblage at the site, Screaming Loon may be a residential base camp and could easily be a counterpart to the numerous smaller logistic or special-function locales that characterize both the riverine and coastal contexts of the Straits region.

In general, southern Lower Michigan poses a somewhat different scenario. Lowered levels in the Great Lakes basins surrounding southern Michigan resulted in greatly expanded land areas for occupation. By ca. 8000 B.P., vegetation change and succession resulted in substantial hardwood communities, most likely with associated changes in faunal composition. Climatic warming during the early and mid-Holocene also catalyzed the establishment of prairie biomes. Significantly, only a handful of primary Early Archaic contexts have been reported for this period. These include bifurcate base points at the Leavitt site (Shott 1993), at the Holcombe site (Fitting et al. 1966), and at 20OK394, which also had a Kessell point (Shoshani et al. 1990). Surface collections have provided the bulk of the data for the Early Archaic (e.g., Brose and Essenpreis 1973), although this has not inhibited attempts at economic or subsistence reconstruction (Arnold 1977). Midcontinent traditions apparently expanded into the southern lakes as hardwood forests progressively transgressed northward. As several have observed (Fitting 1975b; Lovis, Holman, Monaghan, and Skowronek 1994; Shott 1999), however, the bulk of the Early Archaic settlement system probably lies submerged under the raised levels of the Great Lakes.

The archaeological record is scanty after the Paleo-Indian period in southwestern Lower Michigan. Consequently, the behavioral inferences proposed for the region are quite speculative until the onset of the Late Archaic period after ca. 5000 B.P. Postglacial environmental readjustments for the preceding 5,000 years greatly modified the context of human exploitation. Broadleaf mast-producing species were established across the southern Lower Peninsula by at least 8000–7000 B.P. This resulted in the creation of a mixed coniferous/

deciduous community throughout much of the region (Arnold 1977; Mason 1981; Shott and Welch 1984). Gulf-derived atmospheric circulation patterns similar to modern seasonal variability became established by ca. 6000 B.P. (Bryson and Hare 1974). Further, increased rates of stream flow along the St. Joseph River in Berrien County, which have been associated with the Lake Chippewa stage terminated by about 5500 B.P. (Kincare 1984). As discussed in chapters 2 and 3, rebound of the North Bay outlet resulted in the high-water Lake Nipissing stage inundation of coastal and estuarine contexts. The increased vegetational biomass, the establishment of modern fauna, and the presence of recently inundated lake margin contexts provide the important environmental backdrop for Late Archaic occupation of the region. Larsen (1974, 1985b) has argued that climatically induced periodic short-term variations in lake altitudes may have occurred during the Late Archaic and subsequent periods. More recently, others have presented data that supports these or similar cyclical changes in lake level (see discussion in chapter 3). These variations probably figured prominently in regional subsistence strategies (Lovis 1986). It would not be surprising if flooded estuaries and coastal embayments also figured prominently in the seasonal settlement of the Late Archaic in this region as they do elsewhere in the state, such as the Saginaw Valley or the Inland Waterway between Petoskey and Cheboygan (Lovis 1986).

Extensive excavation conducted as part of the US-31 mitigation project along the St. Joseph River in Berrien County provides the majority of the interpretive site data for this period (Garland ed. 1984, ed. 1990). Occupied during a span between 3750 and 2900 B.P., the Rock Hearth and Stover sites are earlier Late Archaic, while the Wymer and Eidson sites are terminal Late Archaic. There is limited evidence for spring occupations at any of these sites, whereas the botanical remains reveal primary late summer/autumn occupation, incorporating a range of nuts, including walnut, hickory, acorn, and beech, as well as sunflower, grape, and hackberry. A structure discovered at the Rock Hearth site is the earliest recorded dwelling for the Michigan Archaic. Other facilities at later sites such as Eidson and Wymer suggest greater incidences of reoccupation during the terminal Late Archaic as well as evidence for plant processing and storage activity. Both of these sites have been characterized as residential hunting camps, although whether a forager or collector type of organizational and mobility strategy was followed cannot currently be determined (Lovis and Robertson 1989). There is, however, a clear intensification of plant food exploitation as part of whichever strategy was practiced, and this has been described as an opportunistic pattern (Egan 1988). In patchy environments with regular risks of periodic resource failure, it is unwise to key an economy too closely to specific resources. Thus, the sites show evidence for a wide range of nut foods, despite their high processing costs, and exploitation of a range of animal foods, with larger meat packages such as deer and elk prevailing. Survey data from the Kalamazoo River basin (Cremin 1982) reveals that as a result of this strategy, Late Archaic site densities increased compared to earlier periods. However, as noted elsewhere, this may well be a consequence of rising lake levels and resultant increased packing of Archaic populations. This data also shows that habitation size decreases commensurately with stream order; the smaller the stream, the smaller the site area.

Central Michigan has few recorded or analyzed Archaic sites. In fact, the majority of chronological, settlement, and subsistence information for the Lower Peninsula of Michigan derives from the rather intensively researched Saginaw Valley region. Interpretations of the Saginaw Valley Archaic have undergone marked reinterpretation in recent years due to substantial excavations at new Archaic-age sites in the region. These include the Middle and Late Archaic Weber I site (Lovis ed. 1989), site 20BY79 (Lovis ed. 1993), the sites at the Marquette Viaduct in Bay City (Lovis ed. 2002), and the Conservation Park site (Beld 1985, 1991).

The Saginaw Valley chronology has been modified to account for new data (Lovis and Robertson 1989), which makes the regional sequence more compatible with that from adjacent regions of Ontario and the greater Midwest. Based on the ^{14}C age estimates associated with the Archaic of southern Michigan, a general chronology can be constructed. The earliest phase of this chronology occurred from 6,200 to 4,500 B.P. and is marked by a late Middle Archaic/early Late Archaic Dehmel Road phase of the Archaic. The Dehmel Road phase is characterized by large side-notched ground-based projectiles such as those found at the Leach site, the Weber I site (see more detailed discussion in chapter 5), the Satchell site, and other locales across central Lower Michigan. Between 4,500 and 3,500 B.P., these point styles give way to a series of stemmed and broad bladed points of the Satchell phase (see Simons 1972, 1979). These types were typically manufactured on argillite, subgreywacke, or a variety of local cherts. A small point horizon follows the previous broad-point horizon and occurs between 3,500 and 2,500 B.P. It is characterized by a series of small, notched and expanding stemmed points in the range of Feeheley, Dustin, Durst, and Innes point types. The terminal end of the small-point phase, which lasted from about 3000 until 2,500 B.P. and may have extended even more recently (Beld 1991), also marks the beginning of a Meadowood phase. This period is characterized by thin side-notched points with a range of blade and base variation that is for the most part consistent with the Meadowood type. The style may have continued into the ceramic-producing Early Woodland period (Beld 1991).

The Middle Archaic has recently been the subject of a major synthesis (Lovis 1999), which will not be duplicated here. Only a limited number of clearly Middle Archaic, Dehmel Road phase, sites are known from the Saginaw Valley. These include the Weber I site (Lovis ed. 1989), the several locales of the Leach site, and the single undiagnostic burial from the Andrews site dated to 5300 B.P. (Papworth 1967). Such a limited array of information precludes comprehensive analysis of settlement systems. However, fauna and flora from Weber I Occupation Zone II suggest a late-summer-through-fall occupation. White-tailed deer, elk, raccoon, muskrat, goose, bowfin, bullhead, and turtle have been identified, although the large cervids clearly dominate the assemblage. The floral remains are dominated by nuts, including acorn and walnut/hickory. This assemblage has been characterized as a "logistic" site probably resulting from repetitive small-scale occupation.

The Bear Creek (Branstner and Hambacher eds. 1994) and Ebenhoff sites (Dobbs and Murray 1993) shed further light on this period, as do the surface deposits at the Leach sites (Mead 1982). Ebenhoff, dated ca. 7000–5300 B.P., has a faunal inventory dominated by mammals with some birds, while Bear Creek has both spring and fall economic indicators. Both of these sites, discussed in more detail in chapter 5, have been interpreted as logistic sites, whereas Leach and Weber I are more likely residential locales. Coupled with scattered point finds, three Middle Archaic site "types" define the settlement system: single or multi-use residential camps, logistic procurement sites, and mobile or transient camps.

The Late Archaic site inventory is more substantial and better able to answer larger questions of settlement system organization and subsistence economy (Robertson et al. 1999). Few single-component Late Archaic burial contexts are known (e.g., the Brandt site; Mead and Kingsley 1985). However, two major burial components of the Late Archaic period, with some transitional Early Woodland contexts, are the Feeheley and Andrews sites. The Feeheley site, with its 15 individuals and a 1980 B.C. ^{14}C age estimate, contains an abundance of copper artifacts, including celts, awls, and beads, as well as shell objects. Covered with red ocher, these flexed burials were wrapped in either bark or fabric for interment. At present, it is not possible to associate the ^{14}C age estimate with the burial component or the occupation with the burials. The primary burial component at Andrews has been dated to 1220 B.C. (Papworth 1967) but may be substantially more recent. Stemmed and larger corner-notched points, birdstones, and other objects may well reveal an Early Woodland placement for the majority of burials at this site. As previously noted, a single Middle Archaic interment was also recovered from this site.

Recent settlement and subsistence studies of the region (Keene 1981; Lovis 1986, 1989; Robertson 1987) have altered several standing interpretations of the Late Archaic in the Saginaw Valley (Taggart 1967; Fitting 1975b). Keene's (1981) work, for example, used an energy maximization approach to develop several economic "seasons" for the region and then derive archaeological expectations that could test the model. Even though his reliance on the earlier Taggart (1967) analysis diminished the practical component of his discussion, the larger heuristic framework of his work does provide a good baseline for matching these observations against archaeological expectations.

Lovis (1986) did precisely this with respect to the question of reliance on nut products for the region. He argued that marked periodicity in the local environment (see Papworth 1967), combined with redundancy of resources between upland and lowland contexts, resulted in a buffering strategy that incorporated high-cost foods into certain components of the subsistence cycle. In later works (Lovis 1989), the evolution of wetlands was investigated to assess relative resource abundance and distribution in the Saginaw Valley system. These studies have concluded that while wetland area remains stable, intraannual variability can exceed interannual variability in this niche and that distributions of wetland niches change markedly between major lake stages. Furthermore, data on resource abundance suggests that as many as 90 individuals could subsist on wetland resources alone during the warm season in this region.

The role of wild gourds in Late Archaic subsistence strategies has also recently become a focus of regional economic research. The carbonized rind of wild *Cucurbita* gourd, accelerator mass spectrometer (AMS) dated to 3840±40 B.P. (Beta 181524; Table 3-1), was identified from a Late Archaic storage/refuse feature context at site 20BY387 in Bay City (Egan-Bruhy 2002; Lovis 2002). This is both an early and far-northern occurrence of this species, which has implications for the relationship between climate change, plant biogeography, and Late Archaic subsistence strategies in the region because it substantially presages the incorporation of domestic squash varieties into local economies. In addition, a seed of domesticated *Cucurbita pepo* squash was discovered incorporated into alluvial sediments during recent excavations at the Green Point site (Demeter et al. 2000). The age (2820±40 Beta-150203; Table 3-1) and context of this seed suggest that Late Archaic populations in Michigan not only used but also grew domesticated squash by about 3000 B.P. In conjunction with other subsistence research, assemblage-related analyses, and the spatial organization of settlement systems, these relationships should be clarified.

Robertson (1987) reappraised the relationship between assemblage composition, site function, and site structure for the Late Archaic using microwear analysis of stone tools as the vehicle for assessing site function. He developed a model of radial mobility for the Saginaw Valley system, with the center of the drainage system acting as a focus for a series of more frequently reused locales. Thus, while assemblages from the center of the system were more abundant and sites larger (e.g., the Schmidt site; Fairchild 1977; Harrison 1966), their function and structure nonetheless remained similar to those from smaller, less dense occupation locales on the peripheries.

Significantly, cycles of lake-level variation both in the long and short run can have an effect on the preservation of sites from the Late Archaic. Buried contexts of Archaic age at Kantzler (Larsen and Demeter 1979), Weber I (Lovis ed. 1989), and Andrews (Papworth 1967) vindicate the propositions of Peebles (1978) and Larsen (1980) that deeply buried alluvial contexts are present and can be explored in the region. This needs to be accommodated in any regional research strategy. More recently (Lovis ed. 2002), radiocarbon sequences from sites 20BY387 and 20BY28 in Bay City have revealed that occupation predating 4000 B.P., during the Nipissing maximum, took place at altitudes well below the commonly accepted Nipissing-stage maximum level. It is possible that Lake Nipissing was either short-lived or that it did not achieve its highest level as currently estimated. This observation underscores the interaction between archaeology and geoarchaeology in field context.

The Early Woodland Period

Traditionally, the Woodland period is marked by the introduction of ceramics as a horizon. In Michigan, this technological innovation occurs at different times in southern Lower Michigan and the remainder of the state. Thus, north of the Canadian-Carolinian transition zone (northern Lower Michigan north of a line from Muskegon to the northern shore of Saginaw Bay) ceramics do not appear until ca. A.D. 0 or a little earlier, whereas in southern Lower Michigan they appear as early as 600 B.C. (Fitting ed. 1972; Garland ed. 1986; Ozker 1982). The Early Woodland, therefore, is a cultural phenomenon primarily associated with the Muskegon River and Saginaw River valleys, and including southwestern and southeastern Michigan. In addition, some Early Woodland occupations also occur in the extreme western Upper Peninsula associated with the northern extension of Wisconsin Early Woodland manifestations.

Three multicomponent sites in the Menominee River watershed of Menominee County in the Upper Peninsula, the Riverside II, Reindle, and Little Cedar River sites, have been assigned to the Early Woodland in this region on the basis of the presence of Dane Incised ceramics (Buckmaster 1979). Some have argued, however, that this pottery is actually of Middle Woodland age or that at least it also extended into the Initial/Middle Woodland period. Fauna and flora found at the sites indicate warm season occupation. Little can be said about the broader pattern of settlement and subsistence for this time period, except that riverbank locations were clearly used by humans during this time period.

The transition to the Early Woodland period took place slightly less than 2,600 years ago (ca. 600 B.C.) in southwestern Michigan. As is true elsewhere in the eastern United States, the Early Woodland is distinguished by the introduction of thick, cord-impressed ceramics that occasionally possess lugs. Garland's (ed. 1986) comprehensive summary of this period in Michigan includes the Moccasin Bluff, Eidson, Rock Hearth, and Stover sites on the St. Joseph River and the Mushroom and Elam sites on the Kalamazoo River, as representative occupations of this time period. Garland (ed. 1986:62) has argued that "there is a predominant Early Woodland settlement pattern of small, seasonal encampments in low-lying site locations near rivers and marshes, where the occupants made use of ceramic vessels." According to Ozker (1982), these vessels were largely used to render and/or store edible nut oils. This is an expected consequence of intensive Late Archaic use of nut resources. Potentially, similar processing procedures may have also occurred during the Archaic, but simply due to the lack of ceramics vessels, we have failed to extract direct evidence from sites to support this. Garland (ed. 1986) notes marked continuity between Archaic and Early Woodland subsistence patterns even in the face of the introduction of an indigenous cultigen (the sunflower, *Helianthus annuus*) into the economy during the Archaic period, a plant that she believes was also used mainly for oils.

Several sites in the Saginaw region relate to the Early Woodland period. These include the Kantzler (Crumley 1973), Fletcher (Lovis 1985), Schultz (Fitting ed. 1972; Ozker 1982), and Bussinger sites (Halsey 1976), as well as site 20LP98 (Lovis ed. 1979), the Bridgeport Township site (O'Shea and Shott 1990), and possibly the Conservation Park site (Beld 1991). Among the significant aspects of this time period is the introduction of thick flower pot–shaped ceramic jars, as well as square and contracting stemmed projectiles. Although Mesoamerican squash (*C. pepo*) was widely believed first introduced into the subsistence economy during the Early Woodland, the AMS-dated *C. pepo* seed from the Green Point site shows that it was actually introduced during the Late Archaic. Ozker (1982) has argued that the introduction of domesticates and the processing of nut oils involving a ceramic technology transformed the scheduling and spacing of Early Woodland subsistence activities. While nuts clearly played a prominent role in Early Woodland activities, Ozker's (1982) research took place before sufficient data was available on Late Archaic nut exploitation in the region and may have affected the way ceramics were viewed relative to this activity. Additionally, given that domesticated squash was actually introduced during the Late Archaic, the assumed relationship between domesticated plants, ceramics, and settlement transformation should be reevaluated or refined.

Beld (1991) has argued that the Meadowood point series of the Late Archaic continues through the Schultz phase of the Early Woodland. His data from Conservation Park, an upland site in Midland County, gives reason to suggest that there may be a functional and seasonal differentiation in projectile point styles between different components of the Early Woodland system. While this proposition can neither be accepted nor rejected at present, the radial mobility model proposed by Robertson (1987) for the Late Archaic may well also explain the variability in site locations, assemblage compositions, densities, and functions that can be observed during the Early Woodland.

Both mortuary and habitation sites from the region give insights into the range of exchange relationships that are present during this period. For example, Stoney Creek and Ten Mile dolomites occur in certain of the smaller mortuary contexts such as Hodges (Binford 1963) and Pomranky (Binford and Papworth 1963; Simons 1989), and Onondaga cherts from Ontario are present in the Conservation Park assemblage (Beld 1991). Exchange affiliations, if not broader social relationships, are clearly oriented to the southeast rather than other areas of the state. This is confirmed by the ephemeral Early Woodland component at the Fort Wayne Mound (Halsey 1968) and in the massive Terminal Archaic/Early Woodland mortuary component at the Williams cemetery site in northwestern Ohio (Stothers and Abel 1993). Recent interpretation of the Williams site has suggested that the funerary context may well have functioned to foster interregional/intergroup interaction, characterized as a "trade fair" acting to enable exchange relationships (Abel et al. 2001).

The evidence from central and southwestern Michigan, on the other hand, which is based primarily on ceramics and lithics, suggests relationships with Illinois rather than Ontario or Ohio. In combination with the eastern Meadowood ties evidenced at Conservation Park, this observation suggests that the Early Woodland in southern Lower Michigan may have multiple origins, as well as include a potential east-to-west differentiation. This has led Garland and Beld (1999) to interpret the circular Early Woodland enclosure/earthwork at Arthurburg Hill as an interregional integration facility, allowing interaction between the Saginaw basin and southwestern Michigan.

The northern extension of this Early Woodland expression is in the mortuary complexes of the Muskegon River drainage (Prahl 1970, 1991), where several mound contexts (Croton Dam Mounds A and B and Carrigan Mound B) produced artifacts typologically similar to those from the Early Woodland component at the Schultz site. Two sixth-century B.C. [14]C age estimates confirm the typological cross dating. Due to a lack of ceramics from these contexts, allow closer affiliations cannot be established. However, site 20LU22 from Leelanau County gives excellent indication of similar affiliations as far north as the Traverse Bay region in northwestern Lower Michigan. Brose (1975) reported a burial cache from this site that included diagnostic artifacts such as a birdstone, blocked-end tubular pipe, Adena and Kramer stemmed bifaces, marine shell beads, and other Early Woodland artifacts. This site has also produced evidence of wild rice (*Zizania aquatica*), a rather early occurrence of this subsistence item in the region.

The Initial and Middle Woodland Periods

The lag in ceramic introduction north of a line from Muskegon to the northern shore of Saginaw Bay (i.e., the Canadian-Carolinian transition zone) makes the Woodland period in this northern region coeval with the onset of the Middle Woodland period to the south. To distinguish between the northern and southern traditions in Michigan, the term Initial Woodland has been employed. The Initial Woodland marks the beginning of the Woodland period in the north (particularly the Upper Peninsula) and the further development of ceramic technology and styles, not to mention other aspects of prehistoric society. It is temporally correlative with the Middle Woodland period to the south.

The Initial Woodland period in the western Upper Peninsula is known from several sites in Menominee, Delta, and Schoolcraft counties. Two well-reported sites from the western Upper Peninsula of northern Lake Michigan are the Summer Island (Brose 1970) and Burnt Bluff caves (Fitting ed. 1968) sites. The former, along with sites such as the Winter site (Richner 1973), attests to the potential for clear stratification of occupational materials in coastal dune contexts. Oval residential structures suggest that several extended families may have occupied this spring/summer season site. The conoidal, tool-impressed ceramics, which lack the cord-impressed surfaces common to North Bay complex material (Mason 1966) from the Door Peninsula of Wisconsin, are more closely related to southern Laurel types from the Straits of Mackinac region. Moreover, the presence of corner-notched and expanding stemmed projectiles, small scrapers, and wedges/bipolar cores confirms a Laurel affiliation. An aquatic emphasis is present in the faunal assemblage. Cleland (1976) has presented the case that spring, shallow-water fishing with nets and individualized fishing were the dominant spring/summer subsistence modes for Initial Woodland populations. They apparently aggregated during the spring and dispersed during other seasons of the year. The latter seasonal aggregation/dispersal cycle is consistent with the model proposed by Brose (1970) for the Summer Island site, where he argued that large mammals probably filled out the seasonal economy. This holds true for eastern Upper Peninsula/Straits of Mackinac Initial Woodland populations as well.

The Spider Shelter site on Bay de Noc is unusual in that it may have been a ritual locale. Projectile point fragments, representing a range of regional Initial Woodland styles, are interpreted as having been shot into the cave from a distance and fracturing on impact with the wall of the cave (Cleland and Peske 1968). It is still not clear what this activity might represent, although Richner (1973) speculated that it might relate to hunting success. He further noted the marked similarity of the lithic assemblage from the Winter site with that from the Burnt Bluff material reported by Cleland and Peske (1968).

Buckmaster's (1979) survey and analysis of the Menominee River drainage recovered five Initial Woodland sites. Based on ceramic decorative techniques, all five sites relate closely to the North Bay complex defined by Mason (1966) on the Door Peninsula of Wisconsin. Limited floral and faunal remains suggest late spring to summer occupation for this group of sites, and Buckmaster (1979) suggests that sites of other seasons may have lower visibility and recovery rates. While some, such as Fitting (1975b), have argued for a historic Chippewa pattern for this region, data is currently lacking to confirm or reject this hypothesis.

Farther east, in Delta County, survey by Franzen (1986, 1987) has revealed a series of smaller Initial Woodland sites classifiable as Laurel primarily on the basis of thin, sandy paste ceramics with multiple bands of tool impressions, a characteristic of early pottery in the region. Corner-notched and expanding stemmed projectile styles, small scrapers, and a bipolar lithic technology taking advantage of small, local raw materials further identify this time period (see Janzen 1968; Brose 1970). Due to the minimal variation between Terminal Archaic and Initial Woodland lithic assemblages in the region, however, it is often possible to confuse the difference between sites of different time periods. It is also likely that ceramics functioned in only certain segments of the seasonal round, suggesting that there may well be aceramic Initial Woodland sites in the region. While Franzen (1986, 1987) discusses the use of the Chippewa model to explain site location, his disenchantment with this approach is reflected in the development of a resource-based locational model that suggests substantial locational flexibility in decisions about seasonal site location.

The southern Laurel tradition is well represented in the eastern Upper Peninsula, Straits of Mackinac, and northern Lower Peninsula. At present, ^{14}C age estimates notwithstanding, it is difficult to place much refined chronological control on the several sites of this time period. For example, based mainly on the ^{14}C chronology from Fort Michilimackinac and the Wycamp Creek sites, Lovis and Holman (1976) have argued that the Initial Woodland intrusion into the Lower Peninsula was a late phenomenon, initiating ca. A.D. 400. Recently collected information from the L'Arbre Croche/Portage site on Little Traverse Bay suggests that this date may be too recent (Lovis et al. 1998).

Middle and Initial Woodland sites from the Sault Ste. Marie, Straits of Mackinac, and northern Lower Peninsula regions are numerous and include portions of the prehistoric components at Fort Brady (Sault Ste. Marie area) and Fort Michilimackinac (Straits area), the Arrowhead Drive site on Bois Blanc Island (Bettarel and Harrison 1962), the Gyftakis and MacGregor sites in St. Ignace (Fitting 1974), and the stratified Ekdahl-Goodreau site west of the Straits on northern Lake Michigan. Additionally, the Portage site on Little Traverse Bay, the Wycamp Creek site, and several smaller sites on the Inland Waterway of northern Lower Michigan, including Sawdust Pile, Columbus Beach, Johnson, and McNeal (MSU field notes), all contain components from this time period. These sites include both coastal and inland locations. Sites from coastal locations at the Straits and along the Lake Michigan lakeshore reveal high artifact densities with abundant ceramics and stone tool inventories and suggest repetitive reuse. Inland sites display lower artifact densities overall. At face value, one could postulate a coastal/interior pattern of seasonal use, with spring/summer aggregation in coastal zones and dispersal into smaller social units during fall and winter. To date, however, no compelling model of Initial Woodland seasonal dynamics has been developed for the region.

Site locations during the northern Middle/Initial Woodland reveal potential in a number of coastal and inland locations. In particular, uplifted lake terraces, both stable and unstable, contain sites of this age. Some, such as Portage, Wycamp Creek, and Ekdahl-Goodreau, are deep and stratified (this is also consistent with the structure of western Upper Peninsula sites such as Summer Island and Winter and the Naomikong Point site west of Sault Ste. Marie). Riverine sites are apparently shallow, quite close to the surface, and fragile. While burials have been encountered at Arrowhead Drive site, this is not a common phenomenon.

What has become increasingly clear is that there are several subregional manifestations of the northern Middle/Initial Woodland in Michigan. In general, these exhibit highly variable subsistence/settlement strategies over a broad area, with generally low population densities, and probably employed ceramic decoration as one vehicle for the symbolizing of group identity (Brose and Hambacher 1999). These subregional traditions, often organized around larger repetitively reoccupied residential sites, may well reflect the first clear archaeological signature of band or family band territories. Furthermore, at a larger spatial scale, the boundary between northern macroregional territories and their more southern counterparts may be rather diaphanous. In this context, the most recent perspective on issues of regionalization, territoriality, and seasonal land use (Brashler and Holman 2004) reveals that at the interface of northern Laurel Initial Woodland and southern Hopewell–related Middle Woodland in northwest Lower Michigan, boundary maintenance may have been low, with noncompetitive scheduling of seasonal resource extraction and a high potential for various forms of social interaction.

In the Carolinian Biotic Province of southern Lower Michigan, the Middle Woodland adaptations are coeval with the Initial Woodland of northern Michigan. Generally characterized by participation in a burial complex known as Hopewell, which employed mounds for disposal of the dead, and associated with riverine types of environments, it was thought that this adaptation was reliant on an agricultural economy (Fitting 1975b). While the Early Woodland inception of Mesoamerican cultigens made this proposition compelling, recent intensive use of recovery techniques, such as flotation, has not revealed archaeological data to support this hypothesis. Rather, the Middle Woodland adaptations of the Saginaw Valley and southeastern Michigan are probably the product of a process of exploitive intensification on local resources. Contrary to patterns in the southern and central Midwest, no evidence for the intensive harvesting of indigenous cultigens has been found at Middle Woodland sites in Michigan. This is true despite the presence of sunflower in some southwestern Michigan sites (Garland ed. 1984, ed. 1990). Recently, Lovis et al. (1996) and Lovis et al. (2001) offered a hypothesis suggesting that intensification of wetland exploitation may have acted as a surrogate for native seed collection in the patchy environments of southern Lower Michigan. This would imply a greater use of aquatic mammals, waterfowl, aquatic tubers, and, as Peebles noted (1978), certain larger shallow water fish species.

Kingsley (1981) argued that drainage characteristics were important considerations in the distribution and abundance of Middle Woodland (ca. 100 B.C. to A.D. 500; Garland ed. 1986) archaeological sites in southwestern Michigan, particularly the Kalamazoo River. There are only two major Middle Woodland occupations in southwestern Michigan, the Moccasin Bluff site on the St. Joseph River (Bettarel and Smith 1973) and the Elam site on the Kalamazoo River (Mangold 1981). Other sites of this age are for the most part isolated "finds" (Cremin 1982). Kingsley's argument hinges on the lack of suitable microhabitats on the Kalamazoo River—chiefly inundated floodplains and backwater lakes—to be conducive to intensive harvesting and collecting adaptations similar to those found in Illinois, where Middle Woodland sites are abundant.

Even given the lack of subsistence data, major habitations, and other factors, this hypothesis remains tantalizing. Assuming that the data from two decades of survey is accurate, this period may have witnessed an adaptive shift toward more centralized habitations, repeatedly reoccupied, in contrast to the preceding dispersed pattern of small (possibly single-occupation) sites. Such a proposition is consistent with a pattern of specific activity-related findspots across a broad landscape, as observed by Cremin (1982). The role of maize in this process of settlement system transformation is not yet known because it has been recovered from only one Middle Woodland context at the Eidson site on the St. Joseph River (Parachini 1984).

East-central Michigan, particularly the Saginaw Bay region, contains a larger number of Middle Woodland sites. These include the stratified Schultz site at Green Point (Fitting ed. 1972) as well as the Kantzler (Crumley 1973), Bussinger (Halsey 1976), 20BY79 (Lovis ed. 1993), Fletcher (Lovis 1985), and Bridgeport Township sites (O'Shea and Shott 1990) in Bay and Saginaw counties. The northernmost extension of this regional Middle Woodland style appears to be through the Muskegon River (Prahl 1970, 1991) and into Antrim County (Lovis 1971) if not farther north (Brashler and Holman 2004).

A few fundamental problems are encountered in recognizing or distinguishing sites of Middle Woodland age. For example, typically such recognition is keyed to the presence of distinctive coiled ceramics with decorative motifs, such as cross-hatching, incising, rocker stamping, and other distinctive attributes. Ceramics, however, may have played a rather restricted role in certain sets of Middle Woodland activities and therefore may be confined to sites of functional or seasonal specificity. This would result in the aggregation of ceramics at certain key locales, such as those enumerated above. A second confounding variable is the fact that certain projectile point styles of the Middle Woodland have been poorly discriminated and are confused with styles of Late Archaic age (Lovis and Robertson 1989; see Fitting 1975a for an example from the Young site). This is not, however, a mere typological problem. Raised water levels in the Saginaw basin during certain segments of the Middle Woodland (Larsen 1985b; Speth 1972) have resulted in the superimposition of Middle Woodland occupations on Late Archaic occupations at Algoma lake stage altitudes. This occurs at least at 20BY79 and well as at the Bussinger and Feeheley sites. Thus, the ability to distinguish between special-function logistic sites of Middle Woodland age and Late Archaic sites is currently difficult. In fact, many sites classified as Late Archaic based on altitude and point types may actually be logistic Middle Woodland camps that simply lack ceramics.

If this is the case, and if wetland intensification rather than food production is the economic adaptation for this time period, then there is no reason to expect that major settlement system transformation should occur during the Middle Woodland. In fact, the implication is that the Middle Woodland should manifest an intensification of the Late Archaic mobility model proposed by Robertson (1987). In the application of this model to the Middle Woodland, then, sites such as Bussinger and Schultz become repetitively reoccupied locales at the center of a radial network of residential mobility, rather than centralized Middle

Woodland villages. It should be recognized, however, that certain locales might take on greater significance in an intensified system. This may explain specific phenomenon at certain locales, such as the circular palisade and mound group at the Schultz site. In such a model, sites such as Kantzler and Fletcher, and possibly Naugle, which have lower overall occupation densities, represent peripheral residential sites. Additionally, aceramic logistic sites should also be present along the wetlands and river drainages radiating away from the center of the basin.

The evolutionary framework of the basin is clearly conducive to the preservation of sites in deep alluvial deposits and in eolian contexts. Some of these sites, such as the Marquette Viaduct locale of the Fletcher site and the Schultz site, preserve stratigraphy (see discussion of these sites in chapter 5). Others, such as Bussinger, do not.

Little can be said about the Middle Woodland occupations of southeastern Michigan, although they may have related broadly to what has been termed the "Western Basin Middle Woodland" (Stothers et al. 1979). The Central and Great Mounds at Fort Wayne (Fitting 1965) in Wayne County include Middle Woodland materials, and regional surveys in the region have also produced either transitional early Late Woodland or Middle Woodland sites (e.g., Brose and Essenpreis 1973). Stothers et al. (1979) conclude that the Maumee River area of Ohio was a center of settlement and population during the Woodland period, that subsistence and economic systems were primarily hunting/gathering, and that burial modes suggest patrifocality. Perhaps more significant to the current summary is the suggestion that raised water-planes in the Erie basin during the Late Woodland period may have resulted in inundation and burying of Middle Woodland-age occupations. Indeed, regardless of any secular variation in lake level, Figure 2-2 shows that the Lake Erie outlet at Niagara Falls is rising faster than the west shore of the lake in Michigan. Consequently, during most of the Holocene, Lake Erie has been transgressive along its Michigan shoreline and over the past 1,500 years (since the end of Middle Woodland) has risen over 1 m due to relative differential uplift alone. By combining this with secular lake-level variation, much of the Middle Woodland Lake Erie shoreline has probably been inundated and associated sites either buried or destroyed.

The Late Woodland Period

The transformations associated with the Late Woodland adaptations of various subregions of Michigan result in rather different mobility patterns (Halsey ed. 1999; Brashler et al. 2000). In large part this is due to changing technology and subsistence patterns that are keyed either to seasonally dense and abundant natural resources or to the transition to an agriculturally based economy. The mode of seasonal mobility patterns in turn can be well associated with the structure of different environments in each subregion.

In the western Upper Peninsula, the presence of major drainages such as the Menominee River provide a context for linear patterns of Late Woodland mobility between lakeshore and interior contexts. Different sets of locational characteristics tend to distinguish between the season of occupation and the function of Late Woodland sites in this context. Buckmaster (1979), basing her interpretations on four groups of locationally distinct sites, presented a model that incorporated aspects of seasonal movement and activity specificity. Warm-season occupations would have occurred on the lakeshore, where population aggregates formed sites of higher artifact density and structural complexity, which are revealed primarily by such factors as post molds, hearths, and storage pits. Conversely, lower density, structurally less complex, smaller occupation sites that are associated with this model are interpreted as hunting camps. The central drainage, Buckmaster (1979) argues, presents evidence of transitional autumn and spring occupation. It was used during movements from the lakeshore to the upper reaches of the drainage. Small logistic locales, probably winter hunting camps, occupy the upper reaches of the drainage. At present, subsistence data are inadequate to determine whether deep-water fall fishing, as proposed by Cleland (1976), operated as part of this system. Recently, evidence of ridged agricultural fields associated with maize cupules, shell-tempered ceramics, and a fifteenth-century A.D. [14]C age estimate have been recovered, which may indicate that horticultural activities could have been incorporated into the local subsistence regime at a larger scale than previously recognized (Buckmaster 2004).

Cultural affiliations for the western Upper Peninsula subregion during the Late Woodland are clearly directed to the south and west in Wisconsin rather than south and east in Michigan. The presence of Madison wares in some abundance, rather than eastern Upper Peninsula and Straits sequence ceramics, reveals that the Menominee system and the Garden Peninsula (Brose 1970) are part of a different system than much of the eastern Upper Peninsula. This is further attested to by the fact that Oneota Upper Mississippian types such as Grand River wares occur across the region at many Late Woodland sites, a rare phenomenon to the east. In addition, individual Oneota occupations also occur in the area (Brose 1970; Buckmaster 1979). Buckmaster (1979) notes that Oneota sites in the Menominee drainage occur in different resource zones than the other Late Woodland occupations. A lack of domestically produced foods and a diverse faunal and floral inventory suggest a broad-spectrum economic base during the Late Woodland.

The Lower Peninsula of Michigan presents a different scenario than the Upper. For example, circular enclosures or earthworks are prominent features of the Late Woodland landscape of southern Michigan. Numerous interpretations of these earthworks have been put forth in the literature during the twentieth century and have been revisited anew in recent years. Current research calls into question some of the earlier work that interpreted these features as defensive works. On the basis of a suite of attributes, McHale Milner and O'Shea (1998) argue that southern and northern earthworks are fundamentally different phenomena. The northern enclosures, in this context, are viewed as ritual precincts situated at ecological and social boundaries and designed to foster exchange interactions between inland hunting-gathering groups that did not practice maize agriculture and coastal societies with access to lacustrine resources and maize (O'Shea 2003). This interpretation is both an interesting proposition and an important alternative hypothesis. Addressing the southern Late Woodland earthworks, particularly in southeastern Michigan, Zurel (1999) envisions the role of these sites as central nodes in a relatively even partitioning of the landscape into social group territories. This is a problem that will undoubtedly attract further concerted attention.

There is a substantial inventory of Late Woodland sites from the region, including Sault Ste. Marie, the Straits of Mackinac, and the northern Lower Peninsula. Together, data from these sites provide abundant information with which to reconstruct late prehistoric patterns of social (Milner 1998; McPherron 1967) and economic organization (Smith 1996). In addition, the presence of stratified occupations such as the Juntunen site (McPherron 1967) and O'Neil site (Lovis 1973, 1990b) provides substantial chronological information for the time period (Milner 1998), as well as demonstrating the potential for coastal environments to preserve deeply buried, stratified Late Woodland contexts.

Perhaps the most compelling economic model for the region at large is that proposed by Cleland (1976). He presents a case for the advent of deep-water gill-net fishing by Late Woodland peoples that is based on changes in site location, fauna, and artifacts. Several lines of evidence are used to draw this conclusion. First, a technological shift occurred from individualized fishing gear such as hooks, gorges, and toggle harpoons to a technology incorporating net-sinkers, presumably employed to weight deep-water nets. Locational shifts, from shallow-water site locales that were used during the Middle Woodland to the addition of sites proximal to deep-water habitats during the Late Woodland, are used as parallel lines of evidence to demonstrate settlement system transformation to fall-season aggregate sites. Finally, faunal data has been incorporated into the discussion to demonstrate the increasing use of deep-water, autumn-spawning fish species during the Late Woodland. In concert, the three sets of information are used to infer an increased reliance on abundant, deep-water fish species such as lake trout and whitefish, which were extracted with gill nets and processed for storage by larger social aggregates.

This model has provoked some discussion in the literature of the upper Great Lakes (Cleland 1989; Martin 1989), specifically related to the structural characteristics of Late Woodland site formation, which Martin (1989) believes reflects longer-term processes rather than short, time-discrete transformations. Martin (1989) argued for greater flexibility in settlement and subsistence strategies during the Late Woodland, flexibility that incorporated gill-net technologies. As certain other sites reveal (e.g., O'Neil [Lovis 1973]), the Late Woodland period in this region has clear spring fishing locations as well. The compatible arguments of Martin and Cleland have been at least partially resolved by the current research of Smith (2004), who reappraised the issue using several decades' worth of new subsistence data. She concludes that the earliest evidence for gill-net technology is still that from the Juntunen site at A.D. 800 but that it is not until ca. A.D. 1100 that it is more commonly incorporated into larger regional strategies at multiple sites across the northern Great Lakes. From an environmental vantage point, it should be noted that recent research on lake-level variation during this period (Larsen 1985b; Lovis 1990c) suggests that any model using stable lake level as an operating assumption probably oversimplifies the Late Woodland decision-making process. As lake levels change, so do the offshore characteristics of many site locales. This entire issue needs to be addressed in greater depth.

Be that as it may, other settlement pattern research gives a clear indication of the cycle of seasonal mobility during the A.D. 700–1000 period of the Mackinac phase in the region. Using site catchment analysis as her analytic method and exploring seasonal resource availability adjacent to known Mackinac phase sites, Holman (1978) reconstructed two potential mobility models. Both models are similar and incorporate a cycle of coastal spring/summer/autumn movement to repetitively reoccupied locations, with late autumn/winter dispersal into dissected interior lacustrine environments. Nuances of difference between these two models revolve around the location of the autumn deep-water location. One incorporates the coastal zone of Lake Michigan into it, while the other keys on the Straits of Mackinac region. This pattern replicates historically documented cycles of Ojibwa mobility in the region. Notably, neither model suggests the use of domestic foods in the subsistence economy; and while time periods within the Late Woodland can be chronologically differentiated, there is currently no reason to suggest additional large-scale transformation of the settlement system during the period.

With the latter point in mind, the chronology of the Late Woodland in the Straits region can be reconstructed from the analysis of McPherron (1967) at the Juntunen site on Bois Blanc Island in the Straits of Mackinac. This sequence begins ca. A.D. 800 with the inception of the Mackinac phase, which is characterized by subconoidal, flared-rim, cord-decorated pottery termed Mackinac Ware. These early Late Woodland styles largely lack collars or castellations. Mackinac Ware declined by ca. A.D. 1000, and the subsequent Bois Blanc phase displayed an increase in Blackduck-related ceramic styles. Vessels of this phase incorporated decorative/manufacturing techniques such as rim and shoulder appliqués, low castellations, globular vessel shapes, and generally straight rim sections. Decoration often included bands of closely spaced corded tool impressions, brushing, and overlapping punctate series. The western cast of the Straits sequence changes markedly with the introduction of Juntunen series pottery from the Juntunen phase (ca. A.D. 1200–1500). McPherron (1967) argues that these Juntunen ceramic styles are more closely comparable to Iroquoian styles from southern Ontario. The eastern relationship, which extends north to the Sault Ste. Marie eastern Lake Superior region, is manifested by strong castellation, collaring, and geometric decorative motifs, including chevrons and vertical and horizontal plats of punctate or stab-and-drag decoration. Based on evidence from the stratified O'Neil site, Lovis (1973) noted that the earlier end of the sequence may lack castellations and favors linear punctate motifs. In addition, he comments that post–A.D. 1500 styles may incorporate curvilinear motifs and broad trailing, while maintaining the geometric characteristics of the motifs. This protohistoric period in the region is termed the O'Neil phase. More recently, Milner (1998) has greatly refined the Juntunen phase sequence and, in a time-space framework, tied ceramic style change to issues of resource uncertainty and consequent social processes.

The mortuary evidence from the Late Woodland is scant. Perhaps the best-reported data derives from the multiple interments recovered from the Juntunen site in the Straits region (McPherron 1967; O'Shea 1988). Multiple interments during the Late Woodland are suggestive of the fact that larger corporate group relationships, such as the lineage, might supercede the importance of individual statuses at death. This would be consistent with the larger regional focus of subsistence activities undergoing a transformation to a fall fishing economy.

A somewhat different sequence is recorded for the west-central portion of the Lower Peninsula, although details of the adaptation have yet to be refined. A Late Woodland sequence with markedly different ceramic styles extends from Grand Traverse Bay south to Oceana and Mason counties, which is roughly consistent with the spatial distribution of the Canadian-Carolinian transition zone. This tradition was initially defined at the Skegemog Point site in Grand Traverse County (Cleland), a large, interior, multicomponent Late Woodland site. The earlier end of this sequence, termed the Bowerman phase, has strong affinities with early Late Woodland manifestations from southern Michigan that will be discussed in subsequent sections. Starting ca. A.D. 900 and lasting through ca. A.D. 1200 is the Skegemog phase. Ceramics from this period display strong affinities with the Mackinac phase of the Straits region. However, the presence of collars on a large proportion of the ware group, with a broader range of rim eversion and punctate decoration that is often in a multiple linear configuration, clearly separates Skegemog from Mackinac. The O'Neil site also has a major Skegemog phase component that is probably logistic in nature (Lovis 1990b) and related to chert procurement at the Pi-wan-go-ning Quarry near Norwood, Michigan (Cleland 1973). The Traverse phase followed the Skegemog phase in the region and is characterized by distinctive sandy paste ceramics, with multiple surface treatments on the same vessel. Decorative techniques include lip scalloping and linear bands of finger pinching. Some of these techniques are reminiscent of the ceramics from the Dumaw Creek site discussed by Quimby (1966). Hambacher (1992) further refined this sequence with a view toward understanding changing Late Woodland boundaries relative to the adaptations to the Canadian-Carolinian transition zone. He concluded, based on ceramic styles, that a distinct adaptation to the transition zone was present by the beginning of the Late Woodland.

While the subsistence economy of this regional tradition remains vague, research at the Point Arcadia site (Hambacher 1988) has clarified one component of the seasonal round. A Traverse phase feature at Point Arcadia, as well as one other feature, produced carbonized maize, and it is possible that food production was an integral part of the subsistence system during the Late Woodland in the transition zone. Other economic items reveal a summer/fall occupancy. These include nut meats and berries, small and medium-sized mammals, and a range of shallow, warm-water fish species probably extracted with seines. Hambacher (1988) suggests that sites such as Point Arcadia acted in a complementary seasonal fashion to interior winter sites, such as those reported by Fitting and Cleland (1969).

The Late Woodland/Upper Mississippian prehistory in southwestern Lower Michigan is marked by several important trends, including a tendency for larger habitation sites to be concentrated on the lower reaches of major river systems, the incorporation of domestic plants as a significant component of the subsistence economy, and an increasing intensification on certain wild resources, both plant and animal (Brashler et al. 2000). The Late Woodland period, from ca. A.D. 500 to 1200, is followed by a post–A.D. 1200 Upper Mississippian period. Although maize has not yet been recovered from Late Woodland or

Mississippian context in the Kalamazoo River valley, it was present at the Moccasin Bluff site on the St. Joseph River (Figure 4-1). Ford (1973) identified it as a developed Eastern complex variety that probably postdates A.D. 1400. Fauna from Late Woodland sites on the Kalamazoo and St. Joseph rivers indicate that substantial palustrine habitats were exploited. Resource specialization, reflected by more intensive extraction, apparently took place during the Upper Mississippian. The Schwerdt site, a specialized fishing station, clearly supports such a position (Cremin 1980).

The overall picture that emerges during the Late Woodland and Upper Mississippian is a system that was gradually in transition from broad-spectrum intensive collecting at seasonal camps to one that became increasingly keyed to specific resources, such as sturgeon and maize, with high productivity, predictability, and storability. These systems were also subject to periodic climatic variation and consequent cyclical changes in wild or domestic resource productivity. Such problems could have been responded to in several ways: by organizing specialized activities in an exploitable area larger than an individual river valley (Cremin 1983), by regularizing symbiotic relationships between adjacent systems with different subsistence economies to buffer resource shortfalls, or even (Larsen 1985b) by periodic north-south latitudinal shifts throughout the entire Woodland period. Clarifying these important issues continues to provide crucial directions for ongoing research in the region.

While some have had the temerity to suggest potential links between late prehistoric assemblages in the southwestern Michigan region and historically documented Native American groups, such assignations continue to remain problematic. The earliest recorded groups in this region are the Miami and the Mascouten (Tanner 1986). The Mascouten, as early as the 1630s, were probably distributed as far south as the Kalamazoo River (Goddard 1978), whereas the Miami, distributed around southern Lake Michigan, probably extended north into the St. Joseph River drainage by the 1670s (Callendar 1978). Clifton (1977), based largely on archaeological evidence, places the Potawatomi in this region between the 1630s and 1640s. Given the spatial movements of indigenous groups as a result of European contact, as well as normal seasonal and longer term cyclical shifts of territory, it is possible that all of these groups may have been temporarily resident in the region during the European contacts of the mid-seventeenth century.

Southern Michigan's Saginaw Valley has one of the greatest densities of Late Woodland sites in the state. Despite this, the general chronology of the period remains poorly known. The important stratified occupation of the Schultz site at Green Point was largely truncated during this time, although a group of thin cord-marked ceramics termed Saginaw Thin dominate the remnant Late Woodland zones (Fitting ed. 1972). Unfortunately, the Late Woodland patterns of residence, refuse disposal, and site formation processes in general do not contribute to the preservation of stratified Late Woodland deposits. Multiple reoccupations of the same locales, such as the Fletcher site (Lovis 1985) and the Bridgeport Township site (O'Shea and Shott 1990); multiple reuse of cultural features, such as storage and refuse pits; and the intensive processing of animal parts for stew preparations all resulted in massive and largely homogeneous cultural deposits. As discussed in chapters 5 and 6, the lack of site stratification during the Late Woodland and better-developed Middle Woodland stratification (particularly in the Saginaw Valley) may also relate to secular variation in climate and related sedimentation cycles. Although not stratified, certain occupations, such as Birch Run Road (Clark 1986), however, display more restricted occupation spans if the ceramic chronology can be used as a clear indicator.

Based on work at the Bussinger site, Halsey (1976) formalized this early Late Woodland period as the Saginaw phase. It is dominated by Wayne ware–style potteries, which could also easily include the Saginaw Thin series. Dating this period has been the subject of recent research (Lovis 1990d, 1990e). Accelerator ^{14}C age estimates on cooking residues on Wayne ceramics from the Fletcher site in Bay City, in concert with other traditional dates from the Saginaw Valley, clearly bracket Wayne ceramics, and the Saginaw phase, between A.D. 600 and 1000. Characterized by cord-impressed, straight-rimmed, globular ceramics, most often with corded decoration, the time period also appears to have clear spatial regularities (Brashler 1981) and is restricted mainly to the Saginaw Valley and southeastern Michigan. Subsequent occupation of the Saginaw Valley is less dense, and the ceramics reveal increasing influence from the Younge tradition of southeastern Michigan and, to a lesser degree, the Upper Mississippian traditions of western Michigan (Brashler and Holman 1985). Although it has been an important area throughout prehistory, the earliest historic accounts from the Saginaw Valley suggest that the area was abandoned at contact.

Discussion of subsistence and settlement systems in the Saginaw Valley region has been the subject of several researchers, including Fitting (1975b), Peebles (1978), Lovis (1985), and Lovis et al. (2001). Cleland (1966) makes the case that large mammals dominated the Late Woodland faunal extraction strategy. This is related to an assumption that agriculture played a significant role in the subsistence economy (Fitting 1975b). Recent interpretations suggest, however, that while maize may have been present during the early Late Woodland, it does not constitute a primary resource prior to A.D. 700–800 in southern Michigan or the Saginaw Valley (Lovis 1985; Lovis et al. 2001; Parker 1996). As Brashler et al. (2000:557) point out:

> Maize is only frequent in contexts that postdate cal A.D. 800–1000, such as the Birch Run Road site (Parker 1986), the Marquette Viaduct locale of the Fletcher site (Lovis et al. 1996), the Schultz site (Lovis et al. 1992; Lovis et al. 2001), the Casassa site (Egan and Monkton 1991), and, most significantly, site 20SA1034 (Parker 1996), where both 8- and 12-row varieties of maize were identified. Analysis of the floral assemblage from site 20SA1034, dated by a suite of ^{14}C assays to ca. cal A.D. 1100, additionally yielded evidence of tobacco, squash, sunflower, and chenopodium-also present at the Marquette Viaduct locale of the Fletcher site (Lovis et al. 1996) and the Schultz site (Lovis et al. 1992)—in quantities sufficient to infer convincingly their intentional production, harvesting, processing, and storage (Parker 1996).

Centralized village constructs (Peebles 1978), therefore, are probably not appropriate to explain the settlement systems of the early Late Woodland in this region. Rather, models that incorporate more mobility and an increasing emphasis on intensive collecting currently appear to have better explanatory potential.

In this vein, several recent complementary models should be explored in greater detail. One model envisions a pattern of seasonal mobility between autumn and winter upland hunting and nut-collecting locales on the fringes of the Saginaw basin to early spring/summer use of the central basin, summer occupation on the coastal zone of Saginaw Bay, and back through the central basin in late summer or early autumn (Lovis 1985). With minor alteration, this is consistent with the model of seasonal mobility proposed by Robertson (1987) for the Late Archaic. Given the scant evidence for domestic food production during this period, there is no reason to believe that major system transformation occurred by the early Late Woodland. Rather, key locales may have shifted their positions in response to increasing population distributions. For example, there is a clear increase in use of the lower reaches of the basin during this time period, a phenomenon absent during earlier periods (Lovis 1985).

Some have argued that an increased use of wetland resources, including tubers, waterfowl, and aquatic mammals, may have sustained the early Late Woodland system prior to the adoption of food production as the dominant subsistence mode (Lovis, Egan, Smith and Monaghan 1994 2001). Post–A.D. 1200 settlement transformation cannot currently be assessed with any accuracy, although it is possible that maize agriculture played a role in the changes observed in the system. While certain sites, such as Bussinger (Halsey 1976), have evidence of post-Wayne occupation, decreases in occupational intensity at this and other sites (Fletcher site, Lovis 1985; Schultz site, Fitting ed. 1972) reveal that early Late Woodland site locations are being utilized less often, and less intensively, by late Late Woodland peoples. The nature and causes of this transformation remain important research questions in the region.

The broader relationships of the early Late Woodland in the Saginaw Valley are well reflected in the mortuary data from this time period. Halsey's Saginaw phase (Halsey 1976) designation for this segment of the Late Woodland is based on a comparative analysis of burial data from the Bussinger site with other early Late Woodland complexes across the Midwest and East. He defines the Wayne Mortuary complex on the basis of broad similarities in the funerary program across the Saginaw Valley, southeastern Michigan, northern Ohio, and parts of southern Ontario. Flexed and bundle burials with ceramics, marine shell beads, axes and adzes, minerals such as limonite and hematite, fauna including turkey leg bones, pendants, and other paraphernalia characterize this mortuary complex. Variations in inventory, according to Halsey (1976), are status related. He views this complex as the product of a larger egalitarian social system. The comparative analysis suggests similarities with Intrusive Mound in Ohio and the Kip Island phase in New York.

The Late Woodland prehistory of southeastern Michigan is intimately tied to adjacent portions of Ohio and Ontario in the western Lake Erie and southern Lake Huron basins, as well as the Lake St. Clair basin. Stothers, in several works, and Krakker (1983) have summarized the chronology of this region into five phases modified from Fitting's (1965) analysis of the Younge tradition. Sequentially, these include the early Late Woodland/transitional Middle Woodland Wayne phase (A.D. 600–800), the Riviere au Vase phase (A.D. 800–1000), the Younge phase (A.D. 1000–1200), the Springwells phase (A.D. 1200–1350), and the Wolf phase (A.D. 1350–1500+). A significant factor in consideration of subsistence trends for the entire Late Woodland in this region is the relatively early (eighth century A.D.) presence of maize at the Sissung site (Fitting 1970), demonstrating its relatively early incorporation into the economy.

Independent lines of inquiry other than flora have been used to assess the direction of transformation in this region. Krakker (1983), for example, uses settlement pattern trends to infer the transition to a maize agricultural economy. Specifically, he documented increases in site size during the post–A.D. 1300 period and a shift in site location to locales maximizing the availability of arable land. Larger sites in agriculturally suitable locations, with a relatively stable site population, allowed him to conclude that human populations remained relatively stable through this transformation. On a comparative level, the similarities in trends between the Saginaw Valley and southeastern Michigan need to be recognized: post–A.D. 1200/1300 shifts in settlement and the adoption of previously known cultigens on an intensive basis.

Stothers et al. (1983) further argue that these trends result in greater intercommunity competition for resources. This argument carries some weight if one views the decline in nonlocal exchange materials in the post-Riviere au Vase period, as witnessed by Halsey (1976) in the definition of the Wayne Mortuary complex, as an expression and consequence of increased boundary maintenance between competing local economic units. The presence of palisades and circular earthworks is consistent with this hypothesis. Parallel trends have been noted for the distribution of cherts as well, with smaller distribution patterns characterizing the later Late Woodland system (Luedtke 1976); the exchange networks appear to contract in extent. Thus, the changes wrought by the rather late adoption of maize agriculture in southern Michigan had major ripple effects through other parts of the social and economic systems.

Mortuary data from this later segment of the Late Woodland is best known from sites such as Riviere au Vase (Fitting 1965), Paint Creek (Sauer and Dunlap 1979), and the later burials from the Bussinger site (Halsey 1976). Increasing emphasis on larger group affiliation, rather than individual statuses, is apparently reflected in the incorporation of multiple individuals into single mortuary facilities. This process is often in the absence or low incidence of mortuary objects. Individuals are generally secondarily rearticulated, in whole or part, in elongated pits, with substantial superpositioning occurring. The decreasing importance of individual status in favor of larger corporate group affiliations is consistent with the transition to larger nucleated settlements inferred for this later, agricultural time period (see O'Shea 1988).

Summary

Michigan's environments, both past and present, express tremendous heterogeneity of composition. This diversity is in turn reflected in the rather substantial differences in precontact human adaptive strategies observed both temporally and spatially across the state, as well as in the types of questions archaeologists ask about these strategies, as the preceding sample of problem orientations in Michigan prehistory starkly reveals.

Because of its relatively recent deglaciation, Michigan has been subject to a variety of postglacial readjustments in physical environment, including landform, vegetation, and fauna, largely on a north-to-south time-transgressive basis. Some of these readjustments were marked, such as the opening of entire new land areas for occupation, the extinction of megafauna, the establishment of mature forests of varying composition, and substantial changes in the levels and spatial configurations of the Great Lakes themselves. The modern environment is the current end product of these cumulative changes and in turn reflects this environmental history. The present configurations of riverine, wetland, and lacustrine drainage systems in the state are less than 10,000–15,000 years old. Systems in the southern part of the Lower Peninsula were established during the earlier part of this interval and are also somewhat better developed. Large parts of the northern Lower Peninsula and the Upper Peninsula of Michigan, which became free of glacial ice or emerged from under glacial lakes after 10,000 B.P., are characterized by extensive wetland and lake systems that have undergone a much shorter period of development.

Marked north-south differences in vegetation communities also exist. In general, deciduous forests dominated to the south in the Lower Peninsula, and coniferous forests predominated in the north. These general forest communities were separated by a broad transition zone that extended north of a line from Muskegon to the northern shore of Saginaw Bay (Albert et al. 1986). This zonation of vegetation is partially a result of climatic difference and partly depends upon differences in soil (more loamy soils in the south and more sandy soils in the north), the latter of which reflects specific deglacial histories. The faunal composition of these different vegetation communities varies considerably, and it should be recognized that such differences were and are present in northern and southern Great Lakes fish populations as well. The interface between Great Lakes aquatic and terrestrial environments was also significant to past economies (Brashler et al. 2000), although the nature of this interface changed over time. Finally, the differences in temperature and precipitation regimes and solarization potential, when loosely translated to frost-free days or growing season, create widely varying potential for the use of indigenous or tropical cultigens between northern and southern regions in later prehistory. However, the geographical location of these northern and southern zones, particularly the transition zone, probably fluctuated throughout the Holocene (Larsen 1985b). Such geographical zonation during the middle and late Holocene generally corresponds with the linked depositional-climatic cycles that were outlined in chapter 3. Additionally, the effects that these cycles had on archaeological site formation and preservation are significant and are discussed in chapter 6.

From a prehistoric settlement and subsistence perspective, this data is important because it shows that the actual climate is dynamic and that conditions for specific regions varied through time. For example, during the Little Ice Age, average temperatures were apparently regionally depressed relative to today, which probably resulted in a reduction of the number of frost-free days throughout the region. These harsher conditions probably affected late prehistoric populations in southern Michigan more than those in northern Michigan, particularly as these conditions are related to Late Woodland horticulture in the Saginaw Valley and southwestern part of the state (Monaghan and Hayes 2001). Conversely, during warmer episodes, such as the relatively mild mid-Holocene

Hypsithermal (ca. 7000–5000 B.P.) or the late Holocene Medieval Warm (ca. 1000–800 B.P.) interval, a relatively longer growing season and milder climatic conditions may have extended much farther north than at present. This may have not only allowed northward extension of horticultural adaptations during the Late Woodland but may have also permitted expansion of more native, more southern plants such as gourds (*Cucurbita pepo*) into the northeastern and Great Lakes region during the mid-Holocene (Cowan and Smith 1993; Hart and Asch Sidell 1997). As archaeologists, we must recognize the significance of a dynamic Holocene environment and account for its effects on prehistoric population dynamics when formulating settlement and subsistence models.

The several theoretical approaches, archaeological research agendas, research questions, and problem orientations reflected in the preceding overview represent ongoing attempts to understand the way that past populations solved the problem of adapting, over both time and space, to such a highly variable environment. Although environment does not necessarily dictate human adaptation, it does provide important limitations and constraints to the kind and structure of those settlement and subsistence systems that are possible. The social and behavioral issues associated with the interaction between human populations and food resources of varying abundance, reliability and predictability, in the context of a changing physical environment, provide a clear focus for Michigan archaeology. In their attempts to understand how past populations responded to highly variable and dynamic contexts, archaeologists in Michigan have addressed different dimensions and different scales of inquiry. Regardless of dimension or scale, however, a fundamental requisite to such inquiries is an understanding of the preserved archaeological record: what is the nature of the record, how was it formed, and how does it reflect the original population of sites (Lovis and O'Shea 1994; Lovis and MacDonald 1999)? The answers to such questions require that the archaeological data be placed in its proper ecological, geological, and environmental context. The remaining parts of our discussion will address certain of these issues from an ecologically based, multi- or cross-disciplinary perspective, with the goal of developing a model for site burial and preservation in fluvial and/or littoral environments of southern Lower Michigan.

CHAPTER FIVE

Location and Description of Buried and Stratified Sites in Michigan

Geological and Cultural Controls for
Site Burial and Stratification

(With Contributions by M. J. Hambacher)

The Distribution and Environments for Buried Archaeological Sites in Michigan

The discovery and proficient excavation of stratified archaeological sites are critical to an understanding of temporal and spatial change in prehistoric human settlement. Because such sites occur in settings that have commonly been reoccupied, they leave a long-term record of cultural change that integrates with associated natural, environmental transformations. Thus, these sites provide an extended record of cultural change as well as registering how those changes correspond to environmental modifications. Numerous buried sites occur throughout Michigan, the more significant of which are shown in Figure 5-1. Those buried sites that have been identified are generally concentrated in three main areas: along the Great Lakes shoreline in extreme northwest Lower Michigan, along the lower Grand and Kalamazoo rivers, and southeast of Saginaw Bay in Bay and Saginaw counties. The majority of buried sites in northwest Lower Michigan occur as a result of shoreline processes, mainly related to eolian sand deposition. Burial of these sites occurred relatively late (i.e., Middle and Late Woodland). Sites in southern Lower Michigan, on the other hand, include a range of occupational ages from the Middle Archaic through terminal Late Woodland and historic periods. This last group of sites, in the Saginaw Bay region, represents the greatest concentration of buried sites in Michigan (Figure 5-1 and Table 5-1) and is discussed in greater detail below.

Although not subject to detailed predictions, several important prehistoric sites in Michigan were discovered preserved under relatively thick sequences of nineteenth- and twentieth-century urban fill deposits. These sites have been found even in the industrialized and downtown locales of many urban areas. Two of the more dramatic examples of these sites occur in Bay City and Grand Rapids. In downtown Bay City, the CERT site (20BY365), which includes stratified, Middle-to-Late Woodland deposits, was discovered effectively sealed under more than 3 m of nineteenth-century fill (Demeter et al. 1994), while in the

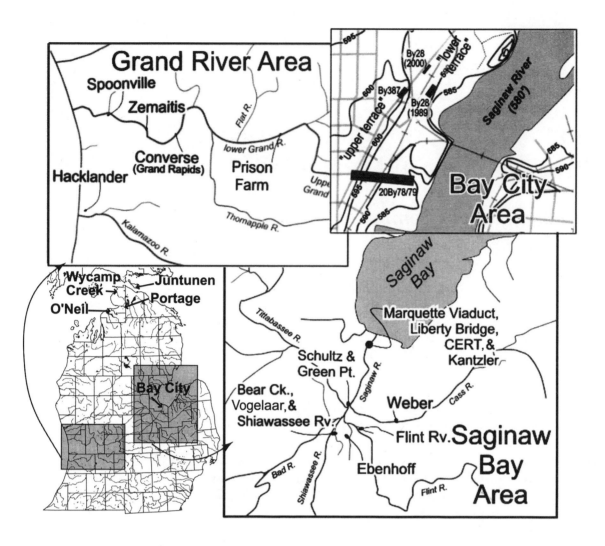

Figure 5-1. Lower Michigan, showing the location of buried and/or stratified archaeological sites discussed in chapter 5.

nearby upland, a few blocks away from the river, undisturbed, in situ Late Woodland "midden" deposits were found directly under a sidewalk (Hambacher, Dunham and Branstner 1995). More recently, an up to 1-m-thick, Late Archaic-through-Late Woodland midden associated with the Converse Mound site (20KT2) was discovered under 2–3 m of nineteenth-century fill along the Grand River in downtown Grand Rapids (Hambacher et al. 2003). This site was believed completely destroyed when Euro-American settlers removed the related mounds in the mid-nineteenth century and industrialized the waterfront. Remarkably, considerable portions of this midden were undisturbed even though a foundry, numerous utility trenches, a parking lot, a flood-control wall, and a six-lane expressway bridge (US-131) were all constructed on the site during the past 150 years. These sites were discovered using normal deep-testing methods, and their preservation confirms several important factors that control site preservation in urban areas. First, because they are generally wet and tend to flood, "filling" rather than "cutting" usually was the first dominant activity that occurred along waterfronts (see Lovis 2004 for an extended discussion of this

Location and Description of Buried and Stratified Sites in Michigan

Table 5-1. Major Stratified Archaeological Sites in Lower Michigan

Drainage	Site	Archaeological Period(s)	Burial Age	Burial Process
Saginaw	Weber I (20SA581)	Archaic–Woodland	Middle Holocene (Nipissing)	Alluvial-Shoreline
Saginaw	Ebenhoff (20SA596)	Archaic	Middle Holocene (Nipissing)	Shoreline-Eolian
Saginaw	Schultz (20SA2)	Transitional Archaic–Woodland	Late Holocene (post-Algoma flood)	Alluvial
Saginaw	Green Point (20SA1)	Transitional Archaic–Woodland	Late Holocene (post-Algoma flood)	Alluvial
Saginaw	Bear Creek (20SA1043)	Archaic–Woodland	Middle Holocene (Nipissing) and Late Holocene (post-Algoma flood)	Alluvial-Shoreline
Saginaw	Shiawassee River (20SA1033)	Woodland	Late Holocene (premodern-Little Ice Age flood)	Alluvial
Saginaw	Marquette Viaduct (20BY28)	Transitional Archaic–Woodland	Late Holocene (post-Algoma flood) and Historic	Alluvial
Saginaw	CERT (20BY365)	Woodland	Historic	Urban fill
Grand	Converse (20KT2)	Woodland	Historic	Urban fill
Grand	Zemaitis (20OT68)	Woodland	Late Holocene (post-Algoma flood)	Alluviation
Kalamazoo	Hacklander	Archaic–Woodland	Middle Holocene (Nipissing)	Alluvial-Shoreline
Lake Michigan	Juntunen	Archaic–Woodland	Late Holocene (premodern-Little Ice Age flood)	Shoreline
Lake Michigan	Portage	Archaic–Woodland	Late Holocene (post-Algoma flood)	Eolian
Lake Michigan	O'Neil (20CX18)	Woodland	Late Holocene (post-Algoma flood)	Shoreline-Eolian
Lake Michigan	Wycamp Creek	Woodland	Late Holocene (post-Algoma flood)	Shoreline-Eolian

and other urban taphonomic processes). Consequently, the settlement surface was sealed from general urban disturbance relatively early. Thus, when more extensive structures were built on the sites, this fill actually protected the archaeological deposits. Second, because hand excavation predominated during the nineteenth century, footing and basement preparations were often minimal and tended to be only as wide as absolutely required. This also tended to minimize the lateral disturbance of such sites. Finally, because they are placed on generally filled wetland, basement excavations for factories were often avoided from a structural stability standpoint. Thus, once built, these buildings, with their shallow, minimal footings, tended to further protect the site, particularly if concrete was poured as a floor in the building.

Regardless of whether burial occurred by natural or cultural processes, the effective discovery of buried or stratified sites requires a balanced, multidisciplinary team of scientists from a variety of disciplines to integrate earth science information and methods with the traditional anthropological focus of archaeological research. Examples of such approaches include the US-31 and US-23 surveys (Dunham et al. 1995; Dunham, Hambacher, Banstner, and Banstner 1999) as well as several pipeline corridor studies. In fact, one of the better and most successful examples of this approach is the cultural resources effort associated with the 1990–1991 Great Lakes Gas Transmission Pipeline (GLGTP) expansion project (Branstner 1990a, 1991; Branstner and Hambacher eds. 1994). Investigations undertaken during this project led to the identification and excavation of several previously unknown buried sites. In addition, 19 prehistoric sites were tested and data-recovery efforts conducted at seven sites in the vicinity of St. Charles, southern Saginaw County, alone. Five of these Saginaw County sites yielded buried and/or stratified prehistoric archaeological deposits. Part of the success of the GLGTP survey derives from the fact that conditions in the Saginaw Bay region are apparently right for burial and preservation of archaeological sites. At least eight buried sites exist in the southern part of the Saginaw Bay region in Saginaw and Bay counties. The reasons for the relative abundance of buried sites involve a combination of factors relating to Holocene lake-level fluctuations, the topographic and hydraulic properties of particular drainage basins, and specific, often unique characteristics of individual site location. These factors are discussed in greater detail below.

Geological Processes Controlling the Location and Burial of Archaeological Sites in Michigan

Although a variety of cultural factors, ranging from strategies of resource exploitation to population dynamics and perhaps even to simple human choice, may dictate the location and preservation of archaeological sites, these factors are difficult to quantify. Therefore, from the perspective of predicting site burial, we will focus mainly on the physical processes relating to availability of land surface and potential burial of sites in various geologic environments. From the perspective of geological processes, two main circumstances dictate the occurrence and preservation of archaeological sites in the Great Lakes region: in order for humans to occupy a site, the area must be both ice-free and above lake level (i.e., not under water). Given these criteria, deep burial of sites results mainly from depositional processes that occur during lake transgressions and ice-margin fluctuations, or more generally within shoreline and stream channel environments. In addition, sites within any environmental setting (upland, floodplain, lakeshore, etc.) may also be buried by eolian deposition. Despite the fact that eolian buried sites are numerous in Michigan, particularly in the northwestern part of the state, they are not the focus of this book. Eolian processes can occur nearly anywhere on the landscape where conditions are favorable and are not necessarily indicative of or related to human settlement. Thus, predicting the probability of whether an archaeological site was buried within a specific eolian landform is probably not possible.

Excepting general eolian processes, the main site burial mechanisms include (1) direct burial under glacial sediment (till, outwash, eolian, etc.) during readvances of the ice margin, (2) direct burial under lacustrine sediments during a transgression of a lake, (3) burial by shoreline processes (littoral and/or eolian), and (4) burial along streams by channel alluviation. As discussed below, only the last two factors, shoreline and alluvial burial, are considered relevant to this book because they offer a greater potential for predicting the location of deeply buried archaeological sites. This is suggested not only because sedimentation rates are typically high in these areas, allowing rapid burial of sites, but also because the paleoenvironment can in part be assumed by analogy with modern floodplains and shorelines. Moreover, these landforms are important places for human settlement because they are frequently ecotonal and offer a relatively greater range of nearby environments to exploit for subsistence. Sites are, consequently, often reoccupied, leaving a long-term record of human settlement.

The general regions that may contain sites buried by ice-margin readvance and lake transgression (points 1 and 2 above) can be defined based on an understanding of glacial and lake-level history discussed previously (see chapter 2). For example, the geological and cultural histories of the area indicate that Paleo-Indian sites buried under glacial sediment must be inside of the Greatlakean ice border (i.e., 11,500 B.P. margin; Figure 2-6) in the northern Lower and Upper peninsulas of Michigan. As was also true for eolian landforms, however, the probability that a buried site underlies a specific location is nearly impossible to assess. The morphological and environmental evidence along the present ground surface, which may indicate potential for human habitation, would have been obliterated during either lacustrine inundation or ice advance. Furthermore, given the potential for either reworking or destroying sites in ice-marginal or subglacial environments, the probability of preserving any valuable archaeological information during glacial readvances (or even by ice-marginal processes) is very low. Designing a sampling strategy to test for sites buried by such processes is probably futile. Sampling for sites buried during lake transgressions, however, may be more productive because rapid sedimentation might allow preservation of at least some archaeological information. The absence of surficial morphological and environmental evidence for buried sites on the lake plain itself dictates that such sampling would be most productive if confined along or near the paleo-shoreline developed during the maximum transgression. These areas can be predicted based on the age and location of specific shorelines and the regional settlement history. While both shoreline and interior regions of the Great Lakes were affected during numerous late glacial and Holocene fluctuations in lake level, the interior includes relatively few shorelines formed after human settlement. Except during the waning stages of Lake Chicago and within the Straits region, the interior of southern Lower Michigan was not directly inundated after about 12,000 B.P. By 10,000 B.P., significantly lower than modern lake stages (Stanley and Chippewa; Tables 2-1, 2-2) existed throughout the upper Great Lakes. Because few Holocene-age raised beaches are found in the interior of Michigan, burial of archaeological sites by shoreline processes was mainly associated with the mid-Holocene Nipissing transgression and the establishment of modern lake level (i.e., after ca. 5000 B.P.).

The burial of archaeological deposits by shoreline processes (point 3 above) is likely, but such deposits are probably only haphazardly preserved. Shorelines consist of facies formed in both erosional and depositional environments. They typically include such deposits as relatively high-energy littoral (foreshore) sediment that makes up the strand along the shore margin and more sporadic, catastrophic storm deposits that typically form the back-berm of the beach. Additionally, marsh deposits commonly developed in swales, which often mark older beach sequences, behind beach berms, while eolian deposits, such as dunes and sand sheets, can occur across the landform. Shoreline landforms are dynamic and evolve. Even such minor 1- or 2-m fluctuations in lake level as those observed during recent times (Figure 3-1) may result in significant shoreward or landward migration of these facies (Larsen 1985b; Thompson 1992; Thompson and Baedke 1995). Very complex sequences of superimposed, partly preserved near-shore, littoral, and eolian sediments, sometimes separated by paleosols, underlie landforms of the Great Lakes shorelines. Archaeological sites are also preserved within the buried paleosols, although the preservation potential is variable depending on the depositional environment. For example, during transgressions, sites found along back-berm, swale margins may be preserved as they are rapidly buried by eolian or storm deposits. Conversely, these same processes would be likely to at least partly erode sites found on the beach berm as sediment was vigorously reworked within the littoral environment during transgressions. During regressions of the lake, on the other hand, sites located on the berm might be preserved if rapidly buried by eolian sand. These processes are particularly important during the post-Nipissing, late Holocene climate-induced lake-level variation, whose numerous raised beaches may have represented important locations for human occupation. Moreover, these lake transgressions also probably accelerated stream channel alluviation near the mouths of streams and, acting in concert with alluvial process, may have been significant to archaeological site preservation during specific intervals.

Of all the factors considered in this study, stream alluviation is probably the most significant for burial of archaeological sites. In fact, throughout most of the Midwest, alluvial landforms are probably the first and most obvious environments considered for archaeological site burial. Because lake-level variations exert significant influence on the alluvial record in the upper Great Lakes, buried archaeological sites probably are especially likely within alluvial landforms that lie close to stream base level. Drainage systems developed near the margins of the Great Lakes basins are generally graded to a specific base level controlled by the water-plane altitude of a specific lake in the basin. If the base level is lowered during a regression of the lake, the stream will respond by incising its channel. During transgressions, however, base level is raised, and the stream will respond by "raising" its channel through alluviation. Sites that occur along the margin of streams may be buried during such an alluviation event. The rate and magnitude of such alluviation are controlled mainly by the rate and magnitude of the transgression and by the "upstream" distance of the site. In general, sites are most rapidly and deeply buried nearest to the lake margin and during a rapid rise of several or more meters in lake level. Importantly, even if the transgression does not actually flood the site, the site can be buried simply as a response to changes in regional base level associated with the transgression.

Although lake-level influence was restricted to within several kilometers of the Great Lakes shorelines, stream channel alluviation also may have been significant in specific areas and was controlled mainly by specific hydraulic characteristics of the drainage system. For example, floodplains that lie upstream from places where stream channels are constricted and narrow or where erosionally resistant material (i.e., bedrock, indurated clay and silt, etc.) floors the valley are also areas of potential accelerated alluviation. Climate changes also resulted in variation in alluviation rates within streams and also influenced variations in lake level. More details about the role that climate change, lake-level variation, and stream hydrology played in archaeological site burial are discussed in chapter 6.

Location and Description of Major Buried Archaeological Sites in Southern Lower Michigan

As previously noted, the most important known buried or stratified sites in southern Lower Michigan are confined mainly to either the Saginaw Bay region or the lower Grand River valley (Table 5-1 and Figure 5-1). Discussions of these sites are arranged based on their geographic proximity. Thus, sites located near Bay City and Saginaw are presented first and include Schultz (20SA2), Green Point (20SA1), CERT (20BY365), and Marquette Viaduct (20BY28). Next, one site found near Frankenmuth, Weber I (20SA581), is described, followed by several sites from southern Saginaw County, including Shiawassee River (20SA1033), Bear Creek (20SA1043), Ebenhoff (20SA596), and Flint River (20SA1027). Finally, one site found along the lower Grand valley, Zemaitis (20OT68), will be described. Additionally, because at least a part of the Vogelaar site is stratified, it supplies important data for the lake-level history of Lake Huron and is also significant to understanding a complex of sites in the southern Shiawassee lowlands (Shiawassee River and Bear Creek sites). A discussion of the related Vogelaar site (20SA291) has also been included.

A brief discussion of the stratigraphy and geological significance of these sites follows. First, locational information and general geographic and ecological background information are presented for each site. This is followed by a brief outline of the stratigraphy. Finally, the importance of dates/data from these sites to reconstructing regional geological history or developing models of archaeological site burial is addressed. Discussions of these issues are necessarily abbreviated and focus more on the significance of the overall stratigraphy to the regional Holocene depositional history and processes of site burial than to the specific archaeology that has been reported. The interested reader is referred to the original references or site reports for greater details concerning specific aspects of the stratigraphy, the archaeological material found, or the overall significance of the site to human settlement and cultural history.

Schultz (20SA2) and Green Point (20SA1) Sites

LOCATION AND BACKGROUND. The Schultz and Green Point sites occur at Green Point, a 1–2-km² alluvial landform developed at the confluence of the Tittabawassee and Saginaw rivers. Green Point occurs at the south end of the City of Saginaw, Saginaw County, Michigan, in the NW1/2 of Sec. 2, T11N R4E and the SW1/4 of Sec. 35, T12N R4E (Figure 5-1). These sites are probably the best-known and most-studied stratified sites in Michigan. The fact that these sites have been prominently mentioned throughout this book indicates their importance in understanding late Holocene environmental change as well as the prehistoric settlement of Michigan. The archaeological significance of the area that includes these two sites has been known since the late nineteenth century. However, the area was first intensively investigated by professionals from 1959 to 1964 (Fitting ed. 1972; Wright 1964), again in 1991 (Lovis, Egan, Smith, and Monaghan 1994; Lovis et al. 2001), and most recently in 2000 (Demeter et al. 2000). Taken together, these studies reveal a 1–3-m-thick, well-stratified, 3,000-year-long record of human occupation within the changing late Holocene environment.

Physiography, hydrology, and geology all played an important role in the formation of the archaeological deposits at Green Point. For example, the comprehensive stratification that makes the site area so important archaeologically is a direct result of the hydraulic constriction of the drainage from a large portion of central Michigan. This constriction generated extensive local levee and flood-plain sedimentation during episodic Holocene flood events. Green Point, which currently lies only 2 m above Lake Huron (the base level for the Saginaw River), was dramatically affected when the level of Lake Huron rose or fell ±2 m, in part due to the numerous secular variations in the Holocene climate (see previous discussion; Larsen 1985b; Lovis et al. 1991).

The Schultz and Green Point sites occur along the Saginaw River about 20 km south of Saginaw Bay and are situated near the northeast margin of the broad, topographically low Shiawassee flats. These flats generally define the region inundated during the Nipissing phase of the Great Lakes and include most of the lower portions of the Cass, Flint, Shiawassee, Bad, and Tittabawassee drainage basins. The locations of these sites are significant because they lie at the "mouth" of the flats where these rivers all merge to form the Saginaw River (Figure 5-1; Lovis, Holman, Monaghan, and Skowronek 1994). The Saginaw River then flows north through a gap in the Port Huron Moraine and discharges into Saginaw Bay at Bay City, about 20 km from Green Point. Thus, during both prehistoric and historic times, human groups using natural transportation networks through the flats must have passed by Green Point. The importance of this location is demonstrated by the extensive, long-term prehistoric occupation at Green Point. The occupation of these locales probably began when the present drainage configuration was established (i.e., ca. 3000 B.P.) and was more or less continuous until historic contact.

STRATIGRAPHY. Speth (1972) was the first to establish a detailed and comprehensive stratigraphic sequence for the Schultz site. It included 10 units (1–10; Figure 5-1) that were defined based on cultural-temporal, pedological, and/or sedimentological criteria from deposits at the Schultz site. In order to integrate this stratigraphy with that of earlier work at the Green Point site (Wright 1964) as well as to place the depositional history of the area into a more comprehensive framework, the ten stratigraphic units were consolidated into five major depositional phases (I–V; Speth 1972) using indicators of relative flood intensity. These depositional phases still represent a baseline for understanding the depositional history at the site, and later work at Green Point by Lovis et al. (1996), Lovis et al.

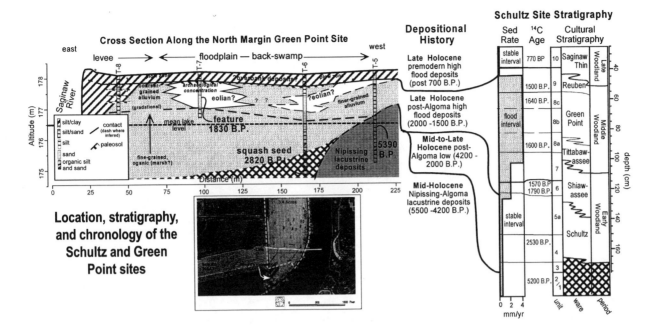

Location, stratigraphy, and chronology of the Schultz and Green Point sites

(2001), Demeter et al. (2000), and Monaghan and Hayes (2001) refined Speth's stratigraphy into a regional framework based on more recent research in the Saginaw Bay region (Figure 5-2). The discussion of the site stratigraphy is based mainly on this more generalized framework.

The basal units at Green Point are mid-Holocene sands related to the Nipissing transgression and are devoid of cultural material. The ^{14}C ages of detrital wood collected from the sand are 5500–5000 B.P., which supports a Nipissing age for the sand (Figure 5-2; Speth 1972; Demeter et al. 2000). Backhoe trenches placed in both the Schultz (Lovis, Egan, Smith, and Monaghan 1994; Lovis et al. 2001) and Green Point (Demeter et al. 2000) sites indicate that the Nipissing sand forms a relative upland, implying that the river eroded a shallow, >3-m-deep "trough" through the sand as it cut its valley north to Saginaw Bay after the Nipissing and Algoma high-water phases (Demeter et al. 2000). Although not observed in the Green Point area, data presented in chapter 3 indicates that the downcutting probably occurred when Lake Nipissing fell to essentially modern level just after ca. 4000 B.P. (Monaghan 2002). Thus, the Saginaw River, which is so important to the settlement of the Green Point site, formed after ca. 4000 B.P. and probably rapidly incised its channel.

That the Saginaw River had extensively downcut at Green Point after 4000-3500 B.P. is supported by ^{14}C age estimates of 2820 B.P. on a domesticated squash seed that was collected from slack-water fluvial deposits 330 cm below the surface (Figure 5-2). The age of the seed and the fact that it was from a domesticated squash indicate that humans had settled Green Point by at least 3000 B.P. The floodplain, however, was not yet stabilized by the Late Archaic, and the area must have included extensive mudflats that actually lay nearly 2 m below present lake level (Figure 5-2). This data not only supports the notion that Saginaw Bay

Figure 5-2. Stratigraphy and depositional history of the Schultz site (after Lovis et al. 2001) and the Green point site area (after Demeter et al. 2000 and Monaghan and Hayes 2002b). See Figure 5-1 for generalized location of the site in the Saginaw Bay area.

had achieved modern levels well before 3000 B.P., as is suggested by other data collected throughout the region (see discussion in chapter 3), but also that the level fell well below modern by ca. 3000 B.P.

Although detailed archaeological and ecological data are rare at Green Point for the period before about 3000–2500 B.P., gastropod (Brose 1972) and wood charcoal (Lovis et al. 1996; Lovis et al. 2001) analyses suggest that the floodplain stabilized during the Early Woodland (ca. 2500 B.P.), and a wet-mesic forest locally covered the point. Additionally, the faunal assemblage (Cleland 1966; Luxenberg 1972) suggested a cooler climate, and the gastropod, floral, and sedimentological data show that occasional dry periods became common after 2500 B.P. and, consequently, flooding probably became relatively rare during this time.

The dry conditions ended and flooding dramatically increased during the Middle Woodland. [14]C age estimates suggest that this occurred after about 2000 B.P. At the Green Point site, about 2 m of sediment was deposited between ca. 2800 and 1800 B.P., and sedimentation was probably concentrated in the latter part of this interval. In fact, data from the Schultz site sequence indicates that sedimentation rates greatly accelerated after 1800 B.P. This is most apparent near the river where nearly 1 m of sediment was deposited in the "channel area" during a brief Middle Woodland interval of episodic flooding between 1800 and 1600 B.P. (Figure 5-2; Lovis, Egan, Smith, and Monaghan 1994; Lovis et al. 2001). A similar period of extensive flooding prior to 1800 B.P. was also noted by Demeter et al. (2000). The period of most intense flooding occurred mainly during the Green Point phase Middle Woodland occupation of the site (Units 8a–c; Figure 5-2), which is also the period of greatest occupation (as measured by high ceramic densities and high frequencies of lithic and subsistence materials; Lovis et al. 2001). Importantly, the presence of discrete, discontinuous Middle Woodland cultural deposits supports the episodic nature of flooding and shows that people periodically occupied the site as the floodplain accreted (Lovis, Egan, Smith, and Monaghan 1994; Lovis et al. 2001).

Extensive flooding ended soon after 1500 B.P., during the transitional Middle-to-early-Late Woodland occupations of the site. Lovis et al. (2001) suggest that occupational intensity falls off dramatically during this period (Figure 5-2). [14]C age estimates and sedimentation rates from both the Green Point and Schultz sites suggest that floodplain stability probably dominated during the Late Woodland until at least 800 B.P., with environmental conditions probably similar to those suggested for the "flood stable" Early Woodland (Lovis et al. 2001). Demeter et al. (2000) also suggested that flooding increased again during the very late prehistoric or early historic period and proposed that a "buried sand dune ridge" beneath a 50–100-cm-thick cap of finer-grained alluvium suggests a return to more rapid, intensive flooding. Because at least the lower part of the clay-rich alluvium is not plow-disturbed, flooding probably initiated during late prehistoric times and is probably associated with the cooler, wetter conditions of the Little Ice Age (Monaghan and Hayes 2001).

Discussion and Significance. Several important archaeological observations can be made from the Green Point sequence. Lovis et al. (2001) showed that during the Middle Woodland, flooding was episodic over an interval of a few hundred years and that people periodically occupied the floodplain during the period. The record of middle and late Holocene environmental change was also significant for developing site burial and locational models as well as for understanding how humans related to these changes. The downcutting of the Saginaw River channel, for example, suggests that the Algoma phase probably ended by 3500 B.P. when Saginaw Bay fell to at least modern levels and broad mudflats fronted relative sandy upland at Green Point. The discovery of a 2820 B.P. domesticated squash seed within these mudflats deposits reveals that humans must have settled Green Point during the Late Archaic and probably cultivated domestic plants. The floodplain was apparently stabilized by 2500 B.P. when warmer-dryer conditions predominated and the Saginaw River was probably graded to a lower-than-present level of Lake Huron. Extensive flooding apparently returned after 2000 B.P. when deposition accelerated and levee formation increased throughout the area. In at least one place, more than 1 m of sediment was deposited over a 200-year interval. Given that the site lies only a few meters above the modern level, such dramatic sedimentation likely reflects a higher-than-present level of Lake Huron (Speth 1972). The floodplain once again stabilized by about 1500 B.P., which probably indicates that lake level likewise returned to at least modern level. Extensive flooding and probably associated high lake-levels returned just prior to Euro-American settlement of the region.

From a prehistoric settlement and site burial standpoint, several interesting points emerge from the Green Point area. The lack of paleosols and even the hint of preserved, buried ground surfaces within or below the Nipissing sequence suggest that the transgression was apparently vigorous and probably destroyed any early or middle Holocene archaeological record that may have existed. A different pattern dominated the post-Nipissing, late Holocene interval, suggesting that although transgressions occurred, they resulted in preservation of the archaeological record. Relative floodplain stability dominated during the Late Archaic and Early Woodland periods and again during most of the Late Woodland period. Rapid alluviation, on the other hand, characterized the Middle Woodland and Mississippian/Late Woodland periods. This pattern suggests that stratification of sites in the area should be more common during the Middle Woodland and very late prehistoric periods and relatively uncommon during the Late Archaic and Early and Late Woodland periods. Although late Holocene sites of any archaeological period could be buried in the area, the actual alluvial burial events are likely concentrated in the intervals between 2000 and 1500 B.P. and again after ca. 800 B.P.

CERT Site (20BY365)

LOCATION AND BACKGROUND. The CERT site (20BY365) is located within Bay City, a few hundred meters east of the eastern bank of the Saginaw River (Figure 5-1). It lies along the west edge of Water Street between 13th and 14th streets and was discovered during deep testing of the U.S. Environmental Protection Agency (EPA) proposed Center for Environmental Research Training (CERT). The site was excavated by Demeter et al. (1994) and consists of a 20–40-cm-thick, dark, organic-rich, prehistoric cultural deposit directly overlain by about 3.5 m of historic-age fills. Although a few small, minor examples of historic-age artifacts were found within the upper part of the cultural deposit, the artifacts within the deposit are mainly of prehistoric age and consist of prehistoric pottery sherds, polished- and chipped-stone tool fragments and flakes and fire-cracked rock. Apparently, the early formation of the 3.5-m-thick historic fill sequence effectively sealed and preserved the underlying prehistoric surface. Consequently, in situ prehistoric cultural information contained within the deposit was preserved from later, more extensive disturbance associated with industrial development along the Saginaw River.

In addition to the artifacts, several culturally related features as well as associated bone, shell, and charcoal and other botanical remains were preserved. In at least one place, probable fluvial deposition has truncated the cultural deposit and separated it into two stratigraphic units. These are informally referred to as the "upper" and "lower" cultural zones.

A ^{14}C age estimate of 1070±100 B.P. (Beta-69036; Demeter et al. 1994) from a composite sample of charcoal collected from the upper cultural zone suggests that the site was occupied during late prehistoric time. This age is supported by the occurrence of a possible Late Woodland pottery sherd collected from the upper cultural zone. Because of the lack of datable material, no absolute age estimate was obtained for the lower cultural zone. Based on comparison of deposition events established for the Marquette Viaduct site located along the west bank of the Saginaw River a few kilometers downstream from the CERT site, however, this part of the cultural deposit was probably formed during the Middle Woodland period.

STRATIGRAPHY. Seven major stratigraphic units were defined at the site based on cultural-temporal, pedological, and sedimentological criteria (Demeter et al. 1994). More recently, Monaghan (2002) and Monaghan and Hayes (2001) have placed the CERT site into a regional depositional framework by relating the seven-unit stratigraphy to the depositional history at Green Point and other sites in the Bay City area. The following discussion of the CERT site stratigraphy and depositional history is placed in this more generalized, regional framework, particularly in reference to the nearby Marquette Viaduct site (Figures 5-1, 5-3).

The base of the sequence at the CERT site includes dense, fissile diamicton. The dense and fissile structure of the diamicton suggests that it was probably deposited as basal till by lodgment processes during the formation of the Port Huron and Bay City moraines about 13,000 B.P. The total thickness of this unit is not known, and only the upper meter was exposed during excavation. The diamicton is overlain by a 10-cm-thick, poorly sorted sand and gravel deposit ("mid-Holocene fluvial"; Figure 5-3). The contact between this unit and the diamicton occurs at an altitude of about 177.5 m, is erosional, and is marked by a discontinuous gravel lag on the diamicton surface. The presence of the lag suggests erosion of the upper surface of the diamicton by vigorous water flow. Given the altitude of the lag and the lake-level history for Saginaw Bay, the erosion occurred after about 4000 B.P. and represented early stages of fluvial sedimentation of the Saginaw River at Bay City. A few faint cross-beds within the upper part of the unit also indicate a generally northward flow of water, a direction consistent with the modern flow in the river (Demeter et al. 1994).

The lower sand and gravel grade upward into a dark-gray-to-black sandy horizon that contains abundant cultural material ("Middle Woodland"; Figure

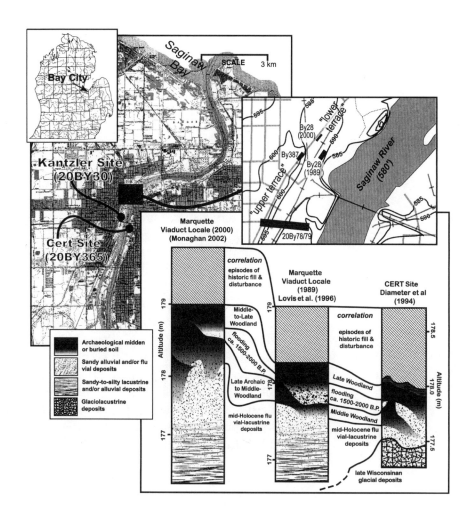

Figure 5-3. Location and stratigraphy of the CERT and Marquette Viaduct sites. The locations of several other important archaeological sites are also shown (after Demeter et al. 1994; Lovis et al. 1996; and Monaghan 2001). See Figure 5-1 for generalized location of the site in the Saginaw Bay area.

5-3). The lower cultural zone is discontinuous and in some places has been eroded. It is about 20 cm thick and generally massive, with a few northward-dipping, shallow cross-beds in the lower part of the zone. The dark color derives from additions of organic material associated with natural soil-forming processes and organic debris from prehistoric human activity. These factors indicate a period of relative stability at the site and suggest that flooding was probably infrequent.

The lower cultural zone is overlain by a discontinuous, variably thick coarse sand and gravel deposit ("flooding ca. 2000–1500 B.P."; Figure 5-3). The contact between it and the lower cultural zone is erosional, and an unknown amount of the lower cultural zone was apparently removed. A few faint cross-beds within the thickest part of the unit suggest northward water flow. The top of the unit lies at an altitude of about 178.2 m. The upper sand and gravel grade upward into the upper cultural zone, which, unlike the lower cultural zone, was continuous and 20–30 cm thick ("Late Woodland"; Figure 5-3). It includes abundant cultural material and several cultural features. Although diagnostic artifacts were not found, a ^{14}C age estimate of a composite of charcoal from the upper cultural zone averaged 1070 B.P. (Demeter et al. 1994), which is consistent with a Late Woodland occupation of the site.

The upper cultural zone grades into a few-centimeters-thick peaty sand that includes large pieces of wood and bark. These lie at an altitude of 178.3 m and probably represent organic material dumped on the site during the mid-nineteenth century. In fact, the bark layer, which occurs at the top of the unit and is commonly found at the base of historic deposits throughout the Bay City area, is probably scrap obtained from lumber mills in the area. The peaty sand, however, may be prehistoric and could indicate that wet, marshy conditions predominated at the site during very late prehistoric time. Wet conditions probably result from increased groundwater levels associated with a rise in lake level. The top of the CERT site sequence consists of a 3–3.5-m-thick historic fill. The lower part of the fill includes thin layers of clay, silt, ash, and diamicton that contain abundant mid-nineteenth-century Euro-American artifacts.

SIGNIFICANCE AND DISCUSSION. Even though the lower cultural zone at the CERT site has neither diagnostic artifacts nor an absolute chronology, comparison with known fluvial and lake-level histories of the area suggests that it probably developed sometime between 3000 and 1600 B.P. The actual occupation, however, was probably toward the latter part of this interval. As such, the lower cultural zone is at least Middle Woodland in age. Because only a small part of the site was excavated, older, undiscovered Late Archaic and Early Woodland occupations may also be present at the site. In fact, a similar-age occupation and cultural sequence as that of the CERT site was noted at the nearby Marquette Viaduct site (see discussion below; Figure 5-1; Lovis et al. 1996; Monaghan 2002) and includes extensive Late Archaic-to-Middle Woodland artifacts within a "lower" cultural zone (Figure 5-3).

A rise in lake level resulted in increased flooding at the site, partial truncation of the lower (i.e., "Middle Woodland"; Figure 5-3) cultural zone, and deposition of the upper sand and gravel at the CERT site. A similar interval of increased flooding was noted for the Schultz and Green Point sites (Figure 5-2) and occurred 2000–1500 B.P. This interval is probably correlative at CERT (Monaghan and Hayes 2001; Monaghan 2002). Similarly, a partial truncation of the Middle Woodland occupation horizon also occurred within parts of the Marquette Viaduct site and was dated to about 1800 B.P. (Lovis et al. 1996). The upper cultural zone is continuous across the site, and a ^{14}C age estimate indicates that it represents a Late Woodland occupation beginning about 1000 B.P. By late prehistoric time, wet, marshy conditions predominated at the site, and the site may not have been habitable (Demeter et al. 1994).

The discovery of the CERT site is significant not only because it includes intact prehistoric artifacts and deposits but also because natural stratigraphic breaks in the occupation sequence allow isolation of cultural components of differing ages. In addition, the site also contains well-preserved bone and botanical debris as well as prehistoric cultural features. Although common on the west bank of the Saginaw River at Bay City (see discussion of Marquette Viaduct site below), such cultural information, in stratigraphic context, is generally lacking from the east bank.

Marquette Viaduct Site (20BY28)

LOCATION AND BACKGROUND. The Marquette Viaduct site occurs along the west bank of the Saginaw River in Bay City, Bay County, Michigan (Figure 5-1). Technically, the site is considered the southwestern locale of the Fletcher site (20BY28), a large multilocale, multicomponent area that includes a late-prehistoric-to-historic Native American cemetery. It is bounded on the west by Marquette Avenue, on the south by the Michigan Central Railroad tracks, on the west by the Saginaw River, and on the north by the Fletcher site proper. Professional work at the site occurred in 1967, 1968, 1970, 1989, and, most recently, 2000 by Michigan State University (Lovis et al. 1996; Lovis ed. 2002). This most recent phase of work focused on a portion of the site that was buried under 3–5 m of middle-to-late-nineteenth-century road fills. The geomorphological work done during the 2000 study generally agrees with the results of the earlier studies (Monaghan 2002).

During the more recent phase of work at Marquette Viaduct, the site was found to spread across different landforms that are informally referred to as the "upper" and "lower" terrace. For historic reasons, these locales have been given different site numbers but include overlapping cultural sequences. The "upper" terrace locale (20BY387) occurs at an altitude of 182–183 m and lies on a beach that has been associated with Lake Algoma (Larsen and Demeter 1979; Monaghan 1991, 1993). It includes an extensive, mainly Late Archaic pit field dated to 4200–3500 B.P. (Lovis ed. 2002; Monaghan 2002). The "lower" terrace locale lies on the modern floodplain of the Saginaw River at an altitude of about 178 m. It includes Late Archaic-through-Late Woodland cultural materials and represents the actual buried Marquette Viaduct site discussed in this section. Because the upper terrace is not "stratified" and was buried under historic fills rather than naturally deposited sediment, its stratigraphy will not be discussed in detail. However, as discussed in chapter 3, the timing for occupation on these terraces is significant for interpreting the geological history of the upper Great Lakes and establishes that Lakes Nipissing and Algoma were both abandoned by at least 4000 B.P. while modern Lake Huron must have formed prior to 3500 B.P. (Monaghan 2002; Monaghan and Hayes 2001). The bulk of the following discussion focuses on the thick, partly stratified cultural and depositional sequence that underlies the "lower" terrace.

Lovis et al. (1996) showed that the "lower" terrace of the Marquette Viaduct site included a 50–80-cm-thick, Middle-to-Late Woodland midden that was buried by 30–50 cm of sandy fill, probably during the late nineteenth or early twentieth century (Marquette Viaduct Locale [1989]; Figure 5-3). The midden is underlain by middle-to-late Holocene fluvial and/or littoral sand and gravel. The modern ground surface of the site lies at an altitude of about 180 m, while the base of the midden occurs at 179 m (1–2 m above the level of Saginaw Bay). Significantly, in a few places the midden is separated into two components by discontinuous gravel deposits. A ^{14}C age estimate in the midden suggests that the intervening gravel was deposited after about 1800 B.P. (Lovis et al. 1996), which generally corresponds with deposition of a similar gravel lens at the CERT site (see previous discussion).

A similar sequence was observed at the site when a different block was excavated more than a decade later (Lovis ed. 2002). This block actually occurred under the "north" ramp of the Marquette Avenue railroad viaduct. It was about 1 m higher and 100 m west of the 1989 excavations (Figure 5-1) and also included preserved Late Archaic and Early Woodland deposits near the base of a nearly 2-m-thick cultural sequence. Like that of the 1989 excavation, a discontinuous, normally culturally sterile layer separated the cultural deposits of the 2000 block into two components: an "upper," mainly Middle and Late Woodland unit and a "lower" unit that includes the Late Archaic-through-Middle Woodland cultural material (Marquette Viaduct Locale 2000; Figure 5-3; Monaghan 2002). Monaghan (2002) and Monaghan and Hayes (2001) attempted to place the Marquette Viaduct site into a more regional depositional framework (Figure 5-2). The following discussion is aimed at placing a simplified site stratigraphy into this generalized framework.

STRATIGRAPHY. Deposits at the Marquette Viaduct site consist mainly of variably textured fluvial and shallow lacustrine/alluvial sand and gravel. Cross- and tabular-bedded fluvial sand and gravel mark the base of the sequence across the entire site. These gravels probably represent fluvial and/or littoral sediment deposited after Lake Algoma receded (ca. 4000 B.P.; Monaghan 2002). The minimum age for the gravels is suggested by ^{14}C age estimates of 3800 B.P. from cultural features in the 2000 excavation blocks (Monaghan 2002). Importantly, the presence of 3800 B.P. cultural features a few meters higher than modern lake level indicates that Lake Algoma had been abandoned by about 4000 B.P., and modern Lake Huron formed prior to the initial site occupation (>3800 B.P.).

The basal gravels grade upward into an 80–120-cm-thick, medium-to-coarse-textured sand. Occasionally, discontinuous fine-gravel cross-beds occur within the lower 10–30 cm of the unit. The upper 30–50 cm of this sand is a gray-to-dark-brown sandy midden that contains abundant Middle-to-Late Woodland artifacts and cultural features. In general, more Middle Woodland artifacts occur deeper in the midden, while Late Woodland artifacts are more abundant near the top. This is particularly true for the 1989 excavation, where ^{14}C age estimates from cultural features near its base indicate the midden was formed mainly after about 2000–1800 B.P. (Lovis et al. 1996). Such an age is consistent with the preponderance of Middle and Late Woodland artifacts.

The lower part of the sand in the 1989 excavations (below the base of the midden), however, also contains sporadic cultural material. This includes Archaic and Early Woodland artifacts that occur in eroded, secondary context within the gravelly cross-beds (Lovis et al. 1996). However, in situ Late Archaic cultural features and deposits that date between ca. 3800 and 3500 B.P. occur within the base of the "lower" unit in the 2000 block. This differential preservation of Archaic occupation suggests that significant erosional and reworking processes took place in discrete areas of the site. Moreover, although people certainly lived in the area during the Early Woodland and Late Archaic periods, based on the 1800 B.P. age of the buried, truncated feature near the base of the 1989 cultural sequence, that occupation was differentially preserved by a flooding and erosional period that occurred sometime during the Middle Woodland period.

The top of the sequence in both the 2000 and 1989 excavations is marked by a sandy fill that is historic in age. The fill is thickest (1–5 m thick) over the 2000 excavation block (Monaghan 2002). It probably represents grade and fill material associated with railroad yard construction and maintenance as well as roadbed associated with the construction of the nineteenth-century Marquette Avenue railroad viaduct (Monaghan 2002).

SIGNIFICANCE AND DISCUSSION. In places, discontinuous fluvial gravel deposits separate the midden in both the 1989 and 2000 excavations into two components, an "upper" and "lower" midden (Figure 5-3; Lovis et al. 1996; Monaghan 2002). The lower midden in the 1989 excavation units is only sporadically preserved but did include some in situ Middle Woodland artifacts and features. In the 2000 block, the lower midden is well preserved and included abundant Late Archaic-through-Middle Woodland artifacts and features. The oldest of these features dated between 3800 and 3500 B.P. and indicated extensive and early occupation of the Saginaw River floodplain. The upper midden, on the other hand, is continuous across the site and includes extensive Middle and Late Woodland cultural material.

Both the upper and lower parts of the midden include well-defined cultural features that provide evidence for the timing of major flooding across the site. For example, a ^{14}C age estimate on charcoal from a remnant feature found in the lower midden within the 1989 excavations units yielded an age of 1740 B.P. (Beta-26380). The age of this feature, which was truncated by about 20 cm of cross-bedded gravel, implies that extensive scouring and redeposition occurred at the site soon after about 1800 B.P. (Lovis et al. 1996). The lack of cultural artifacts within the gravel, coupled with its sedimentology, suggests rapid deposition in a high-energy environment. A similar age is suggested for the "sterile" zone that separates the upper from the lower midden in the 2000 excavation block (Monaghan 2002). Here, however, the site was only minimally affected by the flooding when deposition of the discontinuous "sterile" zone occurred. The lesser impact on the cultural deposits within the 2000 block probably relates to the fact that it is topographically about 1 m higher than the 1989 block.

Extensive flooding and rapid accretion of sediment were also noted at Green Point, located 15–20 km upstream, between 1800 and 1600 B.P. (Figures 5-1, 5-2, 5-3; see previous discussion). Unlike the Green Point sequence, however, occupation apparently did not occur on the Marquette Viaduct lower terrace during the high flood interval. Given that timing for the Middle Woodland flood event at the Marquette Viaduct site generally corresponds with a regional rise in lake level (Larsen 1985b; Monaghan and Hayes 1998, 2001; Monaghan and Schaetzl 1994; Thompson and Baedke 1999), the site may have actually been under water at that time. Such submergence could also explain the lack of occupation during this interval at the site. Moreover, the fact that the topographically higher 2000 block, which is also farther from the river, was not significantly eroded during the flooding indicates that this locale was probably high enough or far enough away from the river to avoid extensive erosion or alluviation and may have been only briefly submerged. This data places a generalized upper limit on the altitude of the post-Algoma high lake-level of about 178 m (Figures 3-2, 5-3).

Findings from the Marquette Viaduct site are significant for reconstructing the late Holocene lake-level sequence and flood history of the region. Clearly, the erosion of the lower midden and deposition of the "sterile" zone at various parts of the Marquette Viaduct site correlate well not only with the Green Point sequence but also with a similar-age gravel lens at the CERT site in Bay City (see discussion above). As discussed below, the CERT sequence is also identical with the depositional sequence found at the Bear Creek site, which is located nearly 30 km upstream and much further inland, and apparently also correlates with flooding that the buried a paleosol and associated archaeological components at the Zemaitis site in the lower Grand River valley. The widespread occurrence of site burial during this interval suggests that extensive flooding was probably basinwide either by or just after 2000 B.P.

Weber I Site (20SA581)

LOCATION AND BACKGROUND. The Weber I site is located on the south bank of the Cass River about 3 km downstream from the village of Frankenmuth, Saginaw County, Michigan (SE1/4 of Sec. 28, T11N R6E; Figure 5-1). It was discovered by Brunett (1981a, 1981c) during a Phase I survey for the replacement of a bridge at the site and was subsequently excavated by Lovis (ed.1989). The site is multi-component and stratified, with evidence of occupation that spans the Middle Archaic through the Late Woodland periods. The site is significant because it includes a Middle Holocene human occupation deposit that was buried during the Nipissing transgression. Because Lovis (ed. 1989) recognized the similarities in processes of site development outlined by Larsen (1980) within the Weber I site, an interdisciplinary strategy that brought together specialists in archaeology, geology, and pedology was developed to decipher site sedimentology, stratigraphy, and formation history. The results of this work showed that Weber I contains an in situ Middle Archaic horizon that includes cultural features as well as diagnostic artifacts that date between about 6200 and 4500 B.P. (Monaghan, Lovis, and Fay 1986; Lovis ed. 1989). In fact, the distribution of artifacts suggests that the main occupation occurred near the end of that interval. The Middle Archaic horizon is overlain by Nipissing-age alluvial and lacustrine deposits, which are in turn overlain by Late Archaic, Woodland, and nineteenth-century occupation horizons.

STRATIGRAPHY. The base of the Weber I sequence is represented by a massive, medium-to-fine-grained sand (Figure 5-4). The age and total thickness of this sand are unknown. However, it may relate to shallow lacustrine or littoral deposition near the shore of Lake Elkton, a late-phase late Wisconsinan lake (ca. 12,500 B.P.; Monaghan, Lovis, and Fay 1986). The sand is overlain by an 8–10-cm-thick, dark, silty sand that contains abundant Middle and early Late Archaic cultural material and features. This unit is informally referred to as the "lower" cultural zone. The dark color resulted from the long-term accumulation of organic material in the A-horizon of a paleosol, both by natural pedogenic processes and by additions of human occupational debris (i.e., plant and animal waste, etc.). Although massive and generally mixed by human occupation, the silty-sand texture of the zone probably derives from alluvial (overbank) deposition. ^{14}C age estimates from features in the lower cultural zone suggest that occupation occurred between 6200 and 4500 B.P., which agrees with the general range of diagnostic artifacts (Monaghan, Lovis, and Fay 1986; Lovis ed. 1989). More detailed study of the age distribution of diagnostic artifacts further suggested that the main, most intensive occupation probably occurred near the end of that interval (Monaghan, Lovis, and Fay 1986).

The lower cultural zone is overlain by about 50 cm of laminated, noncalcareous sand and silt. The laminae are 2–4 cm thick and include alternations of lighter fine sand and darker silty sand. The contact of this unit with the lower cultural zone is sharp and horizontal and occurs at about 180.5 m. These factors indicate that the contact with the lower cultural zone is erosional (Monaghan, Lovis, and Fay 1986). These sediments represent shallow lacustrine deposition in an "estuary-like" embayment of Lake Nipissing (Lovis ed. 1989; Monaghan, Lovis, and Fay 1986). The 4500 B.P. age for part of the lower cultural zone indicates that the site was occupied until relatively late in the Nipissing transgression.

Massive, 35–60-cm-thick, brown, sandy silt overlies the laminated sediment. The upper 15 cm of this zone is composed of dark gray, clayey-to-sandy silt and contains abundant Late Archaic cultural material. It is informally referred to as

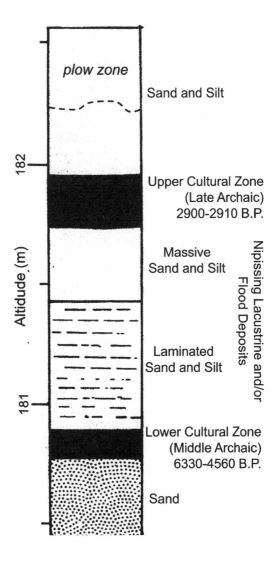

Figure 5-4. Stratigraphy of the Weber I site (after Monaghan et. al. 1986). See Figure 5-1

the "upper" cultural zone. The dark color indicates that it represents the A-horizon of a paleosol that has been augmented by organic additions related to human occupation. [14]C age estimates of cultural features suggest that the age of the upper cultural zone is about 3000–2900 B.P. The massive structure and sand-silt texture imply overbank alluvial deposition for the overall unit. The formation of a paleosol at the top of the unit, coupled with the ^{14}C age of associated occupation, suggests that the floodplain stabilized after about 3000 B.P.

A 50-cm-thick, massive, brown, silty sand overlies the lower cultural zone and extends to the modern ground surface. Although generally mixed by recent plowing, the zone does include pockets of undisturbed Late Woodland cultural material.

SIGNIFICANCE AND DISCUSSION. The excavation at Weber I provides evidence that human occupations were submerged and buried as Lake Nipissing back-flooded the Cass River valley. The relatively "thin" nature of the lower cultural zone may indicate that the pre-Nipissing channel of the Cass River was cut deeply enough that the river only rarely flooded the Weber I site. Alternatively, because the contact of the lower cultural zone with the overlying Nipissing sediment is erosional, an unknown portion of the pre-Nipissing alluvium, and lower cultural zone, may have been lost to erosion. The fact that much of the archaeological debris in the lower cultural zone is late in the dated range for the occupation (i.e., post-5000 B.P.), however, suggests that not much was lost. Furthermore, the late occupational age also implies that humans were probably attracted to the area because of the environmental changes that resulted during the last phases of the Nipissing transgression (i.e., wetter conditions and/or more "sluggish" flows of the Cass River). Considering the paleoenvironments of the Weber I and Ebenhoff sites (see below), both of which are "shoreline" locales, Middle and early Late Archaic populations were certainly attracted to shoreline environments. The differences in shoreline environments for these sites (embayment along a river versus "open" beach-dune shoreline), however, also indicate that a variety of shoreline types were exploited during the middle Holocene. These factors are significant for predicting buried site locations during the Nipissing transgression. In many places, the environmental conditions present today were vastly different during the Middle Holocene. In fact, in many places, such as the Shiawassee lowland near Saginaw Bay, all evidence of the pre-Nipissing landscape is now buried.

The age of the upper cultural zone indicates that fluvial conditions along the Cass River had stabilized prior to about 3000 B.P. This suggests that modern lake levels were also maintained by that date. The fact that the paleosol that marks the upper cultural zone contains mainly Late Archaic materials indicates that the environmental conditions that attracted Archaic people to the Weber I site were not the same as those that attracted Early-to-Middle Woodland populations. The occurrence of Late Woodland and nineteenth-century artifacts in the alluvium overlying the upper cultural zone suggests that flooding increased again in late-prehistoric-through-historic time. This is probably correlative with the pre-modern flood phase and is related to cooler, wetter conditions during the Little Ice Age as well as nineteenth-century land-clearing and agricultural practices.

Shiawassee River Site (20SA1033)

LOCATION AND BACKGROUND. The Shiawassee River site is a small, transitory Late Woodland encampment dating to the fifteenth century A.D. (Branstner and Hambacher eds. 1994). It includes at least part of the surface horizon (A-horizon) paleosol, which occurs sub-plow zone and about 50 cm below the present ground surface. The paleosol and associated archaeological occupation were buried during extensive alluviation associated with the premodern (Little Ice Age) flood phase. The site lies along the west bank of the Shiawassee River and is located in the NW1/4 of Sec. 22, T10N R3E, St. Charles Township, Saginaw County, Michigan (Figure 5-1). The surface of the Shiawassee River floodplain near the site is nearly level and ranges in altitude between 181 and 182 m. It slopes slightly toward the river (i.e., east-west). Other notable physiographic features in the vicinity include a series of isolated relatively small dune ridges. One major north/northeast-trending dune ridge, informally referred to as the "Casassa dune," occurs on the east side of the Shiawassee River. This dune ridge is particularly significant because it includes a large archaeological site, the Casassa site (Figure 5-1), that contains evidence of Late Archaic-through-Late Woodland occupation (Branstner and Hambacher eds. 1995a; Monaghan 1995a). A number of tributary streams are also located in the vicinity of the site. For example, Deer Creek flows into the Shiawassee River approximately 1 km south of Shiawassee River, while the original course of Carson Drain apparently joined the river about 0.5 km south of the site. Bear Creek, whose valley carried the bulk of the Shiawassee drainage prior to about 2,000 years ago (Monaghan and Schaetzl 1994), lies approximately 1 km to the east.

The occurrence of archaeological materials in the immediate vicinity of the Shiawassee River site has been known for quite some time. In fact, the quarter section in which the site lies is designated as 20SA129 in the State of Michigan Archaeological Site Files. While 20SA129 is a generalized site locale, local avocational archaeologists (Ron Burk, personal communication 1991) have indicated that archaeological materials often occur as "hot spots" on the low rises that dot the floodplain along the Shiawassee River. Prior to the 1991 discovery of buried deposits at the Shiawassee River site, however, no cultural materials had been reported from the locale. Prior to mechanized deep testing within the project corridor, the Shiawassee River site had escaped detection by standard surface survey techniques even though it was only shallowly buried. The first Phase I survey of the pipeline corridor (Weir 1981), as well as a subsequent survey (Branstner 1990a), relied on surface inspection and failed to identify the site. Only through the aegis of systematic mechanized deep testing conducted as part of the 1990–1991 GLGTP survey was the existence of the Shiawassee River site revealed. During this survey and subsequent excavation, the presence of a paleosol containing Late Woodland cultural materials was discovered. The paleosol occurs about 50 cm below the modern ground surface and extends across a ca. 30-m diameter area immediately adjacent to the modern levee (Branstner 1991). During data-recovery efforts, the plow zone was removed from the site area to allow close interval testing of the stripped area (50 1-m² units). A 37-m² block was excavated from the main occupation area (Branstner and Hambacher eds.

1994; Figure 5-5). In order to identify the eastward extent of the site, two trenches were excavated into the levee, and a single test unit was placed on the east side of the levee.

Stratigraphy. Soil and sediments at the site are generally poorly drained, sandy silt to silt loam (Iaquinta 1994; Monaghan and Schaetzl 1994) and are fairly uniform across site. Most of the variability in the stratigraphy was related to the amount of the surface horizon paleosol preserved and to the intensity of the B-horizon expression. The type profile for the site was developed from trenches excavated into the levee and from the adjoining excavation block and was subdivided into six strata. These strata generally correspond to naturally occurring soil horizons (pedology) and were constructed based partly on archaeological expression and partly on sediment characteristics.

Stratum 1 (S-1) represents the modern plow zone (Ap) horizon (Figure 5-5). It is typically 30 cm thick and consists of dark-brown-to-dark-yellowish-brown, sandy silt. Although most of the plow zone was stripped from the site prior to excavation, the final several centimeters were systematically excavated and screened (Branstner and Hambacher eds. 1994). Importantly, small amounts of cultural material, most of which occurred in the area adjacent to the levee, were recovered from the unit.

Stratum 2 (S-2) is a buried (Ab) horizon that occurs immediately below and is partly truncated by the plow zone. It typically consists of a black-to-dark-gray loam to silty loam and was virtually devoid of prehistoric cultural materials. In the main excavation block, S-2 was mainly restricted to the southwestern quadrant. Where present, S-2 was typically only 2–3 cm thick, but it did become up to 10 cm thick near the southern edge site. A dip in the surface of this otherwise nearly level horizon suggests the presence of a small, northward-trending erosional rill a short distance west of the main occupation area.

Stratum 3 (S-3) is a 4–6-cm thick, sporadic, light-gray-to-white, silty fine sand and has weathered to an eluviated (E) horizon associated with the overlying Ab horizon (S-2; Figure 5-5). As with the overlying S-2, only a very small number of artifacts were present in S-3. The S-3 unit commonly occurs 25 m from the levee, which is also west of the main occupation area.

Stratum 4 (S-4) consists of 10–30-cm-thick, yellowish-brown-to-dark-brown fine sand that has weathered into a Bw soil horizon (Figure 5-5). S-4 includes the majority of the cultural materials, which are also most abundant in the central portion of the main excavation block.

The last four strata, Strata 5–8 (S-5 through S-8; Figure 5-5), are devoid of cultural material. S-5 is a 50-cm-thick, pale-brown-to-light-yellowish-brown, bedded fine sand and has weathered into E/Bt-horizon. S-5 is truncated 2–3 m east of the excavation block, most likely by a disturbance associated with original levee construction. Strata 6–8 represent a series of C soil horizons at the site. Typically, this sequence consists of 20-cm-thick, pale brown, bedded fine-to-medium sand that is underlain by 10-cm-thick, brown-to-strong-brown, compact, clayey medium sand. The site is underlain by glaciolacustrine clay.

Discussion and Archaeological Significance. Prehistoric usage of the Shiawassee River site centers around a single, small, short-term, Late Woodland

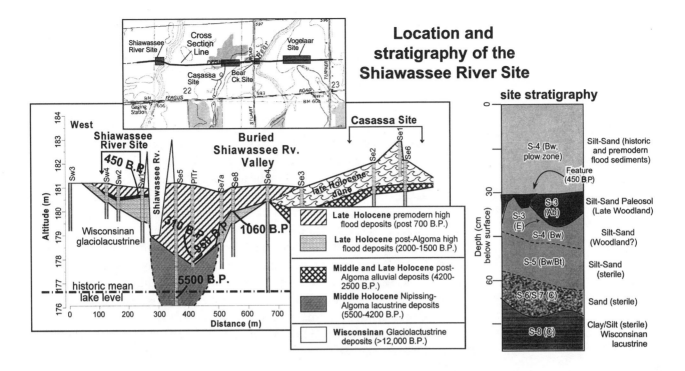

seasonal encampment dating to the fifteenth century A.D. An oval area (8 x 10 m) paralleling the modern levee, with a concentration of cultural debris centered around two hearths, forms the main occupation area and was the focus of the Phase III investigations (Branstner and Hambacher eds. 1994). Although no ceramics were present, an array of stone tools, chipping debris from late-stage manufacture and maintenance, a modest amount of fire-cracked rock, animal bone, and paleobotanical materials were recovered from the excavations. About 85 percent of the artifacts occurred in a 37.5-m² excavation block and related test units adjacent to the modern levee along the river.

A series of 50 1-m² test units were systematically excavated across a 22-m-wide area west of the main excavation block to search for other buried occupation areas. However, only a very diffuse scatter of materials was present. Several minor artifact clusters and a diffuse hearth attest to the repeated usage of this locale over time. One cluster consists of a biface fragment, a retouched flake, a thin scatter of debitage, and a little fire-cracked rock, none of which were temporally diagnostic. The second area, located along the northern edge of the site west of the excavation block, contained a small hearth remnant, a projectile point and a few flakes, and fire-cracked rock pieces scattered across a 9-x-10-m area. The projectile point, an Early Woodland period Schultz Straight Stemmed point (Ozker 1982), was recovered from just below the base of the paleosol 6–7 m from the hearth. Additionally, a Middle Woodland Schultz Small Expanding Stem point was collected from the surface along the levee of the excavation area.

Figure 5-5. Generalized stratigraphy of the Shiawassee River site (after Hambacher and Branstner 1994 and Monaghan and Schaetzl 1994). See Figure 5-1 for generalized location of the site in the Saginaw Bay area.

119

The cultural material in the main excavation block is the result of a single occupation that was centered around two hearths (Branstner and Hambacher eds. 1994). The distribution of cultural material around these features consists of a narrow zone of elevated artifact densities across the central portion of the block immediately west and north of the southern of the two hearths. These materials are largely restricted to the upper 20 cm of S-4. The southernmost hearth, Feature 3, is a circular basin about 85 cm in diameter and 15 cm deep. It contained a zone of charcoal at its base as well as most of the subsistence remains recovered from the site. Bone from this feature is dominated by the remains of at least 11 fish, including sucker, shorthead redhorse, and bass/sunfish. Small mammal, turtle, and several bird bones were also noted. The fish remains suggest that the site was occupied during a brief period in May, when these species traveled upstream to spawn (Smith 1994). Botanical material from Feature 3 is restricted to wood charcoal, primarily oak along with some hickory and maple, and a single corn kernel (Egan 1994). Charcoal from the feature produced a radiocarbon date of 450±50 B.P. (Beta-56115; Branstner and Hambacher eds. 1994). The second hearth associated with the main occupation is similar in form to and slightly smaller than Feature 3. However, it contained only wood charcoal, primarily hickory and a little bit of oak, and no subsistence remains. This suggests that the hearths served different functions or were used at different times.

Artifacts associated with the main occupation area reflect a restricted range of activities primarily revolving around fabrication/tool maintenance tasks and expedient processing activities. Tools include a triangular biface, bifacial preform fragments (all broken during manufacture), a drill, end scrapers and wedge-like tools, a chipped slate tool that may have been used for fish processing, and a possible grinding stone fragment. Chipping debris, which in this case is largely a by-product of late-stage tool manufacture and maintenance, shows a similar distribution, with a slightly higher density southwest of Feature 3. A small amount of fire-cracked rock also occurs mainly southwest of Feature 3. Although limited in scope, two trenches placed in the levee indicated that S-2 was truncated but did not include a significant amount of cultural material.

In summary, although the Shiawassee River site lies in a plowed agricultural field, no evidence of prehistoric occupation was noted along the modern ground surface. Mechanized deep testing and subsequent excavations, however, indicated that a shallowly buried and spatially circumscribed occupation occurred at the site. The fact that the upper portion of the paleosol (S-2) was truncated by the plow zone and that extremely little cultural material was present in the plow zone suggest that only limited occupation occurred at the site and was confined mainly to areas adjacent to the river. It also suggests that most of the sediment above S-2 accumulated after the occupation of Shiawassee River site took place. This corresponds with Monaghan and Schaetzl's (1994) "pre-Modern high" lake stage in the Huron and Saginaw basins. Furthermore, the occurrence of an Early Woodland projectile point near the top of S-4 suggests that the general site area was a fairly stable surface for some 2,000 years prior to the Late Woodland usage of the site. This situation may reflect the fact that prior to 1500–1000 B.P., most of the water flow ran through the Bear Creek channel, and what became the modern Shiawassee River was perhaps only a small, higher-order stream (Monaghan and Schaetzl 1994).

Bear Creek Site (20SA1043)

LOCATION AND BACKGROUND. The Bear Creek site is a stratified seasonal extractive encampment with intermittent short-term occupations spanning the late Middle Archaic through early Late Woodland periods (ca. 4200–950 B.P.). This site represents one of the few in Michigan that contain sealed and undisturbed archaeological deposits dating to the Middle Archaic period. Notably, all of the sites identified in Michigan that include buried Middle Archaic occupations have been discovered in the Saginaw Bay region, and three of these sites (Weber I, Bear Creek, and Ebenhoff) were located by mechanized deep testing associated with cultural resources management (CRM) projects (Lovis ed. 1989; Dobbs and Murray 1993; Branstner and Hambacher eds. 1994). By virtue of its stratified deposits, artifact assemblages, and preserved floral and faunal remains, the Bear Creek site is reflective of the evolution of the post-Nipissing landscape and human response to those changes in the Saginaw Valley. The site was occupied from about 4200 B.P. (Archaic) until about 900 B.P. (Late Woodland). It includes a sequence of deposits that records the middle-to-late Holocene environmental and cultural development of the Saginaw Bay region. The fact that most of the Shiawassee River drained through Bear Creek instead of its current channel prior to about 1500 B.P. (Monaghan and Schaetzl 1994) is significant to the location, function, and ultimate abandonment of the Bear Creek site.

The site is situated along the west bank of Bear Creek and lies in the NW1/4 of Sec. 23, T10N R3E, St. Charles Township, Saginaw County, Michigan (Figure 5-1). The site lies adjacent to the northeastern terminus of the Casassa dune, an extensive southwest-trending complex of Nipissing- and Algoma-age beaches and dunes with prehistoric occupations stretching along most of its ca. 2-km length (Branstner and Hambacher eds. 1995a). A similar southeast-trending beach and dune ridge complex about 0.5 km away, on which the Vogelaar site (Figure 5-1) is situated, forms the eastern margin of the Bear Valley. Although Bear Creek was dredged and channelized during the twentieth century, its present channel position approximates that of late prehistoric times. The western edge of the site area was originally bounded by a wetland extending along the edge of the Casassa dune. From a site location standpoint, the 180.7 m altitude places it at or near the mouth of Bear Creek during Nipissing II and Algoma times (ca. 4200–3500 B.P.; Monaghan and Schaetzl 1994).

Despite its location in an active agricultural field, several previous surface reconnaissances along the GLGTP corridor did not find prehistoric cultural material at Bear Creek (Branstner 1991; Weir 1981). Only when the area was tested using mechanized deep testing associated with the 1990 survey was the Bear Creek site identified. The Phase I, II, and III work showed that the site consists of a ca. 1-m-thick, stratified, mid-to-late Holocene alluvial sequence that contains lithic debitage, ceramic debris, fire-cracked rock, and animal bone (Branstner 1991; Branstner and Hambacher eds. 1994). A well-developed paleosol occurs within the middle part of the alluvial sequence and was preserved generally undisturbed beneath the plow zone. Artifacts occur in abundance within and just above the paleosol but are relatively rare within the plow zone. Late Wisconsinan glaciolacustrine clay forms the base of the sequence. Data-recovery efforts at the site involved the excavation of 73 m² (15 percent of the project area). The excavations focused on a 37-m² rectangular area adjacent to the creek. Five 2-m² and seven 1-m² units also were excavated at 2–4 m intervals west of the main excavation, while nine other test units were systematically placed across a 10-m-wide area south of the main excavation area (Branstner and Hambacher eds. 1994).

STRATIGRAPHY. Surface soils along Bear Creek consist of somewhat poorly drained silt loam (Iaquinta 1994). This, however, reflects only the upper portion of the Bear Creek site stratigraphic sequence. Excavations and ¹⁴C age estimates reveal that a variable sequence of generally fine-textured overbank and/or slack-water sediments, which gradually accumulated during the past 4,200 years, characterizes the site (Monaghan and Schaetzl 1994). Because depositional rates were not uniform during the late Holocene, the relative thickness and the state of preservation of the archaeological deposits were variable. In addition, numerous crayfish burrows partly mixed deposits at the site.

Six stratigraphic units (S-1 through S-6) were defined for the Bear Creek sequence. The plow zone, however, consisted of a 30–40-cm-thick, grayish-brown-to-black, silty-clay loam. Artifacts recovered from the lower units indicate that the plow zone sediment had accumulated since the early Late Woodland period (i.e., post-1500 B.P.). The rate of alluviation at the site, however, probably slowed once the main flow of water shifted west into the Shiawassee Valley. Because it was generally devoid of cultural material, the plow zone was stripped from the site prior to excavation and was not assigned a formal stratum number.

Stratum 1 (S-1) represents the first sub-plow zone horizon at the site (Figure 5-6). It is the thickest horizon at the site and also contains the lowest density of cultural material. Across the site, it varied nonuniformly from clay-rich to more silt- and sand-rich. Vertical distribution of the artifacts in S-1 was also not uniform. Based on a marked increase in the density of artifacts and a gradual darkening of the soil matrix near the base of the unit, Stratum 1 was divided into two subunits (S-1.1 and S-1.2). Interestingly, the distinction between these subunits was not apparent either chemically or texturally (see Table 4 in Monaghan and Schaetzl 1994).

Subunit S-1.1 includes all of S-1 except the lower ca. 10 cm. It consists of a heavily mottled, dark-yellowish-brown-to-dark-grayish-brown, silty-clay loam. Occasional thin, pale brown sand stringers are present, particularly in the northern part of the site nearest to Bear Creek. The thickness of S-1 is related to its distance from the creek. Near the creek, it is 20–40 cm thick and thins to 10–20 cm thick beyond about 20 m from the bank. S-1 was absent in the central part of the site. The only diagnostic artifact from S-1.1 was a Jack's Reef Corner Notched point, which corresponds to the late Middle Woodland through early Late Woodland periods (ca. 1450–950 B.P.; Justice 1987). The age is in general agreement with a ¹⁴C age estimate of 1870±80 B.P. (Beta-57997; CAMS-4571) obtained from charcoal near the base of S-1.1, and corresponds with the reinitiation of alluviation at the site associated with the post-Algoma high-water phase (Monaghan and Schaetzl 1994). S-1.2 marks the base of S-1 and is 5–10 cm thick. It is distinguished by an increase in artifact density and a slightly darker color than the overlying S-1.1. As such, S-1.2 represents the transition from the fluvial stability indicated by the underlying paleosol and more intensive alluviation at the site. Two diagnostic artifacts were present near the base of S-1, a Late Woodland Raccoon Side Notched point (ca. 1450–950 B.P.; Justice 1987) and a small, relatively narrow triangular point (post-1200 B.P.; Justice 1987).

Stratum 2 (S-2) consists of the buried surface (2Ab) soil horizon of a paleosol and is indicative of relative fluvial stability at the site (Figure 5-6). This buried surface horizon is about 20 cm thick and consists of dark-to-very-dark-grayish-brown-to-gray, silty-clay loam. The surface of S-2 exhibits minor relief (ca. 0.5 m), and the highest altitude (180.3 m) occurs in the north-central part of the site. S-2 slopes gradually downward near the creek, suggesting that the ancestral Bear Creek did not have steep, sharply defined banks. Several erosional features, whose formation both pre- and postdate the paleosol, are evident. For example, the paleosol formed within one such rill but was also disrupted (truncated) by another rill elsewhere. A drape of S-2 also lined part of the edge of Feature 4, which is a large (2 m in diameter and 0.7 m deep), poorly defined basin that served as a trash disposal area. This feature may have originally formed by fluvial activity. Most of Feature 4 was apparently infilled during S-2 time. S-2 is discontinuous and was poorly developed in the western and southern parts of the site (i.e., farther from Bear Creek near Stuart Road).

The age and span of time represented by S-2 and the formation of the paleosol are anchored by two ^{14}C age estimates as well as by diagnostic artifacts. The older age estimate, 2510±80 B.P. (Beta-56425; CAMS-3836), was derived from charcoal from near the base of the paleosol, while the younger, 2250±50 B.P. (Beta-56118; CAMS-3817), was derived from a partially mineralized elk femur that was recovered from the center of Feature 4. The age and the relationship between the dated bone and the paleosol drape within Feature 4 suggest that the feature pertains to the later stages of paleosol development. Projectile points from Stratum 2 include an Innes/Merom Expanding Stem point and an *affinis* Norton Corner Notched point. The former point belongs to the Late Archaic small-point tradition (ca. 3500–2700 B.P.; Lovis and Robertson 1989; Ellis et al. 1990), while the latter is diagnostic of the early Middle Woodland period (ca. 2200–1700 B.P.; Justice 1987; Montet-White 1968). A triangular biface similar to Pomranky and Meadowood cache blades (ca. 3000–2500 B.P.; Lovis and Robertson 1989; Spence et al. 1990) is probably also indicative of the Late Archaic period. The archaeological data, the ^{14}C age estimates from S-1 and S-2, and the pedology of S-2 suggest that the paleosol was probably formed over a 1,000-year span and corresponds with the post-Algoma low-water phase (Monaghan and Schaetzl 1994).

Stratum 3 (S-3) is a gray-to-grayish-brown and dark-yellowish-brown, variably thick, heavily mottled, silty clay and, compared to S-2, represents a period of increased fluvial activity along Bear Creek (Figure 5-6). Although some minor weathering associated with B-horizon development probably occurred during the development of the overlying 2Ab (S-2) unit, very limited evidence for it was noted in S-3 or lower stratigraphic units. Occasional thin sand stringers, similar to those noted in S-1, also occur in S-3, particularly near the creek. The stratum was generally 8–10 cm thick but was >15 cm thick in some areas. This variation in thickness was largely due to undulations of the bounding units (S-2 and S-4). Additionally, the lower boundary for S-3 was not always clear. In the southern end of the site, for example, S-3 was differentiated only by a decrease in artifact density and finer texture than the lower units. The intensity of fluvial activity at the site during deposition of S-3 is evidenced by erosion of the underlying units in the south-central part of the site. The basin that forms Feature 4 was eroded at this time, as were numerous other small-scale erosional rills that mark the surface of Stratum 4.

The age of S-3 derives mainly from correlation with regional lake-level fluctuations and from one projectile point. Increased fluvial activity is linked with the rise to the Algoma stage around 4000–3800 B.P. As a consequence, Lake Algoma probably transgressed to the site and periodically may have even inundated it (Monaghan and Schaetzl 1994). A broad-bladed, corner-notched projectile point similar to Brewerton styles was recovered near the base of S-3. Brewerton phase materials span the transition from the Middle Archaic to the Late Archaic and are variously dated 5000–3600 B.P. (Ellis et al. 1990; Justice 1987; Lovis ed. 1989). While the S-3 sequence may span 1,000 years, it probably formed within a shorter time period indicated from the beginning of Lake Algoma to the formation of modern Lake Huron at about 3400 B.P. (Monaghan and Schaetzl 1994).

Stratum 4 (S-4) is a gray-to-dark-gray, variably thick, sandy clay and represents the lowest unit containing cultural materials at the site (Figure 5-6). Its surface is irregular and undulates across most of the site. The contours of this stratum closely follow those of the underlying hummocks of sand forming Stratum 5. While S-4 is typically 6–12 cm thick, it can vary by as much as 15–20 cm within an excavation unit. This variability is particularly well expressed across the central and northern parts of the site. The stratum was eroded across much of the southern half of the site, where it was largely represented by thin (2–3 cm), discontinuous patches. The surface of S-4 generally lies at 179.9 m but ranges from 179.7 to 180.4 m.

The age of S-4 is based on a ^{14}C age estimate as well as on two diagnostic projectile points. A small amount of bone from S-4 yielded an age of 4250±50 B.P. (Beta-56311; CAMS-3835), while a charcoal sample derived from elsewhere (610±70 B.P.; Beat-5998; CAMS-3835) clearly does not reflect when S-4 formed but rather indicates mixing by bioturbation. A large corner-notched projectile point was recovered from S-4 in the same excavation unit as the 4250 B.P. age estimate. Although no direct typological counterpart was identified, the point is distinctly different from that found in S-3. It probably belongs to a series of highly variable, Late Archaic corner-notched forms and has a general affinity with the Brewerton series points. In addition, a reworked Raddatz Side-Notched point was recovered from S-4 and is related to the Dehmel Road phase of the Middle Archaic period (ca. 7000–4000 B.P.; Lovis and Robertson 1989).

Stratum 5 (S-5) and Stratum 6 (S-6) represent the basal portions of the stratigraphic sequence at the site (Figure 5-6). S-5 is yellowish-brown-to-pale-brown sand that rests unconformably on S-6, which is dark-yellowish-brown-to-reddish-brown glaciolacustrine clay. S-5 is very discontinuous across the site and commonly forms small erosional rills and hummocks. A thin layer of reddish brown pea-sized gravels was occasionally sandwiched between S-5 and S-6. The small amount of cultural material present in S-5 probably derived from bioturbation rather than from human occupation. The deposition of S-5 has been linked with the regression of Nipissing II waters from the site area shortly before 4300 B.P. (Monaghan and Schaetzl 1994).

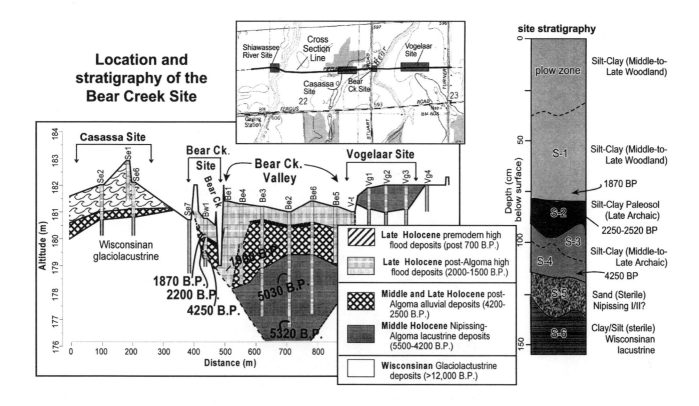

Figure 5-6. Stratigraphy of the Bear Creek site (after Monaghan and Schaetzl 1994). See Figure 5-1 for generalized location of the site in the Saginaw Bay area.

DISCUSSION AND ARCHAEOLOGICAL SIGNIFICANCE. Beginning shortly after its emergence from Nipissing II, the Bear Creek locale was intermittently used for the extraction of food and other economic resources for nearly 4,000 years. Over the millennia and in the face of environmental changes associated with the evolution of the regional landscape, the Bear Creek site has exhibited both continuity and change in its use by prehistoric populations. Initial use of the site occurred related to S-4 deposition. Gastropod data indicates a relatively dry and stable surface at this time, while the recovered fish remains are indicative of a relatively cool, fast-moving stream (Smith 1994). Recovered floral remains indicate the presence of mesic and wet-mesic forest communities in the vicinity (Egan 1994). A series of small, short-term, seasonal encampments focused on the area immediately adjacent to the creek marked the site at this time. Tools recovered from S-4 include projectile points and point fragments, mid- and late-stage bifacial preforms, a recycled biface fragment, expedient flake tools, an anvil, manos, a possible grinding platform, and a chipped slate preform. These tools generally relate to maintenance and fabrication activities associated with hunting and plant collection. The widest array of animal species extracted at the site are found in S-4. While cervids, muskrat, and turtle dominate the S-4 faunal assemblage, beaver, raccoon, dog, several duck species, ruffed grouse, brook trout, brown bullhead, and sucker also occur (Smith 1994). Floral remains from S-4 indicate that hickory, black walnut and walnut family nuts, and aquatic tubers were also collected at the site during this time (Egan 1994). This data indicates that the Middle Archaic occupation occurred primarily during the warm season and extended into the fall.

Commensurate with a rise in lake levels and an associated increase in fluvial activity in this part of the Bear Creek valley, the intensity of usage of the Bear Creek site decreased markedly during S-3 deposition. Not only does the intensity of occupation decrease, but the focus of the occupied area also shifts westward away from the creek bank, which probably reflects generally wet conditions in the area. However, the general structure of the occupation remains the same. As with S-4, the tool assemblage, which includes a projectile point, a bifacial preform, an end scraper, wedgelike tools, and cores, usually reflects hunting and processing activities. No tools commonly associated with plant-processing activities (i.e., grinding equipment) were present in S-3. Faunal exploitation continues to focus on deer, muskrat, and turtles, although black bear, dog, ruffed grouse, a small duck species, and five species of fish are also present (Smith 1994). Collection of hickory, butternut, and walnuts also took place (Egan 1994). This data indicates that the Middle-to-Late Woodland occupation associated with S-3 deposition occurred during the spring and fall.

The most intensive occupation at the Bear Creek site related to the formation of S-2, which represents a time of relative fluvial stability associated with the post-Algoma low-water stage. Commensurate shifts in the local environment are also evident. Wood charcoal indicates an apparent increase in mesic species, reflecting a general drying of the area in comparison to S-3. Gastropod and faunal data also indicate that Bear Creek became a slower, more sluggish stream during this period. Despite these environmental shifts, however, the overall structure of the occupation is very similar to that of the earlier Archaic period. The tool assemblage is reflective of hunting and butchering, hide-processing, and tool maintenance/fabrication tasks, as well as plant processing. S-2 tools include projectile points, bifaces, end scrapers, wedgelike tools, an abrader, a conical pestle, a ground slate tool, a hammer/mano, flaked cobble, and grinding platform fragments. The faunal assemblage is dominated by deer, elk, and muskrat, although woodchuck, dog, black bear, raccoon, beaver, teal, freshwater drum, several varieties of turtle, and a fox snake also occur (Smith 1994). Exploitation of plants continued to focus on walnuts, although hickory nutshell and mulberry and hawthorn seeds are also present (Egan 1994). Unlike the previous Archaic occupation, however, the floral and faunal data from S-2 indicate that the Early-to-early-Middle Woodland occupation at the Bear Creek site was primarily during the fall, winter, and spring.

The intensity of the usage of the Bear Creek site again decreased as a consequence of flooding during the deposition of S-1. The decrease in site usage was not dramatic until the beginning of S-1.1 deposition ca. 1800 B.P. The data recovered from S-1.2 suggests some degree of continuity with the previous occupations. Tools emphasized the extractive nature of the occupations as well as the maintenance of active tool kits. These tools include projectile points, a bifacial preform, an end scraper, a combined graver/scraper, wedgelike tools, and a hammerstone. Deer, elk, muskrat, and raccoon were the primary species targeted during this period, although dog, black bear, a small duck, stinkpot, and turtle are also represented (Smith 1994). Interestingly, no fish were found. Walnut and hickory are the primary nut species exploited during this time (Egan 1994).

While the structure of the occupations and the range of animal and plant species are similar to those of S-2, the season of occupation reverted back to the spring and fall.

S-1.1 represents the terminal phase of prehistoric usage of this site. During this period, the Shiawassee River drainage shifted from Bear Creek to its present channel adjacent to the Shiawassee River site (Monaghan and Schaetzl 1994). As a consequence, Bear Creek was eclipsed as a focal point of prehistoric extractive strategies. The low density of material from S-1.1 reflects a similar pattern of occupation that began during the waning portion of the Middle Archaic. Tools include a projectile point, expedient flake tools, and grinding platforms. Fauna from S-1.1 include the familiar focus on deer, muskrat, raccoon, and elk but also include black duck and turtle (Smith 1994). Floral remains include walnut and hickory nutshells and a small amount of terrestrial and aquatic tubers. During S-2 deposition, a late spring and fall occupation is indicated.

In summary, beginning about 4200 B.P. and continuing until about 900 B.P., occupation at Bear Creek focused on exploiting a variety of wetland and terrestrial species of flora and fauna. While the occupational intensity varied, a degree of continuity in the structure of settlement and exploited food species existed from the Middle Archaic through early Late Woodland periods. Deer, elk, muskrat, and raccoon were the primary animal species hunted, but a variety of fish, birds, and amphibians were also harvested, most likely on an opportunistic basis. Nuts, specifically walnuts and hickory, were the primary floral species exploited by all occupations at Bear Creek. Geologic data, coupled with the radiocarbon evidence and diagnostic tools from the site, showed how these occupations integrated with the changing environment. These environmental changes, moreover, were directly tied to regional fluctuations of Great Lakes water levels and to the corresponding evolution of the post-Nipissing landscape of the Saginaw Bay region. In part, due to the rarity of such sites, the excavations at the Bear Creek site have added another dimension to our understanding of Middle and Late Archaic and Woodland adaptations.

Vogelaar Site (20SA291)

LOCATION AND BACKGROUND. The Vogelaar site is a large, 60-hectare site complex in the SE1/4 of the NW1/4 of Sec. 23, T10N R3E, St. Charles Township, Saginaw County, Michigan (Figure 5-1; Branstner and Hambacher eds. 1995b). It includes evidence of intermittent occupation that spans the end of the Middle Archaic through the Late Woodland. The major occupations, however, occur during the Late Archaic and Middle Woodland periods. Additionally, geoarchaeological studies at the site provided evidence of fluctuating lake levels (Nipissing and Algoma) as well as secular variation of wetland and floodplain conditions during the middle and late Holocene. This data supplements the more detailed record from the Bear Creek site. How prehistoric humans and their cultural systems articulated with this changing environment was an important dimension of the archaeological research at the site.

The sprawling Vogelaar site complex is situated on a Nipissing and Algoma beach and late Holocene dune complex that overlie erosionally resistant glacial and glaciolacustrine clay. Most of the site occurs at an altitude of 185–190 m, although the occupation on the northern portion of the site occurs at an altitude of < 180 m. Situated at the junction of a former embouchure of the Shiawassee River and Bear Creek, the Vogelaar site landform not only forms the eastern rim of the 500-m-wide paleo–Bear Creek valley but also overlooks broad expanses of wetlands to the north. Relative lowland also occurs east of the site. The Bear Creek site, discussed previously, contains a similar archaeological record and is situated on the opposite side of the Bear Creek valley, about 500 m west of the Vogelaar site. The abundance of surrounding wetland and floodplain environments, coupled with the variety of associated forest and animal communities, was likely the primary factor that attracted human populations to the Vogelaar site.

The richness of the archaeological deposits at the Vogelaar site has been well known for at least a century. Until property access was denied by the current landowners several decades ago, it was a popular spot among the local artifact collectors. Among the earliest mention of the general site area is Dustin's (1930) notation of the "Bear Creek Cemetery" as a major prehistoric occupation. Prior to the 1990 and 1991 investigations, professional research at the site was limited to brief investigations conducted by the University of Michigan Museum of Anthropology in the 1960s and late 1980s (Farrand 1990; Papworth 1967). The 1980 survey of the GLGTP corridor identified the site as an extensive and significant Archaic and Woodland complex, the northern edge of which was bisected by the pipeline corridor (Weir 1981). Important to this study is that all of these earlier investigations focused on the topographically higher areas of the site and generally ignored the relative lowland that marked the eastern margin of the Bear Creek valley. The Phase I and II investigations associated with the GLGTP project were the first to explore the western flank of the Vogelaar ridge. One of the explicit goals of this work was to assess the potential for buried cultural deposits (Branstner 1991).

The 1990 and 1991 investigations at the site included a 30-m-wide transect across the northern site margin (Phase II; Branstner 1991), while data-recovery efforts focused on an 8-x-150-m impact corridor in the topographically higher portions of the site (Branstner and Hambacher eds. 1995b). As part of these investigations, a backhoe trench and several test units were excavated in a topographically low area adjoining the western flank of the Vogelaar ridge (informally designated as "Vogelaar's woods"). This area also marked the edge of the Bear Creek valley. Examination of the deposits in this part of the site is the focus of the following summary.

STRATIGRAPHY. The distribution of soil types at the Vogelaar site reflects the general topography and depositional history of the area. Somewhat poorly drained loam and sand underlie the main, topographically higher parts of the site, while very poorly drained silt loams occur in the low-lying areas associated with Vogelaar's woods (Iaquinta 1994). This soil also marks the mouth of a small, intermittent drain extending along the southwestern edge of the Vogelaar ridge. Conceivably, this drain may have been more active during periods of higher lake levels and increased fluvial activity in the region. The modern characterization of the soils at the site primarily pertains to the upper portions of the deposit at the site and, in the case of the Vogelaar's woods area, does not adequately describe the deeper sediments. A four-unit allostratigraphic sequence was developed by Monaghan (1995b) for Vogelaar's woods and is largely based on the stratigraphic sequence exposed by the backhoe trench (Figure 3-4). Unit I, the uppermost unit, represents historically disturbed sediment. Cultural materials were abundant in Unit I but occurred in historically disturbed contexts. Because of differences in the nature of this zone across the overall site area, it was divided into two subunits, Ia and Ib. Subunit Ia represents the modern A-horizon in the lower-lying Vogelaar's woods and is black-to-dark-grayish-brown silt loam. It was largely disturbed during the construction of the 1960s' pipeline. Subunit Ib is very-dark-grayish-brown-to-grayish-brown plow zone that was present across the higher altitude areas of the site. No evidence that the plow zone also extended into the Vogelaar's woods area was noted. Unit I was typically 25–30 cm thick, although in some areas it was up to 60 cm thick.

Unit II is massive-to-faintly-bedded sandy-silt and silt loam. These deposits include middle-to-late Holocene alluvium and colluvium that contain abundant cultural materials. Because no temporally sensitive artifacts were recovered, however, the cultural relationships and precise timing of the sequence with the sequence occurring at the main site area remain unknown. Unit II was divided into two subunits, IIa and IIb, based on the presence of paleosol in the deposits. The upper portion, IIa, consisted of dark-gray-to-dark-grayish-brown silt loam. The thickness of IIa is variable, but in the backhoe profile IIa was approximately 60 cm thick. The horizon thins eastward, eventually pinching out some 5 m to the east of the trench. It was not present in the main site area on the topographically higher Vogelaar's ridge. IIb is 45 cm thick, with color and texture similar to IIa. It is, however, separated from IIa by a paleosol. The presence of the paleosol indicates an interruption of alluvial accumulation in this area, and it has been correlated with the paleosol at the Bear Creek site. As with IIa, IIb also pinches out a short distance east of the type profile and was not present on Vogelaar's ridge.

Unit III is pale-brown-to-yellowish-brown, massive-to-faintly-cross-and-tabular-bedded, medium-to-coarse sand. It was derived by littoral and/or shallow lacustrine processes and can be traced across both Vogelaar's woods and ridge. In Vogelaar's woods, Unit III, which was rich in mollusks and macroplant remains, contained no cultural materials. This probably reflects the fact that this topographically low area was inundated by Lakes Nipissing and Algoma during the deposition of Unit III. Elsewhere, however, Unit III did include some in situ cultural material. The sand grades upward into interbedded sand, silt, and clay in the upper parts of Unit III. The transition from Unit II to III is gradational, most likely reflecting a gradual change from a shallow lacustrine (Nipissing II and Algoma) to an alluvial depositional environment. Three ^{14}C age estimates were obtained for Unit III. The first two, 4400±80 B.P. (Beta-47862) and 4320±70 B.P. (Beta-47879), derived from detrital wood recovered from near the base of the unit in Vogelaar's woods. These relate to the Nipissing II transgression in the Bear Creek area. A third date, 4780±100 B.P. (Beta-78825), obtained from a feature located on Vogelaar's ridge, suggests that the site was also used during the Nipissing phase. This age may reflect periodic, low-density occupation during occasional, minor Lake Nipissing lows, as is indicated at the Ebenhoff site (see below). Alternatively, this feature could represent a remnant occupation that took place prior to the Nipissing I maximum (ca. 4700 B.P.; Monaghan, Lovis, and Fay 1986) and was mostly destroyed during the transgression.

Unit IV marks the base of the sequence and is dark-yellowish-brown and brown-to-slightly-grayish-brown glaciolacustrine clay. The contact between Units IV and III is erosional and occurs about 2 m below the ground surface in Vogelaar's woods.

DISCUSSION AND ARCHAEOLOGICAL SIGNIFICANCE. The Vogelaar site contains evidence of human habitation stretching back at least until the waning stages of the Middle Archaic period. While all but the highest points of the Vogelaar site would have been inundated during the Nipissing maximum (ca. 4700 B.P.; Monaghan, Lovis, and Fay 1986), diagnostic projectile points and a ^{14}C age estimate indicate that at least minor occupation occurred prior to and/or during the Nipissing maximum. During Nipissing II and Algoma high-water phases, the site was rimmed to the north and west by shallow lacustrine and shoreline wetland environments. The importance of the Vogelaar locale as a critical, resource-rich area is attested to by both the high density of cultural materials and the temporal breadth of the prehistoric occupation at the site. Data-recovery efforts at a small portion of this extensive site area revealed the presence of significant Late and Terminal Archaic, Middle Woodland, and early Late Woodland occupations. The relatively lower intensity of Early Woodland occupations at the site may reflect environmental changes related to the stabilization of Bear Creek during the post-Algoma low-water phase. During this time, occupation may have shifted to topographically lower areas nearer to Bear Creek, such as the Bear Creek site (see discussion above), or may have simply concentrated on another part of Vogelaar's ridge north or south of the area investigated during the 1991–1992 GLGTP project.

The main occupations at Vogelaar site clearly occurred on the higher, better-drained areas adjacent to Vogelaar's woods. Here, however, the shallow nature of the deposits, coupled with the intensity of site use through time and only limited soil accretion, resulted in a confusing palimpsest of overlapping archaeological deposits. Limited excavations in the Vogelaar's woods area indicated that while the area was less attractive to human occupation, it nonetheless contained a >1-m-thick sequence of low-to-moderate-density cultural materials in Unit II. Although no diagnostic artifacts were recovered, the materials probably began to accumulate shortly after 3500 B.P. The origin of the cultural material in Unit II, which apparently actively accreted throughout most of the late Holocene, is uncertain. The cultural material may have derived from primary occupation, from "over-the-hill" waste-disposal patterns, or from a combination of the two. Variability in the density and structure of the archaeological deposits suggests that the latter explanation is the most probable. Moreover, vertical distribution of the artifacts is not uniform, indicating periodicity in the intensity of use of this area. One peak in artifact density occurs near the base of Unit II, while another occurs associated with the paleosol that marks the break between subunits IIa and IIb. The vertical distribution of artifacts is reminiscent of that noted at the Bear Creek site. Furthermore, the increase in the density of materials between the impact corridor and the test units excavated a short distance to the south suggest that the occurrence of prehistoric materials is, in part, a function of their relative position along the western flank of the site and the stream draining the wetland area south of the site.

The lack of temporally diagnostic materials from Vogelaar's woods hampers understanding the timing and duration of the use and relationship of this area compared with the larger site complex. The few projectile points recovered from this area were relatively high in the soil profile (Levels 2–3) and generally reflect Middle Woodland styles. One point, a generic corner-notched specimen, however, has typological affiliations with either Late Archaic or Middle Woodland styles. Minimally, this data suggests that use of Vogelaar's woods ceased after the Middle Woodland period, which generally corresponds to a similar decrease in use of the site at large during the Late Woodland period. Lithic artifacts from this area consist of small numbers of fabricating and processing tools (bifacial preforms, wedges, perforators and denticulates, and utilized flakes). In addition, late-stage lithic reduction and expedient flake tool production debris, as well as fire-cracked rock, were present.

Faunal and floral remains were also recovered from Units I and II. Although generally poorly preserved, the bone indicated that a rich diversity of terrestrial and aquatic species occurred at the site. These include deer, muskrat, beaver, raccoon, bird, and several varieties of turtle and fish. Freshwater drum predominates the fish assemblage and suggests that a sluggish, slow-moving stream was periodically present near the site. Although botanical remains from the archaeological deposits were limited, low densities of acorn and walnut shell, along with several types of weedy seeds, occurred. Whether these reflect the local, natural environment or are the by-products of human exploitation is not certain. Overall, the types of archaeological remains recovered from the Vogelaar's woods area, however, are very reminiscent of those from the Bear Creek site. The occupations at the Vogelaar site were probably of short duration and primarily geared toward extraction and processing.

In summary, the archaeological deposits at the Vogelaar site provide a nearly 5,000-year-long record of intermittent human occupation at this resource-rich locale. While Vogelaar's woods was not the focus of prehistoric occupation, excavations within it provided an important component for understanding the structure of prehistoric use of the site. This data provided further indications of how prehistoric populations oriented themselves on the landscape as well as their land-use patterns within a changing Holocene environment. In addition, the preservation of botanical and faunal remains from Vogelaar's woods provides a further dimension not only to prehistoric human subsistence but also to how the site's environmental changes related to fluctuations in the hydrological system along Bear Creek. The investigations in Vogelaar's woods also illustrate the importance of examining the lower-density occupational fringes of sites. For sites like Vogelaar, these more poorly drained areas are commonly ignored to concentrate on higher, better-drained, more densely occupied site areas. Although areas with higher occupational densities do provide greater varieties of cultural materials, in such areas individual components of occupations related to each specific time period are often difficult to separate.

Ebenhoff Site (20SA596)

LOCATION AND BACKGROUND. The Ebenhoff site is an extensive multicomponent occupation area containing artifacts from the terminal Paleo-Indian/Early Archaic (ca. 10,000 B.P.) through Woodland periods (Dobbs 1993). Situated in the center of Sec. 20, T10N R4E, Albee Township, Saginaw County, Michigan, the site lies along the northern fringe of an east-west-trending, 181–183-m Nipissing and Algoma beach and dune complex (Dobbs and Murray 1993; Figure 5-1). The present site surface occurs at an altitude of about 181 m and includes two low knolls. The Ebenhoff landform is bounded on either side by intermittent streams. Fairchild Creek, which is tributary to Misteguay Creek, lies about 800 m to the east, and a second, channelized stream lies about 1.2 km west of the site. The Shiawassee flats lowland extends to the north, while small wetland areas border the southern margin of the Ebenhoff site landform. Critical to the Ebenhoff site's formation, preservation, and discovery is its location along the Nipissing and Algoma shoreline complex. The gently undulating nature of the local terrain today disguises the configuration of the middle Holocene paleo-landscape.

The 1980 GLGTP survey identified the site as a scatter of lithic debris, but because of a lack of diagnostic artifacts and poor surface reconnaissance conditions, the site was considered insignificant (Weir 1981). Similarly, the subsequent 1990 survey of the site also failed to recover temporally diagnostic artifacts (Branstner 1990a). Enough questions were raised about the significance of the Ebenhoff site during the 1990 survey, however, to prompt further testing. This included 66 1-m² archaeological test units and a series of backhoe trenches. The test excavations not only recovered a small number of Early Archaic, Transitional Archaic, and potentially Middle Woodland projectile points but, more important, identified the presence of a series of interbedded, discontinuous lenses of "paleosol" or organic-rich zones between 50 and 80 cm deep (Branstner 1991). Additionally, a ^{14}C age estimate of 12,210±110 B.P. (Beta-40239) from peat 150 cm below the surface from one of the deep-test trenches suggested pre-Nipissing archaeological deposits might be preserved at this locale (Branstner 1991). Based on this information, data-recovery efforts were undertaken along a 175-m-long impact corridor but focused on the site's western knoll. Two blocks (informally, Area 3 [4 x 16 m] and Area 4 [4 x 25 m]) about 30 m apart, as well as a series of 1- x -2-m test units between and adjacent to the blocks, were excavated. These units totaled 234 m² and generally penetrated 1–2 m below the surface (Dobbs and Murray 1993).

STRATIGRAPHY. The subtlety of the landform at Ebenhoff site along with the effects of plowing masked the full nature of the archaeological and geologic deposits at the site. From a soil-genesis standpoint, the site occurs at the transition between somewhat poorly drained sands (Iaquinta 1994). These do not, however, adequately reflect the variability in subsurface conditions. The site includes a deep, complex sequence that preserves variable portions of an evolving middle Holocene landscape (Beaverson and Mooers 1993; Dobbs and Murray 1993). Although the deposits span the Holocene and Early Archaic artifacts were found within the site area, most of the deposits and associated artifacts are Nipissing and younger in age (i.e., post-5000 B.P.; Dobbs and Murray 1993).

Six stratigraphic units were defined at the site (Beaverson and Mooers 1993; Figure 5-7). The first unit is the 30-cm-thick, sandy-loam plow zone. Projectile points representing all of the components present at the Ebenhoff site have been recovered from plow zone contexts. The few artifacts forming the low-density occupation on the eastern knoll of the site are restricted to the plow zone (Branstner 1991).

A 1-m-thick sequence of very fine eolian sand that includes thin layers of fine sand and silt underlies the plow zone and is informally referred to as the "upper fine sand" (Beaverson and Mooers 1993). A thin, discontinuous, weakly developed paleosol occurs in the upper part of the sand (about 30 cm below the plow zone). The morphology of the paleosol across the site suggests that the paleoground surface gently undulated, much as it does today. Several large, Late Archaic corner-notched projectile points were recovered within or directly above the paleosol (Dobbs and Murray 1993) and represent the majority of points recovered during the 1991 excavation. They are similar to Feeheley series points, which broadly date between 5000 and 3000 B.P. (Lovis and Robertson 1989). One of the projectile points found below the paleosol at Ebenhoff is similar to a large corner-notched point from the subpaleosol 4200 B.P.-age lower cultural zone (Stratum 4) at the Bear Creek site. While certainly predating the Bear Creek paleosol, the formation of the Ebenhoff paleosol probably corresponds with the increased landform stability that resulted during the waning of the Nipissing II and Algoma high-water phases (i.e., after ca. 4000 B.P.).

The lower two-thirds of the upper sand unit also includes small-scale laminations and small- and large-scale eolian structures (Beaverson and Mooers 1993). These are particularly evident in Area 4, where up to 1-m-high cross-beds are present. Organic- and clay-rich laminae drape the foresets of these beds and are most common in the lower 50–75 cm of the upper sand unit. These may represent sediment drapes within a shallow-lacustrine environment. Medium-grained, shallow-lacustrine sand deposits also form ramplike structures, which are separated by finer sediment layers and drapes along the base of dune beds. The tops of these features were indistinct and often grade into the eolian sands that formed the upper third of the unit. The basal contact of the unit is abrupt and marked by relatively continuous peat beds. Artifacts were present throughout much of this stratigraphic unit and also occur as concentrations in small depressions in the surface of the peat (Beaverson and Mooers 1993).

The upper sand unit is underlain by a 10–20-cm-thick peat (Beaverson and Mooers 1993). The peat occurs most commonly as organic infillings in small depressions. It thins appreciably from east to west and eventually pinches out. Three ^{14}C age estimates were obtained from the base of the upper sand unit and the underlying peat in Area 4 (between ca. 80 and 120 cm below surface; Figure 5-7). These provide an indication of the age of the base of the Ebenhoff sequence (Dobbs and Murray 1993). Two of these, 4660±90 B.P. (Beta-47379) and 6040±110 B.P. (Beta-47065), represent composites of two charcoal scatters in sand lenses 90–100 cm below the surface and were collected from adjacent excavation units. In addition, an uncharred oak log found in the basal peat produced a ^{14}C age of 4720±50 B.P. (Beta-51001). The 6040±110 B.P.-age sample was considered erroneous based on its stratigraphic position in relation to the other two dates and rejected from further consideration (Dobbs and Murray 1993). However, this date may actually indicate that older, pre-Nipissing materials were reworked and incorporated into the peat deposits at the site or that the stratigraphy is far more complex. The fact that a 12,000 B.P. peat deposit (Branstner 1990a) also occurs at the site supports this conjecture.

As noted above, occasional artifact lags occur in small, wave-formed depressions in the surface of the peat. Whether these reflect brief usage of the surface during lower-water periods is not clear. Regardless, however, they were apparently eroded and redeposited during higher-water or storm events (Dobbs and Murray 1993). Their presence within Nipissing and Algoma beach sediments clearly indicates that humans lived along an active Nipissing and Algoma shoreline.

The peat grades into a 40-cm-thick, very-fine-to-fine sand and silt that includes discontinuous clay laminae. This unit is informally referred to as the

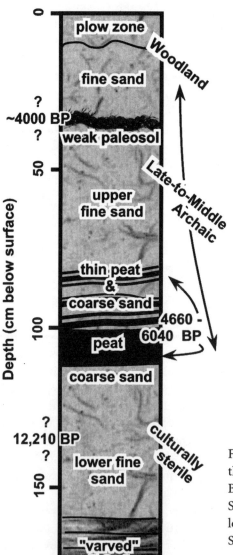

Figure 5-7. Stratigraphy of the Ebenhoff site (after Beaverson and Mooers 1993). See Figure 5-1 for generalized location of the site in the Saginaw Bay area.

"lower fine sand" (Beaverson and Mooers 1993). A small number of artifacts were recovered from the top of the sand near the peat; whether they are intrusive is unclear (Dobbs and Murray 1993). Although not cross-bedded, small-scale de-watering structures (i.e., flame, break-outs, etc.) commonly disrupt the tabular sand beds and lamella. Disturbances, possibly associated with frost-heaving and bioturbation processes, were also noted (Beaverson and Mooers 1993). As organic content (peat layers) decreased downward in the unit, the number and thickness of silt and clay interbeds increased. Ultimately, these grade into varved (laminated) clay and mark the base of the Ebenhoff sequence (Beaverson and Mooers 1993). These laminated sediments probably represent deeper water deposits associated with glacial Lake Arkona and early Lake Saginaw (Beaverson and Mooers 1993) and are late Wisconsinan. No cultural material was present in this horizon.

DISCUSSION AND ARCHAEOLOGICAL SIGNIFICANCE. The Ebenhoff site provides a 10,000-year-long record of prehistoric settlement in southern Michigan. Surface collections from the site indicate the diversity of archaeological materials present. For example, three Paleo-Indian lanceolate points, one of which has affinity to Scottsbluff points while another has a pseudoflute on one side, indicate that occupation first occurred 11,000–10,000 B.P. (Dobbs 1993). The presence of a few LeCroy, Hardin Barbed, and Thebes cluster points, as well as a few possible Kirk and Fox Valley points, shows that sporadic usage of the site continued through the Early Archaic. These early point styles, however, represent less than 10 percent of the diagnostic artifacts in the Ebenhoff surface collection. Additionally, projectile point styles typically associated with the Middle Archaic period, such as Raddatz Side-Notched varieties, are not represented. All the diagnostic artifacts pertaining to these early occupations were recovered from the surface of the site and were not observed during any of the excavations. This suggests that early Holocene cultural deposits were probably destroyed during the Nipissing transgression. Moreover, the provenance of these early points is not certain and may derive from elsewhere on the Ebenhoff property rather than the actual site area under discussion.

Pollen data from the site indicates that the local paleoenvironment during the Nipissing regression was essentially modern (Beaverson and Mooers 1993). A mixed local forest community was dominated by oak, beech, poplar, elm, ash, and hemlock but also included pine, spruce, cedar, and several varieties of nut trees. The site apparently occurred at the edge of a wetland with encroaching sand dunes. At times, particularly during deposition of the lower part of the sequence, lake level rose and inundated the site. In fact, the high percentage of grasses among the pollen samples indicates that the repeated small-scale transgressions and regressions at the site prohibited the development of a permanent plant community along the edge of the wetland (Beaverson and Mooers 1993). The existence of a marsh environment in the area is also reflected by the presence of willow and alder as well as bulrush, smartweed, cattail, wormwood, goosefoot, and fern. Although bone recovered from the site was too fragmentary to permit species identification, the assemblage was apparently dominated by large-to-medium-sized mammals, with lesser numbers of small mammals, bird, turtles, and fish.

The majority of the prehistoric occupation of the site occurred during and just after the Nipissing and Algoma phases. Most of the diagnostic artifacts recovered from the excavations and in the Ebenhoff surface collection are Late Archaic (Dobbs 1993; Dobbs and Murray 1993) and are typologically closely related to the Feeheley complex. Archaeological remains were unevenly distributed throughout the profile, with the majority of the material associated with the upper fine sand. Five informal archaeological "contexts," or groupings, of artifacts were defined at the site (Dobbs and Murray 1993). These, however, can generally be stratigraphically grouped into three main contexts: in the eolian sand above the paleosol, in the eolian-to-lacustrine sand within and below the paleosol, and in the lacustrine-to-eolian sand-peat transitional zone at the base of the upper fine sand.

The greatest proportion of the cultural material from the site occurred above the paleosol and in the plow zone (Dobbs and Murray 1993). For example, in Area 4, about half of the debitage, 80 percent of the tools, and nearly 75 percent of the cores and fire-cracked rock occurred in this context. Artifact densities were generally highest 20–30 cm below the plow zone, which is just above the paleosol. The tool assemblage from this context suggests that hunting, butchering, and processing of animals, along with tool maintenance, were the primary site activities. In addition, a small amount of mammal and bird bone, as well as the only ceramic (Late Woodland) sherds recovered from the site, also occurs above the paleosol. These sherds, along with several Middle and Late Woodland points from the Ebenhoff surface collection (Dobbs 1993), indicate that site use was far less intense after the Late Archaic period. It also suggests that the paleosol formation predates about 3000 B.P. and that the dunes were subsequently reactivated. The age of this reactivation is unknown.

High artifact densities, as well as most of the bone found at the site, also occur in contexts within or just below the paleosol. Artifact distributions are vertically and horizontally discontinuous across the site. Artifact concentrations are commonly associated with the paleosol and with organic- and clay-rich laminae marking the tops of the dune foreset beds (Dobbs and Murray 1993). In some areas of the site, an up to 30-cm-thick zone of sterile sand occurs within the lower sand unit, lending stratigraphic context breaks to small discrete areas. In other areas of the site, however, artifact abundances remain consistent across the paleosol. Most of the artifacts from and below the paleosol consisted of debitage and fire-cracked rock (see Table 7 in Dobbs and Murray 1993). A projectile point from below the paleosol is typologically similar to a 4200 B.P. point recovered from the base of the Bear Creek sequence and indicates that dunes were active as late as 4200 B.P. or slightly more recently. Given the post–4200 B.P. fluctuations in Nipissing II and Algoma suggested from the Vogelaar's woods and Bear Creek sequences, this age also implies that minor inundations of Nipissing and Algoma probably continued after the deposition of most of the upper fine sand. If so, the potential for erosion and redeposition of artifacts is high throughout the sequence.

Artifacts, mainly debitage and a small amount of fire-cracked rock, were also recovered from the lower portions of the sequence within the peat-sand transition zone (Dobbs and Murray 1993). Not only were artifacts from this context discontinuous across the excavations, but there was also proportionately far fewer of them compared with the overlying cultural deposits. Although artifacts within this context represented only about 5 percent of the total assemblages (see Tables 7 and 8 in Dobbs and Murray 1993), when found, they occurred in discrete clusters.

In summary, the Ebenhoff site includes a sequence of stratified Middle-to-Late Archaic archaeological deposits associated with a middle Holocene shoreline/ dune complex. Additionally, the site also records important geomorphological and paleo-environmental data about the development of the local landscape. Similar to the Bear Creek site, a degree of continuity in the Middle-to-early-Late Archaic settlement and subsistence regimes is indicated at the site. Occupations through the period were a series of short-duration hunting and processing camps (Dobbs and Murray 1993). Although the Ebenhoff site contains mainly Late Archaic occupations with only a minor Woodland component, other nearby areas include extensive Woodland occupations (e.g., Shiawassee River, Flint River, Bear Creek, and Schultz). The fact that the Ebenhoff site was essentially abandoned after the Late Archaic, as was the similar-age Weber I site, indicates that the original attraction of the area must have changed after about 3000 B.P. The most obvious, related environmental change is the abandonment of the middle Holocene shorelines and subsequent reconfiguration of the drainage and wetland boundaries in the area to accommodate modern lake level.

Flint River Site (20SA1034)

LOCATION AND BACKGROUND. The Flint River site is a small, Late Woodland agricultural camp situated along the west bank of the Flint River in the S1/2 of the NW1/4 of Sec. 27, T10N R5W, Taymouth Township, Saginaw County, Michigan (Figure 5-1; Branstner 1990a; Dobbs et al. 1993). The site consists of several overlapping archaeological components that are buried under about 50 cm of alluvium. Based on 14 ^{14}C age estimates, it was occupied between 800 and 600 B.P. The Flint River site illustrates a previously unrecognized site-type within Saginaw Valley Late Woodland settlement systems. In addition to the intact archaeological deposits, cultural materials were recovered from apparently reworked and roughly contemporaneous deposits west of the main occupation area. At the site, the valley of the Flint River is broad and marked by well-defined bluffs that rise 4 m above the river. The Flint River channel occurs at an altitude of about 179.5 m (about 3 m above Saginaw Bay), while the surface of the site varies in altitude from 183 to 184.5 m. Upstream from the site, the gradient of the river is relatively steep (0.7 m/km) but becomes flatter downstream from the site (0.15 m/km). The occurrence of a gradient inflection at the Flint River site, which approximately coincides with the upstream limit of the middle Holocene Nipissing transgression, has greatly influenced the late Holocene depositional potentials and patterns for the surrounding floodplain.

The Flint River site was identified during the GLGTP 1990–1991 deep-test survey (Branstner 1990a). Because the Flint River site was buried by a mantle of alluvium, the site was not detected by standard surface reconnaissance and shovel-testing techniques during previous CRM surveys (Branstner 1990a; Weir 1981). The 1990 Phase I investigations identified the presence of Late Woodland ceramics, debitage, and fire-cracked rock in a possible buried soil about 50 cm below the ground surface. Potential archaeological deposits in the sediments underlying the paleosol extended to a depth of about 1 m. Fluvial activity in the valley near the site, and therefore the potential for the burial of archaeological remains, was also indicated by a ^{14}C age estimate of 910 B.P. (Beta-40294) 230 cm below the surface in a trench adjacent to the site. Further testing of the site traced a 10–20-cm-thick, black paleosol across a 70-X-20-m area. It was largely confined to a ca. 20-m diameter area about 60 m west of the riverbank (Branstner 1991). The over- and underlying alluvium was up to 5 m thick and mainly consisted of undifferentiated dark brown silt. An isolated piece of fire-cracked rock at a depth of 1 m indicated other deeply buried deposits may also exist at the Flint River site.

In order to expose the archaeological deposits at the Flint River site, the "sterile" overburden was removed. Data-recovery efforts focused on two areas (Dobbs et al. 1993). The first area was an 87-m^2 excavation block centered over the original paleosol identified by Branstner (1991). The second area focused on a cluster of 28 pit features centered approximately 18 m west of the riverbank. The fact that this part of the site was not noted in a backhoe trench placed in this area resulted because the paleosol was indistinct and because artifacts were largely restricted to the features themselves. Thus, unless the trench actually bisected a feature, sampling error could easily result in a "missed" site. Several small excavation units (2–3 m^2) were also placed in isolated areas between 15 and 35 m west of the excavation block, where shovel tests identified the presence of either artifacts or a paleosol

STRATIGRAPHY. The Flint River site occurs within a band of very-poorly-to-somewhat-poorly drained silt loam (Iaquinta 1994). The general stratigraphy of the site was not complex and consists of a 5-m-thick sequence of silty- and fine-sand alluvium. A discontinuous paleosol occurs in the upper part of the alluvium, while discontinuous organic stringers occur at greater depths (Branstner 1991). Cultural materials were largely associated with the upper 50 cm of the deposits, although, reflecting the site's location on an active floodplain, a degree of reworking of the sediments and redeposition of artifacts at greater depths was also identified at the site (Dobbs et al. 1993).

The site lies on a low, natural levee along the river. The site topography influenced the structure and location of the archaeological deposits. The pit cluster that comprises the site occurs at the highest point of the levee. From there, the paleo-ground surface sloped gently west, decreasing by 0.7 m at the main excavation block and by 1.3 m at the western site margin (Dobbs et al. 1993). The upper stratum of the site at the levee is dark-brown, silty-clay loam that was considered "post-settlement alluvium" (PSA) (Dobbs et al. 1993). The upper 30 cm of PSA is partially plow-disturbed and thins progressively away from the levee. It is absent in the main excavation block. Although a thin (ca. 5-cm) zone of dark-grayish-brown, silty clay underlies the PSA in the levee, no buried paleo-Ab-horizon was identified.

The dark organic zone that was initially identified as a paleosol is restricted mainly to lower-lying areas of the floodplain west of the levee (i.e., away from the river). It occurred within the main excavation block as well as across a

218-m² area located 15–45 m farther west (Dobbs et al. 1993). A 40-cm-thick stratigraphic sequence was defined in the main excavation block. It consisted of a thin, dark-grayish-brown-to-black, silty-clay loam that was underlain by 10 cm of dark-yellowish-brown, silty clay. This was, in turn, underlain by a thin zone of dark-brown, silty clay and 15 cm of yellowish-brown, silty clay. Within the main excavation block, artifacts occurred mainly within the upper 10–30 cm of the stripped surface, although sometimes they were up to 40 cm deep (see Appendix C in Dobbs et al. 1993).

West of the main block, the stratigraphic sequence was slightly different. It consisted of 15–20 cm of dark-brown-silt-to-dark-grayish-brown, silty-clay loam that was underlain by 15–50 cm of dark-brown, silty-clay loam. The base of the sequence consisted of 15–20 cm of very-dark-gray, silty-clay loam. Other thin (less than 10 cm), discontinuous organic stringers were also noted in these units at varying depths. Although these stringers did not contain artifacts, a single piece of fire-cracked rock was associated with one about 1 m in depth. The dark color of the paleosol in the main excavation block and other low-lying areas resulted from organic accumulation in "standing water," rather than long-term soil development (Dobbs et al. 1993). Additionally, artifacts were also transported along the back edge of the levee some distance downslope.

DISCUSSIONS AND ARCHAEOLOGICAL SIGNIFICANCE. The Flint River site is a multicomponent Late Woodland agricultural camp that was occupied 800–600 B.P. Two primary areas of the site were investigated: a group of 23 pit features clustered along a low natural levee adjacent to the river and a cluster of three pit features about 20 m away from the river. The features at the site were grouped into a series of five clusters based on their spatial relationships to one another and suggest the presence of a number of different activity areas at the site (Dobbs et al. 1993). These clusters include small, basin-shaped hearths; small, basin-shaped pits (presumably associated with food processing); and large trash pits. The features contained abundant floral and faunal materials that were critical to identifying site activities and season of occupation (Parker 1996).

The artifact assemblage was modest and was dominated by ceramics and subsistence remains. The recovered ceramics consisted of nearly 4,700 sherds and a minimum of 16 vessels representative of two distinct wares: Wayne and Riviere wares (Dobbs et al. 1993). Wayne ware dominated the site, with 10 vessels that included undecorated, cord-marked, and fabric-impressed as well as Wayne Punctate vessels. Four Riviere ware vessels were recovered and included Vase Tool Impressed and Corded as well as Macomb Interrupted Linear vessels. Two vessels were unclassified. Except in a large trash pit, the distributions of the two ceramic ware types are mutually exclusive. Further ceramic cross-mends of Wayne ware vessels link the largest feature cluster with a smaller, nearby cluster and with the main excavation block. Similarly, cross-mends among the Riviere ware vessels also occur across the same three areas of the site.

Few lithic artifacts were recovered, and most occurred in features. These included < 200 flakes, a blade, a core, and a moderate amount of fire-cracked rock (Dobbs et al. 1993). The debitage reflects mainly late-stage reduction sequences, such as tool refurbishing or the manufacture of expedient flake tools. The paucity of lithic artifacts indicates that the tasks carried out at the site did not require extensive use of chipped stone tools and that tools were probably carried away after each episode of occupation.

The floral and faunal remains from the features represent some of the most important data retrieved from this site. Both were ubiquitous in the features. Floral remains included a variety of domesticated crops as well as collected nuts, seeds, fruits, grasses, and sedges. Wood charcoal reflected items that were either grown on site or collected during the occupations (Parker 1993). Maize, both Eastern Eight Row and some Midwestern Twelve Row varieties, occurred in all but four of the features and is the dominant cultigen at the site. Other domesticated remains included cucurbits, sunflower, and tobacco. A variety of wild plant resources were also exploited. Although not numerous, nuts were represented mainly by acorns, with lesser amounts of butternut, hickory, black walnut, and pignut hickory. Seeds were primarily *Chenopodium*. A broad array of fruits, including nightshade, huckleberry, sumac, elderberry, blackberry/raspberry, grape, blueberry, bunchberry, pin cherry, and plum, also occurred.

The faunal assemblage indicates that hunting was not an important activity conducted at the site (Martin and Richmond 1993). While faunal materials occurred in 27 features, half of the assemblage derived from two large trash pits. Small mammals, like vole and southern bog lemming, dominate the assemblage, while red squirrel and muskrat, along with lesser numbers of beaver, woodchuck, hare, raccoon, martin, skunk, and mink, also occur. Only a few large animals, such as deer and immature black bear, occur at the site. A small amount of bird bone, dominated by grouse and wild turkey with lesser amounts of woodpecker, passerine songbirds, duck, and loon bone, also occurs. Fish, which represents about 20 percent of the bone, includes Centrarchids (bass and sunfish), suckers (especially redhorse), yellow perch, and walleye, with fewer northern pike/pickerel catfish, bowfin, and gar. The age of the site is anchored by a series of 14 ^{14}C age estimates. These consist of date-pairs from six different features and are also the underlying basis for identifying two separate cultural components at the site (Dobbs et al. 1993). By using the calibrated two-sigma standard deviation, along with the ceramic types recovered from the dated features and ceramic cross-mends between features, two separate periods of occupation were identified between 796 and 656 B.P. (Dobbs et al. 1993). The earliest component is associated exclusively with Wayne-tradition ceramics and most likely dates to 796–735 B.P., although calibrated intercepts also occur at 876–874 and 821–815 B.P. The second component is represented by a mixture of Wayne- and Riviere-tradition ceramics and has a calibrated date range of between 693 and 661 B.P.

The ^{14}C chronology of site occupation and post–910 B.P. age for the alluvium in the flood basin west of the levee are similar to the depositional pattern at the Shiawassee River site. Up to 230 cm of deposition occurred within the Flint River floodplain over the past 900 years, while about 50 cm of sediment were deposited on the levee after occupation (ca. 600 B.P.). Although some "postsettlement" alluviation occurred at the site, as indicated by the +30-cm-thick plow zone, most of the post–910 B.P. sediment probably relates to increased alluviation associated with the premodern high lake-level (Little Ice Age flood events). The site area is naturally prone to flooding because it occurs at an inflection point from a relatively steep to more shallow channel gradient. Additionally, because the river lies only 3 m above Saginaw Bay, the site area is particularly susceptible to inundation during high-water levels of the Great Lakes. Importantly, artifacts were apparently transported downslope from the levee into the flood basin by flood events. The fact that these artifacts are generally absent from the plow zone suggests a protohistoric-to-prehistoric (i.e., presettlement) age for deposition. If most of the sediment that buried the Flint River site was PSA, then transported artifacts should also occur in the plow zone. The relatively thick deposition in the flood basin (230 cm since 910 B.P.) probably reflects the fact this area may have been an abandoned channel prior to 910 B.P. and was therefore a natural low spot that promoted deposition of fine-grained and organic-rich alluvium. Additionally, as an abandoned channel, it probably acted as a flood chute early in its history, and during this time even small floods contributed to its infilling. This could explain the difference in sediment thickness between it and the levee. The poor development of the "paleosol" is not surprising given the fact that it represented only a few hundred years of pedogenesis.

In summary, the Flint River site was a specialized warm-season agricultural camp used during the summer or early fall (Dobbs et al. 1993) that was buried by late prehistoric flooding associated with the premodern high-water levels of the Great Lakes. The lack of structural remains or a sheet midden associated with the pit clusters, as well as the moderate number of artifacts, indicated that occupation of the site was for only brief periods of time. Moreover, these occupations probably related to the tending of crops and to gathering and processing wild plant resources. The emphasis on small mammals and fish in the faunal assemblage is consistent with an expedient procurement strategy and suggests that hunting took place on an "as needed" basis. Furthermore, the location of the site on an active floodplain may have contributed to its short-term nature. Periodic inundation of the site during the premodern high-flood episode may have contributed to the lack of a sheet midden associated with the main feature cluster by eroding cultural debris from the levee and redepositing it in the lower-lying flood basin.

Zemaitis Site (20OT68)

LOCATION AND BACKGROUND. The Zemaitis site is located on the north bank of the Grand River in Ottawa County, Michigan, about 45 km upstream from the mouth of the river at Lake Michigan (Figure 5-1). The site is stratified and includes a late Holocene paleosol with associated archaeological material. The ground surface at the site varies in altitude from 183.5 m at the levee crest to 181 m in the back-swamp flood basin (Brashler and Kolb 1995). The altitude of river level at the site is about 180 m, which is approximately 3 m above the mean level of Lake Michigan and about 3–4 m below the top of the Grand River levee. Professional work at the site occurred in 1970, 1975, 1993, and 1994 as field schools from Grand Valley State University. The more recent phase of work focused on a buried portion of the site (Brashler and Garland 1993; Brashler and Kolb 1995).

The Zemaitis site sequence includes thick basal, late Wisconsinan "scroll-bar" sand and gravel that are overlain by 1–3 m of levee overbank, floodplain, and back-swamp organic-silt alluvial deposits (Brashler and Kolb 1995; Figure 5-8). The base of the levee sand is marked by the A-horizon of a well-developed middle-to-late Holocene paleosol. The paleosol includes Late Archaic-to-Early Woodland cultural material, while the overlying alluvium contains Middle-to-Late Woodland artifacts and features. ^{14}C age estimates indicate that the paleosol was buried sometime between 2200 and 1800 B.P.

STRATIGRAPHY. Brashler and Kolb (1995) informally divided the Zemaitis site depositional sequence into two main units: Soil-Sediment Package 1 (SSP1) and Soil-Sediment Package 2 (SSP2). The boundary between these units is marked by a buried surface (2Ab) soil horizon of a paleosol. SSP1 consists of crudely bedded, medium-to-coarse-grained sand and loamy sands. These are related to late Wisconsinan scroll-bar formation and are fluvial in origin (Brashler and Kolb 1995). This unit also forms the core of a levee, while the morphology of the levee partly derives from a remnant late Wisconsinan fluvial bar form. A paleosol, which includes Ab, Eb, and Bt soil horizons, formed on the top of this sequence. Lamella in the Bt horizon of the soil suggest that it underwent at least 3,800 years of development (Brashler and Kolb 1995). A ^{14}C age estimate from an archaeological feature extending from the Ab horizon of the paleosol yielded an age of 2200 B.P. (Beta-65115; Brashler and Garland 1993). Although this feature contained no diagnostic cultural material, the few points found in SSP1 were usually Terminal (Late) Archaic Dustin-Lamoka-Durst-type points. These points are somewhat older than indicated by the 2200 B.P. age of the feature, which implies that an Early Woodland occupation must have also occurred at the site.

SSP1 is overlain by SSP2 sand-to-loamy-sand alluvium. These sediments are generally coarsest on the levee and finer within back-swamp and flood-basin areas. Fluvial-style laminations were observed on the back side of the levee, indicating fluvial deposition (Brashler and Kolb 1995). Minor eolian sand deposits occur in a few isolated areas and are concentrated on the back side of the levee. Ten ^{14}C age estimates were derived from cultural contexts within SSP2. These range from 1840 to 790 B.P. Together with the SSP1 date, these suggest that burial of the SSP1 paleosol occurred sometime between 2200 and 1840 B.P. Abundant archaeological materials were recovered from SSP1, and most occurred in the upper part of the deposit. Diagnostic artifacts are consistent with the ^{14}C chronology and include a sherd and few points that mainly relate to the Middle and early Late Woodland. Brashler and Kolb (1995) suggest that deposition of SSP1 was rapid and may have represented only one flood event. They further attribute the vertical distribution of artifacts within the SSP2 profile to biomechanical mixing processes and suggest that such processes also have destroyed evidence for any depositional or cultural stratigraphy within SSP2.

In a few places near the crest of the levee, the upper 50 cm of SSP1 consists of an ephemeral, remnant, poorly developed surface soil (Ab) horizon that is overlain by 40–50 cm of grayish brown fine sand (Brashler and Kolb 1995). The upper 20 cm of this sand is plow-disturbed. Some of the archaeological features seem to originate from the buried A-horizon beneath this sand. Furthermore, although artifacts are associated with the buried A-horizon, the overlying brown sand and the overlying plow zone are devoid of artifacts. Brashler and Kolb (1995) suggested an eolian origin for these sands but also indicated they may derive from flood deposition on the levee.

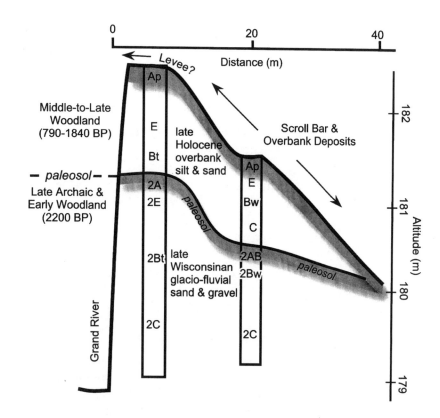

Figure 5-8. Stratigraphy of the Zemaitis site (after Brashler and Kolb 1995). See Figure 5-1 for generalized location of the site in the Saginaw Bay area.

DISCUSSION AND ARCHAEOLOGICAL SIGNIFICANCE. Geomorphologically, the most significant aspect of the Zemaitis site is the presence of a buried 2200 B.P. paleosol. The similarities in the sedimentological and cultural sequences at the Zemaitis, Schultz, and Bear Creek sites, despite the fact that the sites occur in different basins with diverse hydraulic configurations, are remarkable. Each of these sites includes a Late Archaic-to-Early Woodland (ca. 2500–2200 B.P.) midden or paleosol that was buried by extensive flood sediments about 2000–1700 B.P. Evidence for similar-age intensive flooding was also noted at the Marquette Viaduct and CERT sites in Bay City (see discussion of these sites above) and, as discussed in chapter 6 (see Figure 6-1), elsewhere in the Northeast and mid-Atlantic regions.

The discontinuous Ab horizon and overlying sand that comprise the upper 50 cm of SSP2 at Zemaitis are also of interest. Although possibly eolian, Brashler and Kolb (1995) indicated it could represent flooding on the levee. The fact that the sand occurs at the top of the sequence and is devoid of artifacts indicates that any associated flooding is relatively late and probably rapid. Based on minimum ^{14}C ages for archaeological material in the underlying SSP1 archaeological deposits, it must postdate about 800–700 B.P. Increased flooding along the Grand River is consistent with high lake-level and cooler, wetter conditions related to the Little Ice Age. If correct, the upper sand at Zemaitis is correlative with the upper part of the sequence from the Shiawassee River and Flint River sites in the

Saginaw Bay region, as well as with numerous other basins around the Great Lakes and the eastern United States (see Figure 6-1; Hayes and Monaghan 1997; Monaghan and Hayes 1997, 1998, 2001). The similarities in the ages of these cultural and associated sedimentological sequences have important implications not only for archaeological site burial and correlations of regional climate cycles but also for the reconstruction of prehistoric settlement and subsistence.

Significance of the Buried Archaeological Sites Distributions for Predictive Models

An important goal of our work is to develop a probabilistic model or framework that predicts where buried archaeological sites could or should occur. The locations of the relatively few sites that have been buried, discovered, excavated, and subsequently reported on is an important starting point for model development. In southern Lower Michigan, the majority of buried prehistoric archaeological sites discovered to date occur in three main environments: urban settings, eolian landforms, and floodplains. Site burial within each of these settings, however, occurs through very different kinds of processes, some of which severely constrain our ability to predict which areas within each environment might be more likely to include buried sites. In urban settings, such sites occur under fills or accretional deposits related to historic urbanization, whereas along shorelines, which relate mainly to modern or middle-to-late Holocene lake levels, they occur stratified in dunes formed during episodes of eolian reactivation. Although these two burial processes (urbanization and eolian reactivation) are important, they are probably not significant for the development of a probabilistic buried site predictive model. Their lack of significance for modeling purposes does not mean that sites that have been buried in these landforms are not important. Rather, urban landscapes and eolian features only rarely provide a set of specific physical or environmental parameters from which to assess the probability that archaeological sites could lie buried within them.

Eolian and urban landscapes by themselves are probably poor predictors of archaeological site potential and location. This is particularly true for urban settings. Except for their presence on the landscape, the urban fill and dune sand deposits that have buried sites possess few morphological, sedimentological, or environmental factors that may indicate the likelihood that either preserved Holocene surfaces or archaeological sites might be buried within them. Because many of the same cultural and environmental factors apply to the choice of settlement locations during both the historic and prehistoric periods (i.e., factors such as resource availability and transportation along rivers), some urban settings are also likely to encompass significant prehistoric archaeological sites (e.g., the Converse site in Grand Rapids and the Marquette Viaduct and CERT sites in Bay City; Table 5-1). Moreover, because prehistoric archaeological sites are often concentrated along river or lake waterfronts, which are low spots in the landscape, they are also likely to be filled in during the early phases of urbanization (see Demeter et al. 1994; Hambacher et al. 2003; Lovis ed. 2002). Unfortunately, even though burial of such sites during urbanization may be common, areas of high probability can seldom be distinguished from those of low probability. This is suggested because the actual filling procedures are largely unrelated to either climate change or natural processes. Furthermore, because such activities often completely altered the prehistoric landscape (Lovis 2004), only very broad environmental indications remain to suggest what types of environments might be hidden under accumulated accretionary deposits.

Similar issues exist for site burial within eolian landforms. Shoreline habitats are important components to prehistoric economic systems throughout prehistory (see chapter 4), and, as evidenced in northwestern Michigan (Table 5-1), archaeological sites may have commonly been buried within the associated dune complexes. Moreover, unlike the urban filling processes, eolian activity in Michigan during the late Holocene, particularly for the Great Lakes shoreline dune complexes, can be broadly correlated with lake-level cycles (Arbogast et al. 2002) and may therefore directly relate to the types of regional climate cycles discussed in chapter 3. Even though they can be clearly distinguished by their distinct morphology (i.e., barken, parabolic, longitudinal, etc.), dunes themselves present few surface clues from which to evaluate the buried-site potential within individual dune deposits. For example, the depositional processes responsible for their formation dictate that dunes are composed of a very limited range of sediment, mainly medium- and fine-grained sand, regardless of age, origin, or size. Consequently, one dune generally looks the same as another from a geological standpoint. Although archaeologically certain dune environments may be more productive and important than others, that data is not understood well enough to place it in a predictive framework for dune and shoreline environments.

From the standpoint of developing a predictive framework, stream alluviation is probably the most significant process and context for deep burial of archaeological sites. The majority of the buried sites discussed in this chapter were buried under mantles of alluvium. Moreover, most of the sites discussed in this chapter were buried during extended periods of episodic flooding apparently related to one of a few regionally pervasive climate cycles. These cycles have been described in detail in chapter 3 and have important implications for site burial but also have influenced both the development and visibility of the archaeological record idiosyncratically for distinct cultural periods. The utility of floodplain and other alluvial landforms in predicting archaeological site burial locations derives from the fact that they are typically composed of a great variety of sediment types and textural classes that reflect variability in specific depositional environments. Silt and fine-sand alluvium, for example, are generally associated with accretionary, relatively low-energy depositional environments, while coarse sand and gravel are typically deposited in higher-energy, often erosional fluvial environments. Thus, by mapping coarse versus fine-grained sediment on the floodplain, the relative potential for site preservation and burial can be determined spatially. These issues and how they relate to the development of a buried site predictive model are discussed in chapters 6 and 7.

One of the most important observations concerning the chronology and distribution of alluvially buried archaeological sites is the broad correlation apparent between episodes of site burial across various river drainages within the southern Michigan study region. Similarities in the sedimentological and cultural sequences for several stratified sites in the Grand River and Saginaw valleys, despite the fact that the sites occur on opposite sides of southern Michigan, for example, are significant for formulating a predictive framework, even if we recognize that such distant systems are graded to connected lake basins, that is, Lakes Michigan and Huron, respectively. The implication of such correlative alluvial sequences is particularly significant because similar flood histories have been noted throughout the eastern United States (see Figure 6-1; Monaghan and Hayes 1997, 1998; Hayes and Monaghan 1997). From a site-locational standpoint, however, determining whether these evident similarities in depositional sequence and environment are coincidental, or rare, or idiosyncratic, is an important question to address. Unfortunately, at present, insufficient numbers of river systems in Michigan have been either appropriately or intensively tested to determine whether this pattern is general. In addition, deep testing too often focuses only on whether archaeological resources are present, rather than on multidisciplinary approaches designed to understand the interplay between the geomorphology, chronology, depositional history, and archaeology of the floodplain or alluvial valley. One of the underlying goals of our work has been to raise archaeological awareness concerning the importance of transforming site excavation from an archaeology-specific and site- or project-specific approach into an interdisciplinary framework in which geologists, pedologists, archaeologists, and other specialists work collaboratively to understand how past populations behave within the site landform, reconstruct site or multisite depositional and site formational processes, and discover what this data reveals about the dynamic natural and cultural processes of the region. In chapters 6 and 7, we show how all of these factors can be integrated to develop a probabilistic framework for predicting where buried archaeological sites may occur.

Part Two

Site Burial Conceptual Models,
GIS Predictive Framework, and Deep Test
Methods and Standards

CHAPTER SIX

Predicting Archaeological Site Burial in the Great Lakes Region

Integrating the Archaeological and Earth Sciences Perspectives

Introduction

Numerous investigations undertaken over the past several years have revealed a distinctive pattern of Holocene-age alluvial landform construction, soil formation, and human occupation along rivers in the Great Lakes region. The results of many of these studies have been described in previous chapters and provide the basis for defining a pattern of Holocene climate variation and evaluating the response of natural and human systems to that pattern. Taken together, these data show that the middle and late Holocene, particularly after ca. 4000 B.P., is generally characterized by a pattern of broad, possibly millennial-scale cyclical variations in climate. Most of the data described in previous chapters derives only from geoarchaeological studies in Michigan. To place the Michigan data in a larger context, however, we must also include additional data from research projects spanning the lower Great Lakes in New York as well as the mid-Atlantic region of Pennsylvania, Virginia, Maryland, and Delaware (Figure 6-1B). This data will add a larger dimension to our understanding of variability in the middle and late Holocene environment and provide a test of the regional extent of some of the long-term patterns that we have noted in the Michigan data. As with the studies on which Part I of this volume is based, much of the data from outside Michigan also derives from geoarchaeological work associated with deep testing or archaeological site excavations from the Great Lakes regions of Ontario (Crawford et al. 1998) and New York, particularly associated with the construction of the Empire Pipeline (Monaghan and Hayes 1994a, 1994b, 1994c, 1994d; Weir et al. 1992; Weir et al. 1994). In addition, data from deep-testing studies in the mid-Atlantic and northeastern regions has been described and summarized by Monaghan and Hayes (1998, 1999, 2001) and Hayes and Monaghan (1997).

Data from the geoarchaeological studies undertaken around eastern North America reveals that similar trends in general environmental change occur throughout the Great Lakes and mid-Atlantic regions, particularly during the late Holocene (Figure 6-1). By integrating these regional data sets within the framework of Holocene environmental change, we have formulated a model that interrelates alluviation, soil formation, and archaeological site taphonomy into a dynamic, sedimentary framework. This model is conceptual and describes how the accumulation and character of floodplain archaeological deposits articulate with the attending sediment and soil record. It centers on how the floodplain record is altered because of changing sedimentation and weathering rates.

A focus on alluvial settings to develop a model of how, why, and when buried and stratified archaeological sites form makes a great deal of sense from an archaeological, as well as a geological, perspective. Because they are significant for human economic activities (such as food production and transportation), alluvial settings are important locations for archaeological sites. Additionally, such settings along streams, particularly near stream confluences, are relatively easy for prehistoric people to relocate and thus are typically reoccupied, leaving a long-term record of cultural change. This reoccupation is important given that alluvial landforms are constructed by net sediment accretion related to active stream channel migration and episodic flooding. Variability in the hydraulic characteristics of streams results in soil formation on the floodplain during periods of stability or in the construction, partial erosion, and burial of successive terrace surfaces, as well as any attending soil and archaeological deposits, during more dynamic periods. Taken over thousands of years, the stratigraphy of the sediment, soil, and archaeological deposits preserved in the resultant floodplain package indicates time-transgressive variation in the formation and human utilization of alluvial terraces. By comparing and noting commonalities in the

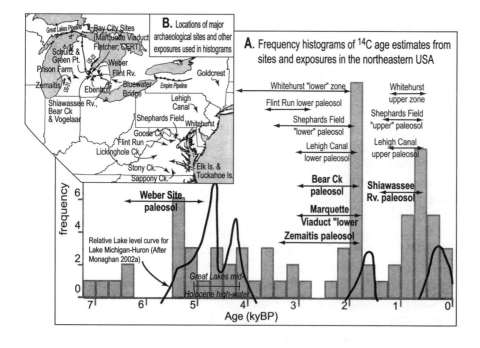

Figure 6-1. Histogram of ^{14}C age dates reported from selected alluvial locales and archaeological sites in the northeastern United States. Location of sites shown in insert map (B). Horizontal axis of histograms shows ages in ^{14}C years B.P. (grouped in 250-year intervals; vertical axis shows frequency of dates within each interval). The age and duration of buried and stratified sites are shown on the histogram (A). Sites from Michigan in bold. Lake-level curve for Lake Michigan-Huron (after Larsen 1985b) shown in gray dash line (after Monaghan and Hayes 1997, 1998, 2001).

alluvial and occupational histories from adjacent as well as far-flung drainage basins, major, regionally significant intervals of environmental change can be constructed.

This chapter will concentrate on three relatively simple ideas. The first focuses on delineating the role that cyclical deposition plays in forming and preserving archaeological sites. It builds on the fact, presented in chapter 3, that mid-to-late Holocene drainages in the Great Lakes region are characterized by variable, but generally short-term, periods of active floodplain sedimentation (see Figures 3-2, 6-1). These periods represent intervals when relatively more frequent and greater magnitude floods occurred, which consequently allowed more rapid and greater sediment accretion on the floodplain. These more active periods of alluviation are separated by generally longer intervals of relative fluvial quiescence or even in some cases of actual active landform degradation. Importantly, we believe that these "high-flood"/"low-flood" intervals are probably driven by significant regional, or perhaps even worldwide, climate events.

Our second idea follows axiomatically from the temporal variation in which sediment accumulates on the floodplain surface. It postulates that periods of active flooding and sediment accretion are followed by more extended times of relatively limited flooding. The formation and episodic burial of stable archaeological middenlike surfaces at several important archaeological sites in Michigan were discussed in chapter 5, while the periodic intervals of relatively greater flooding were outlined in chapter 3. The role that weathering of floodplain surfaces and sediments plays in affecting the visibility of buried archaeological components that may occur within an alluvial sequence has important ramifications not only for the formation of buried archaeological horizons but also for the accurate reconstruction of long-term trends in Holocene human settlement and subsistence patterns.

The first principle for understanding buried site formation is that archaeological horizons must have initially formed on the ground surface. This is true even if that surface now lies buried under thick alluvium. When deep features, such as pits, first formed, they must have extended from the surface. Even limited experience with the discovery of sites that occur at the modern ground surface demonstrates that the thicker and more artifact-rich an archaeological deposit is, the more visible and more easily found it will be on the floodplain. This is true for buried components observed in stratigraphic context as well, regardless of the exploration methods employed. This observation leads to an important quandary for archaeology site discovery and investigations. Site formation, development, and thus visibility in the stratigraphic record are largely time-dependent processes. The most visible and easily discovered sites are also the largest and most intensively and probably longest-occupied sites. Conversely, the smaller, shorter-term occupations, which contain fewer artifacts and features, are less visible and consequently less likely to be discovered, particularly in buried contexts. The dilemma for archaeological research, which will be discussed in more detail below, is that these small, more ephemeral sites may also be the most likely types to yield single-component cultural information delineating culturally specific, prehistoric human subsistence and settlement activities. Their low visibility in the stratigraphic record may result in significant loss of important settlement or subsistence information for entire classes of sites.

The occurrence of buried occupation middens and horizons and how they interact with natural processes are important from an archaeological perspective and are also significant geomorphologically because they reflect a basic, underappreciated element of floodplain development that actually controls the visibility of the archaeological record: the mean residence time of a horizon within a particular part of the weathering environment. For example, the extent of weathering on the floodplain surface, and consequently soil and archaeological site development, is controlled largely by the near-surface, mean residence time of a stratum. In terms of our discussion in this chapter, near-surface mean residence time is the length of time a specific stratum forms the ground surface on the floodplain without being buried by additional stream deposits. Data presented in chapters 3 and 5 demonstrated that the amount of time a particular stratum or stratigraphic unit lay at or near the ground surface was quite variable during the Holocene. Moreover, the duration of time that some particular stratigraphic or cultural unit lay on the surface is clearly dependent on how fast sediment accreted on the floodplain. The longer a stratum lay at or near the ground surface, the greater the weathering and the more soil development that occurred. From an archaeological standpoint, such variation in sedimentation and soil formation has important site taphonomic ramifications.

This, then, leads to the third idea, which is also the most important one for the purposes of this discussion. It examines how the notions of time-dependent accumulation of cultural material, cyclical deposition of alluvium, and near-surface, mean residence time of archaeological horizons interact to structure the preservation, stratification, types, and quality of archaeological sites that ultimately occur in floodplain settings. The development of the archaeological record in a stratigraphic sequence is largely dependent on the near-surface mean residence time of a particular host stratum. A host stratum is the stratigraphic unit that actually contains the archaeological material, features, and any other cultural record that encompass the archaeological site. Longer residence times in a near-surface context not only allow for more intense soil formation but also for the development of a thicker, more artifact-rich, and more easily recognized archaeological deposit. The downside of these circumstances is that the longer the deposit lies at the ground surface, the more natural and human agents act to disturb artifact and feature contexts. Conversely, rapid and deep burial generally preserves context because artifacts and features are isolated from direct surface disturbance and because they become stratigraphically separate from later occupation. By alternately occupying and accreting sediment on the floodplain, a stratified site eventually forms. A major emphasis of this chapter is directed toward understanding the role Holocene climate change played in sedimentation, soil formation, and human settlement patterns in order to deconstruct the nature and significance of stratification at archaeological sites.

Site formation and stratification processes are broadly tied to Holocene climate cycles. Chapters 2 and 3 presented how these cycles have been surrogately measured in Michigan through fluctuations in Great Lakes water levels as well as through episodic alluvial events (Arbogast et al. 2002; Larsen 1985b; Monaghan and Hayes 1997, 1998, 2001; Monaghan and Schaetzl 1994; Thompson and Baedke 1997, 1999). In order to understand the development of the archaeological record in alluvial environment and place it a proper process perspective, the linkages between climate change, lake-level variations, and the alluvial record introduced in chapter 3 will be reexamined and expanded by including data from other areas in the lower Great Lakes, Northeast, and mid-Atlantic regions.

Holocene Climate, Lake Levels, Alluviation, and Archaeological Sites

The middle and late Holocene is an archaeologically important period because it represents the development of "modern" climate and fluvial conditions in the Great Lakes region. By about 5000 B.P., the relatively warm-dry conditions of the Hypsithermal began to give way to the cooler-wetter conditions of the Xerothermic. In the upper Great Lakes, this period is also dominated by isostatic uplift and transgressive lake sequences. In chapters 2 and 3, we described how the classic outlet-controlled and climate-controlled models interact to more fully describe the middle and late Holocene variation in levels of both the modern and ancestral Lakes Michigan and Huron. The former model provided the generally accepted framework for the sequence of ancestral lake phases in the upper Great Lakes during most of the twentieth century, while the latter has only been recently embraced (see chapters 2 and 3; Figures 3-1, 3-2). In brief, the outlet-controlled model is based on the correct, but simplistic, notion that as the sole isostatically depressed North Bay outlet rebounded during the early Holocene, water in the Huron-Michigan basins transgressed, rose more than 100 m, and finally reached a base level 7 m above present to form Lake Nipissing. The North Bay outlet was abandoned 5000–4000 B.P., when it rose above the St. Clair River at Port Huron and established the present-day outlet configuration. Channel incision at Port Huron resulted in a progressive regional regression of lake level, and the most recent data shows that essentially modern levels were achieved before 3500 B.P. (Figures 3-1, 3-2). Although it broadly explains changes in Holocene lake level, the outlet-controlled model cannot account for the smaller-order, shorter-term variations that are particularly evident during the late Holocene (Figures 3-1, 3-2). These apparently reflect water-level responses to minor, short-term fluctuations in climate, which appear on lake-level curves constructed to depict the general, decades-to-centuries-scale lake cycles (Figures 3-1, 3-2; see also Larsen 1985b; Monaghan and Schaetzl 1994; Monaghan and Hayes 1998, 2001; Thompson 1992; Thompson and Baedke 1997, 1999). However, despite the fact that they broadly agree, the exact timing, duration, and magnitude of each curve vary somewhat (Figure 3-1). Such differences probably occur for a number of reasons, including the difficulty in determining the age and magnitude of lake-level events from field exposures as well as the fact that many of these lake-level events within individual curves are either minor in scope or not truly regional levels.

Even if they cannot agree on causes of the Holocene lake-level changes in the upper Great Lakes, most researchers concur that regional rises in water level occur when more water is input into the lake than can drain from the basin and that larger-scale, more long-lasting fluctuations in water level probably result from major changes in climate. The extent to which various specific factors affect lake level has been and continues to be the subject of much research. Certainly, obvious elements such as the season of precipitation (winter versus summer), amount of evapotranspiration around the basin, total seasonal snowpack amounts, and duration of precipitation events all affect the level of the Great Lakes to varying degrees. Individually, however, these tend to be short-term, year-by-year, seasonal factors that sometimes cancel each other out. Notably, the variation in the hydraulic input-output of the lakes that results in decades-to-centuries-long secular variation in basinwide water levels likely resulted from regional, or even continental-wide, long-term variation in climatic-related factors. Ultimately, these various factors combine to create relative climate extremes that result in the regional changes in water level. For example, increased rainfall combining with decreased evapotranspiration during extended wet-cool periods puts and keeps more water in the basin. Increased rainfall during these periods also raises regional groundwater levels, increases base-flow in rivers, and probably also results in more frequent and greater magnitude flooding. Conversely, increased evaporation of the lake surface combined with decreased precipitation (including snowfall) during dry-warm periods results in less water input into the basin. Regionally, these conditions also result in lowered groundwater tables, decreased base-flow, and, consequently, less frequent and less extensive flooding.

Although lake-level variation during most of the middle and late Holocene probably resulted from a combination of isostatic rebound and secular perturbation of regional climate, a major exception to this occurred earlier, as drainage was progressively transferred from North Bay to Chicago to Port Huron during Nipissing. Because the channel at Port Huron was eroded, widened, and otherwise reconfigured during this time, lake level may have varied because of modifications in the channel hydraulic properties rather than through strictly climatic permutations. Such changes could account for some of the short-duration variation suggested by Larsen (1985b) between about 5000 and 3000 B.P. (see Figures 3-1, 3-2) and, if so, may not reflect climatic variability at all. The issue of discerning climate-controlled from hydraulic-controlled lake-level changes underscores the underlying problem of using shoreline and nearshore sedimentological data as a surrogate measure of relative climate change. Because the sedimentological characteristics caused by changes in the littoral environments related to higher or lower lake level, for example, are the same regardless of the cause, the mid-Holocene, small-magnitude lake-level changes related to the reconfiguration of the upper Great Lakes outlet channel during the Nipissing and Algoma phases are nearly impossible to distinguish, based on shoreline sedimentology, from those caused by variation in climate. Shoreline processes are the same during lake-level excursions regardless of cause. Moreover, any small, cyclical lake-level variations during Nipissing I, which represents the maximum Nipissing level achieved (Lewis 1969; Larsen 1985b), would also be difficult to detect because of the transgressive nature of the event. This is suggested because much of shoreline evidence for minor 1–2-m variation similar to that observed during the late-Holocene-to-historic period (see chapter 3) may have been destroyed as lake level progressively rose during the transgression. In other words, the minor variations would have been overwhelmed by the grosser changes that occurred as the lake level rose to its maximum. Noting such water-level variability during the waning of the Nipissing phase and throughout the Algoma phase would be similarly difficult. This is suggested partly because the differences between Nipissing I, Nipissing II, and Algoma are about 2 m each, respectively, which is generally in the range of expected "climate-related" variation (Larsen 1985b; see also Figure 3-1). Additionally, the time difference between these events is 300–500 years in duration, which is within the range of many of the late Holocene secular lake-level variations (see Figure 3-1). Hence, many of the smaller-order lake-level variations observed during the mid-Holocene may be climate driven, may relate to outlet reconfiguration, or may be coincidental. In fact, they may also just be artifacts of preservation during the progressive Nipissing-to-modern-lake-phase regression. Importantly, we simply cannot distinguish these factors from each other based on shoreline data alone.

Some of the uncertainties of discerning climate-controlled from hydraulic- or outlet-controlled lake-level changes are lessened by focusing on changes in more inland stream channel sedimentation rates and modes. In fact, streams may be somewhat less sensitive than lake-level variation to minor perturbations in rainfall or temperature. Thus, their hydraulic changes may better reflect the longer-scale, more significant climatic fluctuations. Minor, shorter-term or seasonal changes in flooding are simply not well preserved in the floodplain record or can be related to developmental alluvial sequences without distinctive sedimentological or stratigraphic breaks. Moreover, if preserved and recognizable as distinctive events, they are usually associated with individual stream valleys and along only some of the stream reaches. In fact, as discussed below, most of the streams in the regions do not record many of the Holocene lake-level cycles discussed previously (Figure 3-1). Stream channel sedimentation, however, is not entirely independent of lake-level fluctuation. Rather, rising level in the Great Lakes enhances (or diminishes) sedimentation regimes near stream mouths, especially when regional climatic conditions promote extensive alluviation throughout the drainage basin.

Regardless of the cause of the minor transgressions and regressions of the upper Great Lakes during the late Holocene, they would have had significant effects on the sedimentary and hydraulic characteristics of rivers and streams draining into the lake. During high-water events, for example, stream base-level would have progressively risen, resulting in lowered stream gradients and greater potentials for floodplain aggradation. If related to wetter-cooler conditions, floods during such periods would have been even more intense, causing even more accretion. When the lake level fell during subsequent regressive phases, on the other hand, base-level lowered and stream gradients increased. Consequently, aggradation decreased, and, if related to warmer, dryer periods, flooding became more limited. Clearly, from the standpoint of buried archaeological site potential, the greatest impact on stream alluviation associated only with transgressing lake level is near the mouth of the river, while farther upstream, the effects would be less. Thus, the alluvial record of stream segments near the shorelines of the Great Lakes, although important, is likely affected at least as much by lake-level variation as by strictly climate-related processes. Stream channel alluviation in more upstream portions of the valley, on the other hand, is probably controlled more by climate-related phenomena and thus may be more likely to reflect pervasive, regionally extensive climate changes. The stratigraphy of floodplains in these areas may be more important for developing large-scale models of site burial and understanding the linkage between site burial, flooding, and secular variations in climate. By focusing on correlating periods of increased sedimentation between valleys around the region, particularly in upstream portions and from regions outside of the Great Lakes, with temporally equivalent variation in levels of the Great Lakes, better surrogate measures for more regionally pervasive changes in the longer-term climate may emerge.

As was true for lake level, however, alluvial events may also occur that are independent of climatic variation. Changes in the rate or timing of alluvial events within an individual drainage basin can occur, for example, because of natural or catastrophic changes in the morphological characteristics of the surrounding basin uplands. These changes include factors such as decreased vegetation on valley hillslopes, which promotes increased runoff, or catastrophic landslides along the valley walls. Even cutoffs of stream meanders can alter the rate of alluviation on short reaches of a river. Thus, only by observing streams where episodes of alluviation are registered in both the upstream and downstream portions of the river can the relative importance of climate factors be deduced. Furthermore, intervalley as well as interregional comparisons of alluvial events can shed light on larger-scale events. If similarly timed episodes of stream channel alluviation occur in adjacent and far-flung drainage systems, then even stronger evidence for significant regional long-term climate change can be proposed. If the water-level cycles shown in Figure 3-1 reflect significant regional variations in climate, then they should also be reflected in both upstream and downstream reaches of rivers throughout the region. Ultimately, this should be reflected as multiple sequences of several stacked, buried surfaces across large expanses of the floodplain. Geoarchaeological and geomorphological deep testing within the Great Lakes region, however, shows that although multilayer floodplain sequences are relatively rare, they occur in a few predictable intervals. We suggest that this reflects the importance of regional, long-term climate change in determining basinwide alluvial episodes.

Cycles of Late Holocene Alluviation and Archaeological Site Burial

Rather than using fluctuations in the levels of the Great Lakes alone as a measure of regionally pervasive, long-term climate change, identifying time periods when regional stream alluviation overlaps the intervals of high water-levels of the Great Lakes may offer a more complete picture of Holocene environmental change. Information collected from river valleys throughout the Great Lakes, Northeast, and mid-Atlantic regions will be used to augment the previously presented data from Michigan. This data includes the ages and duration of middens and other occupation horizons or buried paleosols from numerous stratified or buried archaeological sites as well as detrital organic material that has been incorporated in alluvial sediment that overlies these archaeological deposits. In addition, where available, dated organic material reported from alluvial sequences at other deep-test locations has also been included. By mapping the alluviation episodes from throughout the areas mentioned above and by comparing their ages with the duration of occupation horizons, we hope to demonstrate that temporally correlative clusters of flood intervals could be traced regionally.

The data clearly shows that not only do the ages of alluvial intervals cluster, so do the ages and durations of buried occupation horizons (Figure 6-1). The flood intervals are indicated by clustering of histogram bars marking the ^{14}C ages of organic material collected from alluvial sequences (Figure 6-1A). The height of each of the bars in the histogram indicates the number of dates that occur within consecutive intervals of 250 ^{14}C years (uncalibrated). The more dates that occur within a specific interval, the higher the histogram bar. Thus, a regionally pervasive flood event is implied when many dates cluster within a relatively brief interval of time. For example, the clusters of dates that occur about 2000 B.P. and about 500 B.P. probably mark significant regional flood intervals. The ages and general durations of the archaeological horizons and/or buried paleosols that occur within alluvial sequences are also plotted on the histogram. The duration of each is represented by the length of the horizontal lines that occur below the site names (Figure 6-1A). The locations of the sites are shown on the insert map (Figure 6-1B).

The age and duration of occupation horizons and paleosols, which broadly indicate length of human occupation at the site, cluster into a few distinct groupings. These are most apparent just prior to 2000 B.P. and 500 B.P. (Figure 6-1A). Importantly, terminal ages for occupation of these buried horizons, which probably correspond with the timing of site burial, match with major clusters of ^{14}C ages that mark significant episodes of alluvial deposition. The implication for this relationship is crucial for developing a model describing episodic site burial during the late Holocene: groups of similar-age archaeological horizons and paleosols were buried by regionally pervasive alluviation events. We believe that the more or less discrete groupings of paleosol and/or relatively long duration occupation horizons, and well as the relatively high numbers of ^{14}C ages grouped into specific, mainly short, time intervals, are significant. This data supports our contention that significant regional deposition cycles dominate the late Holocene throughout the Great Lakes, Northeast, and mid-Atlantic regions. This is suggested because these intervals occur within far-flung basins around the region and therefore likely represent more than just local, brief perturbations in precipitation or hydraulic characteristics of individual drainages. Rather, the regional overlap of the flood intervals, indicated by the groupings of alluvially derived ^{14}C ages, and the stable periods, indicated by the age and duration of paleosols and buried occupation horizons, both suggest that regionally correlative variations in climatic patterns must have occurred. Given that the overlap of data during specific intervals is recorded in river valleys from the Chesapeake Bay region to northern Michigan (Figure 6-1B), this pattern may be continental or even global in scope.

More detailed scrutiny of Figure 6-1, particularly in reference to the lake-level data presented in chapter 3 (Figure 3-2; Monaghan and Schaetzl 1994), indicates that three major alluvial intervals occur in the Great Lakes region. Based on the generalized temporal extent of the clusters of ^{14}C ages (i.e., histograms in Figure 6-1A), these intervals constitute regionally pervasive but relatively short-term periods of extensive alluviation. The oldest of these intervals occurs about 5000–3000 B.P., the second 2000–1500 B.P., and the final one after about 600 B.P., just prior to European contact. Not surprisingly, these also roughly correspond with the high lake-level events defined by Monaghan and Schaetzl (1994) and Monaghan (2002). Based on their ^{14}C ages, the oldest of these in Michigan is associated with the Nipissing transgression, although the latter part (ca. 4000–3500 B.P.) may correspond with regional cooler-wetter conditions related to the Xerothermic and the development of the modern Lakes Michigan and Huron. Increased flooding during the interval was presumably related both to transgressing, high-water phases of Nipissing I and to hydraulic conditions of the Port Huron outlet as the modern lake level formed. That the flooding in the Great Lakes region may be at least partly related to climatic conditions is indicated because a similar increase in sedimentation associated with the end of Hypsithermal has been noted in the Mississippi Valley (Bettis and Hajic 1995).

A second, younger interval, from 2000 to 1500 B.P., also occurs during the late Holocene and is marked by a relatively tight cluster of many dates. In Michigan, this interval is apparently related to increased flooding correlative with a late Holocene post-Algoma high-water phase discussed in chapter 3. It occurs throughout the region and is particularly evident by site burial along many major drainages in the mid-Atlantic and Great Lakes and has been noted in the mid-Atlantic and Northeast (Hayes and Monaghan 1997; Raber and Vento 1990) and the Great Lakes (Monaghan and Hayes 1997, 1998, 2001; Monaghan and Schaetzl 1994). The regionally pervasive nature of this event is particularly evident because sites were buried along nearly every major stream in the mid-Atlantic during this interval (Figure 6-1B).

The youngest flooding interval occurs after about 600 B.P. and is almost certainly related to increased flooding during the Little Ice Age, a worldwide cool-wet period. Although it is mainly prehistoric, some of the increased alluviation after about A.D. 1700 may reflect increased sediment input into the drainage due to accelerated erosion related to land-clearing activities during Euro-American settlement. This is probably more important and problematic within the mid-Atlantic region than in Michigan, because Euro-American land clearing was not extensive in the upper Great Lakes until after the middle nineteenth century. In Michigan, the interval is related to the premodern high-water phase described in chapter 3. That increased alluviation during a similar time period has been noted in the Great Plains (Bettis and Mandel 2002), the Northeast and mid-Atlantic (Hayes and Monaghan 1997; Monaghan and Hayes 2001; Raber and Vento 1990), and Great Lakes (Monaghan and Hayes 1997, 1998, 2001; Monaghan and Schaetzl 1994) indicates the regional extent of the interval.

The three major flooding intervals noted apparently represented relatively short-duration (only a few-hundred-year-long) events and are separated from each other by longer (several-hundred-year-long) periods of comparative fluvial quiescence. Interestingly, the latter two of these "high-flood"/"low-flood" periods form cycles that are about a millennium in duration (Monaghan and Hayes 1997, 1998, 2001). At least in Michigan, alluviation associated with the earliest period, which relates in part to the Nipissing and Algoma interval in the Great Lakes, is probably not strictly or completely climate controlled. As discussed above, it may also reflect flooding caused by basinwide reconfiguration of the upper Great Lakes drainage system. Insufficient numbers of sites, particularly away from the Great Lakes shoreline, exist to test this argument. We believe, however, that the two other late Holocene flood intervals, as well as the intervening stable periods, are mainly related to secular changes in the regional climate. The clear association of the post–600 B.P. premodern high flood interval with the Little Ice Age, for example, may also mean that the preceding stable period, the premodern low, is related to warmer, milder conditions during the Medieval Warm interval (Monaghan and Hayes 2001; Monaghan and Schaetzl 1994).

The dated samples used to isolate the pattern of Holocene deposition (Figure 6-1A) derived from a mixture of in situ and detrital organic materials. The ^{14}C sample base used to identify the pattern of the alluviation episodes (i.e., the bars of the histogram shown Figure 6-1A), for example, was derived mainly from detrital materials collected in floodplain sequences. Only rarely were in situ samples of organic materials included. The data used to show the "stable" periods (i.e., the horizontal bars marking the duration of occupation or paleosol; Figure 6-1A), on the other hand, was mainly collected from occupation horizons at buried or stratified archaeological sites. These samples and the overall occupation horizon were in place and not reworked. In fact, the identification of these in situ occupation horizons, although relatively few in number, is essential for reconstructing the chronology of episodic flooding. These horizons provide the actual measures for the timing and duration of the periods of stability and mark intervals when little alluvium accumulated on the floodplain surface. This is because these horizons do not date the alluvial "events" of the sequence. Rather, they mark where the ground surface was throughout the stable periods, allow measurements of relative sediment accretion on the floodplain, and record the duration for intervals of fluvial quiescence. In addition, the fact that these horizons derive from archaeological sites allows for even more detailed measures of the full duration of floodplain stability. The material cultural ages of artifacts from the horizons not only provide a check on the reliability of ^{14}C dates taken from the horizon but can also extend the chronology because they themselves provide a range of absolute time measurements by cross-referencing them to dated sequences at other sites. Furthermore, through repeated occupation, these horizons provide data on human responses to local and regional environmental change.

Several stratified archaeological sites in Michigan (Figures 3-1, 5-1) include occupation and soil horizons that were buried by various of the three major regional flood events discussed above and discussed in detail previously (see chapters 4 and 5). Archaeological sites reflecting the Nipissing-to-Algoma alluvial events include the Ebenhoff, Weber I, and Bear Creek sites in the Saginaw Bay region (Figure 5-1). In addition, sediments related to the Nipissing transgression were also identified from the Schultz, Green Point, Vogalaar, and Bear Creek sites (Fitting, ed. 1972; Monaghan and Schaetzl 1994; Wright 1964; Figure 5-1). Excellent examples of stratified sites related to the 2000–1500 B.P., late Holocene flood interval in Michigan include the Bear Creek (Branstner and Hambacher, eds. 1994) and Schultz sites (Fitting, ed. 1972; Lovis, Egan, Smith, and Monaghan 1994; Lovis et al. 2001) in the Saginaw Bay region and the Zemaitis site (Brashler and Kolb 1995; Brashler and Mead 1996) along the Grand River in western Michigan (Figures 3-1, 5-1; see also chapters 3 and 5). Each of these sites contains a well-developed paleosol and associated Late Archaic-to-Early Woodland occupation overlain by post–2000 B.P. flood deposits.

By combining the ages and detailed sedimentary histories of buried archaeo-logical sites with the sketchier alluvial histories from around the Great Lakes and broader northeastern United States, a model describing the processes re-sponsible for site formation in alluvial settings can be constructed. This is actu-ally more of a "conceptual framework" than a model and describes the relationship between environmental change and archaeological site formation in alluvial landforms. By understanding that archaeological sites are formed by the unique relationships that artifacts and features have with sedimentation and pedogenesis, the details of both the environmental and human record can be more easily teased apart. Importantly, this can result in a better understanding of just how the environment and cultural spheres interact and represents the basis on which the locations of buried sites might be predicted within a proba-bilistic framework.

Summary of Depositional Cycles, Climate, and Archaeological Site Formation Processes

The relationships between floodplain development, climate, and cycles of allu-viation are integrated and summarized in Figure 6-2. These relationships have important effects on and partly structure the archaeological record that may be preserved within the floodplain stratigraphy. The summary depicts the three millennial-scale deposition cycles identified during the mid to late Holocene (Figures 3-2, 6-1) and diagrammatically illustrates how these cycles relate to fluc-tuation in relative floodplain alluviation rates (shown along the horizontal axis) through time (represented by the vertical axis). Additionally, correlations with important regional climatic events are also suggested. Although the exact causes for the cyclical deposition pattern (Figure 6-2) are unknown, its correlation with distinct, long-term, regional climatic fluctuations is probably more than coinci-dental. For example, if the temporal correspondence of the most recent flood interval with the Little Ice Age and the preceding period of quiescence with the Medieval Warm is analogous with the earlier cycles, then increased flooding re-sults from long-term changes to cooler, wetter climates, while the intervening intervals of quiescence reflect relatively warmer, dryer periods. Moreover, the timing and regional extent of these cycles then must reflect millennial-scale changes in regional, if not continental, climate. These relationships further imply that the broad interval of limited flooding and soil formation prior to 2000 B.P. and the dramatic increase in alluviation between 2000 and 1500 B.P. may demonstrate that a similar pattern in climate fluctuation occurred between 3000 and 1500 B.P. These factors have clear import for Late Archaic as well as Early and Middle Woodland settlement and subsistence models.

In addition to its importance for understanding the impact of short- and long-term changes in Holocene climate and reconstructing prehistoric human settlement systems, the cyclical depositional pattern (Figure 6-2) also has critical implications for locating buried archaeological sites. The basic premise of our thesis, and its significance to modeling and predicting site burial, rests on the assumption that variability in the responses of streams to changes in climate results in distinct fluctuations in the rate of sediment accretion and that these correspond with climate cycles that are correlative across the region. These

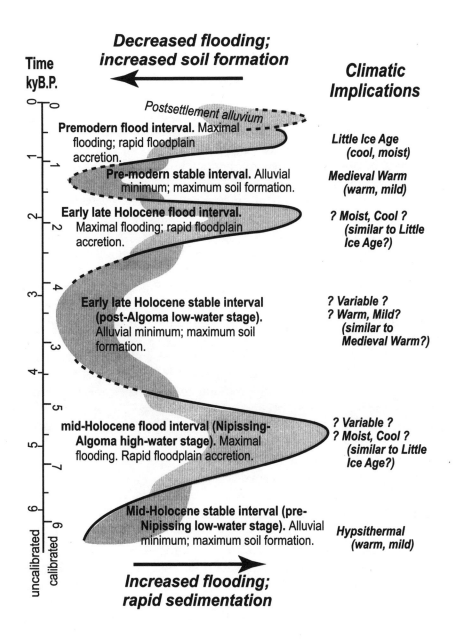

Decreased flooding; increased soil formation

Time kyB.P.

Climatic Implications

Postsettlement alluvium

Premodern flood interval. Maximal flooding; rapid floodplain accretion.

Little Ice Age (cool, moist)

Pre-modern stable interval. Alluvial minimum; maximum soil formation.

Medieval Warm (warm, mild)

Early late Holocene flood interval. Maximal flooding; rapid floodplain accretion.

? Moist, Cool ? (similar to Little Ice Age?)

Early late Holocene stable interval (post-Algoma low-water stage). Alluvial minimum; maximum soil formation.

? Variable ? ? Warm, Mild? (similar to Medieval Warm?)

mid-Holocene flood interval (Nipissing-Algoma high-water stage). Maximal flooding. Rapid floodplain accretion.

? Variable ? ? Moist, Cool ? (similar to Little Ice Age?)

Mid-Holocene stable interval (pre-Nipissing low-water stage). Alluvial minimum; maximum soil formation.

Hypsithermal (warm, mild)

uncalibrated   calibrated

Increased flooding; rapid sedimentation

Figure 6-2. The millennial-scale cycles in major alluvial and lake transgressive episodes during the middle and late Holocene in the upper Great Lakes region (after Monaghan and Hayes 1997, 1998, 2000).

depositional cycles have important and predictable consequences for the archaeological record in floodplains and dictate the types of processes that will act to preserve or destroy associated archaeological sites. Consequently, not only are the types of archaeological sites that may form on the floodplain surface circumscribed by the processes of floodplain development, but those processes are reflected in the very archaeological record preserved at the site as well. For example, greater temporal variation in cultural material within a vertically discrete, relatively thin deposit, such as the multicomponent, middenlike sites that commonly occur in Michigan, implies limited alluvial accretion, rare flooding, and general floodplain stability. Conversely, more limited temporal diversity within a thick unit indicates rapid accretion of the floodplain and more intensive flooding.

The secular variation in deposition during the late Holocene places limits on the types of archaeological sites that can occur in floodplain settings in Michigan, limits that are essentially independent of cultural processes. During periods of stability, the floodplain surface undergoes extended periods of weathering and greater soil development. Sites formed during such times have longer near-surface residence time and are better developed, both archaeologically and pedogenically. During more dynamic periods, however, accelerated rates of alluviation lead to the construction, partial erosion, and burial of successive terrace surfaces and any attending soil and archaeological deposits. Sites formed on the floodplain during such intervals have significantly shorter near-surface residence times and may also have a greater potential for erosion. Such limitations will probably result in the formation of buried archaeological sites with greater apparent visibility during certain time periods, such as when middenlike sites are more commonly developed. These site types are more visible simply because they are easier to see and more likely to be found than the thinner, more artifact-poor, shorter-term occupation horizons typically formed during intervals of rapid alluviation.

Over time, the stratigraphy of the sediment, soil, and archaeological deposits preserved in the floodplain provides a time-transgressive record of the formation of alluvial landforms as well as of human subsistence and settlement. Regional correlations of major occupation horizons provide timing and durations for periods of regional alluvial stability, just as basin-by-basin correlations of episodes of alluviation provide timing for periods of regional flooding. Taken together, these data provide the foundation of a model that systematically interrelates climate change to landform development.

The Model for Archaeological Site Formation in Alluvial Settings

Figure 6-3 summarizes the interrelationships between floodplain sedimentation, soil formation, and archaeological site development described throughout this chapter. The graph on the left side of the diagram is similar to Figure 6-2 and includes the three "flood" periods proposed above. The right side of the diagram shows how variations in flooding through time relate to floodplain accretion and archaeological site formation by depicting the stratigraphy at an "idealized" floodplain archaeological site. During intervals of relatively limited flooding, which are indicated when the line shown the left side of the diagram (informally, the "flood-line"; Figure 6-3) moves to the left, sediment only very slowly accretes on the floodplain surface. This results in a relatively longer near-surface residence time for the stratum (i.e., a "stable" ground surface) and, concomitantly, more intense pedogenesis. Even though a relatively long time interval is indicated (see left side of Figure 6-3), these stable periods are represented by vertically quite limited deposits on the archaeological side of the diagram (see right side of Figure 6-3). This reflects only limited alluviation during the interval.

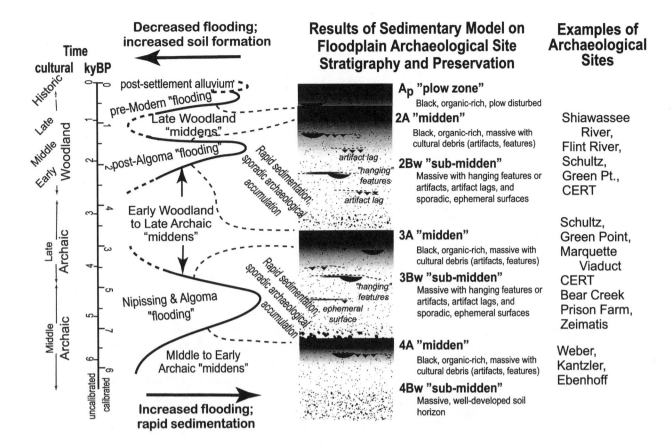

Time cultural kyBP

Decreased flooding; increased soil formation

Results of Sedimentary Model on Floodplain Archaeological Site Stratigraphy and Preservation

Examples of Archaeological Sites

Historic
Late — Middle — Early   Woodland
Late Archaic
Middle Archaic

post-settlement alluvium
pre-Modern "flooding"
Late Woodland "middens"
post-Algoma "flooding"
Early Woodland to Late Archaic "middens"
Nipissing & Algoma "flooding"
Middle to Early Archaic "middens"

Rapid sedimentation; sporadic archaeological accumulation

artifact lag
"hanging" features
artifact lag

ephemeral surface
"hanging" features

uncalibrated / calibrated

Increased flooding; rapid sedimentation

A$_p$ "plow zone"
Black, organic-rich, plow disturbed

2A "midden"
Black, organic-rich, massive with cultural debris (artifacts, features)

2Bw "sub-midden"
Massive with hanging features or artifacts, artifact lags, and sporadic, ephemeral surfaces

3A "midden"
Black, organic-rich, massive with cultural debris (artifacts, features)

3Bw "sub-midden"
Massive with hanging features or artifacts, artifact lags, and sporadic, ephemeral surfaces

4A "midden"
Black, organic-rich, massive with cultural debris (artifacts, features)

4Bw "sub-midden"
Massive, well-developed soil horizon

Shiawassee River, Flint River, Schultz, Green Pt., CERT

Schultz, Green Point, Marquette Viaduct CERT Bear Creek Prison Farm, Zeimatis

Weber, Kantzler, Ebenhoff

Longer residence time in a near-surface context not only allows for greater soil formation but also for the development of a much thicker, more artifact-rich archaeological deposit. Because only very limited alluviation occurs during this interval, however, the contexts for artifacts and features are commonly disturbed. This is because the longer an object lies on the ground surface, the greater the probability of its displacement. Also, given that these floodplain locales are highly desirable for human habitation, people return to the same site year after year. The longer the ground surface remains unchanged, the more artifact mixing will occur during the periodic reoccupations of the site. Common site activities like pit digging, for example, typically mix the upper few tens of centimeters of sediment by intruding into older deposits, burying younger artifacts, reexcavating older tools, and generally mixing the soil within 10–20 cm (or more) of the ground surface. Over time, these and similar processes form a sometimes >50-cm-thick, dark, organic-rich, "middenlike" deposit, as has been described from several sites in the region (see chapters 4 and 5).

These deposits are commonly rich in cultural debris but are also often poor, or at best obscure, in archaeological context. Because of the lack of reliable internal stratigraphy, such horizons are frequently more like plow zones than

Figure 6-3. The interrelationships between lake-level variation, floodplain alluviation, and archaeological site formation based on the millennial-scale cycles (after Monaghan and Hayes 1997, 2000).

"undisturbed" archaeological deposits; even the most careful and detailed excavation method will often recover only marginally reliable vertical and contextual information. In the absence of intact vertical stratigraphy, Archaic points may lie within Late Woodland pits, while cord-marked pot sherds may be mixed in Archaic fire-pits. Thus, because they commonly represent 1,000–2,000 years of occupation, these midden sites are a challenge to use for reconstructing subsistence and settlement information for specific time periods or for understanding the spatial distribution of temporally related artifacts. In fact, given the uncertainty in the vertical or horizontal position of any specific artifact, making significant statements about their cultural context and meaning is problematic (see O'Shea and Shott 1990 for an example of this problem).

Unlike the previous stable, "low-flood" period, during the intervals of increased flooding, which are indicated when the "flood line" moves toward the right (Figure 6-3), sediment rapidly accretes on the floodplain surface. As a consequence, the previous ground surface (or soil or archaeological site) is buried and at least partly removed from near-surface forms of disturbance. The more frequent and intense the flood periods, the more rapid and deep the stratum and related archaeological deposits are buried. This is not to say, however, that only one large flood occurred during these intervals. In fact, we believe that these flood intervals commonly lasted for a few centuries and may have included several very large floods with smaller-magnitude floods occurring relatively frequently in between the larger. Evidence for this exists at many sites, most notably at the Schultz, Green Point, and Bear Creek sites in the Saginaw Bay region (Figures 3-1, 5-1, 5-3).

In fact, in Michigan, flooding was quite extensive, particularly during the Middle Woodland period in the Saginaw River drainage basin (Branstner and Hambacher, eds. 1994; Lovis, Egan, Smith, and Monaghan 1994; Lovis et al. 2001; Monaghan and Schaetzl 1994). Evidence for multiple flood events can be noted in the stratigraphic records from sites in the area, supporting the idea that the flood intervals did not represent a single event but rather embodied a few-centuries-long period of comparatively more frequent and more intensive flooding. At the Schultz site, for example, flooding just after 1800 B.P. is indicated by a 50–70-cm-thick, coarse, poorly sorted sandy silt that was deposited during a brief (200–300 years) interval (Lovis, Egan, Smith, and Monaghan 1994; Lovis et al. 2001; Speth 1972; see also chapter 5). The period of most intense flooding occurred mainly during the Green Point phase Middle Woodland occupation of the site, which is also the period of greatest occupation (as measured by high ceramic densities and high frequencies of lithics and subsistence materials). Multiple floods were demonstrated by Lovis et al. (2001), who noted that numerous discrete, discontinuous Middle Woodland cultural deposits occur throughout this "flood" layer. Their presence attests to the fact that flooding was episodic during the interval and also shows that people could periodically occupy the floodplain at the site during the interval. This data indicates that the site was likely only seasonally flooded and probably did not even flood each year. Moreover, the altitude of this sequence of Middle Woodland occupations also allows an approximate upper limit to the lake level associated with the post-Algoma high-water interval (Figure 3-2). If the level of Lake Huron was actually high enough to flood most of the Schultz site, as suggested by Speth (1972), it was only for a very brief period of a few years.

Similar, but older (ca. 4000–3500 B.P.) Archaic-age, discontinuous cultural zones also occur below a Transitional-to-Early Woodland (2500–2200 B.P.) "midden" (paleosol) at Bear Creek, located about 15 km upstream from Schultz (Figure 5-1; Branstner and Hambacher, eds. 1994; Monaghan and Schaetzl 1994). As at Schultz, the Bear Creek midden is overlain by a 20–30-cm-thick sequence of fine-grained alluvium that was deposited during an increase in flooding after about 1900 B.P. (Monaghan and Schaetzl 1994). Correlative depositional sequences were also described at the Marquette Viaduct locale of the Fletcher site in Bay City (Figure 5-3), where a Middle Woodland feature from the lower portion of a Woodland midden was truncated by extensive flooding soon after 1740 B.P. (Lovis et al. 1996). In addition to the extensive data from the Saginaw Bay region, an archaeological occupational horizon that was also buried by flood deposits after about 2000 B.P. occurs at the Zemaitis site along the lower Grand River on the opposite side of the state from Saginaw Bay (Figures 3-1, 5-1; Brashler and Kolb 1995). The floods at the Zemaitis site were apparently extensive, because they overtopped a 2–3-m-high natural levee and ultimately raised the levee by another 1–2 m (Brashler and Kolb 1995).

Such zones and layers as evidenced at the Schultz and Bear Creek sites probably represent brief occupations on ephemeral floodplain surfaces and as such are often very difficult to recognize or trace. At best, they occur related to poorly formed A/C soil horizons. More commonly, the associated buried ground surface is usually elusive in a profile and typically may only be traced by minor variations in sediments (i.e., texture, organic content, etc.) or by connecting sporadic, ephemeral cultural features and occasional artifacts that appear to "hang" or "float" in an otherwise massive alluvium (Monaghan and Hayes 1997, 1998). Regardless of their apparent dubious context, these artifacts, particularly when related to ephemeral surfaces and/or "hanging" features, can be in situ and probably occur along remnants of short-lived ground surfaces (Figure 6-3). Just because they are unrelated to obvious surface soil horizons does not mean that they were "dragged down by tree roots" or rodents or termites or other such commonly postulated phenomena. Their occurrence in what is today's subsoil horizon is not necessarily related to bioturbation or biomantle processes.

The recognition of the types of ephemeral buried archaeological horizons, zones, and layers described above is significant to understanding site-development processes in dynamic floodplain environments. They actually represent short-term, sometimes even one-time, occupations. Even though they may not include abundant artifacts or features, the primary archaeological context of these zones is often preserved. Importantly, just because artifacts or features occur in the B horizon or subsoilcontext and are not related to any obvious surface soil horizon does not preclude their being in situ. Because the floodplain is such a dynamic environment, with the potential for concurrent rapid sedimentation and erosion, the excavation of associated archaeological sites is a complex process necessitating a multidisciplinary format. Developing an excavation strategy, not to mention postexcavation interpretation, for such sites may require more background and a greater breadth of experience in soil and earth science than is standard in most anthropology programs. The interrelationships of cyclical deposition to floodplain accretion, weathering processes, and archaeological site formation are complex. Working out how the various components that make up the archaeological, soil, and sedimentary packages interact to form floodplain sites is a process that should be undertaken jointly in a multidisciplinary research framework that incorporates the expertise of archaeologists with that of earth and soil scientists.

Summary and Discussion of Significance of the Model to Site Discovery

A model relating floodplain sedimentation, soil formation, and archaeological site development (Figure 6-3) was formulated by integrating more than two decades of geoarchaeological research in Michigan. It is based on the premise that sites were buried episodically during relatively brief, few-hundred-year-long, climate-driven intervals of more intense and higher-frequency flooding. In Michigan, these intervals occurred between about 5000 and 3500 B.P., between 2000 and 1500 B.P., and just prior to European contact. The high-flooding intervals are separated by longer periods of relative fluvial quiescence, when flooding was significantly less. During these intervals, only limited accretion occurred on the floodplain surface, allowing great weathering and more developed soil profiles to form. Taken as a whole, we believe that these high-to-low flood intervals reflect secular changes in regional climate that not only affected stream hydraulics and sedimentation and caused cyclical variations in the level of the Great Lakes but also affected human subsistence systems by altering environmental conditions. From a site predictive standpoint, our model of cyclical burial of sites also structures the archaeological record by limiting the types of sites that might be occur on floodplains during specific cultural periods. Importantly, the types of site formation and preservation processes resultant from the secular changes in deposition are generally independent of time-specific cultural processes. Through time, our model (Figure 6-3) predicts that archaeological "middenlike" sites will form more frequently on the floodplain during periods of floodplain stability and that more sites that commonly include stacked ephemeral, discontinuous, but culturally more cohesive occupation horizons should develop during intervals of rapid floodplain accretion.

The earliest flooding interval noted in the model during which archaeological sites may be regularly buried is related to the Nipissing transgression (Nipissing I) and subsequent regression through Nipissing II and Algoma. As such, increased flooding during this interval is at least partly related to isostatic rebound and hydraulic reconfiguration of the Port Huron outlet. However, it also correlates with regional, cooler, moister middle Holocene climatic changes that occurred as the Hypsithermal ended. At least one significant buried middenlike Middle Archaic site, Weber I (Figure 5-4), which represented nearly 1,500 years of occupation (Monaghan, Lovis and Fay 1986), was buried during this interval. Additionally, somewhat younger stratified Middle and early Late Archaic deposits buried in accretionary deposits related to the Nipissing transgression have been noted at the Ebenhoff site (Figure 5-7). These deposits occur within beach deposits and are partly reworked (Dobbs 1993). Middle or early Late Archaic ephemeral horizons and artifacts, which probably represent similar short-term occupation, also occur in stratified context at the Bear Creek site (Figure 5-6). The stratification of these deposits apparently occurred as alluvium or "estuary-like" deposits accreted during the Nipissing transgression (Monaghan and Schaetzl 1994).

Importantly, each of these Middle and early Late Archaic occupations is overlain by younger, relatively well developed, middenlike horizons formed during subsequent Late-to-Terminal Archaic and/or Early Woodland occupations at these sites. At Weber I, the Middle and Late Archaic occupation midden horizons are separated by culturally sterile silt deposited during and after the Nipissing transgression. At Ebenhoff and Bear Creek, the Late Archaic-to-Early Woodland middens overlie the late Middle and early Late Archaic accretionary deposits. Diagnostic cultural artifact and ^{14}C age estimates collected from these various middens indicated that the latter part of the Late Archaic and the Early Woodland periods occurred during an interval of relative floodplain stability, and most of the Middle Archaic is probably also associated with an interval of similar fluvial stability. The end of the Middle Archaic and the early part of the Late Archaic periods, on the other hand, are associated with active alluviation and accretionary deposits.

A similar pattern of floodplain occupation and deposition occurred during the Early and Middle Woodland periods. Early Woodland sites, for example, are often associated with generally stable floodplains and formed relatively thick, middenlike horizons. These horizons represent proportionally long cultural records that even can include Late Archaic material. As was true during the early Late Archaic, by the end of the Early Woodland flooding became more common again and began to bury the Late Archaic and Early Woodland middens on previously stable floodplains. Flooding was apparently regular and relatively intense between 2000 and 1500 B.P., and examples of occupation horizons buried during this flooding occur throughout Michigan. An Early Woodland midden, for example, was buried at Bear Creek after about 1900 B.P. (Figure 5-6). At Zemaitis (Figure 5-9), a similar-age occupational horizon, which also included Late Archaic materials, was buried after about 2000 B.P. As discussed above for the waning Middle and early Late Archaic periods, similar stratified or accretionary occupation zones formed during the 2000–1500 B.P. flood interval related to the Middle Woodland. Stratified Middle Woodland occupation zones have been noted at the Schultz and Green Point sites (Figure 5-2), while buried, eroded, and stratified Middle Woodland occupation was noted at the Marquette Viaduct locale of the Fletcher and CERT sites (Figure 5-3).

After about 1500 B.P., during the early Late Woodland, floodplains once again stabilized and allowed extended periods of occupation with only limited alluviation. This interval of fluvial stability is probably associated with a mild climate related to the Medieval Warm interval. As a result of little alluvial accretion and generally mild conditions, extensive, thick, well-developed Late Woodland middenlike deposits commonly occur on floodplains throughout Michigan. Just prior to European contact, however, flooding again accelerated, most likely related to the worldwide, cooler, moister climate of the Little Ice Age. The relatively thick middens at several archaeological sites were buried during this interval.

The cyclical depositional pattern (Figure 6-2) and site formation processes (Figure 6-3) outlined in this chapter occur not only within the Great Lakes regions but also more broadly across the northeastern United States (Figure 6-1). They are particularly apparent and regionally extensive associated with the late Holocene intervals (i.e., the flooding between 2000 and 1500 B.P. and related to the Little Ice Age). Importantly, the duration and regional persistence of these cycles suggest that millennial-scale cyclical variation from a longer-duration, warm-dry to a shorter-term, cool-moist climate generally characterizes the late Holocene in the Great Lakes region. These changing intervals are particularly significant in the more northern regions, such as the upper Great Lakes, where even minor fluctuations to cooler-wetter, or alternatively warmer, climates could have had significant effects on subsistence resources. Such changes would have had especially important ramifications during the Late Woodland, when horticultural activities became more important in the subsistence systems of the Great Lakes region.

Although the late Holocene climate cycles are important in themselves and probably influenced prehistoric settlement and subsistence patterns, the depositional framework associated with these intervals also structured the archaeological record preserved in the floodplain and may have affected site visibility differentially during specific cultural periods. During periods of limited flooding, alluvium was only slowly accreted on floodplain surfaces. As a result, thick, well-developed, multicomponent midden deposits probably formed more frequently, resulting in more visible archaeological horizons in floodplain stratigraphies. During periods of more intensive flooding, however, the floodplain surface rapidly accreted, leaving less time for a particular horizon to exist in a near-surface weathering environment. Consequently, although occupation still certainly occurred, it resulted in stacked, thinner, more discontinuous horizons with fewer artifacts and features. Such horizons are generally less visible than their midden counterparts and probably less likely to be found during deep testing. Thus, given the pattern of deposition in Michigan (Figure 6-3), Middle Archaic, late Late Archaic-through-Early Woodland, and Late Woodland occupations probably formed such multicomponent horizons more frequently than during the early Late Archaic or Middle Woodland. If so, sites associated with the former periods may be more frequent in floodplains than those of the latter periods.

That climate and archaeological site burial are linked and change cyclically is significant from both a settlement and site discovery perspective. Instead of alluvially buried sites confined only to the margins of the Great Lakes in Michigan, as was believed just a few decades ago, the model developed in this chapter suggests that site burial may occur in any fluvial basin where conditions are favorable for extensive floodplain accretion but that such accretion is more frequent during specific intervals. The challenge for developing effective and efficient site discovery strategies is delineating the hydraulic factors and basin characteristics that dictate site burial and preservation. Chapter 7 represents an attempt to systematize this data into a predictive framework by mapping the potential for buried sites based on environmental criteria using Geographic Information System (GIS) techniques.

From a larger research perspective, the ideas presented in this chapter are significant to a more refined understanding of prehistoric behavioral processes. In order to refine settlement and subsistence models and test whether they are accurate reflections of human behavior, the entire range of archaeological site types present in the region must be discovered and excavated. If buried archaeological horizons remain undiscovered, then a whole subpopulation of important sites will be ignored, which can only result in an incorrect understanding of prehistoric settlement patterns in the area. Additionally, not only must the buried sites that occur be found, but we must also determine how depositional patterns can enhance or limit the visibility and preservation of the archaeological record. How confident are we that certain environments, such as floodplains, are not underrepresented in the archaeological record? If sites of specific ages are more common than others, how much of the difference is due to cultural processes, and how much is a function of site taphonomy? How much and what parts of the archaeological record are missing due entirely to natural processes? Understanding the interplay between chronology, depositional patterns, climate, local ecology, and cultural selection processes for site location is critical to addressing this problem.

Geoarchaeological data from alluvial settings provides important indicators of time, location, and relative fluvial stability throughout the Holocene. Certainly, buried and stratified sites, which are generally rare, hard to discover, and perhaps underrepresented in syntheses of prehistoric settlement systems, can provide some of the cleanest data as to context. However, such sites also offer special problems in excavation, problems that are best solved by involving other related Quaternary disciplines, such as geology, pedology, and botany, each of which brings a different approach and perspective to the solution of several related research questions.

CHAPTER SEVEN

A GIS Framework for Predicting Site Burial Potential in Southern Lower Michigan

Introduction

As we have shown throughout this book, the state of deep testing in Michigan has improved over the past few decades to the point that scientists trained in geology and geoarchaeology are routinely integrated into local and regional site discovery strategies. This has occurred, at least in part, because archaeologists have recognized that decisions concerning the how and where of deep testing for archaeological resources should be founded on sound, scientifically based earth science information, information that is best provided in an interdiscipline-based research environment. How this type of interdisciplinary research occurs has likewise been progressively transformed from idiosyncratic, site-specific descriptive applications to more regional-level applications that emphasize secular environmental change and landform-scale depositional processes. Consequently, long- and short-term geological processes, such as sedimentology and pedology, that are not strictly archaeological and their relationships to landform construction have become fundamental to buried site discovery plans. The emphasis of this project has been to integrate earth science information and methods with the more traditional anthropological focus of archaeology. This approach underscores the importance we place on a sound multidisciplinary approach to archaeological research. Although the general factors controlling archaeological site burial are understood through the kind of regional integration provided in Part I of this study, the actual sedimentation at a specific locale is fundamentally controlled by local, basin-specific variables. Even though the distribution patterns of archaeological sites, in particular those associated with site burial and preservation, are certainly linked to many of the long-term patterns of sedimentation outlined in Part I, their significance to and impact on a particular floodplain location cannot be fully understood isolated from specific, distinct local and regional drainage basin developments that sometimes have nothing to do with regional patterns.

In fact, such locally specific depositional patterns compel most deep-test reports to focus on more or less idiosyncratic and site-specific interpretations rather than on regional integration. This is not a criticism but rather results because such studies are project, not model, driven and are mainly descriptive rather than theoretical. They provide a detailed account of the depositional history for a geographically specific buried alluvial or archaeological sequence from a particular site, rather than develop a framework from which the location of other buried archaeological sites could be predicted. However, just how local, site-specific data and regional environmental factors articulate, in the context of discovering buried archaeological sites, is important to developing a framework that may predict the occurrence and distribution of buried sites. To create such a predictive framework or "model" requires the integration of site-specific, regional, and theoretical data. It is toward this end that this chapter is directed.

Although the situation has improved somewhat for more of those studies undertaken during the past decade, the selection of specific areas that may require deep testing has frequently been more haphazard than scientific. This is in part because clear criteria to establish areas that should be tested were often lacking. Clearly, various levels of geographical and geological data complexity could be applied to establish such criteria. At the most elementary level, for example, the mere spatial extent of the recent, Holocene-age floodplain landform can be used to establish the boundaries of deep-test locales. This simplistic criterion is based on the assumption that areas beyond defined Holocene floodplains are unlikely to include buried archaeological sites, while areas within floodplains might include such sites. Although this seems easy to apply, establishing even this simplistic criterion on the ground is unfortunately not as transparent or straightforward as it might seem. Floodplains, for example, are only sometimes mapped in detail and, when they have been, are often defined based on stream hydrograph and flow-duration data collected over the last 50–75 years. As mentioned below, the Federal Emergency Management Agency (FEMA) has primarily used this type of data to delineate 100- and 500-year flood pools for insurance standards. While this may be fine for present or even future floodplain development, which is the purpose of such FEMA maps, it can only partly represent the prehistoric conditions or extent of floodplains. Because historic changes in streams—such as levee construction, channelization, dam construction, land clearing, and paving of surfaces, to name a few-have all altered stream hydrology, the modern floodplain, as defined by these criteria, may not even approximate that of the past. Moreover, even if a stream reach remains relatively pristine and unaltered from its prehistoric configuration, as we have demonstrated throughout this monograph, the Holocene climate itself has been quite variable. At times in the past, climate was more like today, while at other times it was very different. Consequently, a floodplain defined using modern climate criteria may only vaguely resemble the configuration of a past floodplain developed under, for example, cooler, moister conditions associated with the Little Ice Age. Of even greater import are the potential differences between early, middle, and late Holocene floodplains, particularly for streams located near the shores of the Great Lakes. This is important because cultural resource management (CRM) issues in Michigan should be concerned as much with the Early and Middle Archaic as with the Late Woodland. For example, because the 7–15-m differences between Nipissing and modern lake levels greatly altered stream base level, the extent and configuration of Nipissing floodplains may be vastly different than those present today. Comparison, definition, or even recognition of early

Holocene floodplains along streams that were graded to lakes that were as much as 100 m lower than today is still more problematic. Indeed, a great deal of early Holocene floodplains now lies submerged under the Great Lakes.

Much more complex and detailed data concerning floodplains and stream reaches within entire drainage basins is required to address many of the problems mentioned above. This data, unfortunately, is not now and may never be available at the scale and coverage needed. In order to effectively model or interpret floodplain formation and distribution during the entire Holocene, precise field mapping, along with detailed three-dimensional subsurface reconstruction and chronology, must be undertaken. Projects with this aim have been undertaken elsewhere, most prominently in Minnesota, where several million dollars were spent over a number of years to develop a model, informally referred to as MnModel, that predicts the location of buried archaeological sites within the state. MnModel is holistic in approach and involved the development of a three-dimensional approximation of sedimentary environments (shorelines, floodplains, fluvial terraces, etc.) that might include buried deposits and places them into Geographic Information System (GIS) coverages. These were then meshed with other GIS coverages that showed such factors as the distribution of archaeological sites as well as numerous other environmental variables. Ultimately, one of the goals of MnModel was to integrate all of these data to produce a GIS framework that ranked landforms based on the probability they might include buried archaeological sites. Such an endeavor, while certainly important and worthwhile, would require financial and time commitments that were beyond the scope of this project. Instead of the comprehensive, relatively expensive and labor-intensive approach of MnModel, we chose to approach the problem by developing a simpler, albeit less complete, framework that focuses on the characteristics of the floodplain that may predict the potential for including buried archaeological deposits as the fundamental criterion for archaeological site burial.

While the issues involved with defining areas of archaeological site burial potential discussed above may seem daunting, we believe that many of the problems can be minimized by placing multiple geographical data sources within a spatial framework and analyzing their interrelationships through GIS. Using GIS to provide the framework for developing a buried site potential model is actually a middle level of complexity between mere floodplain definition and complete floodplain characterization, as was done with MnModel. Because we believe that data standardization as well as easy information exchange and updating of the database are desirable characteristics, the GIS framework was set up using one of the most commonly used packages: GIS Environmental Systems Research Institute (ESRI) software package ArcVIEW GIS (version 3.2). The file coverages could then be more easily distributed to other users. Furthermore, in order to directly merge with other state spatial coverages, the Michigan GeoRef coordinate system (an oblique mercator projection developed by the Michigan Department of Natural Resources that displays spatial data throughout Michigan; see *www.michigan.gov/documents/DNR_Map_Proj_and_MI_Georef_Info_20889_7.pdf* for more information about Michigan GeoRef) was employed to project spatial information geographically. Additionally, the coverages were generally developed from data that was formulated at the approximate resolution of the United States Geological Survey (USGS) 7.5' (1:24,000 scale) quadrangle map. Thus, although data may appear to be a higher resolution, its resolution is not more accurate than 1:24,000.

The objective for the construction of the GIS was to establish the relationship between deep-test locations and buried archaeological sites with various other spatial environmental information. In this fashion, we hoped to develop a framework that predicts the likelihood, or probability, of discovering deeply buried archaeological deposits within counties of southern Lower Michigan. This probability coverage, therefore, is based on the relationship that previously discovered buried archaeological deposits have with other environmental criteria. Ultimately, it depicts a synthetic GIS overlay that integrates the information from Part I of this study (i.e., the general geological and archaeological background and locations of buried archaeological sites) and Part II (the synthetic model for site burial during the Holocene) with a series of overlays from the GIS mapping program to predict areas of high, moderate, and low potential for buried archaeological resources in the southern Lower Peninsula of Michigan

The GIS database was constructed mainly to assist the Michigan Department of Transportation (MDOT), as well as other state and federal agencies, plan for and manage deeply buried archaeological deposits within southern Lower Michigan. Overall, it was designed to group floodplains into categories based on measures of their relative potential for buried archaeological deposits. The real utility of this GIS, however, is ultimately in planning. By defining areas based on their potential for buried archaeological resources, future MDOT projects might be better prepared to address many of the more problematic aspects of CRM. Once they have been identified, areas of high potential for buried resources could either be avoided or tested for the presence of buried archaeological resources early in the site selection process. This could minimize delays or surprises during project development. The remainder of this chapter describes how this coverage was produced, how it can be used, and its limitations.

The GIS Database and Conceptual Framework

The GIS framework database constructed for this project synthesized archaeological, physiographic, and geological data for two purposes. The first was to better understand archaeological site preservation and destruction processes in the southern part of Michigan's Lower Peninsula. This aspect of the project focused especially on those processes resulting from changes in the flow characteristics of Michigan's major rivers that may have affected archaeological site burial. A second purpose for constructing the database was to provide MDOT with the basic location, data quality, and other information pertaining to previously examined deep-testing locations in the region.

The project study area was broadly defined based on political boundaries and to a certain extent physiographic regions. It included only counties in southern Lower Michigan and generally focused on an area south of an east-west line connecting the towns of Manistee on the west and Oscoda on the east (Figure 7–1). This area was selected mainly because it included the majority of deep-testing locations in Michigan, its geographical extent was relatively manageable, and it included a variety of large drainage systems with differing characteristics. In fact, several of the largest, most archaeologically significant fluvial systems in Michigan occur within the study area. These include: from western Michigan, the St. Joseph, Kalamazoo, Grand, Muskegon, and Manistee rivers, which all drain into Lake Michigan; from eastern Michigan, the Bell, Saginaw, Cass, Flint, Shiawassee, Bad, Tittabawassee, Pine, Rifle, and AuGres rivers, which drain into Lake Huron; and from southeastern Michigan, the Huron, Rouge, and Raisin rivers, which drain into Lake St. Claire or Lake Erie.

To achieve the secondary project goal, a database and point polygon coverage were constructed to provide locational and other basic information pertaining to previously investigated deep tests, as well as buried and/or stratified archaeological sites that occur within the study area. We hoped that this data could allow us to distinguish the major environmental factors that affect site formation and preservation processes along the river systems mentioned above. Once these factors were recognized, the places within the drainage basins where archaeological materials are likely to be buried in situ or where preservation is limited could be identified and mapped. Furthermore, by relative ranking of areas where archaeological potential is high, along with ranking areas where the likelihood of subsurface preservation seems slight, we hoped to provide MDOT's CRM program and planners with an important tool to aid in construction design considerations for future projects. Finally, by placing this data within a statewide GIS framework, we could provide a single source that summarized the results of more than two decades of deep testing in southern Michigan. Thus, CRM firms or other researchers could have relatively easy access to what is otherwise highly disparate data.

Data Collection and Sources for Coverages

Data collection occurred in two phases. First, archaeological reports pertaining to deep testing for buried archaeological sites were identified and examined from the collections at the Michigan State University Consortium for Archaeological Research, the archives of the Office of the State Archaeologist, and the personal libraries and collections of the authors. These consisted mainly of reports on the results of CRM-related deep-testing projects but in a few instances also included unpublished research and the results of yet-to-be-completed CRM studies. A bibliography of these reports and references, together with their location names, related deep-testing statistics, and summary of deep-test results (if available) are tabulated in files on the accompanying CD-ROM. If detailed and geologically comprehensive trench descriptions were included, these are also tabulated in the accompanying CD-ROM by their deep-test location name.

Once they were identified, the reports were then examined as to the relevance of their contents for this study. Applicable sections were photocopied for future use, and the results of the deep-testing components of these studies were abstracted to summarize data considered useful for predicting site burial processes or for understanding local and regional depositional and/or geomorphological history. The types of information included focused on such factors as the

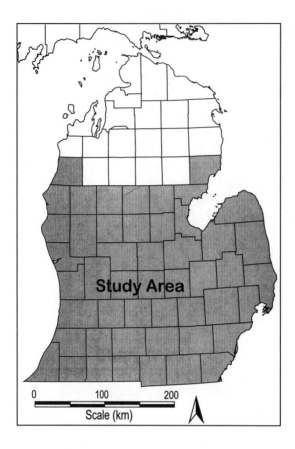

Figure 7-1. Counties within the study area of southern Lower Michigan.

location and nature of any known archaeological sites in the project area and the location, nature, and contents of deep tests (boreholes, backhoe trenches, etc.) in the project area. In addition, the training and background of both field personnel and report authors were noted. This information often provides a set of criteria related to the relative reliability of the conclusions presented in the studies. For example, a lack of appropriately trained personnel with professional credentials in geomorphology, geology, and/or the other geoarchaeological sciences, either on site for the fieldwork or as a report author, might call into question conclusions concerning the stratigraphy, depositional history, sedimentology, pedology, and geomorphology. Although recognizing the obvious, thick, archaeological-rich midden soils or extensive paleosol sequences might seem simple and obvious to professional archaeologists with even minimal earth science background, identifying and understanding the significance of more subtle, ephemeral buried soils and surfaces require more extensive training and experience in earth science disciplines. Understanding and recognizing depositional environments, sedimentary sequences, and associated pedological development within a stratigraphic sequence require specific training and extensive field experience. Even more critical to this enterprise, however, is to properly understand the significance of the absence of such deposits within a stratigraphic sequence. This requires even broader and more specialized training.

Table 7-1. Counties Studied in Southern Lower Michigan and Availability of Countywide GIS Coverages

County	SSRGO[1]	Q-FRM[1]	County	SSRGO	Q-FRM
Allegan	No	No	Livingston	No	Yes
Arenac	No	Yes	Macomb	Yes	Yes
Barry	Yes	No	Manistee	No	Yes
Bay	Yes	Yes	Mason	Yes	No
Berrien	Yes	Yes	Mecosta	No	No
Branch	No	No	Midland	Yes	No
Calhoun	No	Yes	Monroe	Yes	Yes
Cass	No	No	Montcalm	No	No
Clair	No	No	Muskegon	Yes	Yes
Clinton	Yes	Yes	Newaygo	No	No
Eaton	No	No	Oakland	Yes	Yes
Genesee	Yes	Yes	Oceana	Yes	No
Gladwin	Yes	No	Osceola	No	No
Gratiot	No[2]	No	Ottawa	No	No
Hillsdale	Yes	No	Saginaw	Yes	Yes
Huron	No	Yes	Sanilac	No[2]	No
Ingham	No	Yes	Shiawassee	Yes	No
Iosco	Yes	Yes	St. Clair	Yes	Yes
Isabella	No	Yes	St. Joseph	Yes	No
Jackson	No	Yes	Tuscola	Yes	No
Kalamazoo	No	No	Van Buren	No	No
Kent	No	Yes	Washtenaw	No	No
Lapeer	No	No	Wayne	Yes	Yes
Lenawee	No	No			

Note: All other GIS coverages discussed in text, except for the SSURGO and Q3-FIRM data shown, exist for each county listed.
[1] SSRGO = SSURGO soil data, Q-FIRM = FEMA Q3-FIRM flood insurance data; Yes = coverage used to construct archaeological potential maps; No = coverage not used.
[2] Coverage exists but became available after October 2002 when the archaeological potential maps were constructed.

The archaeological sites and deep-test locations identified in this phase of data collection were selected because the printed materials associated with them provide a wealth of information as to the time period of the occupation of the sites and the nature of their depositions (stratified, surface, or subsurface). Once the basic deep-testing locations were identified and reports collated, a second round of data collection was undertaken. This involved acquiring a variety of ArcVIEW and ArcINFO compatible coverages from several different sources. Coverages contained various types of physiographical, geological, hydrological, and political data (see Table 7–1) and focused on data collected from both state- and countywide formats.

Several statewide data coverages were acquired to assess their utility in designing the Archaeological Site Potential Framework. These were, for the most part, obtained from the Michigan Department of Natural Resources (DNR) and included Bedrock and Quaternary geology as well as statewide coverages of soils, topography, and other miscellaneous geographic frameworks. Most of these coverages were generally derived either directly from digitized, large-scale, statewide paper maps or from generalizing and "lumping" data sets from more detailed coverages. For example, the topographic data was derived from the 90-m^2-grid digital elevation model (DEM), which is a relatively coarse grid for understanding details of the ground surface slopes. The soil coverages were derived from the STATSGO, a digital general soil association map developed by the National Cooperative Soil Survey that consists of broad-based inventory of soils compiled by generalizing more detailed soil survey maps. The STATSGO data was collected in 1-x-2-degree topographic quadrangle units (i.e., 1:250,000-scale map), and the minimum area delineated was about 1:544. Statewide geological maps (Bedrock and Quaternary) are based on even smaller-scale coverages. These were digitized from 1:500,000-scale maps and have been even more generalized from the original paper map coverages.

Unfortunately, most of the statewide GIS coverages for the study area proved inadequate for our purposes. The scale was simply not fine enough to allow for detailed analyses of fluvial, textural, or other environmental characteristics of floodplains. Indeed, digitally enlarging these maps to scales greater than was originally constructed still does not improve the original map accuracy and can even cause misinterpretation of the data.

Countywide formats are, not surprisingly, more useful mainly because they are more detailed. These coverages focused mainly on topographical coverages and base maps. For example, from the Michigan DNR we obtained a set of 30-m interval DEMs of Michigan counties as well as a set of 1:24,000 digital raster graphics (DRG) of USGS quadrangle maps (assembled at the county level) and USGS digital orthophoto quadrangles (DOQ). Several base maps useful for display purposes were also compiled as part of the initial exploratory coverages. These base maps include county-level maps depicting political boundaries, major and minor waterways, and inland lakes and were derived mainly from the Michigan Geographic Framework Base file (MiGFB).

Coverage accuracy for each of these databases is quite variable depending on what the database was used for or the original data source from which they derive. For example, DRG coverages consist of scanned, 8-bit TIFF-format, georectified, 1:24,000-scale, 7.5' USGS quadrangles. Each georectified TIFF file includes a world file that enables GIS software to place the TIFF file in space. The quadrangles have been merged into county files by removing the map collars and merging individual DRG quadrangles from the county. Thus, these maps represent countywide coverages, and, because they are simply scanned paper maps, they maintain the accuracy of the original USGS 7.5' quadrangle map. The DOQ coverages were similarly constructed and have like levels of accuracy and constraints. In fact, most of the base maps used in this study are generally accurate to about 1:24,000 (i.e., the USGS 7.5' quadrangle map).

Not surprisingly for a study whose primary goal is to predict archaeological site locations in alluvial settings, the definition, lithology, and extent of floodplains within the study area are of particular significance. Although no actual digital representations of real "floodplains" were found within the study area, a few coverages were located that provided either surrogate representations of floodplains or included data from which the floodplain extent could be approximated. For example, the United States Department of Agriculture, Natural Resources Conservation Service (USDA-NRCS) provides detailed soil survey information in GIS-ready format. These coverages represent Soil Survey Geographic (SSURGO I and II) database standards for county-level soil survey coverages. As opposed to statewide soil association (STATSGO) coverages, SSURGO coverages are very detailed. This data was acquired for counties where such coverage was available (see Table 7-1) and includes several important data pertaining to ground slope, surface and subsurface textures, and hydric properties. Importantly, flood-prone soils and, in some instances, floodplain soils are also designated.

According to the USDA-NRCS, the SSURGO coverage was developed to depict digital information about soil features on or near the surface of the earth. It embodies a digital soil survey and is generally the most detailed digital soil spatial data available from the USDA-NRCS. The SSURGO coverage was prepared either by digitizing maps or by revising previously digitized maps based on remote-sensing data. The maps were derived from a 7.5' quadrangle format. The coverage includes a detailed, field-verified inventory of soils and nonsoil areas, which normally occur in a repeatable pattern on the landscape. Additionally, these areas must be able to be cartographically displayed at the scale mapped. After compilation by the USDA-NRCS, the soil data was manually compared to the original "paper" map source and corrected as needed. Digitization accuracy was established using USGS quadrangle maps at 1:24,000. Thus, increasing the map scale digitally beyond the 1:24,000 scale does not actually enhance the relative accuracy of the SSURGO data. Importantly, SSURGO data, however accurate, was collected based on countywide maps and was not altered at borders to match soil units from adjacent counties. A defined standard or level of confidence in the interpretive accuracy of the map varies with the kind and intensity of field investigations. Field investigations and data collection, however, were of sufficient detail to name map units and to identify accurately and consistently areas of about 1.8 hectares. More details of how the SSURGO data was used as an aid in constructing the archaeological site potential framework coverage is discussed below.

In addition to soil information provided by the SSURGO data, maps showing the extent and recurrence interval of areas that may flood have been developed by FEMA. These are actually flood insurance risk maps and typically delineate, among other things, the 100- and 500-year flood levels. FEMA has produced digital copies of these, designated as Q3-FIRMs.

The Q3-FIRMs were developed by FEMA to provide the basis for floodplain management, mitigation, and insurance activities for the National Flood Insurance Program (NFIP). These maps were constructed to assist in providing the basic data by which to enforce the mandatory purchase requirement of the Flood Disaster Protection Act. Thus, the Q3-FIRM maps are intended to provide flood-risk data rather than map specific floodplain distributions. The flood-hazard areas were determined using statistical analyses of records of river flow and rainfall and were originally compiled as countywide, paper FIRM maps. Moreover, the paper maps were digitized to construct the Q3-FIRMs, and accuracy was tested by manually comparing the digital data with the original paper maps. Digitization accuracy was consistent with mapping at a scale of 1:24,000, and horizontal control was established using USGS quadrangle maps at 1:24,000. Thus, increasing the map scale digitally does not enhance the relative accuracy of the Q3-FIRM flood data. Importantly, the Q3-FIRM data, however accurate, was collected based on countywide maps. The coverages were not altered at any county border to match adjacent counties. Additionally, the completeness of the data reflects the original source map, and certain complex features were sometimes eliminated or generalized because of map scale and legibility constraints. Only 2.6 km^2 drainage areas were compiled.

Based on its availability, the Q3-FIRM flood potential coverage was acquired for selected counties. Practical experience with the Q3-FIRM data from FEMA shows, however, that floodplain delineation is relatively inaccurate. In many cases, 100- and 500-year floodplains, particularly in smaller tributary streams, were often up to a few hundred meters offset from the actual stream locations. Consequently, this data only provided a guide to the relative significance and extent of potential floodplains in counties where Q3-FIRM coverage was available. The Q3-FIRM polygons were commonly adjusted to "fit" clear, geomorphologically consistent floodplains. More details of how the Q3-FIRM data was used as an aid in constructing the archaeological site potential framework coverage is discussed below.

In addition to the coverages mentioned above, a few coverages were constructed either from derivatives of these previously obtained coverages or as separate coverages based on other criteria. From the onset of the project, certain types of information and coverages emerged as critical data. These include two primary data sets: the location and distribution of Holocene-age floodplains within the study area and the extent of surface area that was submerged during the mid-Holocene high-water phase of Lake Nipissing. The importance of the former is clear. Because of the focus on alluvially buried archaeological sites, determining the distribution of floodplains was central to the project. The importance of the extent of Nipissing submergence, however, may not be as clear but is based on the clear association of most buried sites with the Nipissing lake plain (e.g., see Figures 3-2, 5-1).

Coverages delineating the distribution of Holocene floodplains were developed by combining the 100- and 500-year flood pools as defined by the FEMA Q3-FIRM coverage with the distribution of floodplain indicator soils as defined in the SSURGO database. In some areas, this data was augmented with unpublished mapping and fieldwork by the authors. Sometimes, mapping other soil units that are not commonly or typically associated with floodplain alluvium aided in defining the maximum possible, reasonable extent of the floodplain. This was accomplished by mapping soil units that intersect or lie within 100 m of rivers and streams in the area. The boundaries of these soil types were then adjusted to fit within the likely morphologically reasonable floodplain boundaries. In addition, gaps in these derivative coverages were filled, where possible and reasonably detectable, based on morphological consideration and the experience of the authors. When appropriate and when the data or drainage basin was of sufficient importance to justify it, floodplains were also extended into adjacent counties, where the surrogate data was not available, using a similar combination of morphology, experience, and "educated guesses." Once all of these various coverages were merged, the boundaries of the resultant polygons revealing the extent and distribution of resultant floodplain coverages were checked by hand. The floodplain polygons were first overlaid on 7.5′ DRG maps to study and adjust their distribution. Where they clearly extended outside of morphologically reasonably constrained floodplain boundaries, the polygons were adjusted to fit. Additionally, where polygons did not "fill" clearly definable valleys or only partially covered Holocene terraces, they were expanded to provide reasonably accurate representation of the extent of Holocene floodplain or terrace sediments.

As has been pointed out in many places throughout this book, the Nipissing transgression was a significant event within the upper Great Lakes region and greatly affected sedimentation along streams in southern Lower Michigan, particularly near the margins of the Great Lakes. In fact, the flat lacustrine and nearshore plains that formed within the area submerged by Lake Nipissing, particularly that area rimming Saginaw Bay, continued to influence alluvial deposition and floodplain formation throughout the late Holocene (these factors have been thoroughly discussed in chapters 2, 3, and 4). For example, previous deeptest studies within the Saginaw Bay region (notably the Great Lakes Gas Transmission Pipeline study; Monaghan and Schaetzl 1994) indicated that thick, middle-to-late Holocene alluvial sequences characterize much of the area within the Nipissing lake plain. Many of these sequences have buried pre- and post-Nipissing maximum paleosols within them that sometimes include Middle Archaic-through-Late Woodland archaeological deposits. Moreover, such sites are particularly abundant near the limit of the Nipissing transgression (see Figures 3-3, 3-5, 5-1). That these site locations do not result exclusively from habitation along the active Nipissing shoreline is demonstrated by the fact that the majority of sites do not even contain Middle Archaic cultural materials, which would have been contemporaneous with Lake Nipissing, but instead are mainly made up of Late Archaic and Woodland deposits. (The Weber I and Ebenhoff sites are important exceptions to this statement. However, even these sites include significant post-Nipissing Late Archaic horizons.) Rather than shoreline occupation, this clustering of sites near the Nipissing maximum reflects an interplay of both natural sedimentary and cultural site-selection processes. These in turn result from the interrelationship between a variety of ecological factors unique to the area. For example, the Nipissing shoreline typically marks a significant change in the gradient of rivers and streams from relatively steeper gradients inland from the shoreline to essentially flat stream profiles between mid-Holocene beaches and the present Great Lakes shoreline. Consequently, the amount and rate of sedimentation dramatically increase near this boundary, which results in the development of thick, late Holocene accretionary alluvium.

Cultural selection processes likely also influenced site clustering along the Nipissing shoreline. This is particularly true in the Saginaw Bay region. Here, the Nipissing beach approximates the margin of the Shiawassee lowland, a broad wetland area that generally corresponds with the area inundated by Lake Nipissing. Inland from the lowland, the region predominately includes upland forests.

Because the mid-Holocene shoreline zone is ecotonal between upland forest and wetland habitats, it was especially attractive for generalized resource exploitation. Even later in prehistory, during the Woodland period, this area maintained its ecotonal relationship between wetland and upland forests, although the extent of these environments probably expanded or contracted during the cyclical changes in late Holocene climate. The occupants of late prehistoric archaeological sites situated along the margin could probably exploit a wide variety of resources from both wetland and upland habitats. Given the significant relationship between the Nipissing shoreline and submerged lake plain to buried and stratified archaeological sites, constructing a GIS coverage that shows the extent of the mid-Holocene high-water phases within the study area is important for predicting where buried or stratified archaeological sites may occur.

A coverage showing the distribution of areas submerged by mid-Holocene high-water levels was developed based on the altitudes and positions of the previously mapped Nipissing beaches or other shoreline indicators. Because the mid-Holocene shorelines in the upper Great Lakes are subject to differential isostatic rebound, the altitude of beaches actually increases north and east in the upper Great Lakes basin (see Figure 2-2). For example, near Chicago, the maximum altitude of Nipissing beaches occurs at about 183 m asl, while near Sault Ste. Marie, correlative beaches lie at about 198 m. Thus, a coverage that showed the extent of areas submerged by Nipissing could be constructed using the altitude of beaches from a variety of geographic locales in Lakes Michigan and Huron. This coverage was derived based on previously mapped Nipissing maximum beaches from several areas in Wisconsin, Illinois, Indiana, and Michigan, as well as Ontario, compiled by Leverett and Taylor (1915) and Larsen (1985a), as well as on unpublished fieldwork by the authors. The locations of beaches from these areas were then plotted on a statewide map, and, based on their altitudes, a contour map "grid" was created that approximated or "modeled" the shoreline during the Nipissing maximum. To allow direct comparison, the derived grid of the "Nipissing" shoreline was constructed using the same interval and size as the 30-m DEM of the modern ground surface. Thus, by comparing the values of spatially identical nodes of these grids, the extent of Lake Nipissing could be estimated. For example, nodes of the "Nipissing" grid that had altitude values greater than those of the "DEM" grid must mark areas that were submerged during Nipissing. On the other hand, grid nodes of the "DEM" whose values were greater than those of the "Nipissing" grid represented areas that were also dry land during the Nipissing maximum. These two grids were then further manipulated to create a simple "presence-absence" coverage showing the maximum extent of Lake Nipissing.

Once the coverage was established, the limits of the areas submerged by Lake Nipissing were also inspected by hand for obvious mismatches with known beaches. Where the "modeled" shoreline did not approximate the mapped beaches, the coverage was adjusted to fit, based on the experience of the authors. In addition, gaps, errors, or other unusually complicated "orphaned" or "island" features within or just outside of Lake Nipissing were filled, deleted, or otherwise adjusted to fit within reasonable boundaries based on rational morphological consideration of what the configuration of the Nipissing shoreline probably looked like.

Constructing the Stratified Archaeological Sites and DTL Point Coverage

Using data collected from archaeological reports, deep-test descriptions, and other information from the Office of the State Archaeologist, two major coverages were created in ArcVIEW. The first of these is a point coverage that is primarily descriptive and focuses on the locations and physical parameters of buried and stratified archaeological sites in addition to the deep test locations (DTLs). The second, discussed in detail in the next section, is a derivative coverage modeling the probability that a specific locale will include buried prehistoric surfaces or archaeological deposits.

The first of the coverages constructed was a descriptive point source location map showing the distribution of DTLs. The coverage included not only the DTL for which adequate locational of information was available but also the stratified or buried archaeological sites from southern Lower Michigan (Figure 7-2 and Table 7-2a, 7-2b). The variety of information that was included within the Coverage Attribute Table (CAT) was considered the most useful for predictive modeling, general display, or giving users a detailed citation to return to the original data source for further information. Included within the CAT were names and various designations (numbering systems) that uniquely described each location; the nature of the burial, stratigraphy, or sedimentation (if any) at the site; basic data about what was discovered at the site (i.e., archaeological material, ^{14}C age estimates, etc.); and the principal citation for information about the site (i.e., the authors, date of publication, and title of the report). To allow easier analysis, basic environmental and geographical background information was also included. This data represented information that could be spatially

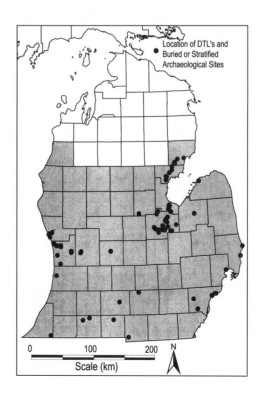

Figure 7-2. The distribution of DTLs and buried or stratified archaeological sites within the southern Lower Michigan study area.

Table 7-2a. Deep-Test Locations in Southern Lower Michigan.

County	Basin	River	Project	DTL Name	Classification	Reference
Arenac	Au Gres	Big Creek	US-23 1996	DTL-5	Not Assessed	Monaghan 1996a
Arenac	Au Gres	Au Gres Rv	US-23 1996	DTL-6	High-Moderate	Monaghan 1996a
Arenac	Rifle	Pine Rv	US-23 1996	DTL-3	Low	Monaghan 1996a
Arenac	Rifle	S Br Pine Rv	US-23 1996	DTL-1	Low	Monaghan 1996a
Arenac	Rifle	Pine Rv	US-23 1996	DTL-2	High-Moderate	Monaghan 1996a
Arenac	Rifle	Rifle Rv	US-23 1996	DTL-4	High-Moderate	Monaghan 1996a
Bay	Saginaw	Saginaw Rv	Marquette Viaduct 1995 Survey	Marquette Viaduct 95	Low (Nipissing inundation)	Monaghan 1994
Bay	Saginaw	Saginaw Rv	Bay Cty. Broadway Improvement	Broadway Improvement	Moderate	Hambacher et al. 1995
Bay	Saginaw	Saginaw Rv	EPA CERT Project	EPA CERT	Moderate	Demeter et al. 1994
Bay	Saginaw	Saginaw Rv	Fletcher SiteBay City	1987 testing at Fletcher	Low (Nipissing inundation)	Prahl 1987b
Bay	Saginaw	Saginaw Rv	Karn Plant Pipeline Bay Co	Karn Plant	Moderate-High	Robinson et al. 1993
Bay	Saginaw	Saginaw Rv	Liberty Bridge Project	20BY79	Moderate-High	Monaghan 1993
Bay	Saginaw	Saginaw Rv	Marquette Viaduct 1987 survey	Marquette Viaduct (1987)	High	Lovis et al. 1996
Bay	Saginaw	Saginaw Rv	Marquette Viaduct 2000 Survey	Marquette Viaduct (2000)	Low	Monaghan 2002
Bay	Saginaw	Saginaw Rv	West Rv Drive Bay City	West Rv Drive Bay City	Moderate-High	Larsen and Demeter 1979
Berrien	St. Joseph	St. Joseph Rv	Vector Pipeline	Vector DTL-1	High–Very High	Monaghan and Hayes 1999
Berrien	St. Joseph	St. Joseph Rv	Vector Pipeline	Vector DTL-1	High	Monaghan and Hayes 1999
Branch	St. Joseph	Coldwater Rv	Tristate Pipeline	20BR47	Low	Dunham et al. 1999
Calhoun	Kalamazoo	Kalamazoo Rv	Vector Pipeline	Vector DTL-4	Low	Monaghan and Hayes 1999
Hillsdale	Maumee	W Fork W Br St. Joseph Rive	M49 Bridge Replacement	M49 Bridge, Camden	High–Very High	Weir et al. 1984
Huron	Sebewaing	Lake Drainage	Section 35 Caseville	Section 35 Caseville,	Low (Nipissing inundation)	Brunett 1982
Ionia	Grand	Grand Rv	Deep Testing at Prison Farm Site	Prison Farm Site	High-Moderate	This report
Iosco	Au Gres	Au Gres Rv	US-23 1996	US-23 DTL-8	High-Moderate	Monaghan 1996a
Iosco	Au Gres	Au Gres Rv	US-23 1996	US-23 DTL-9	High-Moderate	Monaghan 1996a
Iosco	Au Gres	Au Gres Rv	US-23 1996	US-23 DTL-7	High-Moderate	Monaghan 1996a
Iosco	Au Sable	Dead Creek	US-23 1996	US-23 DTL-11	Not Assessed	Monaghan 1996a
Iosco	E. Br. Au Gres	E Br Au Gres Rv	US-23 1996	US-23 DTL-10	High-Moderate	Monaghan 1996a
Jackson	Grand	Grand Rv	Vector Pipeline	Vector DTL-5	High-Moderate	Monaghan and Hayes 1999
Jackson	Grand	Grand Rv	Vector Pipeline	Vector DTL-5	Not Assessed	Monaghan and Hayes 1999

(table 7-2a cont.)

County	Basin	River	Project	DTL Name	Classification	Reference
Kent	Grand	Grand Rv	East Side Retention Basin	East Side Retention Basin	Moderate-High (Inadequate Data)	Frankforter 1989
Kent	Grand	Grand Rv	Gerald Ford Museum	Gerald Ford Museum	Moderate-High	Monaghan 2002
Kent	Grand	Grand Rv	US-131 S-Curve Project	20KT2	Moderate-High	Monaghan and Hayes 2001
Macomb	Belle	Salt Rv	Ameritech Trench	Utility Trench	Low	Payne 1995
Midland	Chippewa	Pine Rv	Great Lakes Gas Pipeline	Pine Rv	Low	Branstner 1991; this report
Muskegon	Grand	Mona Lake	Survey in Norton Township Muskegon	Mona Lake Location	Low	Caiser 1978
Muskegon	Grand	Lake Drainage	Survey in Norton Township Muskegon	Sherman Rd Location	Low	Caiser 1978
Muskegon	Muskegon	Muskegon Rv	Muskegon Utility Reconstruct	Western Ave Reconstruct	Moderate-High	Kern et al. 1983
Ottawa	Grand	Grand Rv	—45 Crossing of Grand Rv	—45 Crossing of Grand Rv	Not Assessed	Roper et al. 1984
Ottawa	Grand	Grand Rv	US-31 1996	US-31 DTL-1	High-Moderate	Monaghan 1996b
Ottawa	Grand	Grand Rv	US-31 1996	US-31 DTL-2	Not Assessed	Monaghan 1996b
Ottawa	Macatawa	Pigeon Rv	US-31 1996	US-31 DTL-4	High-Moderate	Monaghan 1996b
Ottawa	Macatawa	Macatawa Rv	US-31 1996	US-31 DTL-5	High-Moderate	Monaghan 1996b
Saginaw	Cass	Cass Rv	Dehmel Rd Bridge Replacement	Dehmel Road Bridge	Very High	Brunett 1981c
Saginaw	Flint	Flint Rv	Great Lakes Gas Pipeline	Flint Rv	High–Very High	Branstner 1991; this report
Saginaw	Flint	Mistequay Ck	Great Lakes Gas Pipeline	Mistequay Ck	High	Branstner 1991; this report
Saginaw	Flint	Mistequay Ck	Great Lakes Gas Pipeline	Mistequay Ck	High	Branstner 1991; this report
Saginaw	Flint	Pine Run	Great Lakes Gas Pipeline	Pine Run	High–Very High	Branstner 1991; this report
Saginaw	Flint	Flint Rv	Shiawassee Flats Levee Project	Flint Rv	Very High	Weikel 1985
Saginaw	Saginaw	Saginaw Rv	Block 81 of Hoyt's Plat	Block 81 of Hoyt'sPlat,	Low (Nipissing inundation)	Brunett 1981a
Saginaw	Saginaw	Cheboyganing Ck	Cheboyganing Ck Wetland	Cheboyganing	High	Monaghan 2003c
Saginaw	Saginaw	Saginaw Rv	Croaty St Wetland Project	Croaty Wetland Green Point	Very High	Demeter et al. 2000
Saginaw	Saginaw	Saginaw Rv	CSO in Saginaw	Emerson and Fitzhugh	Moderate-High	Taylor et al. 1992a
Saginaw	Saginaw	Saginaw Rv	Saginaw CSO Facilities	Salt/Fraser and Weber	Moderate-High	Taylor et al. 1992b
Saginaw	Saginaw	Saginaw Rv	Emerson, Fitzhugh, Salt/Fraser and Weber	Emerson, Fitzhugh, etc.	Moderate-High	Taylor et al. 1992a
Saginaw	Saginaw	Saginaw Rv	Emerson, Fitzhugh, Salt/Fraser and Weber	Emerson, Fitzhugh, etc.	Very High	Taylor et al. 1992a

(table 7-2a cont.)

County	Basin	River	Project	DTL Name	Classification	Reference
Saginaw	Saginaw	Saginaw Rv	Naval Reserve Center, Saginaw	Naval Reserve Center	Moderate-High	Shannon 1982
Saginaw	Saginaw	Saginaw Rv	Saginaw CSO Control Facilities Project	CSO Control Facilities	Moderate-High	Demeter et al. 1995
Saginaw	Saginaw	Saginaw Rv	Saginaw CSO Control Facilities Project	CSO Control Facilities	High	Demeter et al. 1995
Saginaw	Saginaw	Saginaw Rv	Saginaw Plant Landfill	Schultz-Green Point	Very High	Russell et al. 1981
Saginaw	Shiawassee	Shiawassee Rv	Deer Ck Bridge Replacement	Deer Ck	Moderate	Monaghan 1985
Saginaw	Shiawassee	Bad Rv	Great Lakes Gas Pipeline	Bad Rv, North Fork	High–Very High	Branstner 1991; this report
Saginaw	Shiawassee	South Fork Bad Rv	Great Lakes Gas Pipeline	Bad Rv, South Fork	Very High	Branstner 1991; this report
Saginaw	Shiawassee	Bad Rv	Great Lakes Gas Pipeline	Bad Rv, North Fork	High–Very High	Branstner 1991; this report
Saginaw	Shiawassee	Bear Ck	Great Lakes Gas Pipeline	Bear Ck	Very High	Monaghan and Schaetzl 1994
Saginaw	Shiawassee	Bear Ck	Great Lakes Gas Pipeline	Ebenhoff Dune	Low (Nipissing inundation)	Branstner 1991; this report
Saginaw	Shiawassee	Shiawassee Rv	Great Lakes Gas Pipeline	Shiawassee Rv	Very High	Monaghan and Schaetzl 1994
Saginaw	Shiawassee	Bear Ck	Great Lakes Gas Pipeline	Vogelaar Site	High–Very High	Monaghan and Schaetzl 1994
Saginaw	Shiawassee	Shiawassee Rv	Spaulding Wetland	Spaulding Wetland	High	Monaghan 2003b
Saginaw	Shiawassee	Swan Ck	Swan Ck. Bridge Replacement	Swan Ck	High–Very High	This report
Saginaw	Tittabawassee	Tittabawassee Rv	Boat Launch Saginaw Co	Boat Launch	Low	Prahl 1987a
St Clair	Black	Lake Drainage	ANR Intercostal Link Pipeline	St Clair Rv	Low	Robertson et al. 1994
St Clair	Black	Lake Drainage	Blue Water Bridge Plaza Revision	Blue Water Bridge Plaza	Low (Nipissing inundation)	Weir et al. 1983
St Joseph	St. Joseph	Portage Rv	Vector Pipeline	Vector DTL-3	Very High	Monaghan and Hayes 1999
St Joseph	St. Joseph	Rocky Rv	Vector Pipeline	Vector DTL-2	Moderate-High	Monaghan and Hayes 1999
Tuscola	Cass	Cass Rv	Chippewa Landing Park, Caro	Chippewa Landing Park	Moderate-High	Brunett 1981a
Wayne	Clinton	Lake Drainage	Ambassador Bridge Project	North Study Low Area		Demeter et al. 1996
Wayne	Clinton	Lake Drainage	Prince Hall Place Development	Prince Hall Place Site	Low	Branstner 1990
Wayne	Clinton	Lake Drainage	Sheridan Place Development	Sheridan Place Site	Low	Demeter et al. 1980
Wayne	Clinton	Lake Drainage	Stroh Brewing Co, Detroit	Stroh Brewing	Low	Branstner et al. 1983
Wayne	Huron	Huron Rv	M2 West Road near I-275	—2 West Road	High–Very High	Miller et al. 1992
Wayne	Rouge	Lower Rv Rouge	I-275 Bike Path (Rouge Rv)	1-275 DTL-1	High–Very High	Monaghan 2003a

Table 7-2b. Buried or Stratified Archaeological Sites in Southern Lower Michigan.

County	Drainage Basin	Nearest Stream	Site Name	Site Number	Buried Site Potential	Reference
Allegan	Kalamazoo	Kalamazoo Rv	Hacklander Site	20AE78	High-Moderate	Kingsley 1981
Bay	Saginaw	Saginaw Rv	Marquette Viaduct (2000)	20BY387	Low (Nipissing inundation)	Lovis 2002
Bay	Saginaw	Saginaw Rv	Kantzler Site	20BY30	Low-Moderate	Larsen and Demeter 1979
Bay	Saginaw	Saginaw Rv	CERT Site	20BY365	Moderate	Demeter et al. 1994
Bay	Saginaw	Saginaw Rv	Marquette Viaduct (2000)	20BY28c	Moderate-High	Lovis 2002
Bay	Saginaw	Saginaw Rv	Marquette Viaduct (1989)	20BY28b	Moderate-High	Lovis et al. 1996b
Ionia	Grand	Grand Rv	Prison Farm	20IA58	High-Moderate	Brashler and Mead 1996
Kent	Grand	Grand Rv	Converse Site	20KT2	Moderate-High	Hambacher 2002
Kent	Grand	Grand Rv	Converse Site	20KT02	Moderate-High	Hambacher 2002
Ottawa	Grand	Grand Rv	Zemaitis Site	20OT68	High-Moderate	Brashler and Mead 1996
Saginaw	Flint	Flint Rv	Flint Rv Site	20SA1034	High–Very High	Dobbs et al. 1993a
Saginaw	Shiawassee	Bear Ck	Vogelaar Site	20SA291	High–Very High	Branstner and Hambacher 1995b
Saginaw	Shiawassee	Bear Ck	Ebenhoff Dune Site	20SA596	Low (Nipissing inundation)	Dobbs et al. 1993b
Saginaw	Shiawassee	Bear Ck	Casassa Site	20SA1021	Moderate	Branstner and Hambacher 1995a
Saginaw	Shiawassee	Bear Ck	Bear Ck	20SA1043	Very High	Branstner and Hambacher 1994
Saginaw	Saginaw	Saginaw Rv	Green Point Site	20SA01	Very High	Wright 1964
Saginaw	Tittabawassee	Tittabawassee Rv	Schultz Site	20SA02	Very High	Fitting 1972
Saginaw	Shiawassee	Bad Rv	Shiawassee Rv Site	20SA1033	Very High	Branstner and Hambacher 1994
Saginaw	Cass	Cass Rv	Weber I Site	20SA581	Very High	Lovis 1989

Table 7-3. Attribute Information for the Southern Michigan DTL and Buried Archaeological Site File.

Attribute	Explanation and Discussion of Attribute Values
ID	Represents a unique integer numeric locator to identify each point in the file. Numbers greater than 999 represent buried or stratified archaeological sites; numbers less than 1,000 represent DTLs.
LOCALE	Represents a unique integer numeric locator to identify larger grouping of deep-test locations (i.e., projects that include more than 1 DTL). Numbers greater than 999 represent buried or stratified archaeological sites; numbers less than 1,000 represent DTLs.
LOCALE_ID	Represents a unique integer numeric locator to identify each point within the larger grouping of LOCALE.
PROJECT_NA	Represents a unique alpha numeric code (PROJECT_NA) to identify larger grouping of DTLs (i.e., projects that include more than 1 DTL). This is a descriptive name for attribute LOCALE as either a DTL project name or archaeological site informal name

(table 7-3 cont.)

Attribute	Explanation and Discussion of Attribute Values
DTL_SITE	Represents a unique alpha numeric code to identify each point within the larger grouping of PROJECT_NA. Descriptive name of either an individual DTL or the formal county-coded archaeological site number.
TRENCH	Represents an alpha numeric code (TRENCH) to identify each individual point based on description in original data source. Descriptive name of a DTL Trench.
SITE_TYPE	Represents an alpha numeric code of the type of the location or site represented by the point. DTL = Deep Test Location SITE = Archaeological Site
ARCHMAT	Represents an integer numeric code designating if archaeological material was found at the point. 0 = No archaeological material found 1 = Archaeological material found
PALEOSOL	Represents an integer numeric code designating if buried soil (paleosol) was found at the point. 0 = No buried soil (paleosol) found 1 = Buried soil (paleosol) found
C14	Represents an integer numeric code designating if a ^{14}C age estimate (radiocarbon date) was performed on sample(s) found at the point. 0 = No 14C age estimate performed 1 = 14C age estimate performed
TYPE	Represents an alpha numeric code of the type of the location or site represented by the point. DTL-T = Individual trench location from DTL DTL-L = Point location of a DTL. There was not enough information in original source report to determine the location of individual trenches. SITE-St = Stratified archaeological site SITE-B = Buried (not stratified) archaeological site
URBAN_FILL	Represents an integer numeric code designating if urban or historic (cultural) fill occurs at the point. 0 = No Urban Fill 1 = Urban Fill present
ARCHPOT	Information about the potential of the area in which the point lies to contain alluvially buried archaeological sites. It is derived from matching the point location with the Southern Michigan Buried Archaeological Site Potential (SMBASP) map coverage (see table 7-4 for values and further information).
CLASS	Information about the potential of an area to contain alluvially buried archaeological sites. It represents an alpha-numeric description of the relative potential based on ARCHPOT value (see Table 7-4 for values and further information).
NIP_SUBMRG	Information about areas that were submerged during the mid-Holocene high-water levels. It is based on the altitudes and positions of the previously mapped Nipissing beaches or other shoreline indicators. Values are integer numeric and are either 1 or 0. NIP_SUBMRG = 1: Area was submerged during the maximum extent of Lake Nipissing NIP_SUBMRG = 0: Area was not submerged during the maximum extent of Lake Nipissing

(table 7-3 cont.)

Attribute	Explanation and Discussion of Attribute Values
COUNTY	Information about the county in which the map unit is located based on county FIPS code. Values are integer numeric.
NAME	Information about the county in which the point is located based the name of the county. Values are alpha-numeric.
BASIN	Name of the drainage basin in which the point is located.
STREAM	Name of the nearest stream to the point.
TOWN	Land survey description of the point. Alpha-numeric description of the tier north or south.
RANGE	Land survey description of the point. Alpha-numeric description of the range east or west.
SECTION	Land survey description of the point. Numeric description of the section (1–36).
QRT_QRT	Land survey description of the point. Alpha-numeric description of the 2nd quarter section.
QRT	Land survey description of the point. Alpha-numeric description of the 1st quarter section.
GEO_ID	Complete land survey description of the point (Town, Range, Section, Qrt-section of Qrt-section).
OTHER	Property description if not part of land survey.
CITATION	Abbreviated bibliographic reference for the source of original data for the point.
REFERENCE	Complete bibliographic reference for the source of original data for the point.

related to the DTL or archaeological sites based on IDENTITY functions in ArcVIEW and included such data as the county, township, and drainage system that the site was located within as well as the predicted potential for buried archaeological material at the locale. More details concerning what fields are included and what they mean are presented in Table 7-3.

Basically, three main categories of "locations" were defined within the point coverage. For a DTL included in the coverage, the location was given either as the position of individual deep-test trenches or, if individual trench locations were not available, the general location of areas that underwent deep testing. In the latter case, the locations of trenches or cores at a DTL were not given in sufficient detail within the original report to plot each of their locations accurately. Similarly, buried or stratified archaeological sites within the study area were also assigned location. The general location of a DTL (i.e., trench positions were not located) or for the buried archaeological sites was usually given as the approximate spatial center of the area under study based mainly on the locations given in the citations listed in the ArcVIEW coverage CAT (see Table 7-2). Importantly, the point position is only an estimate based on the maps or the descriptions presented in the report. It is, at best, located to the USGS 7.5' quadrangle map accuracy. Thus, increasing the map scale digitally beyond the 1:24,000 scale will not actually enhance the relative precision of these site locations.

The majority of DTL reports, particularly for the more recent projects, included enough information to locate individual trenches or cores accurately. Many of the reports actually plotted trenches on some sort of base map or included more detailed descriptions of trench locations based on azimuths and distances to specific landforms or cultural features. In the latter cases, trenches were plotted on the USGS 1:24,000 DRG based on descriptive parameters only, but their locational accuracy could not be double-checked. Where maps were present, either USGS 7.5' quadrangles or site-specific detailed maps, the trench locations could be checked for accuracy. In these cases, trenches were plotted directly on the USGS 1:24,000 DRG and then rechecked against the original map for accuracy. In either case, whether descriptive or map location information was employed, the points were then georectified and added to the ArcVIEW point coverage along with the other information included in the CAT. Regardless of how the trenches were plotted, however, the accuracy of their locations is dependent on the information provided in the citations listed in the ArcVIEW coverage CAT (see Table 7–2). In any case, trench locations were plotted only to the USGS 7.5' quadrangle map accuracy, and digitally enhancing the map scale will not increase their relative precision.

Constructing the Archaeological Site Potential Framework Coverage

One of the more fundamental reasons for undertaking the GIS portion of this study was to construct ArcVIEW coverages that "modeled" or "predicted" the probability of finding buried archaeological deposits within southern Lower Michigan. Predicting the actual location of archaeological sites, however, is exceptionally complicated because site locations are at least partly controlled by distinct, often idiosyncratic, cultural factors. Moreover, people select places to live based not only on cultural reasons but also on environmental criteria. These places usually correspond to locales where significant natural, ecological, or other environmental elements related to subsistence patterns specific to the site's cultural period coalesce with a variety of social and cultural factors that are also particular to specific cultural periods. These latter cultural factors may not relate directly to subsistence and may even be more or less independent of distinct, local environmental conditions. Moreover, cultural practices vary geographically as well as through time and cultural phase. The whole issue of predicting site location is further complicated by other factors. Not only do cultural variables and decisions control site location and may be poorly documented or understood or may vary though time, but so do the natural ecological conditions. Consequently, the isolation of pertinent cultural variables and the complex parameters dictating how they interact with natural environmental conditions is beyond the scope of this project. We have not considered them in constructing the GIS predictive framework for the locations of buried archaeological sites.

Although we have not aimed to predict the specific locations of buried archaeological sites, we have attempted to define areas where the conditions are favorable to site burial. This was done by focusing not on the actual locations of sites but rather on defining places within the study area where buried ground surfaces, or paleosols, are likely both to occur and to have been preserved. The relationship between paleosols, alluviation, and archaeological site location has been discussed throughout chapters 3 and 6. In chapter 6, we presented a model that suggests site burial occurred during specific time periods related to episodic changes in climate. The transference of that model into a GIS coverage is predicated on a few basic assumptions. We suggest that sites will be buried and preserved within broader areas, such as floodplains, only when sedimentation is significant enough and of the correct sedimentological characteristics also to bury and preserve the paleo ground surfaces on which the site lies. In other words, archaeological sites can only be buried if the paleosol that they are associated with is also buried and preserved. The difficulty arises in defining where such places can be found and what sedimentological conditions might be the best predictors of preserved, buried sites. As far as the places are concerned, we have concentrated on defining floodplain, and to a lesser extent shoreline, environments that promote such conditions. These locales were highlighted because, logically, the preservation and burial of paleosols and associated archaeological sites are most common along rivers and streams where sedimentological and geological factors allow periodic, extensive aggregation of sediment. This notion is support by our discussion of buried site locations presented in chapters 4 and 5. These locations indicate that although such sites occur in a wide variety of environments, shoreline and alluvial locales predominate. In fact, even dune-buried sites, such as the Wycamp Creek and Portage sites found near Little Traverse Bay (Lovis et al. 1998; Figure 4-1 and Table 5-1), are typically associated with the shorelines of the Great Lakes and are only rarely found within interior dunes.

Because no coverages exist that digitally delineate their distribution, several different environmental parameters that either are directly associated with or can be used to predict the frequency of flooding and sedimentation were selected to help define floodplains. These were then manipulated and combined into a single derivative GIS map coverage that defines areas where buried surfaces and associated archaeological sites may be preserved. Thus, the buried site potential of the study area was defined through the creation of a composite of the databases and coverages through a series of overlay operations to union, combine, and intersect the diverse types of data from multiple sources into a single GIS coverage.

In order to undertake this operation, each of the diverse coverages within the study area was referenced to a common coordinate and projection system. The Michigan GeoRef coordinate system discussed above was selected as the common projection for map coverages because it is used universally by MDOT for its GIS. Once the coverages were placed in a common map projection, the main task of defining and ranking parts of the study area that might include alluvially buried archaeological deposits could begin. The first step in this process was to define the extent and distribution of floodplains in the area. By necessity, the floodplain became the primary landform of interest because the greatest potential for alluviation, sediment accretion, and site burial is along rivers. Unfortunately, as mentioned previously, because floodplains have not been specifically mapped in Michigan, their distribution can only be deduced based on other indirect, incomplete, or surrogate data. We drew upon several different data sets to collectively define floodplains in the region. Ultimately, these focused primarily on countywide FEMA Q3-FIRM and SSURGO soil data (see previous discussion). To varying degrees of accuracy and among other flood-hazard information, the Q3-FIRM data defines the 100- and 500-year floodplains. Many of the issues and problems related to usage of the Q3-FIRM data have been discussed previously. The most critical topic to consider when trying to apply this data, however, is that the FEMA maps were constructed not to intrinsically map floodplains from a geomorphological perspective but rather to rate areas of land based on their relative flood insurance risk. As a consequence, the distributions of Q3-FIRM floodplains must be carefully considered. For the purposes of this study, they should be scrutinized with an eye toward their geomorphological "reality." Less ambiguous data showing the distribution of floodplains can be derived from the SSURGO soil data. Although soil types are the principal map unit, information about whether a soil type is part of a floodplain, or at least whether it is alluvially derived, is also included as part of the SSURGO CAT database.

By selectively displaying the soils with "floodplain" or "alluvial" attributes and grouping (or unioning) these together with the Q3-FIRM map units that have "100-" or "500-year" attributes, a partial floodplain map was developed for southern Lower Michigan (Figure 7-3). Not surprisingly, the initial floodplain coverage constructed from this data was discontinuous throughout the study, with gaps common along even major streams. This occurred not only because the floodplains are not composed exclusively of alluvial soils but also because the coverage of SSURGO and Q3-FIRM data is incomplete across the area. For example, many counties have only one or the other coverage, and several counties have neither SSURGO nor Q3-FIRM coverage available (see Table 7-1 and Figure 7-3). A generally continuous floodplain was assembled by filling in the gaps of the derivative coverage. This process was performed based on clear geomorphological criteria that were apparent on 1:24,000 DRG quadrangles or by using published nondigital maps or the authors' private field notes as a guide. In addition, counties that did not include either SSURGO or Q3-FIRM data but had sufficient published and private maps that depicted the floodplain were used to extend the more detailed coverage. Ultimately, a single coverage was created that defined the extent of floodplains for about 75 percent of the study area (Figure 7-3).

Once the composite floodplain coverage was constructed, it was used to clip attribute information from various other GIS map coverages. These included such data as slope, geometry, and area of the floodplain, as well as the texture and distribution of soils. Where more complete coverages were available, the relationship of alluvial soils to the 100- or 500-year flood pool and to the Nipissing lake plain was also determined. The data were subsequently unioned or intersected with each other to establish a combined GIS framework that associated several important pieces of baseline geological, environmental, geomorphological, and sedimentological information into one coverage. This collection of information provided the basis for subdividing the floodplains and other landforms of the study area into groups based on their relative site burial potential.

A buried archaeological site potential GIS coverage was developed by ranking localities of the study area based on ascending integer numbers. Broadly, localities were assigned potentials that depended on the relative number and combinations of high-potential predictors present, as well as on the "quality" of data available. The number 1 was assigned to areas representing the lowest potential, while 1,000 represented the highest potential. The value of 0 was assigned to areas where insufficient data was available to reasonably evaluate any sort of potential for buried sites. More details of these values, as well as an explanation

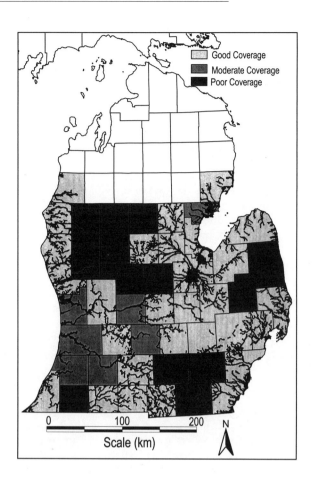

Figure 7-3. The distribution of flood-plains or other flood-prone land-forms (marked by black areas and lines) in the study area. Quality of data used to construct floodplains shown by county: light gray (good coverage) indicates that SSURGO and/or Q3-FIRM data, along with geomorphological data, was used to define floodplains; medium gray (moderate coverage) indicates that floodplains were based mainly on field maps or geomorphological relationships; dark gray (poor coverage) indicates that insufficient data was available to reasonably define floodplain distributions.

for the basis for their designation, are shown in Table 7-4. Of the data available for this study, texture, slope, and the probability of flooding are probably the most important predictors for burial and preservation of paleosols and, consequently, archaeological sites. This is suggested because low-gradient, broad streams that include high suspended sediment load (i.e., fine-grained) tend to be less "erosive" and more "constructive" of floodplains than high-gradient streams with high bed-loads (i.e., abundant coarse-grained sediment) and narrow, steep floodplains (Huisink 2000; Monaghan and Hayes 1997, 1998, 2001; Monaghan and Schaetzl 1994). Considering the GIS data included in this study, this data is readily available only from the SSURGO and Q3-FIRM data sets. Consequently, for areas where these coverages were not integrated into the floodplain map, detailed or specific probability ranking was not performed. Instead, these areas were assigned values that indicate only a broad ranking from relatively low to relatively high (see values 9, 49, and 99 in Table 7-4).

The lowest buried site potential values (i.e., less than 9) were usually assigned to areas that were outside the floodplain. These were categorized as having low potential because the opportunity for significant sediment accretion, and consequently site burial, was minimal. High-potential areas (values greater than 99) occurred within flat, broad, fine-grained floodplains because these areas had the

Table 7-4. Classification Used in Archaeological Site Potential Model.

Code	Class	Explanation of Factors Controlling Class
0	Not Assessed (inadequate coverage)	Explanation: GIS coverages are not complete and not enough information available to create reasonable model of site burial potential. These areas have no detailed soil (SSURGO), Q3-FIRM (FEMA), and flood-plain maps. Deep Test Recommendation: Deep testing may be required. Specific areas should be assessed by geoarchaeologists to determine if deep testing is needed.
1	Low	Explanation: GIS coverages for the area complete enough to show that the potential of finding buried sites is low. These areas are typically not within floodplains, mid-Holocene lake plains, or other areas where site burial is likely. Areas within urban settings, however, may include sites buried by historic cultural fills related to urbanization. Deep Test Recommendation: Deep testing not required.
3	Low (Nipissing inundation)	Explanation: GIS coverages for the area complete enough to show that the potential of finding buried sites is low. These areas typically occur outside of floodplains and show no evidence of alluviation but occur within the Nipissing lake plain. Site burial is not likely but could have occurred during the mid-Holocene (i.e., Ebenhoff Dune site; 20SA596). These areas are confined mainly to the Shiawassee flats (Saginaw Bay region) or along the Great Lakes shoreline. Deep Test Recommendation: Deep testing not required. However, specific areas might need to be tested. These sites could be assessed by trained geoarchaeologists using soil probes, stream-bank exposures, and/or bucket augers to determine if mechanical deep testing is required.
5-8	Low–Moderate	Explanation: GIS coverages complete enough to show that the potential of finding buried sites for the area is low to moderate. These areas are typically either outside or near the margin of floodplains and are often associated with the upper reaches of stream valleys. Areas are sometimes associated with Q3-FIRM (FEMA) 100- or 500-year flood areas that are not directly associated with streams but occur within wetland areas subject to occasional flooding by seasonally ponded water. Site burial is not likely but could occur related to specific conditions. If it occurs, site burial is probably shallow. Deep Test Recommendation: Deep testing not required. However, specific areas might need to be tested. These sites could be assessed by trained geoarchaeologists using soil probes, stream-bank exposures, and/or bucket augers to determine if mechanical deep testing is required.
9	Moderate	Explanation: GIS coverages are incomplete but include enough data to show that the potential of finding buried sites for the area is moderate. These areas usually do not include soil (SSURGO) data but either have Q3-FIRM or other mapped information to define floodplain boundaries. These areas typically form near the margin of floodplains, occur along very minor streams with very narrow floodplains, or occur within the upper reaches of stream valleys. Site burial could occur but is not likely. Deep Test Recommendation: These areas probably require testing. Sites could be initially assessed by trained geoarchaeologists using soil probes, stream-bank exposures, and/or bucket augers to determine if mechanical deep testing is required.
10-40	Moderate	Explanation: GIS coverages complete enough to show that the potential of finding buried sites is moderate. These areas consist of coarse-grained sediment along minor streams or in the upper reaches or margins of major streams. Site burial could occur but is probably not deep. Deep Test Recommendation: These areas probably require testing. Sites could be initially assessed by trained geoarchaeologists using soil probes, stream-bank exposures, and/or bucket augers to determine if mechanical deep testing is required.

(table 7-4 cont.)

Code	Class	Explanation of Factors Controlling Class
49	Moderate–High (inadequate coverage)	Explanation: GIS coverages are incomplete but include enough data to show that the potential of finding buried sites is moderate to high (i.e., greater than code 9). These areas usually do not include soil (SSURGO) data, but either have Q3-FIRM or other mapped information to define floodplain boundaries. These areas typically form the floodplains of minor or major streams but are associated with either narrow reaches or high gradients floodplains. Site burial could occur, but the lack of textural information makes their classification subjective. Deep Test Recommendation: These areas should be deep tested.
50–90	Moderate–High	Explanation: GIS coverages are complete enough to show that the potential of finding buried sites is moderate to high. These areas typically form the floodplains of minor or major streams but are composed on coarse-textured or nonalluvial soils. In major streams, these areas often occur near the floodplain margins. These areas can also be associated with narrow reaches or high gradients of floodplains. Site burial could occur. Deep Test Recommendation: These areas should be deep tested.
99	High–Moderate (inadequate coverage)	Explanation: GIS coverages are incomplete but include enough data to show that the potential of finding buried sites is high to moderate (i.e., greater than code 49). These areas usually do not include soil (SSURGO) data but either have Q3-FIRM or other mapped information to define floodplain boundaries. These areas typically form the floodplains of minor or major streams and are of relatively low gradient but lack textural information to determine the frequency of flooding and likelihood of fine-sediment accretion. Site burial likely to occur in these areas, but the lack of textural information makes their classification subjective. Deep Test Recommendation: These areas should be deep tested.
100–400	High	Explanation: GIS coverages are complete enough to show that the potential of finding buried sites is high. These areas typically form the floodplains of major streams or the lower reaches of minor streams, are of relatively low gradient, and include coarse- and fine-grained flood-prone soils or fine-grained nonalluvial soils. Some of these areas, particularly within the Nipissing lake plain in Bay and Saginaw counties, also occur beyond the obvious floodplains of streams but are composed of flood-prone soils; these areas may include older (i.e., pre-Nipissing) floodplain deposits with buried pre–late Holocene sites or include more shallowly buried younger (Late Archaic and Woodland) sites. Site burial is likely to occur in these areas. Deep Test Recommendation: These areas should be deep tested.
500–600	High–Very High	Explanation: GIS coverages are complete enough to show that the potential of finding buried sites is high to very high. These areas typically form the floodplains of major streams and have wide, very low gradient to flat floodplains. They are composed of thick, fine-grained alluvial soils. These areas are very common in Saginaw, Bay, Midland, and Tuscola counties and along the St. Joseph and Grand river valleys. Site burial is likely to occur in these areas. Deep Test Recommendation: These areas should be deep tested.
700–1,000	Very High	Explanation: GIS coverages are complete enough to show that the potential of finding buried sites is very high. These areas typically form the floodplains of major streams and have wide, almost flat floodplains. They are composed exclusively of thick, fine-grained, flood-prone alluvial soils. The highest probability areas (i.e. 1,000) occur along streams within the Nipissing lake plain, particularly within 3 km of the Nipissing maximum limit. These areas are very common in Saginaw, Bay, and Midland counties. Site burial is likely in these areas. Deep Test Recommendation: These areas should be deep tested.

[1]Numeric code showing the relative potential that an area may contain buried surfaces (i.e., buried archaeological deposits). Numbers range from 1 to 1,000, with lower numbers indicating lower probabilities; 0 = areas not assessed; 1 = lowest probabilities; 1,000 = highest probabilities. Relative ranking within categories is arbitrary or subjective and is based on minor differences in textural, slope, or other environmental conditions.

greatest potential for significant alluviation. Rankings between low and high potential, and well as subdivisions of high potential, were based on the relative numbers and types of "high-potential predictor" attributes found on the floodplain. Thus, floodplain areas that occur within upstream portions of high-gradient, narrow, relatively minor tributary streams, particularly if composed on nonalluvial soils, were usually assigned values representing moderate to low potential. Somewhat broader floodplains along larger, lower-gradient streams were usually assigned moderate potential, particularly if fine-grained alluvial soils were not present. Additionally, portions of broader, major steam floodplains that were either coarse-grained or found near the valley margins of broader floodplains were also designated as having moderate potential.

The high-potential areas are of greatest interest to this study. These were generally associated with broad, flat (low-gradient) floodplains, particularly those composed of fine-grained, flood-prone alluvial soils. In addition, flood-prone areas near the confluence of major rivers with relatively large tributary streams are also relatively high potential. Intuitively, these areas include both cultural and natural reasons for suspecting that they may be high potential because alluvial fans, which are generally accretionary, are commonly associated with such environments. However, the relative ranking for these areas was actually based on the number of "high-potential predictor" attributes found within portions of the floodplain. In general, the "lower" ends of high potential were typically associated with floodplains that had somewhat higher gradients, or were along the lower portions of tributary streams, or had more coarse-grained soils. The upper ends, on the other hand, were composed of fine-grained alluvial soils that formed wide, flat floodplains. Because of the numerous buried archaeological sites clustered within and near the margin of the Nipissing lake plain, particularly in Bay and Saginaw counties, the highest potential for site burial was assigned to floodplains that had the high-potential characteristics (i.e., broad, fine-grained, flood-prone, low-gradient floodplains) and that were within or near the margin of the Nipissing lake plain.

Discussion, Summary, and Conclusions

The overarching objective for the construction of the buried archaeological site GIS framework was to understand how the locations for buried archaeological sites interacted with related geomorphological and environmental information. The underlying goal of this work was to fashion a GIS coverage that "modeled" the distribution of areas of high, moderate, and low potential for buried archaeological resources in the southern Lower Peninsula of Michigan. Additionally, we hoped to assist MDOT, as well as other state and federal agencies, plan for and manage deeply buried archaeological deposits by mapping counties based their relative buried archaeological site potential. This analysis proceeded by first studying the distribution of known buried archaeological sites, compiling the results of any previous deep-test studies, and finally relating this data to other environmental information that may predict the locations of buried archaeological resources. By relating all of these factors, a GIS framework was created that modeled the relative potential of a specific area to contain buried sites.

From the perspective of state and federal agency archaeologists, the most significant application of this GIS model is probably its utility to aid in long-range planning. For example, if the potential for buried archaeological resources of areas can be known, then future MDOT projects might be better prepared to address many of the more problematic aspects of CRM. This is suggested because once they have been identified, areas of high potential for buried resources could then either be avoided or at least tested for the presence of buried archaeological resources early in the site-selection process. If considered early in the project development time frame, delays could be minimized. Moreover, last-minute (and consequently expensive) surprises of complex buried or stratified sites could be eliminated. In order to facilitate this process, two basic GIS coverages were constructed and included in this study.

The first coverage is a point source location map that includes the locations and other significant information for the major stratified or buried archaeological sites as well as all the DTLs from southern Lower Michigan. This data represents a complete list of DTLs that had been reported before January 2003. The information included as attributes within the coverage concentrated on providing environmental, archaeological, or descriptive data about the location of DTLs or buried sites. To allow easy access to further details about the GIS point, a bibliographical reference to the original report is also provided. Details about the attributes included are presented in Table 7-3. The locations of the point within the coverage were plotted on USGS 1:24,000 DRG based on information provided in the original report about the DTL or archaeological site. Importantly, although it was rechecked with the original map, the exact point location is dependent on the information provided in the original citation.

The construction of an ArcVIEW coverage that "modeled" or "predicted" the probability of finding buried archaeological deposits within southern Lower Michigan was one of the central goals of this study. For a variety of sound reasons, however, we did not attempt to predict the actual, specific locations of buried sites directly. Rather, we focused on defining places within the study area where buried ground surfaces, or paleosols, are most likely to occur. This provides an indirect, yet broader, perspective on buried site locations and is probably a more appropriate approach because the cultural and environmental factors that control the archaeological site locations are extremely complicated and poorly understood. The indirect prediction is based on an understanding of the relationships between paleosols, alluviation, and archaeological site formation processes that are fundamental to this study and detailed throughout this monograph. Essentially, we assume that sites are buried within broader areas, such as floodplains, where sedimentological and geological factors allow periodic, extensive aggregation of sediment. Moreover, archaeological sites can only be preserved if the paleosol that they are associated with is also buried and preserved. We have concentrated mainly on floodplain environments, because these landforms offer the best potential for preservation and burial of such paleosols and associated sites.

The floodplain necessarily became the primary map unit in this study. However, because coverages that digitally delineated floodplains throughout southern Lower Michigan did not exist when this project began, they had to be constructed. These were assembled based on several environmental and geo-morphological parameters associated with floodplains rather than by directly mapping floodplains in the field. Important attributes and data from each of these maps were then combined into a composite coverage through a series of GIS overlay operations. Ultimately, the final buried archaeological site potential coverage was produced by ranking localities of the study area based on the presence of specific attributes that predicted the presence and burial of paleosols. Ranking was expressed by ascending integer numbers, with 1 assigned to areas typifying the lowest potential and 1,000 delineating the highest potential. In some cases, not enough information existed within the area to even speculate about the buried site potential. These areas were designated by assigning 0 for buried site potential.

Areas outside of the floodplain were generally categorized as possessing the lowest potential because the opportunity for significant sediment accretion, and consequently site burial, was minimal. The high-potential areas, on the other hand, were generally associated with broad, flat (low-gradient) floodplains composed of fine-grained, flood-prone alluvial soils. Because of the numerous buried archaeological sites clustered within and near the margin of the Nipissing lake plain, particularly in Bay and Saginaw counties, the highest potential for site burial was assigned to floodplains that had the high-potential characteristics described above and that were within or near the margin of the Great Lakes, were covered by fine-grained alluvial soils, and were characterized by low-gradient surfaces.

CHAPTER EIGHT

Recommendations and Procedures for Undertaking Discovery of Deeply Buried Archaeological Sites in Lower Michigan

Importance of an Earth Science Perspective

As revealed in the introductory chapter of this monograph, differing methods and techniques have been applied to the discovery of buried archaeological resources in Michigan during the past several decades. Some of these approaches are well designed, regionally focused, and interdisciplinary in scope. These include, most notably, the regional corridor studies by Monaghan and others of the Great Lakes Gas and Vector pipelines (Branstner 1990a, 1991; Monaghan 1990a; Monaghan and Hayes 1999; Monaghan and Schaetzl 1994), as well as the US-31 and US-23 projects (Monaghan 1999, 1995c). At their best, studies like these aim to integrate earth science techniques with archaeological perspectives in an attempt to gain a better understanding of Holocene depositional patterns and their effects on archaeological site preservation. Their goal is not only to discover whether buried archaeological resources exist at a specific locale but also to evaluate the probability that other buried archaeological resources may occur elsewhere on the floodplain. By broadening the research goals to achieve a more comprehensive picture of local depositional history, the larger question of why a specific location contains or does not contain buried deposits can be addressed. As such, these more broadly conceived projects represent the basis for constructing the predictive framework proposed in this study.

We have sought to show that the general application of these interdisciplinary methods and ideas to deep-site discovery in Michigan over the past two decades has resulted in the recognition of entirely new and previously unknown suites of information about the historic and prehistoric past. This can also be said for our understanding of the archaeological data, as well as for the long- and short-term geological processes responsible for the formation of alluvial landforms. As a consequence of these successes, the scope of such interdisciplinary research has also been transformed from more idiosyncratic and descriptive applications in project-specific context to an increasing awareness of regional-level applications and an emphasis on formation and depositional processes. A fundamental principle of an interdisciplinary approach to the discovery of buried archaeological resources is the concept that site distribution, particularly associated with site preservation, is linked to long-term patterns of sedimentation and cannot be fully understood isolated from local and regional drainage basin development. The articulation of this linkage, in the context of formulating a regional depositional model, is an important underlying objective of this study. Such models, however, cannot be formulated either locally or regionally without sound, reliable data collected from a variety of geological and archaeological contexts.

Our review of deep-test studies in southern Lower Michigan highlighted the fact that many of the deep-test projects conducted in the region have not applied the kinds of interdisciplinary approaches appropriate to the discovery or evaluation of buried archaeological resources. Nor have these studies usually focused on the larger, regional questions described above. Typically, many projects neglected the importance of synthesizing patterns of sedimentation and regional Holocene depositional history with the actual site discovery process and focused more narrowly only on finding archaeological sites. Although more limited in scope and often undertaken by archaeological professionals with only minimal background or training in the earth sciences, some of these studies were nevertheless adequate for site discovery purposes. In fact, a few such projects even located important buried and stratified archaeological sites. These include, most notably, the Weber I site discovered during Phase I work related to the Dehmel Road Bridge replacement study (Brunett 1981a, 1981c). Subsequently, data-recovery efforts were undertaken at these sites (Lovis, ed. 1989) and documented a Middle Archaic occupation that was buried and inundated during the Nipissing transgression (Monaghan et al. 1986). Indeed, the significance of the Weber I site was not realized at the time of its discovery but was only understood during excavation through the efforts of an interdisciplinary research approach (Lovis, ed. 1989). As discussed below, the application of an interdisciplinary approach would have probably been more productive and resulted in a better research design if applied earlier in the project during the Phase I effort.

Because site discovery projects are principally related to cultural resources management (CRM) pursuits and therefore competitively bid, the input of earth science specialists has often been neglected during the early phases of evaluation because of cost considerations. Simply stated, the fewer higher-level (and higher-paid) personnel involved with a project, the lower the cost and the more competitive the price. This is unfortunate because even though many archaeologists, regulators, and project administrators have come to recognize the importance of deep-site discovery, cost considerations continue largely to drive the process. The competitive nature of CRM work means that in the absence of clear-cut guidance and requirements placed on prospective bidders by regulatory agencies in Michigan, project cost will continue to drive deep-test efforts and methods. Guidelines that outline where and when testing for buried sites are necessary have not yet been established in Michigan, except on a project-by-project basis. In addition, neither acceptable methods nor professional standards and criteria are routinely specified for projects. Since the success of such deep-testing projects as the Great Lakes Gas Transmission Pipeline, the CERT and other Bay City area studies, and, most recently, the US-131 (S-Curve) data recovery, this has begun to change. This chapter aims to help this process along by offering an outline for basic standards and methods that should be considered when undertaking deep-testing efforts in Michigan.

Lamentably, over the past few decades the decisions about where and how to explore for buried cultural resources in Michigan have usually rested with the very CRM firms that bid on the project and not with the appropriate state compliance agencies. Consequently, the application of earth science perspectives that can address the types of geoarchaeological issues and problems discussed here are often haphazardly applied to CRM projects in Michigan. Although many firms do include geoarchaeological work in their projects, where cost is critical, substantive deep testing is often ignored, relying instead on, as we mentioned in Part I, "shovel testing a little bit deeper" along floodplains. Hence, projects of this sort not only inadequately protect cultural resources but also often waste valuable opportunities to advance the archaeological sciences. An important goal of this work is to provide the Michigan Department of Transportation (MDOT) and the State Historic Preservation Office (SHPO) basic guidelines for field methods and data collection as well as to suggest minimum standards for reporting the results obtained through deep testing.

Even though, as mentioned above, cost considerations are often the primary limitation for including professional earth scientists in deep-testing projects, philosophical positions can also sometimes constrain accomplishing the types of significant interdisciplinary work we have espoused here. Many regulatory agency administrators and archaeological investigators, for example, believe that earth science and geoarchaeology specialists are hardly needed to simply "discover" buried archaeological sites. Rather, such specialists are considered most "cost-effectively" used during the evaluation or data-recovery phases of the work (i.e., Phase II or III level). Thus, only if a site is found and additional assessment is required to clarify aspects of site stratigraphy, origin, or "intactness" are geoarchaeologists or earth scientists called upon to contribute to the project. We believe that this notion is incorrect and ultimately shortsighted. In fact, earth science methods and perspectives are actually most effectively employed in the earliest phases of a research project, when an understanding of the origin and depositional history of the locale will greatly aid in developing a coherent strategy to guide future work at the site.

A basic understanding of floodplain stratigraphy and depositional history is just as important when buried archaeological material is not discovered as it is when a site is found. Why a site or paleosol occurs within a floodplain sequence or, if not found, what the probability is that either might be found elsewhere at the location are critical questions to answer. The question of why they do or do not occur is best addressed by focusing on the site-specific depositional environments and sedimentology that occur within the stratigraphic sequence. Similarly, gauging the probability that buried soils and sites may occur elsewhere on the local floodplain can only be achieved through an understanding of the depositional history of the floodplain under study.

This is not to say that the research that did not employ geologists or geoarchaeologists was necessarily of poor quality. In fact, some studies were quite thorough in reporting specific sets of details. Our experience working with the published data in Michigan, however, shows that many of these reports were incomplete in some respect or another. These deficiencies generally rendered them insufficient to aid in predicting or understanding site burial potential, other than the presence or absence of archaeological materials or buried organic horizons or "soils." Rather, these studies point to the fact that without clear guidelines and minimum field and reporting standards, both data collection and reporting tend to be inconsistent. By reviewing the previous deep-test efforts, the aspects of these studies that were not adequate can be noted and, more important, the types of changes in methods and reporting that will ultimately lead to improvements in future projects can be proposed.

Knowing just how the floodplain history of a locale integrates with archaeological site formation and preservation is critical for understanding archaeological site taphonomy. Moreover, understanding the ways that site formation processes articulate with human settlement history and ecological or environmental transformation to form and alter the overall archaeological record is also important. Such an understanding can only be achieved through an ongoing dialogue between archaeologists, geologists, pedologists, and those in other geoarchaeological disciplines. In this chapter, we will propose a set of minimum standards for data collection and reporting related to deep-testing studies that will promote this dialogue. To this end, we will outline how the basic earth science approach to developing a floodplain history through a three-dimensional reconstruction of the subsurface can be undertaken. We will also discuss the basic tools, equipment, and personnel necessary for such work and suggest standards for data reporting.

The Three-Dimensional Approach to Floodplain Reconstruction

Any investigations undertaken to discover deeply buried archaeological resources within both large and small fluvial systems should focus on a systematic reconstruction of the geological and depositional history revealed by the stratigraphy of the floodplain sediments. This is best accomplished by developing a three-dimensional model of the subsurface based on systematic, subsurface exploratory methods, such as a series of backhoe trenches or continuous cores, that penetrate important terraces and other fluvial features on the floodplain. The series of trenches or cores should not only sample specific natural and/or cultural features but should also be oriented and positioned in such a fashion that allows construction of a cross section, or series of cross sections, that displays the stratigraphic and lithological relationships and correlations of each geological, pedological, and/or archaeological unit revealed in the subsurface. These cross sections should also aim to link the stratigraphy discovered to the human and natural landform surface features on the floodplain as well as allow buried parts of the landforms to be reconstructed to their original, preburial configuration. In general, lacking other information to guide placement, the preferred orientation for trenches should be perpendicular or transverse to floodplain axis or alluvial patterns expressed on the surface (i.e., terraces, abandoned and active channels, back-swamps, and other geomorphological features). In Michigan, such surface features may reasonably be used as a guide to the subsurface because drainage systems are so relatively young and immature. However, this is not always true. For example, key surface morphological features, such as those associated with the early and middle Holocene prior to the Nipissing transgression, may not be present on the modern floodplain surface. In fact, if partly buried, these may not have any obvious relationship to present channel configurations. Only through detailed reconstruction of the buried landscape can these relationships be properly sorted out. Clearly, experience and specialized training are required to undertake such interpretations.

Although the most important aim of deep-test exploration projects is to discover and evaluate the significance of buried archaeological resources, this effort by itself is incomplete because the probability of the occurrence of archaeological resources elsewhere in the study area cannot be adequately assessed. By broadening the goals of the deep testing to develop a more complete picture of the depositional history of a specific floodplain locale, elements like the stratigraphic locations and the timing of depositional hiatuses representing periods when prehistoric people could have lived on the floodplain can be suggested. Because of its strength in reconstructing depositional history and understanding floodplain evolution, an approach relying on three-dimensional sedimentological techniques should be regularly utilized during all deep-test CRM projects. The goal of discovering and predicting the location of buried archaeological sites naturally goes hand-in-hand with the recognition of buried alluvial deposits, channels, or related Holocene alluvial features and landforms. As revealed in the reference list for this study, these techniques have been commonly used by the authors not only in Michigan but also throughout the Great Lakes and northeastern regions of the United States.

Because the cross section reconstructions rely heavily on the detailed observation of fundamental geological factors, such as sedimentology (sediment bedding, texture, etc.), vertical changes in sedimentary sequences, and the weathering and pedological characteristics of sediments, broad earth sciences training and field experience are critical. Although the actual degree discipline might vary for individual geoarchaeologists who implement such projects (e.g., geology, geography, anthropology, etc.), experience and thorough training in geomorphology, pedology, and sedimentology are important in establishing a minimum level of credentials that should be required to undertake deep-testing work. For example, geoarchaeologists who exclusively study the composition of pottery or of lithic sources but who have no training in the physical properties of sediments are not appropriately trained to undertake deep testing. Furthermore, one or two courses in introductory geology, geomorphology, or physical geography do not represent adequate preparation or credentials for such work. Additional details concerning the minimum qualifications for researchers as well as suggestions for the types of recording methods and equipment needed to undertake deep testing are discussed below.

Field Methods and Standards

A variety of different methods and techniques can be employed to explore for buried archaeological resources. These include mechanical procedures, most commonly backhoe trenching or borehole drilling, as well as various geophysical techniques such as resistivity and geomagnetic surveys or ground penetrating radar (GPR). Although each of these methods has its relative advantages and disadvantages, our experience suggests that despite its brute-force approach, backhoe trenching ultimately offers the most efficient, certain, and cost-effective way of locating buried archaeological resources within floodplain or alluvial settings. The relative merits of these techniques, arranged from the least to greatest impact to archaeological sites, are described below.

Because they usually do not involve any direct subsurface disturbance, geophysical techniques are generally the least intrusive site exploration procedure (Bates 2000; Schurr 1997; Wynn 1986). Unfortunately, unless combined with other direct-sampling methods (e.g., coring), they can also be the least effective at finding sites with any certainty (Bates 2000). Such approaches are generally most effective for large urban prehistoric or historic sites or within urban landscapes where relatively extensive cultural features (such as building foundations and earthworks) and large metal artifacts occur in abundance (Chávez et al. 2001; Hargrave et al. 2002). Certain geophysical methods can also be effectively used to map subsurface features and horizons at large stratified or buried prehistoric sites (Isaacson et al. 1999). The limitations of geophysical approaches for buried site discovery are particularly true for methods that focus on resistivity and geomagnetic techniques (Bates 2000). Considering that they generally rely on the presence of some type of soil or sediment "anomaly," most typically of unknown origin, geophysical explorations usually show some level of positive results (Isaacson et al. 1999). These results can be buried archaeological features but might also represent natural soil and sedimentary anomalies (i.e., well-indurated argillic [B-] subsurface soil horizons, channel fills, peat deposits, etc.). Thus, outcomes for geophysical surveys focusing on exploration for unknown buried sties are typically equivocal and usually require a relatively high degree of interpretation or corroborative data to argue for the presence of archaeological resources (Isaacson et al. 1999). This is particularly true for prehistoric sites, where relatively small and limited cultural features and few if any metal artifacts occur, leading to likely confusion or masking with natural anomalies. More important, even if buried archaeological resources are potentially indicated, subsurface excavation must still be undertaken. Because of cost considerations, this further work is usually done with a backhoe. Consequently, these remote methods are probably better employed during later phases of work related to the exploration of known or newly discovered buried sites, for example, tracing known layers to determine the site boundaries or mapping the remnants of larger-scale features like fragmentary and partially destroyed earthworks (Schurr 1997).

Drilling, using some type of continuous core-recovery equipment, offers a better alternative for exploration but also includes some similar limitations. It has been used extensively in archaeological site investigations (both historic and prehistoric) and buried site exploration, particularly in the CRM environment (Canti and Meddens 1997; Stein 1986, 1991). Continuous sediment cores can be collected using a variety of equipment. These include vibracore devices and split-spoon sampling using a hollow stem auger, as well as common hydraulic equipment brands such as Giddings Drilling Rigs or Geoprobes. In general, coring should be separated from augering. The former yields excellent subsurface information, while the latter does not. Large-diameter bucket augers have been suggested as a quick and inexpensive method of coring (Schuldenrein 1991). Such a technique, however, does not yield continuous, undisturbed core data and cannot give the same quality geological and sedimentological information as other true coring methods (Stein 1991).

Vibracore devices are relatively small and often transportable by an individual. They work by "vibrating" a tube through sediment by partly desegregating the sediment and recover a continuous solid core that is usually 6–10 cm in diameter. Split-spoon sampling is typically performed using a 60-cm-long, 5-cm-diameter core tool that is inserted into a hollow-stemmed auger (larger core devices are sometimes employed). It requires a large, specially equipped drilling truck to transport and run the equipment. The split-spoon coring device is then driven into the ground the length of the spoon (i.e., usually 60 cm) using a hammer-blow tool. It is withdrawn and opened, and the sample is then extracted. The hollow-stemmed auger is subsequently drilled down the length of the split-spoon core, and the operation is repeated. In this fashion, a series of 60-cm samples can be taken to form a more or less "continuous core" of any length. Hydraulic coring devices, such as Giddings and Geoprobes devices, are similar to split-spoon devices but are usually smaller. They are either truck or trailer mounted. To recover sediment cores, a 2.5–5-cm-diameter hollow tube (usually a 1.2–2.2-m long plastic or aluminum) is actually hydraulically "pushed" into the ground the length of the core tube. Once the appropriate depth is reached, the tube is pulled and cut in half (typically with a saw), and the core samples are extracted. Under the best of conditions, these devices can recover sets of cores up to several meters long.

All of the drilling methods mentioned above are relatively nonintrusive (Stein 1986). Depending on the equipment used, only a 2.5–15 cm diameter borehole will actually impact the archaeological deposits. Unlike geophysical methods, however, sediments and soils can be directly observed. Cores are particularly useful to discover where buried soil horizons are present. The typically small-diameter sediment cores that can be recovered using most coring rigs, however, only allow a limited view of the sedimentary sequence (i.e., bedding types and extent) and soil characteristics. Thus, although paleosols might be obvious in the core, the probability of actually recovering archaeological material from it, particularly given the low-density attributes of prehistoric sites characteristically found in Michigan, is small. This is especially true for low-density sites where sediment cores are not likely to include direct evidence for an archaeological site (features, tools, etc.). Consequently, and as was also true for geophysical methods, those areas that evidence the possibility of buried sites ultimately usually must still be excavated to verify the presence of archaeological deposits. Cost, time, and depth of burial combine to dictate that this excavation is usually undertaken with heavy equipment, such as a backhoe.

While not ideal for initial exploration for buried sites, core data can be very effectively employed to trace known, well-defined archaeological deposits within the subsurface, to demarcate site boundaries, or to trace site remnants to determine where excavation blocks should be placed to maximize archaeological information (Canti and Meddens 1997; Stein 1986). Mechanically tracing buried site deposits using these procedures was recently used to establish the limits of a relatively undisturbed site midden and guide the placement of excavation blocks for data-recovery efforts at the Converse site (Hambacher et al. 2003). The research at Converse also points out an important outcome of the early participation of geoarchaeologists. The involvement of a geoarchaeologist during the discovery phase of the Converse site allowed an efficient, timely, and cost-effective appraisal of the relative integrity and importance of the site. Without the early-stage, multidisciplinary approach to this project, it probably would not have been completed within the time constraints placed upon it.

Our experience in the upper Great Lakes region indicates that deep testing for buried archaeological sites can be most efficiently and effectively performed through mechanical trenching using either a rubber-tire or tracked backhoe. With very few exceptions, this is true despite the fact that trenching is one of the most destructive approaches to discovering buried archaeological resources. Except for hand excavation, backhoe trenching is the only technique we know of that will allow the exposure of a relatively long, continuous soil and geological (sedimentary) profile. Such an exposure offers the best potential for actually "seeing" features and artifact concentrations that are directly associated with parts of a buried archaeological site. Additionally, the direct exposure of subsurface horizons also offers an opportunity for controlled testing of deeply buried paleosols for the presence of relatively low-density archaeological materials. In fact, many states actually require controlled archaeological testing of buried surfaces (i.e., A-) soil horizons discovered within floodplain settings. This testing is typically performed by positioning a test unit of specific size (e.g., 50 × 50 cm or 1 × 1 m) from one trench wall, mechanically removing the sediment overlying the paleosol in the test unit, and then hand excavating and screening the sediment from the buried soil horizon. Alternatively, a known volume of sediment (i.e., 10 or 20 1iters) from the buried soil is sometimes sampled from several places along the length of the trench and screened. Either way sampling is done, the artifact concentration of the horizon, expressed as either artifact numbers or weights per unit volume, can be calculated. Together with the presence of other archaeologically significant components (features, bone, organic material, etc.), this data can be used to determine whether further archaeological testing (either Phase II assessment or direct data recovery) is required.

In practice, the sizes of backhoe trenches required to undertake effective testing are quite variable and often dictated by unique conditions in the field. Generally, backhoe trenches should be wide enough to allow inspection of wall profiles. Mechanically, this is most efficiently accomplished using a 1-m-wide backhoe bucket. Aspects of the backhoe, as well as safety standards, often also determine the maximum depth for trenches. For example, the normal backhoe boom, which often extends up to 3–5 m, usually allows a < 5-m-deep maximum depth to the excavation. From a safety perspective, trenches more than about 175 cm deep must be stepped back to meet Occupational Safety and Health Administration (OSHA) standards. In practice, depths for even large backhoe excavation are about 5 m. Consequently, if greater depths are required, coring is probably a better alternative.

The placement and number of trenches excavated at each deep test location (DTL) are necessarily variable and depend on the site testing objectives, topography, and stratigraphy. Sometimes accessibility, either environmental or property ownership, is a limiting factor and can define the ultimate placement of trenches. In any case, a minimum of two trenches (or cores) should be excavated at any DTL to allow reconstruction of the subsurface. In general, trenches should be excavated as narrow and short as possible and still allow a complete disclosure of the stratigraphy and soil profiles. Such trenches are ordinarily approximately 1 m wide and 4 m long, although occasionally trenches need to be extended an additional few meters in length. Overall, the trench should be long enough that the variability in composition, sedimentology, and pedology can be confidently determined, which is frequently dependent on experience. As mentioned above, for safety purposes and to meet OSHA standards for excavations or to allow better exposure of the profile, trenches sometimes need to be widened or stepped back. The amount of stepping depends on the depth and composition of the material excavated. This widening can also help clarify sedimentological and stratigraphic relationships of the subsurface units and contacts.

The maximum depth of trenches at a DTL depends chiefly on the stratigraphy observed within the trench while excavating. Because the major objective of the deep-test excavation is to locate areas of buried archaeological information, the definition of soils and sediments that are of Holocene age is critical. With this in mind, trenches should usually be excavated to a depth defined by the maximum extension of the backhoe boom or until the geoarchaeologist or geomorphologist on the site is reasonably certain that the trench had penetrated late Wisconsinan or older age units (i.e., glacial, glaciolacustrine, glacio-fluvial, bedrock, etc.).

During trench excavation, important information concerning the general lithology, sedimentology, pedology, and extent of each identified stratigraphic unit must be recorded. Such data, particularly including the depth below surface of the top and bottom of each of the units encountered as well as their general thickness, should be measured. Lithologic information such as general color, texture, and lithology of the units as well as that of any minor interbeds or interstratified deposit included within the unit should also be noted according to currently accepted standards (i.e., Munsell soil color charts, Wentworth scale, etc.). Major sedimentological information should include, but not be limited to, bedding (cross-bedded, tabular beds, etc.), sorting, grading, and any deformation observed in the unit. Additional pedological information such as evidence of postdepositional inclusions, transferrals, development of structure, consistency, and bioturbation should be noted. The contact between lithologic units should also be described. Importantly, when encountered, samples of organic material (both floral and faunal) should be collected for possible analysis at a later date (i.e., ^{14}C age estimates and/or faunal or paleobotanical analysis). Details of the lithology, pedology, sedimentology, and thickness of each unit in each trench at each DTL should be presented as an appendix to the deep-test report.

In addition to descriptions of the actual soils and sediments found, details about individual trench depths, widths, and lengths, as well as the number of trenches at each DTL, should be recorded. Although this may seem obvious, our survey of previous deep-test work in Michigan revealed a surprisingly large number of reports that did not include such basic information as trench numbers, sizes, and depths, let alone details of stratigraphic information revealed within the trenches. A more detailed discussion of reporting standards is presented as part of a subsequent section.

The distance between each trench should be measured and the trenches located on a scaled map. In addition, the trenches, ideally each corner, should be recorded using global positioning system (GPS) equipment. In addition, sometimes for CRM-related projects construction survey markers (station markers) are present. Trenches should also be measured and plotted in relationship to these. Construction station markers, if present, should also be included in the sketch map, as should natural and cultural features that occur at or near the DTL (roads, streams, fence and property lines, towers for power lines, etc.). In this manner, the trenches can be more directly related to natural features found on the topographic maps and alignment sheet.

Most of the mapping techniques mentioned above are actually field sketches and drawn without detailed survey methods. Therefore, they cannot be considered highly accurate but should serve rather as augmentation and backup for more accurate survey methods. Today, more accurate and easily obtained locational information is available for recording the actual geodetic position of the deep-test trenches. This data is important and can be obtained by using even relatively inexpensive GPS equipment. Such trench and feature locations obtained through GPS are typically recorded as either Universal Transverse Mercator (UTM) or latitude-longitude designations but can be easily converted to other coordinate systems and map projections. Even more important, they can also be included directly in the Geographic Information System (GIS) framework developed for MDOT as part of this study. For deep-test purposes, GPS accuracy need not be of survey quality. In general, while submeter precision is preferred, the approximate 2–3-m accuracy achieved by most modern Wide Area Augmentation System (WAAS) capable GPS units, particularly those employing postprocessing techniques, is sufficient.

Qualifications for Deep-Testing Researchers

Regardless of methods and techniques, the minimum qualifications expected for researchers and consultants undertaking deep testing should be established. This is particularly true for the techniques that adversely impact archaeological deposits, such as backhoe trenching. Because of its destructive nature, the best possible information should be recovered during the trenching process. If archaeological resources are to be potentially disturbed, then the most information possible should be obtained during the process. In fact, for any of the methods of deep testing mentioned above, the involvement of geoarchaeological or archaeological personnel suitably trained in both earth science and archaeological methods is essential. Specialized training beyond that of archaeological methods is crucial to recognize and interpret the significance of geomorphology, sedimentology, and pedology within an archaeological context. These skills require training well beyond the introductory geology and geomorphology courses required in many archaeological university programs. Although simply identifying the presence of archaeological deposits may meet the more limited goals of site discovery, it inadequately addresses floodplain history or depositional environments. The determination of these two latter objectives should also be important to CRM projects because they can serve as a guide to assessing site integrity and taphonomy or may assist in predicting what other areas of the site may contain intact buried deposits. Moreover, understanding the formational history and depositional environments found on the floodplain is crucial to assess the probability of buried deposits at a DTL. To be useful, however, this data must be collected by scientists who are experienced and thoroughly trained in geomorphology, pedology, and sedimentology.

To provide that such a suitably trained geoarchaeologist is actually present in the field and involved in interpreting and reporting the results, minimum professional credentials should be established for undertaking deep testing. In most states, such credentialing standards are ordinarily required for supervisory archaeological personnel and are sometimes also required for related scientists participating in archaeological projects (e.g., in Pennsylvania). From a practical standpoint, credentials for professionals in charge of deep testing should include at least an advanced degree in one of the earth science fields or from a program that focused on multidisciplinary training in geoarchaeology. In addition, specific class work in sedimentology, geomorphology, geoarchaeology, and pedology or several years of experience should be required. Evidence for fulfilling such professional requirements can be provided in several ways. For example, the degree and class-work requirements could be provided by university transcripts. Professional experience could be demonstrated by a listing of the publications by the researcher and employment history. Ultimately, demonstration of professional credentials can be managed in the same way that archaeologists present their qualifications for certification.

Data Collection, Recording Standards, and Reporting of Results

Once fieldwork related to deep site discovery is completed, a summary of the results of the excavations must also be prepared. Given the variation and irregular nature in the types and quality of information included in past reports, guidelines outlining the minimal, basic standards for presentation should be established. Importantly, these guidelines also dictate a level of consistency in the types of information and ensure a minimum quality to data available for DTLs across the state. Such standards should aim not to hold back innovation or stifle creativity but rather to make sure that certain critical information is always included in reports.

At the very least, a deep-test report should include a description of the project location and geomorphological background. It should also aim to place the DTL in its proper geographical, temporal, and geological framework. Additionally, the deep-test results, including whether archaeological material was recovered, should be included along with the geological and archaeological significance of the DTL. Finally, a descriptive "log" of the stratigraphy, sediments, and sedimentary features encountered in each trench or core should be listed (Table 8-1). Diagrams and maps depicting the surface and subsurface trench and feature relationships should be included. These should aim to clarify or support the information and conclusions presented in the report (Figure 8-1). Although the content and actual organization of the report should ultimately be left to the discretion of the principal investigator, the major aims and goals mentioned above can be addressed through three major sections: Location and Background, Results and Discussion, and Archaeological Potential and Recommendations. The kinds of information and possible organization for these sections are presented below.

Table 8-1. Example of Trench "Log" Suggested for Inclusion in DTL Reports

Trench 8 South side of creek in valley

| Length: | 4.0 m | Width: 1.0 m |
| Altitude: | 184.3 m | Depth: 1.8 m |

Base	Lithology and Description
0.8	**Sand,** black-to-tan, massive-to-faintly-tabular-bedded medium-to-coarse-grained sand; upper 10-20 cm is black, organic-rich, friable A-horizon of soil; lower part is mottled tan and gray, faintly tabular bedded sand.
——	Sharp (paleosol) contact
1.5	**Sand/Silt,** gray-to-tan, medium-to-coarse-grained, clean sand and silt; upper 5-10 cm dark gray, massive sand-silt and may represent **paleosol**? lower part is tabular bedded in upper portion and shows shallow, small-scale, thin (<2-cm thick), cross-beds in the lower part; thin discontinuous layers of fine charcoal common in lower part of the sequence.
——	Gradational contact
2.2	**Peat-Silt-Sand,** gray-to-tan, interbedded (thin, tabular beds) organic silt and sand with interbeds of peat common; fine detrital wood common in organic silt and peat layers.
——	Gradational contact
2.4+	**Organic Sand,** tan-to-gray, tabular bedded, coarse-grained, organic-rich sand; discontinuous; may contain interbeds of fine **gravel** at ca. 240 cm (trench filled with water below 2.4 m)

The Location and Background section of the report should concentrate on describing the geographic location of the DTL (i.e., land survey, geodetic, and descriptive location) and the important physiographic, topographic, and geologic landforms and features that occur near the DTL. This section should also outline how these landforms and features may influence the local geology or archaeology and explain the overall objectives for testing at the DTL. Basic information about the number and placement of trenches should likewise be introduced.

The Results and Discussion section comprises the body of the report. As such, it should describe the general stratigraphy, sedimentology, and pedology observed at the DTL. It should also include an outline of the probable depositional history revealed by trench excavations and describe any archaeological deposits encountered at the DTL. Besides the general summary, a stratigraphic cross section and general location map should also be included (Figure 8–1).

The cross sections provide the basis for a three-dimensional reconstruction of the DTL. They are constructed using the lithologies and sedimentology observed in each trench and should aim to link the various excavations at the site and clarify important aspects of the geological, sedimentological, and pedological history. Correlation of lithologic units between trenches is based primarily either on depositional facies relationships inferred from sedimentological information or on possible chronological relationships. Thus, the cross sections

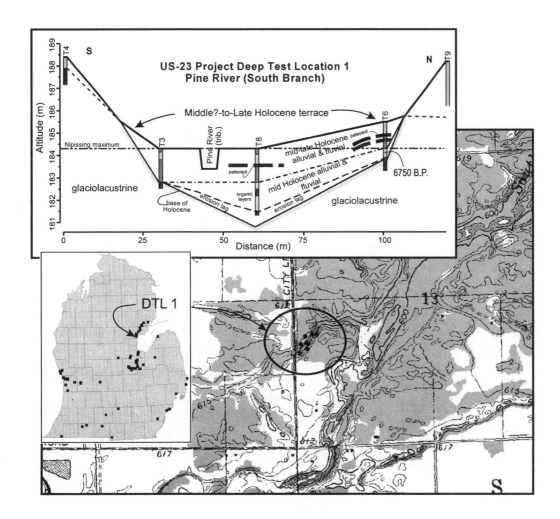

Figure 8-1. An example of the type of map and diagram suggested to include for each DTL.

should be capable of showing positions in the stratigraphy where depositional hiatuses occur, particularly related to buried surface soil horizons (Figure 8–1). Horizons like these suggest floodplain stability and could represent times when archaeological deposits might have been buried. In Michigan, a DTL is usually selected for testing because some sort of evidence for at least a shallow sequence of Holocene-age sediments has been noted. Thus, one of the important attributes of the cross section should be to show where these Holocene deposits occur in the subsurface. It should also depict the contact between Holocene and pre-Holocene (Wisconsinan glacial or older bedrock) deposits.

Ideally, and given that a deep test report summarizes the locations and stratigraphy of the primary DTLs present in southern Lower Michigan, some attempt should be made to associate site-level observations with those made at the subregional or regional level. The underlying premise here is that reconstruction of the depositional histories of fluvial systems or segments of fluvial systems are best and most productively undertaken as part of a larger, ongoing, and cumulative process of data generation and synthesis. Each DTL has the potential to contribute to this larger picture. As such, existing fluvial system data gleaned from other regional investigations must also be incorporated into site-level investigations in order to facilitate even broader syntheses. Notably, and as previously indicated, the new data can be systematically incorporated into existing state agency GIS-organized databases to be employed in future project planning.

Finally, an Archaeological Potential and Recommendations section should be included in the deep-test report. This section should assess and describe the possibility that deep burial and/or preservation of prehistoric cultural information may occur at the DTL. It should draw on both project-specific and regional data. Specific recommendations for further work, if required, should also be noted. Cost and time constraints often mean that the deep-testing process is necessarily broad in its coverage. For example, unlike more detailed, closely spaced shovel tests, backhoe trenches are usually spaced relatively far apart, which can result in accidentally missing more limited, buried archaeological deposits. Consequently, the potential of the DTL for actually including buried archaeological material should not be evaluated based solely on the presence or absence of archaeological deposits. Rather, the report on the DTL should focus on assessing the potential for the burial and preservation of stable land surfaces based on the types of geological processes inferred from the depositional history and deposits revealed at the DTL. The answers to such questions as "Were buried soils, indicating periods of stability, encountered at the DTL?" and "Were floodplain overbank or levee sediments encountered that may include preserved archaeological material?" may guide archaeological recommendations or support further work at the DTL. Alternatively, the widespread presence of coarse-grained, high-energy channel deposits or cross-bedded sand horizons may support conclusions suggesting that the DTL has undergone extensive episodes of erosion and has a low probability of containing prehistoric materials. The deep-test report should serve as support for archaeological conclusions reached at the DTL and should apprise agency or regulatory archaeologists of the confidence that can be placed on the testing results. Mistakes can happen and incorrect conclusions can be reached, but if the basis for those conclusions, incorrect or otherwise, are clearly articulated, then other professionals can judge the work in a fair manner. Ultimately, CRM work, particularly related to more uncertain aspects such as buried site exploration, should aim to avoid surprises and last-minute mitigation of archaeological sites.

Summary and Conclusions

The primary purpose of this chapter was to provide MDOT, the Office of the State Archaeologist, and SHPO basic guidelines for field methods and data collection at DTLs in Michigan. Additionally, we have also suggested minimum standards for reporting deep-test results and have suggested basic qualifications for principal investigators undertaking deep testing. Establishing basic qualifications is a significant step to ensure that professionally competent and useful data is collected at DTLs. Thus, regardless of guidelines for data collection or reporting standards, without qualified researchers actually collecting it in the field, such data remains of dubious quality.

Geoarchaeological personnel who undertake deep testing should be suitably trained in both earth science and archaeology. Specialized training in earth science, in addition to understanding basic archaeological methods, is essential for understanding and placing geomorphological, sedimentological, and pedological data into their proper archaeological context. Credentialing standards, similar to those required for supervisory archaeological personnel, can be established for scientists who direct deep-testing components of CRM projects. These should include an advanced degree in one of the earth science fields or a program focused on geoarchaeology as well as specific background and experience in important subdisciplines (i.e., pedology, geomorphology, sedimentology, geoarchaeology, etc.). Evidence for fulfilling these requirements can be provided through university transcripts and professional résumés that list publications and outline employment histories and research experiences.

Given the wide variety of techniques that can be used for deep testing, we believe that despite its brute-force approach, backhoe trenching offers the most effective, certain, and cost-efficient way of locating buried archaeological resources within floodplain or alluvial settings in Michigan. This is suggested mainly because trenching allows direct exposure of a relatively long, continuous soil and geological (sedimentary) profile. Such an exposure allows direct observation of stratigraphic horizons and any associated cultural features and artifact concentrations and also offers an opportunity for controlled archaeological testing of these strata. Most other techniques, particularly geophysical, yield at best equivocal results and usually still require trenching or hand excavation to verify the presence or absence of buried archaeological material. The numbers, locations, and depths of backhoe trenches at DTLs may be quite variable, often depending on site-specific environmental and stratigraphic circumstances. Consequently, despite the fact that many agencies have guidelines for minimum distances between trenches, the number and placement of trenches are probably best left up to the geoarchaeologists in the field. In some instances, however, coring, which, like trenching, allows direct observation of sediments but has a much lower impact, may be a better alternative. For example, coring may be more suitable when very deep (> 5 m) Holocene deposits are suspected or when known archaeological resources occur at the DTL and would be severely disturbed by trenching.

Although the ultimate goal of a deep-test project is to discover buried archaeological resources, to be most useful it should also concentrate on a systematic reconstruction of the geological and depositional history revealed by floodplain sediments. This is best met by developing a three-dimensional model of the subsurface based on a systematic exploration of important terraces and other fluvial features on the floodplain. Only by understanding the stratigraphic and lithologic relationships between geological and archaeological units can the probability of the presence or absence of buried archaeological deposits be confidently submitted. By addressing the formational history and depositional environments found on the floodplains, instead of the more narrowly focused goal of whether archaeological deposits are present, data can be collected that achieves larger objectives important to CRM. For example, data from such projects not only can serve as a guide to assessing the integrity and taphonomy of the specific site but also can be used to help predict the probability that other environmentally similar floodplain setting contain buried archaeological deposits.

Guidelines delineating the basic standards for presentation of deep-test results should be established. These standards could provide a level of consistency as to the types of information reported and ensure a minimum quality to data available for DTLs across the state. Although details as to the content and organization of a report are ultimately the responsibility of the principal investigator, at the very least a deep-test report should include a description of the project location and geomorphological background and place the DTL in its proper geographical, temporal, and geological framework. Additionally, the geological and archaeological significance of the DTL as well as the presence of archaeological material should be discussed. Diagrams and maps should accompany the report to support or clarify the information and conclusions presented. Finally, and perhaps most important, a descriptive "log" of the stratigraphy, sediments, and sedimentary features encountered in each trench or core should be listed.

The deep-testing studies undertaken in Michigan serve the dual purpose of both supporting archaeological conclusions reached at the DTL and also placing the depositional environment in a regional framework. The overall task of deep testing should aim to inform agency or regulatory archaeologists of the probability that buried resources exist at the DTL. Obviously, if such resources are actually discovered during deep testing, the probability is 100 percent, but if they are not found, then the issue becomes less certain. This is because, just like shovel testing, complete coverage is never possible. Mistakes and incorrect conclusions occur, but if the basis for recommendations, incorrect or otherwise, are clear, they can be judged fairly. Ultimately, surprises and costly last-minute mitigation of archaeological sites must be avoided.

CHAPTER NINE

Summary and Conclusions

Implications for Predicting Archaeological Site
Burial and Human Settlement Patterns in the
Great Lakes Region

Project Summary and Background

Over the past two decades, geoarchaeological investigations focusing on the discovery of deeply buried and stratified archaeological sites have become generally accepted as an important component to Phase I survey in cultural resources management (CRM) projects throughout the Great Lakes region. Unfortunately, neither acceptable methods nor professional standards and criteria, nor even basic guidelines that outline where and when to test for buried sites, have been established in Michigan. To date, choices for deep testing as well as standardized criteria for reports and methods are often ad hoc according to agency managers or left up to individual CRM firms. Although many firms have been visionary and included deep testing as part of their work plan, others have ignored deep testing, relying instead on "shovel testing a little bit deeper" along floodplains. This situation not only inadequately protects our shared cultural resources but also ultimately places firms that desire to perform more comprehensive compliance at a competitive disadvantage. The overall goal of this book is to remedy this situation by aiding the Michigan Department of Transportation (MDOT) and the State Historic Preservation Office (SHPO) to establish guidelines, methods, and minimum reporting standards for deep testing in Michigan.

This book represents the first stage in achieving this overall project goal. We have assembled the disparate pieces of preexisting deep-testing data accumulated throughout Michigan over the past few decades into an integrated framework. It summarizes the results of more than two decades of deep testing and places the results of this work within the framework of the Holocene history and geological processes that control the burial and preservation of such sites. Thus, the emphasis of this book has been to integrate earth science information and methods with the more traditional anthropological focus of archaeology. Using this approach, we have emphasized the importance of a sound multidisciplinary approach to archaeological research. We have presented information regarding the geological and environmental history of the Great Lakes region that focused mainly on lake-level history for ancestral predecessors to the Great Lakes, as well as information related to environmental and climate change during the past 12,000–13,000 years. This period was chosen not only because it covers the main phase of human settlement in North America but also because deglaciation and the physiographic alteration in the region set the stage for development of the modern environment in the Great Lakes region.

By integrating the environmental and archaeological backgrounds, we described the types of geological and sedimentological processes that promote archaeological site burial in certain preferred settings. We also delineated those aspects of Holocene climatic history that enhance site burial during specific time periods and discussed how these factors affected the human settlement systems of the region. We have proposed a regional site burial model that integrates the geological and environmental information into a regional depositional model that describes processes, periods, and depositional environments that promote archaeological site burial. In this fashion, we have attempted to model the buried archaeological sites as a predictable resource.

Geological Background

Today, Lakes Michigan and Huron are considered as a single hydraulic lake basin connected at the Straits of Mackinac, while Lake Superior exists as a separate lake basin and discharges southward over a bedrock threshold near Sault Ste. Marie, through the St. Mary's River, and into Lake Huron. The entire upper Great Lakes system (Lakes Superior, Michigan, and Huron) ultimately discharges through the St. Clair River at Port Huron (Figure 2-1). Modern water levels for Lake Michigan-Huron (176.5 m) and Lake Superior (183 m) are controlled by a balance between the amount of water input to the basin and the amount that discharges through the outlet. Over the past 15,000 years, however, the lakes that occupied each basin (Table 2–1) had vastly different levels. In fact, the present topography and configuration of Michigan were dictated mainly by depositional events associated with the late Wisconsinan Laurentide Ice Sheet (ca. 10,000–20,000 years ago). The configuration of this ice sheet had a significant impact on the drainage patterns and style of deglaciation that developed and ultimately determined the general positions of the major modern river systems in the state as well as the configuration of the Great Lakes that we observe today. The glacial lake system, which was described in detail in chapter 2, is varied and complex. The levels of these lakes varied wildly and sometimes changed catastrophically but were generally controlled by ice-margin fluctuations of the Lake Michigan, Huron-Erie, and Saginaw ice lobes that uncovered, or re-covered, vastly different outlets.

The sequence of Holocene (post–10,000 B.P.) lakes within the Michigan and Huron lake basins includes extremely low-level lakes (Chippewa and Stanley; ca. 10,000–5000 B.P.), higher-than-present lakes (Nipissing and Algoma; ca. 5000–3500 B.P.), and the modern Lakes Michigan and Huron (ca. <3500 B.P.). In general, the Holocene is characterized by regional transgression during the early Holocene to form Lake Nipissing (informally, the "Nipissing transgression"; 10,000–5000 B.P.), followed by a regional regression in lake level (Nipissing I–II and Algoma; 5000–3500 B.P.) to the modern lake level. The water levels attained during this sequence were controlled primarily either by isostatic rebound (transgressive phase) or by erosion (downcutting) of the outlet at Port Huron (regressive phase). Superimposed on this "outlet-controlled" lake sequence is a secondary system controlled by relatively long-term, secular variation in the regional climate.

Site Burial during the Holocene

The burial of archaeological sites results from processes that deposit extensive layers of sediment on the site surface. In the Great Lakes region, the most significant of these processes include burial under lacustrine sediments during lake-level transgressions, burial by shoreline processes (littoral and/or eolian), and burial along streams by channel alluviation. The preservation of sites buried during lake-level transgressions has occurred at several sites in Michigan, but known buried sites are confined mainly to the middle to late Holocene. (Undoubtedly, Early-to-Middle Archaic sites were buried during the Nipissing transgression and are now submerged along drowned river valleys submerged under Lakes Michigan and Huron. Because of the present state of technology, however, none of these areas have been systematically surveyed for archaeological resources [see Lovis, Holman, Monaghan, and Skowronek 1994]. The fact that intact forest beds [Chrzastowski et al. 1991; Hunter 2004] of early to middle Holocene age have been discovered submerged under both lakes suggests that similar age archaeological sites might also be recovered.) Predicting the location of and systematically sampling for such sites can only be productive along or near the paleo-shoreline. In addition, predicting the location of sites buried by stream alluviation may also be fruitful. In fact, because they are appealing for human occupation as well, such environments are excellent places to find archaeological sites, buried or otherwise. Moreover, the locations of abandoned shorelines, alluvial terraces, and floodplains are readily apparent, while paleo-environment and depositional processes can be assumed based on analogy with modern processes. Shoreline sedimentation is dynamic and may include high-energy, littoral (foreshore) deposits formed along the shore margin; storm deposits developed along the back-berm of the beach; marsh deposits in swales behind beach berms; and eolian deposits. Notable examples of sites partially buried by shoreline processes include the Woodland-period Juntunen (McPherron 1967), O'Neil (Lovis 1973, 1990b), and Portage sites (Lovis et al. 1998) in northern Michigan and the Archaic-period Weber I (Lovis, ed. 1989; Monaghan, Lovis and Fay 1986) and Ebenhoff Dune sites (Dobbs and Murray 1993) near Saginaw Bay.

Even more significant than shoreline sites, however, is site burial along rivers and streams. We have used the notion that variability in the hydraulic characteristics of streams results in soil formation on the floodplain during periods of stability or in the construction, partial erosion, and burial of successive terrace surfaces, along with any attending soil and archaeological deposits, during more dynamic periods. Sites buried on floodplains by alluvial processes include the Shiawassee River and Bear Creek sites in southern Saginaw County, the Schultz and Green Point sites near Saginaw, the Marquette Viaduct locale of the Fletcher site, the CERT site (20BY365; Demeter et al. 1994) in Bay City, and the Zemaitis and Prison Farm sites along the lower Grand River in western Michigan. Interestingly, the majority of these sites lie along stream reaches nearer to the Great Lakes rather than more inland (see Figure 5-1). These areas were also greatly affected by the mid-Holocene Nipissing transgression or by the late Holocene, cyclical variation in lake level that occurred during the late Holocene (see Figure 3-2).

Although evidence for the regional climate events that were likely responsible for the late Holocene (i.e., post–3000 B.P.) lake-level excursions occurs throughout the Great Lakes, northeastern, and mid-Atlantic regions (see Figure 6-1), the paucity of more interior, buried sites in Michigan raises some important questions. Is site burial actually more common near the Great Lakes, as the deep-test data from Michigan suggests, or does this distribution simply reflect that archaeologists have failed to systematically test more interior locales? The answers to these questions are important for developing a realistic model that predicts the probability of any specific areas including buried archaeological resources. Part II of this book is devoted to developing such a predictive framework. The fact that relatively few deep-test locales have been investigated from inland locales (see Figure 7-2) may indicate that we just do not have enough data to answer these questions. However, there may be several good reasons, both cultural and environmental, why buried sites may actually be more common near the Great Lakes. Culturally, locations near shorelines may be more attractive from a settlement or subsistence standpoint and thus include more and larger archaeological sites. As pointed out in chapter 3, changes in water levels within lake basins affected alluvial settings near the Great Lakes, creating conditions that enhance sediment accretion and site burial, particularly during wetter periods. Although the potential for alluvially buried archaeological sites may be greater along stream reaches nearest to the Great Lakes shorelines, the regional extent of site burial during specific time intervals also indicates that pervasive variations in the regional climate may affect alluviation rates for stream reaches throughout their drainage basin.

Regardless of the problems that may be associated with the spatial distribution of archaeological sites, the chronology and characteristics of the suite of buried sites in Michigan constitute a basis for developing a predictive model for alluvial and shoreline archaeological site burial. Importantly, the data presented in chapters 3 and 5 shows that the timing for the burial of these sites is not random but rather is linked to episodes of regionally significant environmental changes. By comparing and noting commonalities in the alluvial and occupational histories from adjacent as well as far-flung drainage basins, we have reconstructed at least three major, regionally significant intervals of environmental change during the middle to late Holocene. We have also suggested that these intervals represent periods with high site burial potential along rivers and streams in the Great Lakes region. Because these intervals occur throughout the region and depositional processes resulting from the climatic variation associated with the intervals are predictable, a model was developed to map locations that have a higher potential to include buried archaeological resources.

This model, which relates floodplain sedimentation, soil formation, and archaeological site development, includes three major prehistoric periods of relatively extensive sedimentation: one about 4000–3000 B.P., a second between

2000 and 1500 B.P., and a final period just prior to European contact. These intervals are separated by longer periods of relative quiescence. During these intervals, relatively thick soils formed on floodplain surfaces, and thick, "middenlike" deposits developed at archaeological sites. We believe that these intervals are controlled by major, regional climatic events that not only disrupted stream hydraulics but also probably affected human subsistence systems. The earliest period is related to the Nipissing transgression, and increased flooding during this interval is at least partly associated with isostatic rebound around the basin and with hydraulic reconfiguration of the Port Huron outlet. However, we also propose that at least part of the increased alluviation during this interval occurred because of the regionally cooler, moister middle Holocene climatic changes that occurred as the Hypsithermal ended. Similarly, the second (2000–1500 B.P.) and third periods (just prior to European contact) are also probably related to a cooler, moister regime. This is clearest for the third and most recent interval. Its timing is clearly correlative with the worldwide, cooler, moister climate of the Little Ice Age. Moreover, the relatively thick middens at several archaeological sites that have been buried by this event, and which commonly date to around 1200–800 B.P., probably formed during the warmer-dryer climate associated with the Medieval Warm climatic interval. Thus, by analogy with the Medieval Warm/Little Ice Age cycle, we propose that a similar warm-dry-to-cool-moist cycle also exists for the ca. 3000–2000 B.P. middens that were buried by the 2000–1500 B.P. flood interval. The duration and regional persistence of these cycles suggest that millennial-scale, cyclical variation from longer-duration, warm-dry to shorter-term, cool-moist climate conditions generally characterizes the late Holocene in the Great Lakes region.

We propose from this data that middle-to-late Holocene drainages throughout eastern North America are characterized by variable, but generally short-term, periods of active floodplain sedimentation, which results in more rapid sediment accretion on the floodplain. These intervals are significant because archaeological sites are buried during the alluviation events. The more active periods of alluviation are apparently separated by generally longer intervals of relative fluvial quiescence, or even of actual active landform degradation. During these periods of fluvial quiescence, relatively extensive soil and archaeological "midden" development occurs. We believe that these "high-flood"/"low-flood" intervals are driven by significant regional, or perhaps even worldwide, climate events. Based on the distribution of buried archaeological sites, alluviation is most substantial along floodplains near the margins of the Great Lakes (i.e., within 5–6 m above lake level). The model we propose, however, also suggests that site burial may occur in any fluvial basin where conditions are favorable to extensive floodplain accretion. The challenge is delineating the hydraulic factors and basin characteristics that dictate site burial and preservation.

In spite of the fact that our model is useful in understanding general factors controlling archaeological site burial, local basin-specific variables actually dictate patterns of sedimentation. Despite extensive deep testing, some floodplain systems simply do not contain buried sites or even buried surfaces that might represent parts of the Holocene depositional cycles that we have defined. Large and small archaeological sites, however, are often found in the uplands adjacent to rivers in the area (i.e., US-23 project; Dunham et al. 1995; Monaghan 1995c).

Several ^{14}C age estimates from the alluvial sequences associated with the US-23 project indicate that many of these valleys have undergone extensive reworking during the late Holocene. As a result, only remnants remain of the middle Holocene Nipissing inundation of the valleys and the most recent of our proposed flood cycles. Consequently, most of the Middle-to-Late Archaic and Early-to-Late Woodland deposits would have been destroyed during these erosional events. Whether sites are absent in the valleys because they were eroded away or because they were never there in the first place remains speculative but can be addressed based on the fluvial and depositional histories of the valleys. Unlike the US-23 project, in the absence of deep testing or detailed geomorphologic analysis of the floodplain in other survey areas, the question of whether sites are absent because they were never there or because they were destroyed by fluvial processes cannot be addressed. Clearly, these alternatives have important, but different, ramifications for the structure of regional archaeological settlement and subsistence models. The correct choice of model is important and can only be made when prehistoric human settlement systems are placed within the broader context of the depositional patterns revealed within specific drainage basins. Site distribution, particularly associated with site preservation, is linked to long-term patterns of sedimentation and cannot be fully understood isolated from local and regional drainage basin development.

Archaeological Significance and Discussion

Although this study has focused on deep testing for archaeological resources in Michigan, it also has wider relevance not only in the Great Lakes region but also throughout the northeastern and midwestern United States and most of eastern Canada. Most of this region shares a similar late Wisconsinan and Holocene history of environmental transformation as well as common, often related, archaeological traditions. It has experienced extensive continental glaciation and thus shares the suite of landforms common to such areas. The environmental histories of various parts of the region also share similar developmental, secular changes since deglaciation. The geomorphological processes outlined for Michigan apply over most of the humid eastern half of North America. The general fluvial processes that affect rivers in Michigan, for example, also affect those in Illinois and Ontario. From a CRM standpoint, the issues raised in this study and the solutions and recommendations proposed also largely apply throughout eastern North America. The tendency of humans to focus more intensive settlement along fluvial systems, shorelines, and wetlands has meant that accelerated deposition during moister, more flood-prone time periods commonly buried and preserved these settlements. The fact that such landforms generally remained the focus of settlement throughout the Holocene resulted in the preservation of stacked occupations that often span various cultures of the middle and late Holocene.

The archaeology of Michigan is complex and can be viewed from a variety of perspectives. The perspective employed in this study has a strong ecological or environmental cast. Moreover, our perspective clearly relies on cross- or multidisciplinary collaboration. We believe that research questions and problems are best solved by involving several of the related Quaternary disciplines, such as geology, pedology, and botany, in archaeological research programs. Each of these ancillary fields brings a different approach and perspective to the solution of our related research questions. The ecological, multidisciplinary approach endorsed and applied here reinforces the recognition of some rather central issues of research design in archaeology. Central to this approach is an understanding of the multiple scales of inquiry that are of potential interest to both earth scientists and archaeologists in terms of environmental evolution and the related changes and trajectories of human behavior (Lovis and MacDonald 1999). These issues involve not only obvious physical, taphonomic elements, such as how the environmental transformations described previously alter our understanding of the nature of archaeological site populations and the nature and formation of the remnant archaeological record (Hayes and Monaghan 1997; Lovis, Holman, Monaghan, and Skowronek 1994; Lovis and O'Shea 1994; Monaghan and Hayes 1997, 1998, 2001; Monaghan and Schaetzl 1994), but also the more subtle cultural issues, such as how environmental evolution and dynamics are coupled to human behavioral choices (Jochim 1994).

One of the major tasks in preparing this book was to show how the accumulated data related to a highly dynamic Holocene environment of the Great Lakes pertains to some of the key issues in archaeological research design and CRM. One contribution of this work is the recognition that climate and archaeological site burial are linked and change cyclically. This is a significant observation from both a settlement and site discovery perspective. For example, instead of alluvially buried sites confined only to the margins of the Great Lakes, as was believed just a few decades ago, we have presented a model showing that site burial may occur anywhere in any fluvial basin where conditions are favorable to extensive floodplain accretion. The challenge this model presents is delineating the characteristics that determine when, where, and what conditions are conducive to site burial and stratification. The conclusions reached in this book are applicable at both an academic level, as well as at a more applied level, which can be incorporated into CRM practices. We have also shown the utility of how this information and synthesis can be used to address some rather discrete and long-standing problems of Great Lakes and Michigan archaeology.

While the deglaciation of southern Michigan clearly resulted in major, sometimes catastrophic, environmental change, the effects that these modifications had on human settlement and behavior are complex and not always apparent. Moreover, the severity of ecological change, and consequently the effect on human subsistence and settlement patterns, has varied throughout the Holocene. These differences require scalar distinctions both in the approach to formulating archaeological research questions and in conceptualizing what the archaeological record means for different time periods (Lovis and MacDonald 1999). Clearly, the catastrophic drainage of Lake Algonquin to form Lakes Stanley and Chippewa about 10,000 years ago would have profoundly altered human settlement systems. Additionally, the 5,000-year-long, progressive rise in lake level associated with the Nipissing transgression probably never allowed a firm, predictable resource base for human subsistence systems to stabilize, particularly along shoreline environments. Thus, during the first 5,000–6,000 years of the Holocene, Early-to-Middle Archaic people probably lived in an environment that changed from generation to generation, which must have profoundly affected both their worldview and settlement system. Conversely, the magnitude of ecological change associated with the millennial-scale, more subtle, late Holocene transgressions and flood events is relatively minor by comparison. During this time, Early-to-Late Woodland subsistence was affected to a much lesser extent. Modifications and reorientation of subsistence choices for the predominantly hunter-gathering Early-to-Middle Woodland economies did occur (see Lovis et al. 2001) but were not of the same magnitude as those required during the first half of the Holocene. They required a more subtle reorientation of choice within a similar environmental setting rather than a completely new approach. During the Late Woodland, however, maize horticulture became a more important component of the subsistence economy. While during the more mild climate associated with the Medieval Warm interval (ca. 1000 B.P.) growing maize was possible throughout much of Lower Michigan, climatic deterioration associated with the subsequent Little Ice Age (the premodern flood interval) probably made tropical cultigens less reliable as a resource base after about 800 B.P. Because they were more reliant on horticulture, Late Woodland people had more limited subsistence options as climate changed than did Early-to-Middle Woodland populations.

Scalar differences in ecological changes during the Holocene also have ramifications for human settlement as applied to site location models. Clearly comprehending the relationship between these natural, environmental changes and any associated behavioral choices made by human societies warrants further refinement. The formation processes, as well as preservation potential, of specific archaeological sites have varied for any given time period. A distinct scalar difference exists between understanding the positions and altitudes of uplifted relict beaches as they relate to different time periods (Paleo-Indian, Late Archaic) and the processes responsible for the formation of fluvial systems and the consequent impacts on site visibility and preservation (Early and Middle Archaic, Middle Woodland, terminal Late Woodland). Moreover, such scalar differences warrant markedly different methodological approaches to site survey and excavation. Indeed, the relationship between our operating assumptions about the archaeological record is a linked dimension to the way archaeologists operate relative to this record. While we may recognize that our sample of archaeological sites is incomplete, we do not yet understand what sites are missing from our extant population or why. Moreover, if we do not know what is missing from the record, we cannot really even understand what the population of sites we have studied means in the overall archaeological record or why these sites were preserved. We still treat them, however, as somehow representative of the past (Lovis and O'Shea 1994).

The GIS Framework for Buried Sites and Guidelines for Deep Testing

An important goal of this study was to map the distribution of areas in southern Lower Michigan that may be likely to include buried archaeological resources. Our aim was to assist MDOT, as well as other state and federal agencies, to plan for and manage deeply buried archaeological deposits by mapping specific counties based their relative buried archaeological site potential. This task was approached by constructing a Geographic Information System (GIS) framework that modeled our understanding of how the locations of archaeological sites might have interacted with related geomorphological and environmental information to enhance or diminish site burial potential. We have assumed that floodplains represent the most significant environments for site burial and have oriented our GIS framework around these settings. The GIS analysis proceeded by first studying the distribution of known buried archaeological sites, compiling the results of any previous deep-test studies, and finally relating this data to other environmental information that may predict the locations of buried archaeological resources. Through relating all of these factors together, a GIS framework was created that modeled the relative potential that a specific area may contain buried sites. We ultimately developed two main GIS coverages. The first was a point source coverage that showed where DTLs occurred in southern Lower Michigan and, if available, plotted individual deep-test trenches or cores. Tables of more detailed information concerning these DTLs and trenches were also included and linked to the point source coverages. Second, we developed a polygon coverage that mapped the distribution of areas of high, moderate, and low potential for buried archaeological resources throughout the study area. These coverages, as well as more detailed information on some of the DTLs, are included on a compact disc with this volume.

In formulating the probability GIS coverage, we did not try to predict the actual, specific locations of buried sites directly; rather, we focused on defining places where buried ground surfaces (or paleosols) are likely to occur. The actual prediction of the archaeological site locations is extremely complicated, is poorly understood, and involves integrating cultural and environmental factors that are beyond the scope of this project. Because no floodplain map exists for southern Lower Michigan, one based on a composite of data types was developed for this study. The distribution of floodplains was broadly defined based on several environmental and geomorphological parameters. These parameters form the basis for the buried site potential mapped. This map ranked localities of the study area based on the presence of specific attributes that predicted the presence and burial of paleosols. Areas outside of the floodplain were categorized as generally the lowest potential because the opportunity for significant sediment accretion, and consequently site burial, was minimal. The high-potential areas, on the other hand, were generally associated with broad, flat (low-gradient) floodplains composed of fine-grained, flood-prone alluvial soils. Because of the numerous buried archaeological sites clustered within and near the margin of the Nipissing lake plain, the highest potential for site burial was assigned to floodplains that existed within the area transgressed by Lake Nipissing and that also included the characteristics described above for high-potential areas.

From the perspective of state and federal agency archaeologists, the most significant application of this GIS model is probably its utility to aid in long-range planning. If the buried site potential of areas can be known, then future MDOT projects might be better prepared to address the issue early. Once identified, areas of high potential for buried resources could then be either avoided or at least tested for the presence of buried archaeological resources early in the site selection process. The discovery of complex buried sites at the last minute only leads to expensive delays and surprises.

In addition to the GIS framework and coverages, we have provided some suggestions for very basic guidelines to institute standards for field methods, data collection, and reporting of deep testing in Michigan. However, establishing basic qualifications for deep-test personnel is probably the most important first step to ensure that professionally competent and useful data is obtained from DTLs. Without qualified researchers present in the field, work at DTLs remains of dubious quality regardless of the implementation of clear guidelines for methods or reporting standards. Although geoarchaeological personnel should understand basic archaeological methods, they should be trained primarily in earth science. Such training is essential for understanding and placing geomorphological, sedimentological, and pedological data into their proper archaeological context. Credentialing standards, similar to those required for supervisory archaeological personnel, can be established and should include an advanced degree in one of the earth science fields or from a program focused on geoarchaeology. Personnel should have specific background and experience in important subdisciplines of earth science (i.e., pedology, geomorphology, sedimentology, geoarchaeology, etc.).

Given the wide variety of techniques that can be used for deep testing, we believe that despite its brute-force approach, backhoe trenching offers the most effective, certain, and cost-efficient way of locating buried archaeological resources within floodplain or alluvial settings in Michigan. This is suggested mainly because trenching allows direct exposure of a relatively long, continuous soil and geological (sedimentary) profile. Such an exposure allows direct observation of stratigraphic horizons and any associated cultural features and artifact concentrations and also offers an opportunity for controlled archaeological testing of these strata. In some instances, however, coring, which, like trenching, allows direct observation of sediments but has a much lower impact, may be a better alternative. For example, coring may be more suitable when very deep (>5 m) Holocene deposits are suspected or when known archaeological resources occur at the DTL and would be severely impacted by trenching.

Guidelines delineating the presentation of deep-test results should provide a level of consistency as to the types of information reported and ensure a minimum quality to data available for DTLs across the state. At the very least, reports should include a description of the project location; place the DTL into its proper geographical, temporal, and geological framework; and outline its geological and archaeological significance. Clearly, whether or not buried archaeological deposits were discovered should be a prominent part of in the report. Diagrams and maps should accompany the report to support or clarify the information and conclusions. Additionally, descriptions of the stratigraphy, sediments, and sedimentary features encountered in each trench or core should be listed. Ultimately, the goal of deep testing should aim to inform any agency or regulatory archaeologists of the probability that buried resources exist at the DTL. Obviously, if archaeological deposits are discovered during deep testing, the issue is moot. But if not found, then the possibility the deposits were missed becomes important because, as with shovel testing, complete deep-test coverage is never possible. Even if mistakes occurred and incorrect conclusions were reached, if the basis for those conclusions, incorrect or otherwise, are clearly articulated, then other professionals can judge the work in a fair manner. Ultimately, as professionals, we have certain scientific obligations for presenting the facts as we understand them. These obligations need not conflict with our responsibilities as consultants on environmental projects, however, because our goal should be to avoid surprises for clients that can lead to very costly last-minute mitigation of archaeological sites.

Conclusions

This book is an attempt to systematize what we know, what we do not know, and what we are capable of knowing given the current state of knowledge about the buried archaeological record in Michigan. We must not only understand what we do not or cannot know but also recognize that cyclical alluvial processes can enhance or diminish the preservation and clarity of the archaeological record independent of cultural considerations. Moreover, such enhancements are variable through time. We have approached these issues by integrating archaeological and geological information into a process framework to create a model from which we can predict the potential that a given landscape includes buried archaeological resources. Inherent to this model is a conceptual framework outlining how climate, sedimentation, and site formation processes interact to produce the archaeological record in floodplains. The geoarchaeological model presented here suggests that the preservation of the archaeological record in floodplain environments in Michigan is a complex interplay of climate, lake-level dynamics, and fluvial system evolution. This is a problem at a mesoscale of inquiry, encompassing centuries of environmental change. Our research on the cumulative record of these processes suggests that the interplay of these variables is regular and has resulted in sites from certain archaeological time periods being both more prone to preservation through alluvial burial as well as potentially less visible given current site discovery methods. A better understanding of the impact of these observations may be obtained by placing them in the context of more problem-oriented research.

We have established that three fluctuation cycles occurred within the context of postglacial lake-level readjustment. Each of these affected the preservation and visibility of the archaeological record. The first occurred during the middle Holocene and is associated with the Early and Middle Archaic. The second occurred about 2000 B.P. and is linked with the Middle Woodland period. The last occurred just prior to European contact and is associated with the terminal Late Woodland and protohistoric periods. Each of these fluctuations varied in magnitude and differentially influenced the archaeological record. Our floodplain model, however, suggests that sites associated with each of these fluctuations have the potential to be preserved within or beneath a variably thick mantle of floodplain alluvium. This process has several consequences.

First, we cannot assume that any of these time periods have a representative and recoverable population of sites, site locations, site functions, or seasonal components of the settlement system. This is particularly problematic for older floodplain sites that may have undergone all three of the middle-to-late Holocene cycles and thus are either deeply buried or eroded away. The challenge is delineating the characteristics that determine site preservation, burial, and stratification. If such floodplain sites remain undiscovered, archaeologists will generate an inaccurate understanding of prehistoric settlement patterns in the area. Several researchers have already addressed this issue for the Early and Middle Archaic (Branstner and Hambacher, eds. 1994; Dobbs and Murray 1993; Fitting 1975b; Larsen and Demeter 1979; Lovis, ed. 1989; Shott 2000), while an accumulating body of data corroborates the significance of "missing" sites for reconstructing Middle Woodland settlement patterns (Brashler et al. 1994; Lovis and Robertson 1989). Only recently has this issue even been recognized for the terminal Late Woodland (Dobbs et al. 1993). Any models of mobility, seasonal settlement, or subsistence change must accommodate the potential that significant parts are missing from the settlement system for all of these time periods. Data from alluvial settings, where these missing sites commonly occur, provides important indicators of time, location, and relative fluvial stability throughout the Holocene. Such sites are certainly underrepresented in syntheses of prehistoric settlement systems, even though they can provide some of the cleanest data as to context.

Second, the data presented in this study shows that the structure of the fluvial or wetland environments has not been stable over time. The changes in the lowland components of the Saginaw drainage system during the Middle and Late Archaic, such as the shifting of channels at Bear Creek and the Shiawassee River (Monaghan and Schaetzl 1994), cannot necessarily be associated with modern drainages and landform configurations. Thus, the present drainage conditions may not always be helpful in understanding human settlement patterns even during the late Holocene. This point is particularly clear for the Ebenhoff site, which at the time of Middle-to-Late Archaic occupation was the Great Lakes shoreline but today occurs 20–30 km inland, as well as for the Weber I site, which altered from a Middle Archaic alluvial setting to an "estuarine-like" environment and finally back to an alluvial setting between 6000 and 3000 B.P. (Lovis, ed. 1989; Monaghan, Lovis and Fay 1986). Similarly, the amount of floodplains, levees, and wetlands varied tremendously adjacent to several multicomponent Archaic-to-Woodland sites near Saginaw and Bay City (Demeter et al. 2000; Lovis, Egan, Smith, and Monaghan 1994; Lovis et al. 1996; Lovis et al. 2001; Speth 1972). These variations in nearby ecology indicate that any model of site locational choice must accommodate dynamic and potentially major changes in the position of the fluvial system, the location of shorelines, and the abundance and proximity of wetlands. During the three middle-to-late Holocene transgressive and flood events, the distribution and structure of the drainage, associated wetlands, and their related dynamics also changed. Wetlands became differentially distributed conditioned by the altitude of the Great Lakes water planes and varied markedly over time. During transgressive events, episodic flooding increased, but in the downstream portions of streams inundated by the Great Lakes, stream-flow velocity actually decreased. As a consequence, different fluvial and wetland system dynamics resulted, thereby altering the resource potential of riverine and wetland environments. In the lower parts of the Shiawassee lowland near the Schultz and Green Point sites, for example, this apparently resulted in "wetter" wetlands that included more standing water for longer periods of time. As a consequence, the relative abundance of wild rice and/or certain fish species probably increased at the expense of other resources (Lovis et al. 2001). Human settlements may have also been displaced to higher, less flood-prone altitudes on the floodplains. This resulted in superimposed or mixed occupations. Such alterations must be adequately incorporated into models of seasonal settlement mobility and resource use.

Third, neither can we assume that the visible archaeological record is adequate for the major cultural time periods or that our current discovery methods are sufficient to understand the nature and distribution of archaeological site populations. A most daunting observation is how the premodern deposition impacted on the visibility and preservation of terminal Late Woodland sites situated on floodplains. The model we have presented suggests that entire categories of Late Woodland sites are likely buried beneath mantles of alluvium. These sites are simply not visible on the surface, and site survey projects, particularly related to CRM, warrant the application of subsurface inspection techniques for their discovery. Alternatively, it is also possible that these sites may have been eroded away during the extensive premodern flooding and can never be discovered. While archaeologists have acknowledged this problem for the middle Holocene, such recognition is generally absent for the late Holocene and must be regularly incorporated into research design. Understanding and integrating the floodplain history with archaeological site formation and preservation, human settlement history, ecological and environmental transformation, and the archaeological record are best achieved by ongoing dialogue between archaeologists, geologists, and pedologists.

In sum, the archaeological record of southern Lower Michigan is complex and not easily deciphered. Regularities of natural process in the evolution of drainages in the region can assist in better understanding the nature of this record. The implications of these regularities will influence the operating assumptions, research design, and methods archaeologists bring to understanding and managing the past.

REFERENCES

Abel, T. J., D. M. Stothers, and J. M. Koralewski

2001   The Williams Mortuary Complex: A Transitional Archaic Regional Interaction Center in Northwestern Ohio. In *Archaic Transitions in Ohio and Kentucky,* edited by O. H. Prufer, S. E. Pedde, and R. S. Meindl, pp. 290–327. Kent State University Press, Kent, Ohio.

Albert, D., S. Denton, and B. Barnes

1986   *Regional Landscape Ecosystems of Michigan.* School of Natural Resources, University of Michigan, Ann Arbor.

Alden, W. C.

1918   *The Quaternary Geology of Southeastern Wisconsin.* Professional Paper 106. United States Geological Survey, Washington, D.C.

Allison, L. E.

1965   Organic Carbon. In *Methods of Soil Analysis,* edited by C. A. Black, pp. 1367–1378. American Society of Agronomics, Madison, Wisconsin.

Andrews, J. T.

1970   Differential Crustal Recovery and Glacial Chronology (6,700 to 0 B.P.), West Baffin Island, N.W.T., Canada. *Arctic and Alpine Research* 2:115–134.

Arbogast, A. F., E. E. Hansen, and M. D. Van Oort

2002   Reconstructing the Geomorphic Evolution of Large Coastal Dunes along the Southeastern Shore of Lake Michigan. *Geomorphology* 46:241-255.

Arnold, J.

1977   Early Archaic Subsistence and Settlement in the River Raisin Watershed, Michigan. In *The River Raisin Archaeological Survey Season 2, 1976: A Preliminary Report,* edited by C. Peebles and J. Krakker, pp. 279–376. Museum of Anthropology, University of Michigan, Ann Arbor.

Barnett, P. J.

1985   Glacial Retreat and Lake Levels, North Central Lake Erie Basin, Ontario. In *Quaternary Evolution of the Great Lakes,* edited by P. F. Karrow and P. E. Calkin, pp. 185–194. Special Paper 30. Geological Society of Canada, St. John's, Newfoundland.

Bates, M. R.

2000   Multidisciplinary Approaches to Geoarchaeological Evaluation of Deeply Stratified Sedimentary Sequences: Examples from Pleistocene and Holocene Deposits in Southern England, United Kingdom. *Journal of Archaeological Science* 27:845-858.

References

Beaverson, S. K.

1993   Reconstruction of Late Glacial and Holocene Paleoenvironmental Setting at 20SA596, Saginaw Basin, Michigan. Unpublished Master's thesis, Department of Geology, University of Minnesota, Duluth.

Beaverson, S. K., and H. D. Mooers

1993   *Reconstruction of Late Glacial and Holocene Paleoenvironmental Setting at 20SA596, Saginaw Basin, Michigan.* Reports of Investigations No. 210. Institute for Minnesota Archaeology, Minneapolis.

Beld, S. G.

1985   The Conservation Park Site (20-GR-33). In *Radiocarbon Dating in Gratiot County,* edited by T. Luke, pp. 1–203. Submitted to Michigan History Division. Alma College, Alma, Michigan. Report on file at the Office of the State Archeologist, Lansing, Michigan.

1991   *Two Terminal Archaic/Early Woodland Sites in Central Michigan.* Technical Report No. 22. Museum of Anthropology, University of Michigan, Ann Arbor.

Bettarel, R. L., and S. Harrison

1962   An Early Ossuary in Michigan. *Michigan Archaeologist* 8:37–42.

Bettarel, R. L., and H. Smith

1973   *The Moccasin Bluff Site and the Woodland Cultures of Southwestern Michigan.* Anthropological Papers No. 49. Museum of Anthropology, University of Michigan, Ann Arbor.

Bettis E. A., III, and E. R. Hajic

1995   Landscape Development and the Location of Evidence of Archaic Cultures in the Upper Midwest. In *Archaeological Geology of the Archaic Period in North America,* edited by E. A. Bettis III, pp. 87–113. Special Paper 297. Geological Society of America.

Bettis, E. A., III, and R. D. Mandel

2002   The Effects of Temporal and Spatial Patterns of Holocene Erosion and Alluviation on the Archaeological Record of the Central and Eastern Great Plains. *Geoarchaeology* 17:141–154.

Binford, L. R.

1963   The Hodges Site: A Late Archaic Burial Station. In *Miscellaneous Studies in Typology and Classification,* pp. 124–148. Anthropological Papers No. 19. Museum of Anthropology, University of Michigan, Ann Arbor.

Binford, L. R., and M. L. Papworth

1963   The Eastport Site, Antrim County, Michigan. In *Miscellaneous Studies in Typology and Classification,* pp. 71–123. Anthropological Papers No. 19. Museum of Anthropology, University of Michigan, Ann Arbor.

Branstner, M. C.

1990a   *1990 Great Lakes Gas Transmission Limited Partnership Pipeline Expansion Projects (TCPL-2): Phase I Cultural Resources Inventory Surveys of Pipeline Corridor and Access Roads Associated with Loops 11–14 and Loops 16–17 in Michigan.* FERC Docket No. CP89–892–000, MDOS ER No. 89502. Submitted to Great Lakes Gas Transmission Company and Braun Environmental Laboratories, Minneapolis. Great Lakes Research Associates, Williamston, Michigan. Report on file at the Office of the State Archeologist, Lansing, Michigan.

1990b   An Archaeological Testing Program at the Prince Hall Place Development Site, Detroit, Michigan. Report No. 88187. Great Lakes Research, Associates,

Williamston, Michigan. Report on file with the Office of the State Archaeologist, Lansing, Michigan.

1991   *1990 Great Lakes Gas Transmission Limited Partnership Pipeline Expansion Projects (TCPL-2): Phase II Cultural Resources Evaluations and Mitigative Recommendations (Part A)*. FERC Docket No. CP89–892–000, MDOS ER No. 89508. Submitted to Great Lakes Gas Transmission Company and Braun Environmental Laboratories, Minneapolis. Prepared by Great Lakes Research Associates, Williamston, Michigan. Report on file at the Office of the State Archeologist, Lansing, Michigan.

Branstner, M. C., and M. J. Hambacher

1991   *Data Recovery from Seven Sites in the Saginaw Valley, Michigan: Addendum A*. Submitted to Great Lakes Gas Transmission Company and Braun Environmental Laboratories, Minneapolis. Great Lakes Research Associates, Williamston, Michigan. Report on file at the Office of the State Archeologist, Lansing, Michigan.

Branstner, M. C., and M. J. Hambacher (editors)

1994   *1991 Great Lakes Gas Transmission Limited Partnership Pipeline Expansion Projects: Phase III Investigations at the Shiawassee River (20SA1033) and Bear Creek Sites (20SA1043), Saginaw County, Michigan*. Report No. 93–01. Great Lakes Research Associates, Williamston, Michigan. Report on file at the Office of the State Archeologist, Lansing, Michigan.

1995a   *1991 Great Lakes Gas Transmission Limited Partnership Pipeline Expansion Projects: Phase III Investigations at the Casassa Site (20SA1021) Saginaw County, Michigan*. Report No. 95–01. Natural Resources Group, Minneapolis, and Great Lakes Gas Transmission Limited Partnership, Detroit. Great Lakes Research Associates, Williamston, Michigan. Report on file at the Office of the State Archeologist, Lansing, Michigan.

1995b   *1991 Great Lakes Gas Transmission Limited Partnership Pipeline Expansion Projects: Phase III Investigations at the Vogelaar Site (20SA291) Saginaw County, Michigan*. Report No. 95–02. Natural Resources Group, Minneapolis, and Great Lakes Gas Transmission Limited Partnership, Detroit. Great Lakes Research Associates, Williamston, Michigan. Report on file at the Office of the State Archeologist, Lansing, Michigan.

Branstner, M., and E. Prahl

1983   An Archaeological Cultural Resource Management Investigation of the American Natural Resources, Stroh Brewing Co., and Chene Street Project Sites. Report No. 5811. Great Lakes Research Associates, Williamston, Michigan. Report on file with the Office of the State Archaeologist, Lansing, Michigan.

Brashler, J. G.

1981   *Early Late Woodland Boundaries and Interaction: Indian Ceramics of Southern Lower Michigan*. Anthropological Series 3(3). Publications of the Museum, Michigan State University, East Lansing.

Brashler, J. G., and E. B. Garland

1993   The Zemaitis Site (20OT68): A Stratified Woodland Occupation on the Grand River, Michigan. Paper presented at the Midwest Archaeological Conference, Milwaukee, Wisconsin.

Brashler, J. G., E. Garland, M. Holman, W. A. Lovis, and S. Martin

2000   Adaptive Strategies and Socioeconomic Systems in Northern Great Lakes Riverine Environments: The Late Woodland of Michigan. In *Late Woodland*

Societies: Tradition and Transformation across the Midcontinent, edited by T. Emerson, D. McElrath, and A. Fortier, pp. 543–579. University of Nebraska Press, Lincoln.

Brashler, J. G., E. G. Garland, and W. A. Lovis
  1994   Recent Research on Hopewell in Michigan. *Wisconsin Archeologist* 75:2–18.

Brashler, J. G., and M. B. Holman
  1985   Late Woodland Continuity and Change in the Saginaw Valley of Michigan. *Arctic Anthropology* 22(2):141–152.
  2004   Middle Woodland Adaptation in the Carolinian/Canadian Transition Zone of Western Lower Michigan. In *An Upper Great Lakes Archaeological Odyssey: Essays in Honor of Charles E. Cleland,* edited by W. Lovis, pp. 14–29. Cranbrook Institute of Science. Wayne State University Press, Detroit.

Brashler, J. G., and M. Kolb
  1995   Geoarchaeology and Ceramics at the Zemaitis Site. Paper presented at the Midwest Archaeological Conference, Beloit, Wisconsin.

Brashler, J. G., and B. Mead
  1996   Woodland Settlement in the Grand River Valley. In *Investigating the Archaeological Record of the Great Lakes State: Essays in Honor of Elizabeth Baldwin Garland,* edited by M. Holman, J. Brashler, and K. E. Parker, pp. 181–250. New Issues Press, Kalamazoo, Michigan.

Bretz, J. H.
  1951a   The Stages of Lake Chicago—Their Causes and Correlations. *American Journal of Science* 259:401–429.
  1951b   Causes of the Glacial Lake Stages in Saginaw Basin. *Journal of Geology* 59:244–258.
  1953   Glacial Grand River, Michigan. *Michigan Academician* 38:359–382.
  1955   *Geology of the Chicago Region, Part II—The Pleistocene.* Bulletin 65. Illinois State Geological Survey, Urbana.
  1959   The Double Calumet Stage of Lake Chicago. *Journal of Geology* 67:675–684.
  1963   The Prehistoric Great Lakes of North America. *American Scientist* 51:84–109.
  1964   Correlation of Glacial Lake Stages in the Huron-Erie and Michigan Basins. *Journal of Geology* 72:618–627.

Broecker, W. S.
  1966   Glacial Rebound and the Deformation of the Shorelines of Pro-glacial Lakes. *Journal of Geophysical Research* 71:7089–7105.

Broecker, W. S., and W. F. Farrand
  1963   Radiocarbon Age of the Two Creeks Forest Bed, Wisconsin. *Geological Society of America Bulletin* 74:795–801.

Brose, D. S.
  1970   *The Archaeology of Summer Island: Changing Settlement Systems in Northern Lake Michigan.* Anthropological Papers No. 41. Museum of Anthropology, University of Michigan, Ann Arbor.
  1972   The Mollusc Fauna. In *The Schultz Site at Green Point: A Stratified Occupation Area in the Saginaw Valley of Michigan,* edited by J. E. Fitting, pp. 117–130. Memoir No. 4. Museum of Anthropology, University of Michigan, Ann Arbor.
  1975   The Fisher Lake Site (20 LU 21): A Multi-component Occupation in Northwest Michigan. *Michigan Archaeologist* 21:71–90.

Brose, D. S., and P. Essenpreis
1973 A Report on a Preliminary Archaeological Survey of Monroe County, Michigan. *Michigan Archaeologist* 19(1–2).

Brose, D. S., and M. Hambacher
1999 The Middle Woodland in Northern Michigan. In *Retrieving Michigan's Buried Past: The Archaeology of the Great Lakes State,* edited by J. Halsey, pp. 59–70. Bulletin 64. Cranbrook Institute of Science, Bloomfield Hills, Michigan.

Brown, J. A., and C. E. Cleland
1968 The Late Glacial and Early Postglacial Faunal Resources in Midwestern Biomes Newly Opened to Human Adaptation. In *The Quaternary of Illinois.* Special Publication No. 14. College of Agriculture, University of Illinois, Urbana.

Brunett, F. V.
1981a *A Cultural Resources Inventory Report of the Dehmel Road Bridge Right of Way, Frankenmuth Twp, Saginaw County, Michigan.* Report No. 42781. Submitted to the Saginaw County Road Commission. Saginaw Archaeological Commission, Saginaw, Michigan. Report on file with the Office of the State Archaeologist, Lansing, Michigan.
1981b *A Cultural Resources Inventory Report of the West Portion of the Chippewa Landing Park, Village of Caro, Tuscola County, Michigan.* Report No. 5781, Submitted to Village of Caseville, Michigan. Saginaw Archaeological Commission, Saginaw, Michigan. Report on file with the Office of the State Archaeologist, Lansing, Michigan.
1981c *Further Excavations at 20SA581 and 20SA582, The Weber I and Weber II Sites, Frankenmuth Township, Saginaw County, Michigan.* Report No. 92481 Saginaw Archaeological Commission. Saginaw, Michigan. Report on file with the Office of the State Archaeologist, Lansing, Michigan.
1982 *An Archaeological Survey of a Portion of Section 35, T18N R10E, Village of Caseville, Michigan.* Report No. 71682, Submitted to Caseville Housing Commission, Caseville, Michigan. Report on file with the Office of the State Archaeologist, Lansing, Michigan.

Bryson, R., and F. Hare
1974 *Climates of North America.* Elsevier Press, New York.

Buckley, S. B.
1974 Study of Post-Pleistocene Ostracod Distribution in the Soft Sediment of Southern Lake Michigan. Unpublished Ph.D. dissertation, Department of Geology, University of Illinois, Urbana.

Buckmaster, M. M.
1979 Woodland and Oneota Settlement and Subsistence Systems in the Menominee River Watershed. Unpublished Ph.D. dissertation, Department of Anthropology, Michigan State University, East Lansing.
1999 The Northern Limits of Ridge Field Agriculture: An Example from Menominee County. Paper presented at the 45th Annual Midwest Archaeological Conference, East Lansing, Michigan.
2004 The Northern Limits of Ridge Field Agriculture. In *An Upper Great Lakes Archaeological Odyssey: Essays in Honor of Charles E. Cleland,* edited by W. Lovis, pp. 30–42. Cranbrook Institute of Science, Bloomfield Hills, Michigan.

Buckmaster, M. M., and J. Paquette

1989 The Gorto Site: Preliminary Report on a Late Paleo-Indian Site in Marquette County, Michigan. *Wisconsin Archeologist* 69:101–124.

1996 Surface Indications of a Late Pleistocene and Early Holocene Occupation at Silver Lake Basin, Marquette County, Michigan. In *Investigating the Archaeological Record of the Great Lakes State: Essays in Honor of Elizabeth Baldwin Garland,* edited by M. Holman, J. Brashler, and K. E. Parker, pp. 1–54. New Issues Press, Kalamazoo, Michigan.

Burgis, W. A.

1970 The Imlay Outlet of Glacial Lake Maumee, Imlay City, Michigan. Unpublished Master's thesis, Department of Geological Sciences, University of Michigan, Ann Arbor.

Butterfield, I. W.

1986 Water Configurations in the Human Environment from the Main Algonquin to the Nipissing I Stages of the Great Lakes in the Saginaw Valley, Michigan. *Michigan Archaeologist* 32(3).

N.D. Unpublished field notes. Manuscript on file, Michigan State University Museum and Department of Anthropology, Michigan State University, East Lansing.

Caiser, D.

1978 *Report of an Archaeological Survey in Norton Township, Muskegon County, Michigan.* Report No. 2231. Report on file with the Office of the State Archaeologist, Lansing, Michigan.

Calkin, P. E., and B. H. Feenstra

1985 Evolution of the Erie-Basin Great Lakes. In *Quaternary Evolution of the Great Lakes,* edited by P. F. Karrow and P. E. Calkin, pp. 149-170. Special Paper 30. Geological Society of Canada, St. John's, Newfoundland.

Callendar, C.

1978 Miami. In *Northeast,* edited by B. G. Trigger, pp. 681–689. Handbook of North American Indians, Vol. 15, W. C. Sturtevant, general editor. Smithsonian Institution, Washington, D.C.

Canti, M. G., and F. M. Meddens

1997 Mechanical Coring as an Aid to Archaeological Projects. *Journal of Field Archaeology* 24:97-105.

Chávez, R. E., M. E. Cámara, A. Tejero, L. Barba, and L. Manzanilla

2001 Site Characterization by Geophysical Methods in the Archaeological Zone of Teotihuacan, Mexico. *Journal of Archaeological Science* 28:1265-1276.

Chrzastowski, M. J., F. A. Pranschke, and C. W. Shabica

1991 Discovery and Preliminary Investigations of the Remains of an Early Holocene Forest on the Floor of Southern Lake Michigan. *Journal of Great Lakes Research* 17:543–552.

Clark, C. P.

1986 The Prehistory of the Birch Run Road Site, Saginaw County, Michigan. *Michigan Archaeologist* 32:1–92.

1989 Plano Tradition Lithics from the Upper Peninsula of Michigan. *Michigan Archaeologist* 35:88–112.

Clark, J. L., J. K. Walsh, J. A. Primus, and H. S. Pranger
  1985   A Model of Proglacial Lake Strandline Delevelling during the Past 18,000
          Years: Stratigraphic Implications. Abstract. *Geological Society of America Ab-
          stracts with Programs* 17:283.

Clark, R. H., and N. P. Persoage
  1970   Some Implications of Crustal Movement in Engineering Planning. *Canadian
          Journal of Earth Sciences* 7:628–633.

Cleland, C. E.
  1965   Barren Ground Caribou *(Rangifer arcticus)* from an Early Man Site in South-
          eastern Michigan. *American Antiquity* 30:350–351.
  1966   *The Prehistoric Ecology and Ethnozoology of the Upper Great Lakes Region.* An-
          thropological Papers No. 29. Museum of Anthropology, University of
          Michigan, Ann Arbor.
  1971   *The Lasanen Site: An Historical Burial Locality in Mackinac County, Michigan.*
          Anthropological Series 1(1). Publications of the Museum, Michigan State
          University, East Lansing.
  1973   The Pi-wan-go-ning Prehistoric District at Norwood, Michigan. In *Geology
          and the Environment: Man, Earth and Nature in Northwestern Lower
          Michigan,* edited by H. M. Martin, pp. 85–87. Michigan Basin Geological So-
          ciety, Ann Arbor.
  1976   The Focal-Diffuse Model: An Evolutionary Perspective on the Prehistoric
          Cultural Adaptations of the Eastern United States. *Midcontinental Journal of
          Archaeology* 1:59–76.
  1989   Comments on "A Reconsideration of Aboriginal Fishing Strategies in the
          Northern Great Lakes Region" by Susan R. Martin. *American Antiquity*
          54:605–608.
  N.D.   The Skegemog Point Site: A Late Woodland Village in Grand Traverse
          County, Michigan. Manuscript on file, Division of Anthropology, Michigan
          State University Museum, East Lansing.

Cleland, C. E., M. Holman, and J. A. Holman
  1998   Late Pleistocene Geochronology and the Paleoindian Penetration of the
          Southwestern Michigan Basin. *Wisconsin Archeologist* 79:28–52.

Cleland, C. E., and G. R. Peske
  1968   The Spider Cave Site. In *The Prehistory of the Burnt Bluff Area,* edited by J. Fit-
          ting, pp. 20–60. Anthropological Papers No. 34. Museum of Anthropology,
          University of Michigan, Ann Arbor.

Cleland, C. E., and D. Ruggles
  1996   The Samel's Field Site: An Early Archaic Base Camp in Grand Traverse
          County, Michigan. In *Investigating the Archaeological Record of the Great Lakes
          State: Essays in Honor of Elizabeth Baldwin Garland,* edited by M. Holman, J.
          Brashler, and K. E. Parker, pp. 55–79. New Issues Press, Kalamazoo, Michigan.

Clifton, J.
  1977   *The Prairie People: Continuity and Change in Potawatomi Indian Culture,
          1665–1965.* Regents Press of Kansas, Lawrence.

Coakley, J. P.
  1999   Lake Levels in the Erie Basin: Driving Factors and Recent Trends. In *Proceed-
          ings of the Great Lakes Paleo-Levels Workshop: The Last 4000 Years,* edited by

C. E. Sellinger and F. H. Quinn, pp. 24–29. Technical Memorandum ERL GLERL-113. NOAA, Ann Arbor, Michigan.

Conway, T.
1980 The Heartland of the Ojibway. In *Collected Archaeological Papers,* edited by D. Melvin, pp. 1–28. Archaeological Research Report 13. Historical Planning and Research Branch, Ontario Ministry of Culture and Recreation, Toronto.

Cowan, W. R.
1985 Deglacial Great Lakes Shorelines at Sault Ste. Marie, Ontario. In *Quaternary Evolution of the Great Lakes,* edited by P. F. Karrow and P. E. Calkin, pp. 33–37. Special Paper 30. Geological Society of Canada, St. John's, Newfoundland.

Cowan, C. W., and B. D. Smith
1993 New Perspectives on a Wild Gourd in Eastern North America. *Journal of Ethnobiology* 13:17–54.

Crawford, G. W., D. G. Smith, J. R. Deloges, and A. M. Davis
1998 Floodplains and Agricultural Origins: A Case Study in South-Central Ontario, Canada. *Journal of Field Archaeology* 25:123–138.

Cremin, W.
1980 The Schwerdt Site: A Fifteenth Century Fishing Station on the Lower Kalamazoo River, Southwest Michigan. *Wisconsin Archeologist* 61:280–291.
1982 Perspectives on the Prehistoric Occupation of the Kalamazoo River Valley: The Kalamazoo Basin Survey, 1976–1980. *Michigan Academician* 14:229–238.
1983 Late Prehistoric Adaptive Strategies on the Northern Periphery of the Carolinian Biotic Province. *Midcontinental Journal of Archaeology* 8(1):91–108.

Crumley, C. S.
1973 The Kantzler Site (20 BY 30): A Multi-component Woodland Site in Bay County, Michigan. *Michigan Archaeologist* 19:183-291.

DeCooke, B. G.
1967 Control of Great Lakes Water Levels. *Journal of the American Water Works Association* 59:684–698.

Dekin, A. A.
1966 A Fluted Point from Grand Traverse County. *Michigan Archaeologist* 12:35–36.

Demeter, C. S., and B. Burton
1980 *Archaeological Investigations at the Sheridan Place Development Site.* Report No. R-2229. Commonwealth Cultural Resources Group, Jackson, Michigan. Report on file with the Office of the State Archaeologist, Lansing, Michigan.

Demeter, C. S., and N. F. Demeter
1996 *An Archaeological and Soils Reconnaissance of the North Study Area Ambassador Bridge/ Gateway Project, Detroit, Michigan.* Report No. R-0242. Commonwealth Cultural Resources Group, Jackson, Michigan. Report on file with the Office of the State Archaeologist, Lansing, Michigan.

Demeter, C. S., and G. W. Monaghan
1997 *A Phase II/III Prehistoric Site Evaluation of the Ambassador Bridge/Detroit Welcome Center, Detroit, Michigan.* Commonwealth Cultural Resources Group, Jackson, Michigan. Report on file with the Office of the State Archaeologist, Lansing, Michigan.

Demeter, C. S., G. W. Monaghan, and M. J. Hambacher
2000   *A Phase I Archaeological Evaluation of the Crotty Street Mitigation Wetland: The Green Point/Schultz II (20SA1) Site, City of Saginaw, Saginaw County, Michigan.* Report No. R-0344. Commonwealth Cultural Resources Group, Jackson, Michigan. Report on file with the Office of the State Archaeologist, Lansing, Michigan.

Demeter, S. C., J. A. Robertson, and K. C. Egan
1994   *Phase I/II Archaeological Investigations of the Environmental Protection Agency Center for Ecology Research and Training, Bay City, Michigan.* Report No. R-0175. Commonwealth Cultural Resources Group, Jackson, Michigan. Report on file with the Office of the State Archaeologist, Lansing, Michigan.

Demeter, C. S., J. A. Robertson, and G. G. Robinson
1995   *Phase I/II Archaeological Investigations of the Saginaw CSO Control Facilities Phase B Collectors Site, City of Saginaw, Saginaw Co, Michigan.* Report No. R-0209. Commonwealth Cultural Resources Group, Jackson, Michigan. Report on file with the Office of the State Archaeologist, Lansing, Michigan.

Demeter, C. S., and D. Weir
1983   *A Cultural Resources Investigation of the Chene Park II Site, Detroit, Michigan.* Report No. R-2523. Commonwealth Associates, Jackson, Michigan. Report on file with the Office of the State Archaeologist, Lansing, Michigan.

Dobbs, C. A.
1993   *Projectile Points from 20SA596: Documentation of the Ebenhoff Collection.* Reports of Investigations No. 232. Institute for Minnesota Archaeology, Minneapolis.

Dobbs, C. A., C. Johnson, K. E. Parker, and T. Martin
1993   *20SA1034: A Late Prehistoric Site on the Flint River in the Saginaw Valley, Michigan.* Reports of Investigations No. 229. Institute for Minnesota Archaeology, Minneapolis.

Dobbs, C. A., and M. L. Murray
1993   *Ancient Native American Occupation at 20SA596 in the Saginaw Valley, Michigan.* Reports of Investigations No. 209. Institute for Minnesota Archaeology, Minneapolis.

Drake, R. H.
1980   Lake Whittlesey Outlet Channels and the Late Wisconsinan History of the Michigan Thumb Region. *Michigan Academician* 13:181–197.

Dreimanis, A.
1958   Beginning of the Nipissing Phase of Lake Huron. *Journal of Geology* 66:591–594.
1969   Late-Pleistocene Lakes in the Ontario and the Erie Basins. *Proceedings of 12th Conference on Great Lakes Research*, pp. 170–180.

Dreimanis, A., and R. P. Goldthwait
1973   Wisconsin Glaciations in the Huron, Erie, and Ontario Lobes. In *The Wisconsinan Stage*, edited by R. F. Black, R. P. Goldthwait, and H. B. Willman, pp. 71–106. Memoir 136. Geological Society of America, Washington, D.C.

Dunham, S. B., T. M. Branstner, and M. C. Branstner
1995   *Cultural Resources Surveys: US-23 Corridor Alternates, Arenac and Iosco*

Counties, Michigan. Submitted to Snell Environmental, Inc., Lansing, Michigan. Great Lakes Research Associates, Inc., Williamston, Michigan. Report on file with the Office of the State Archaeologist, Lansing, Michigan

Dunham, S. B., M. J. Hambacher, T. M. Branstner, and M. C. Branstner
1999   *Cultural Resource Surveys: US-31 Corridor Alternates, Allegan, Ottawa and Muskegon Counties, Part 1: 1995 Alternate Corridor Surveys.* Report submitted to the Michigan Department of Transportation, Lansing. Great Lakes Research Associates, Inc., Williamston, Michigan. Report on file with the Office of the State Archaeologist, Lansing, Michigan

Dunham, S.B., K. C. Taylor, and G. W. Monaghan
1999   *Phase II Investigations at Site 20Br47 and Phase I Deep Testing at the Coldwater River Tristate Pipeline Project, Branch County Loop, Girard Township, Branch County, Michigan.* Commonwealth Cultural Resources Group, Inc. Jackson, Michigan. Report on file with the Office of the State Archaeologist, Lansing, Michigan

Dustin, F.
1930   Some Ancient Indian Village Sites in Saginaw County, Michigan. *Papers of the Michigan Academy of Science, Arts and Letters* 14:35–45. Ann Arbor.

Egan, K. C.
1988   Middle and Late Archaic Phytogeography and Floral Exploitation in the Upper Great Lakes. *Midcontinental Journal of Archaeology* 13:83–89.
1994   Floral Remains (20SA1033). In *1991 Great Lakes Gas Transmission Limited Partnership Pipeline Expansion Projects: Phase III Investigations at the Shiawassee River (20SA1033) and Bear Creek Sites (20SA1043), Saginaw County, Michigan,* edited by M. C. Branstner and M. J. Hambacher, pp. 93–102. Report No. 93–01. Submitted to Great Lakes Gas Transmission Company, Detroit, and Natural Resources Group, Minneapolis. Prepared by Great Lakes Research Associates, Williamston, Michigan. Report on file with the Office of the State Archaeologist, Lansing, Michigan.

Egan-Bruhy, K. C.
2002   Floral Analysis of Sites 20BY28 and 20BY387. In *A Bridge to the Past: The Post-Nipissing Archaeology of the Marquette Viaduct Replacement Sites 20BY28 and 20BY387,* edited by W. Lovis, pp. 6.1–6.31. Submitted to City of Bay City and Federal Highway Administration. Michigan State University Museum and Department of Anthropology, Michigan State University, East Lansing.

Ellis, C. J., I. T. Kenyon, and M. W. Spence
1990   The Archaic. In *The Archaeology of Southern Ontario to AD 1650,* edited by C. J. Ellis and N. Ferris, pp. 65–144. Occasional Publication No. 5. London Chapter, Ontario Archaeological Society, London, Ontario.

Eschman, D. F.
1978   Pleistocene Geology of the Thumb Area of Michigan. In *Guidebook, North Central Section,* pp. 35–62. Geological Society of America, Ann Arbor, Michigan.

Eschman, D. F., and P. F. Karrow
1985   Huron Basin Glacial Lakes: A Review. In *Quaternary Evolution of the Great Lakes,* edited by P. F. Karrow and P. E. Calkin, pp. 79–93. Special Paper 30. Geological Society of Canada, St. John's, Newfoundland.

Evenson, E. B.
1973 Late Pleistocene Shorelines and Stratigraphic Relations in the Lake Michigan Basin. *Geological Society of America Bulletin* 84:2281-2297.

Evenson, E. B., W. R. Farrand, D. F. Eschman, D. M. Mickelson, and L. J. Maher
1976 Greatlakean Substage-A Replacement for Valderan Substage in the Lake Michigan Basin. *Quaternary Research* 6:411–424.

Fairchild, J. D
1977 The Schmidt Site: A Pre-Nipissing Village in the Saginaw Valley, Michigan. Unpublished Master's thesis, Department of Anthropology, Western Michigan University, Kalamazoo.

Farrand, W.
1962 Postglacial Uplift in North America. *American Journal of Science* 260:181–199.
1977 Revision of the Two Rivers ("Valders") Drift Border and the Age of Fluted Points in Michigan. In *For the Director: Research Essays in Honor of James B. Griffin,* edited by C. E. Cleland, pp. 74–84. Anthropological Papers No. 61. Museum of Anthropology, University of Michigan, Ann Arbor.
1990 Geological Observations on 20SA620. In *The Bridgeport Township Site: Archaeological Investigations at 20SA620, Saginaw County, Michigan,* edited by J. M. O'Shea and M. Shott, pp. 45–57. Anthropological Papers No. 81. Museum of Anthropology, University of Michigan, Ann Arbor.

Farrand, W. R., and C. W. Drexler
1985 Late Wisconsinan and Holocene History of the Lake Superior Basin. In *Quaternary Evolution of the Great Lakes,* edited by P. F. Karrow and P. E. Calkin, pp. 17–32. Special Paper 30. Geological Society of Canada, St. John's, Newfoundland.

Farrand, W. R., and D. F. Eschman
1974 Glaciation of the Southern Peninsula of Michigan: A Review. *Michigan Academician* 7:31-56.

Farrand, W. R., R. Zahner, and W. S. Benninghoff
1969 *Cary-Port Huron Interstade-Evidence from a Buried Bryophyte Bed, Cheboygan County, Michigan.* Special Paper 123. Geological Society of America, Washington, D.C.

Fillon, F. H.
1972 Possible Causes of the Variability of Postglacial Uplift in North America. *Quaternary Research* 1:522–531.

Finamore, P. F.
1985 Glacial Lake Algonquin and the Fenelon Falls Outlet. In *Quaternary Evolution of the Great Lakes,* edited by P. F. Karrow and P. E. Calkin, pp. 127–132. Special Paper 30. Geological Society of Canada, St. John's, Newfoundland.

Fisher, D.
1984 Taphonomic Analysis of Late Pleistocene Mastodon Occurrences: Evidence of Butchery by North American Paleo-Indians. *Paleobiology* 10(3):338–357.

Fitting, J. E.
1963 The Hi-Lo Site: A Late Paleo-Indian Site in Western Michigan. *Wisconsin Archeologist* 44:87–96.

1965   *Late Woodland Cultures of Southeastern Michigan.* Anthropological Papers No. 24. Museum of Anthropology, University of Michigan, Ann Arbor.

1970   *The Archaeology of Michigan: A Guide to the Prehistory of the Great Lakes Region.* Natural History Press, Garden City, New York.

1974   The Nelson Site (SIS 34). In *Contributions to the Archaeology of the St. Ignace Area,* edited by J. Fitting. *Michigan Archaeologist* 20:121–138.

1975a   Field School at the Young Site, 20SA209, Saginaw County, Michigan. *Michigan Archaeologist* 21:113–152.

1975b   *The Archaeology of Michigan: A Guide to the Prehistory of the Great Lakes Region,* 2d ed. Cranbrook Institute of Science, Bloomfield Hills, Michigan.

Fitting, J. E. (editor)

1968   *The Prehistory of the Burnt Bluff Area.* Anthropological Papers No. 34. Museum of Anthropology, University of Michigan, Ann Arbor.

1972   *The Schultz Site at Green Point: A Stratified Occupation Area in the Saginaw Valley of Michigan.* Memoirs No. 4. Museum of Anthropology, University of Michigan, Ann Arbor.

Fitting, J. E., and C. E. Cleland

1969   Late Prehistoric Settlement Patterns in the Upper Great Lakes. *Ethnohistory* 16:289–302.

Fitting, J. E., J. DeVisscher, and E. Wahla

1966   *The Paleo-Indian Occupation of the Holcombe Beach.* Anthropological Papers No. 27. Museum of Anthropology, University of Michigan, Ann Arbor.

Ford, R. E.

1973   The Moccasin Bluff Corn Holes. In *The Moccasin Bluff Site and the Woodland Cultures of Southwestern Michigan,* by R. L. Bettarel and H. Smith, pp. 188–197. Anthropological Papers No. 49. Museum of Anthropology, University of Michigan, Ann Arbor.

Frankforter, W. D.

1989   *Archaeological Investigation of the East Side Retention Basin Project ER-89052 City of Grand Rapids, Michigan, Combined Sewer Overflow Control.* Report on file with the Office of State Archaeologist, Lansing, Michigan.

Franzen, J. G.

1986   *Prehistoric Settlement on the Hiawatha National Forest, Michigan: A Preliminary Locational Model.* Cultural Resource Management Report No. 4. United States Department of Agriculture, Forest Service, Hiawatha National Forest, Escanaba, Michigan.

1987   *Test Excavation and Locational Analysis of Prehistoric Sites in the Hiawatha National Forest, Michigan: 1985 Season.* Cultural Resource Management Report No. 5. United States Department of Agriculture, Forest Service, Hiawatha National Forest, Escanaba, Michigan.

Fraser, G. S., C. E. Larsen, and N. C. Hester

1975   Climatically Controlled High Lake Levels in the Lake Michigan and Huron Basins. *Anais. Academia Brasileira Ciencias* 47:51–66 (Suplemento).

1990   Climatic Control of Lake Levels in the Lake Michigan and Lake Huron Basins. In *Late Quaternary History of the Lake Michigan Basin,* edited by A. F. Schneider and G. S. Fraser, pp. 75–90. Special Paper 251. Geological Society of America, Washington, D.C.

Fullerton, D. S.

1980   *Preliminary Correlation of Post-Erie Interstadial Events (16,000–10,000 Radio-carbon Years Before Present), Central and Eastern Great Lakes Region, and Hudson, Champlain, and St. Lawrence Lowlands, United States and Canada.* Professional Paper 1089. United States Geological Survey, Washington, D.C.

Garland, E. B. (editor)

1984   *Archaeological Investigations in the Lower St. Joseph River Valley, Berrien County, Michigan.* Submitted to Michigan Department of Transportation, Michigan Department of State, and United States Department of Transportation. Prepared by Western Michigan University, Kalamazoo.

1986   Early Woodland Occupations in Michigan: A Lower St. Joseph Valley Perspective. In *Early Woodland Archaeology,* edited by K. Farnsworth and T. Emerson, pp. 47–83. Kampsville Seminars in Archaeology, Vol. 2. Center for American Archaeology, Kampsville, Illinois.

1990   *Late Archaic and Early Woodland Adaptation in the Lower St. Joseph River Valley.* Michigan Cultural Resource Investigation Series, Vol. 2. Michigan Department of Transportation and Michigan Department of State, Lansing.

Garland, E. B., and S. Beld

1999   The Early Woodland: Ceramics, Domesticated Plants, and Burial Mounds Foretell the Shape of the Future. In *Retrieving Michigan's Buried Past: The Archaeology of the Great Lakes State,* edited by J. Halsey, pp. 125–146. Bulletin 64. Cranbrook Institute of Science, Bloomfield Hills, Michigan.

Goddard, L.

1978   Mascouten. In *Northeast,* edited by B. G. Trigger, pp. 668–672. Handbook of North American Indians, Vol. 15, W. C. Sturtevant, general editor. Smithsonian Institution, Washington, D.C.

Goldthwait, J. W.

1891   High Level Shores in the Region of the Great Lakes and their Deformation. *American Journal of Science* 41:201–221.

1908   A Reconstruction of Water Planes of Extinct Glacial Lakes in the Lake Michigan Basin. *Journal of Geology* 16:459–476.

Goldthwait, R.

1958   Wisconsin-Age Forests in Western Ohio, Pt. 1-Age and Glacial Events. *Ohio Journal of Science* 15:290-319.

Greenman, E.

1943   An Early Industry on a Raised Beach near Killarney, Ontario. *American Antiquity* 8:260–295.

Greenman, E., and G. Stanley

1940   A Geologically Dated Camp Site, Georgian Bay, Ontario. *American Antiquity* 5:194–199.

1941   Two Post-Nipissing Sites near Killarney, Ontario. *American Antiquity* 6:305–313.

1943   The Archaeology and Geology of Two Early Sites near Killarney, Ontario. *Papers of the Michigan Academy of Science, Arts, and Letters* 28:505–531.

Griffith, M. A.

1980   A Pedological Investigation of an Archaeological Site in Ontario, Canada. I. An Examination of the Soils in and Adjacent to a Former Village. *Geoderma* 24:327–336.

References

Halsey, J. R.
1968   The Springwells Mound Group of Wayne County, Michigan. In *Contributions to Michigan Archaeology,* pp. 79–159. Anthropological Papers No. 32. Museum of Anthropology, University of Michigan, Ann Arbor.
1976   The Wayne Mortuary Complex. Unpublished Ph.D. dissertation, Department of Anthropology, University of North Carolina, Chapel Hill.

Halsey, J. R. (editor)
1999   *Retrieving Michigan's Buried Past: The Archaeology of the Great Lakes State.* Bulletin 64. Cranbrook Institute of Science, Bloomfield Hills, Michigan.

Hambacher, M. J.
1988   The Point Arcadia Site (20MT120), Manistee County, Michigan: A Preliminary Consideration of the Williams Collection. *Michigan Archaeologist* 34:81–102.
1992   The Skegemog Point Site: Continuing Studies in the Cultural Dynamics of the Carolinian Canadian Transition Zone. Ph.D. dissertation, Michigan State University, East Lansing. University Microfilms International, Ann Arbor.

Hambacher, M. J., J. G. Brashler, K. C. Egan-Bruhy, D. R. Hayes, B. Hardy, D. G. Landis, T. E. Martin, G. W. Monaghan, K. Murphy, J. A. Robertson, and D. L. Seltz
2003   *Phase III Archaeological Data Recovery for the U.S.-131 S-Curve Realignment Project, Grand Rapids, Michigan.* Report No. R-0446. Submitted to Michigan Department of Transportation, Lansing. Prepared by Commonwealth Cultural Resources Group, Jackson, Michigan. Report on file with the Office of the State Archaeologist, Lansing, Michigan.

Hambacher, M .J., S. B. Dunham, and M. C. Branstner
1995   *Cultural Resource Investigations of the Broadway/Washington Avenue Corridor Project Area, Bay City, Michigan.* Report No. 95–21. Submitted to HNTB Michigan, Inc, Okemos, Michigan and the Michigan Department of Transportation. Great Lakes Research Associates, Inc., Williamston, Michigan. Report on file with the office of State Archaeologist, Lansing, Michigan.

Hansel, A. K., and D. M. Mickelson
1988   A Reevaluation of the Timing and Causes of High Lake Phases in the Lake Michigan Basin. *Quaternary Research* 29:113–128.

Hansel A. K., D. M. Mickelson, A. F. Schneider, and C. E. Larsen
1985   Late Wisconsinan and Holocene History of the Lake Michigan Basin. In *Quaternary Evolution of the Great Lakes,* edited by P. F. Karrow and P. E. Calkin, pp. 39–53. Special Paper 30. Geological Society of Canada, St. John's, Newfoundland.

Hargrave, M. L., L. E. Somers, T. K. Larson, R. Shields, and J. Dendy
2002   The Role of Resistivity Survey in Historic Site Assessment and Management: An Example from Fort Riley, Kansas. *Historical Archaeology* 36:89–110.

Harrison, S.
1966   The Schmidt Site (20SA192), Saginaw County, Michigan. *Michigan Archaeologist* 12:49-70.

Hart, J. P., and N. Asch Sidell
1997   Additional Evidence for Early Cucurbit Use in the Northern Eastern Woodlands East of the Allegheny Front. *American Antiquity* 62:523–537.

Hayes, D. H., and G. W. Monaghan

1997 Archaeological Site Burial during the Holocene: A Case Study Approach to the Mid-Atlantic. Paper presented at the 3rd International Conference on Soils, Geomorphology and Archaeology, Lurey, Virginia.

1998. The Down and Dirty Approach to a Variable Archaeological Record: a Geomorphological Framework for Archaeological Site Formation, Preservation, and Discovery in the James and Potomac River Basins. Paper presented at the Society of American Archaeologists, Seattle Annual Meeting.

Holman, M. B.

1978 The Settlement System of the Mackinac Phase. Unpublished Ph.D. dissertation, Department of Anthropology, Michigan State University, East Lansing.

Holman, M. B., J. Robertson, and R. Kingsley

1983 *An Archaeological Evaluation of Caseville Township Airport, Huron County, Michigan.* Archaeological Survey Report No. 73. Michigan State University Museum, Michigan State University, East Lansing.

Horton, R. E.

1927 *Hydrology of the Great Lakes.* Chicago Sanitary District, Chicago.

Hough, J. L.

1938 The Submerged Valley through Mackinac Straits. *Journal of Geology* 46:365–383.

1955 Lake Chippewa, a Low Stage of Lake Michigan Indicated by Bottom Sediments. *Geological Society of America Bulletin* 66:957–968.

1958 *Geology of the Great Lakes.* University of Illinois Press, Urbana.

1962 Lake Stanley, a Low Stage of Lake Huron Indicated by Bottom Sediments. *Geological Society of America Bulletin* 73:613–619.

1963 The Prehistoric Great Lakes of North America. *American Scientist* 51:84-109.

1966 Correlation of Glacial Lake Stages in the Huron-Erie and Michigan Basins. *Journal of Geology* 74:62–77.

Hruska, R.

1967 The Riverside Site: A Late Archaic Manifestation in Michigan. *Wisconsin Archeologist* 48:145–260.

Huisink, M.

2000 Changing River Styles in Response to Weichselian Climate Changes in the Vecht Valley, Eastern Netherlands. *Sedimentary Geology* 133:115–134.

Hunter, R. D.

2004 Project Drowned Forest: A Study of Prehistoric Underwater Forest in Lake Huron, Michigan. Electronic document, http://www.Oakland.edu/biology/staff/DrownedForest.pdf

Iaquinta, J. L.

1994 *Soil Survey of Saginaw County, Michigan.* United States Department of Agriculture, Soil Conservation Service, Washington, D.C.

Isaacson, J., R. E. Hollinger, D. Gundrum, and J. Baird

1999 A Controlled Archaeological Test Site Facility in Illinois: Training and Research in Archaeogeophysics. *Journal of Field Archaeology* 26:227-236.

Janzen, D. E.
1968 *The Naomikong Point Site and the Dimensions of Laurel in the Lake Superior Basin.* Anthropological Papers No. 36. Museum of Anthropology, University of Michigan, Ann Arbor.

Jochim, M. A.
1994 An Ecological Agenda for Archaeological Research. In *Great Lakes Archaeology and Paleoecology: Exploring Interdisciplinary for the Nineties,* edited by R. I. MacDonald, pp. 5–23. Publication 10. Quaternary Sciences Institute, University of Waterloo, Waterloo, Ontario.

Johnson, T. C., R. D. Stieglitz, and A. M. Swain
1990 Age and Paleoclimatic Significance of Lake Michigan Beach Ridges at Baileys Harbor, Wisconsin. In *Late Quaternary History of the Lake Michigan Basin,* edited by A. F. Schneider and G. S. Fraser, pp. 67–74. Special Paper 251. Geological Society of America, Washington, D.C.

Johnson, W. H.
1976 Quaternary Stratigraphy in Illinois: Status and Current Problems. In *Quaternary Stratigraphy of North America,* edited by W. C. Mahaney, pp. 161–196. Dowden, Hutchinson, and Ross, Stroudsburg, Pennsylvania.

Justice, N. D.
1987 *Stone Age Spear and Arrow Points of the Midcontinental and Eastern United States.* Indiana University Press, Bloomington.

Karrow, P. F.
1980 The Nipissing Transgression around Southern Lake Huron. *Canadian Journal of Earth Sciences* 17:1271–1274.

Karrow, P. F., T. W. Anderson, A. H. Clarke, L. D. Delorme, and M. R. Sreenivasa
1975 Stratigraphy, Paleontology and Age of Lake Algonquin Sediments in Southwestern Ontario. *Quaternary Research* 5:49–87.

Kaszicki, C. A.
1985 History of Lake Algonquin in the Haliburton Region, South-Central Ontario. In *Quaternary Evolution of the Great Lakes,* edited by P. F. Karrow and P. E. Calkin, pp. 109–123. Special Paper 30. Geological Society of Canada, St. John's, Newfoundland.

Keene, A. S.
1981 *Prehistoric Foraging in a Temperate Forest: A Linear Programming Model.* Academic Press, New York.

Kern, J. R., J. Schuldenrein, and C.S. Demeter
1983 *Land Use History for the City of Muskegon, Western Avenue Utility Reconstruction.* Report No. R-2572. Commonwealth Cultural Resources Group, Jackson, Michigan. Report on file with the Office the State Archaeologist, Lansing, Michigan.

Kincare, K.
1984 Geological Age of Point Bar Formation at the Wymer Site. In *Archaeological Investigations in the Lower St. Joseph River Valley, Berrien County, Michigan,* edited by E. Garland, pp. 870–898. Submitted to Michigan Department of Transportation, Michigan Department of State, and United States Department of Transportation. Western Michigan University, Kalamazoo.

Kingsley, R.
1981   Hopewell Middle Woodland Settlement Systems and Cultural Dynamics in Southern Michigan. *Midcontinental Journal of Archaeology* 6:131–178.

Krakker, J.
1983   Changing Sociocultural Systems during the Late Prehistoric Period in Southeast Michigan. Ph.D. dissertation, University of Michigan, Ann Arbor. University Microfilms, Ann Arbor.

Krist, F. J.
2001   A Predictive Model of Paleo-Indian Subsistence and Settlement. Unpublished Ph.D. dissertation, Department of Anthropology, Michigan State University, East Lansing.

Kunkle, G. R.
1963   Lake Ypsilanti: A Probable Late Pleistocene Low-Lake Stage in the Erie Basin. *Journal of Geology* 71:72–75.

Lane, A. C.
1900   *Geological Report on Huron County, Michigan.* Geological Survey of Michigan, Vol. 7, Part 2.

Larsen, C. E.
1974   Late Holocene Lake Levels in Southern Lake Michigan. In *Coastal Geology, Sedimentology, and Management, Chicago and the North Shore,* edited by C. Collinson, pp. 39–49. Guidebook Series 12. Illinois State Geological Survey, Urbana.

1980   Some Personal Views on Needed Archaeological Research in Michigan Archaeology. In *Major Problem Orientations in Michigan Archaeology: 1980–1984, Phase II Completion Report,* edited by J. Mueller, pp. 1–31. Report No. R-2134. Commonwealth Associates, Jackson, Michigan. Report on file with the Office of the State Archaeologist, Lansing, Michigan.

1985a   *A Stratigraphic Study of Beach Features on the Southwestern Shore of Lake Michigan: New Evidence of Historical Lake Level Fluctuation.* Illinois State Geological Survey Environmental Notes, Urbana.

1985b   Lake Level, Uplift and Outlet Incision: The Nipissing and Algoma Great Lakes. In *Quaternary Evolution of the Great Lakes,* edited by P. F. Karrow and P. E. Calkin, pp. 63–77. Special Paper 30. Geological Society of Canada, St. John's, Newfoundland.

1985c   Geoarchaeological Interpretation of Great Lakes Coastal Environments. In *Archaeological Sediments in Context,* edited by J. K. Stein and W. R. Farrand, pp. 91–110. Peopling of the Americas, Vol. 1. Center for the Study of Early Man, Institute for Quaternary Studies, University of Maine at Orono, Orono.

1987   *Chronological History of Glacial Lake Algonquin and the Upper Great Lakes.* Bulletin 180. United States Geological Survey, Washington, D.C.

1999a   A Century of Great Lakes Levels Research: Finished or Just Beginning? In *Retrieving Michigan's Buried Past: The Archaeology of the Great Lakes State,* edited by J. Halsey, pp. 1–30. Bulletin 64. Cranbrook Institute of Science, Bloomfield Hills, Michigan.

1999b   Reconstructing Holocene Lake Level Fluctuations in the Lake Superior Basin. In *Proceeding of the Great Lakes Paleo-Levels Workshop: The Last 4000 Years,* edited by C. E. Sellinger and F. H. Quinn, pp. 20–23. Technical Memorandum ERL GLERL-113. NOAA, Ann Arbor, Michigan.

Larsen, C. E., and C. S. Demeter

1979   *Archaeological Investigations of the Proposed West River Drive, Bay City.* Commonwealth Associates, Inc. Report No. R-2090. Commonwealth Cultural Resources Group, Jackson, Michigan. Report on file with the Office of the State Archaeologist, Lansing, Michigan.

Larson, G. J., and G. W. Monaghan

1988   *Wisconsinan and Holocene Stratigraphy in Southwestern Michigan.* Midwest Friends of the Pleistocene 35th Field Conference Guide. Department of Geological Sciences, Michigan State University, East Lansing.

Leverett, F.

1897   *The Pleistocene Features and Deposits of the Chicago Area.* Bulletin 2. Geology and Natural History Survey, Chicago Academy of Sciences, Chicago.

Leverett, F., and F. B. Taylor

1915   *The Pleistocene of Indiana and Michigan and the History of the Great Lakes.* Monograph No. 53. U. S. Geological Survey, Washington, D.C.

Lewis, C. F. M.

1969   Lake Quaternary History of Lake Levels in the Huron and Erie Basins. *Proceedings 12th Conference on Great Lakes Research,* pp. 250–270. International Associations for Great Lakes Research.

1970   Recent Uplift of Manitoulin Island. *Canadian Journal of Earth Sciences* 7:665–675.

1999   Holocene Lake Levels and Climate: Lakes Winnipeg, Erie and Ontario. In *Proceeding of the Great Lakes Paleo-Levels Workshop: The Last 4000 Years,* edited by C. E. Sellinger and F. H. Quinn, pp. 6–19. Technical Memorandum ERL GLERL-113. NOAA, Ann Arbor, Michigan.

Lewis, C. F. M., and T. W. Anderson

1989   Oscillations of Levels and Cool Phases of the Laurentian Great Lakes Caused by Inflows for Glacial Lakes Agassiz and Barlow-Ojibway. *Journal of Paleolimnology* 2:99–146.

1992   Stable Isotope (O and C) and Pollen Trends in Eastern Lake Erie, Evidence for a Locally-Induced Climatic Reversal of Younger Dryas Age in the Great Lakes Basins. *Climate Dynamics* 6:241–250.

Lovis, W. A.

1971   The Holtz Site (20AN26), Antrim Co., Michigan: A Preliminary Report. *Michigan Archaeologist* 17:49–64.

1973   Late Woodland Cultural Dynamics in the Northern Lower Peninsula of Michigan. Unpublished Ph.D. dissertation. Department of Anthropology, Michigan State University, East Lansing.

1976   Quarter Sections and Forests: An Example of Probability Sampling in the Northeastern Woodlands. *American Antiquity* 41:364-372.

1985   The Role of the Fletcher Site and the Lower Basin in the Woodland Adaptations of the Saginaw Valley. *Arctic Anthropology* 22(2):153–170.

1986   Environmental Periodicity, Buffering, and the Archaic Adaptations of the Saginaw Valley of Michigan. In *Foraging, Collecting, and Harvesting: Archaic Period Subsistence and Settlement in the Eastern Woodlands,* edited by S. Neusius, pp. 99–116. Occasional Paper No. 6. Center for Archaeological Investigations, Southern Illinois University at Carbondale, Carbondale.

1988   Human Prehistory of Southwestern Michigan: A Paleogeographic Perspective. In *Wisconsinan and Holocene Stratigraphy in Southwestern Michigan,* edited by G. Larson and G. W. Monaghan, pp. 43–50. Midwest Friends of the

Pleistocene 35th Field Conference Guide. Department of Geological Sciences, Michigan State University, East Lansing.

1989 Variation in Late Archaic Resource Availability as a Consequence of Lake Level Periodicity in the Huron Basin. Paper presented at the 54th Annual Meeting of the Society for American Archaeology, Atlanta.

1990a Screaming Loon: A Post-Nipissing Site on the Devil's Elbow. *Michigan Archaeologist* 36: 232–252.

1990b Site Formation Processes and the Organization of Space at the Stratified Late Woodland O'Neil Site. In *The Woodland Tradition in the Western Great Lakes: Essays in Honor of Elden Johnson*, edited by G. Gibbon, pp. 195–211. Minnesota Publications in Anthropology No. 4. University of Minnesota Press, Minneapolis.

1990c Native American Resources. In *The Great Lakes Gas Transmission Company Natural Gas Pipeline Corridor (MP 562.6–972.9): A Preliminary Sensitivity Model and Testing Strategy*, edited by M. Branstner, pp. 4–18. Great Lakes Research Associates, Williamston, Michigan. Report on file with the Office of State Archaeologist, Lansing, Michigan.

1990d Curatorial Considerations for Systematic Research Collections: AMS Dating a Curated Ceramic Assemblage. *American Antiquity* 55:382–387.

1990e Accelerator Dating the Ceramic Assemblage from the Fletcher Site: Implications of a Pilot Study for Interpretation of the Wayne Period. *Midcontinental Journal of Archaeology* 15(1):37–50.

1999 The Middle Archaic: Learning to Live in the Woodlands. In *Retrieving Michigan's Buried Past: The Archaeology of the Great Lakes State*, edited by J. Halsey, pp. 83–94. Bulletin 64. Cranbrook Institute of Science, Bloomfield Hills, Michigan.

2002 Conclusions. In *A Bridge to the Past: The Post-Nipissing Archaeology of the Marquette Viaduct Replacement Sites 20BY28 and 20BY387*, edited by W. Lovis, pp. 11.1–11.9. Submitted to City of Bay City and Federal Highway Administration. Michigan State University Museum and Department of Anthropology, Michigan State University, East Lansing.

2004 Backyards, Scrap Yards, and the Taphonomy of Riverine Urban Environments: Bay City, Michigan, as a Case Study. In *An Upper Great Lakes Archaeological Odyssey: Essays in Honor of Charles E. Cleland*, edited by W. Lovis, pp. 127–149. Cranbrook Institute of Science, Bloomfield Hills, Michigan.

Lovis, W. A. (editor)

1976 *Archaeological Investigations within Fisherman's Island State Park: 1976 Season*. Archaeological Survey Report No. 10. Michigan State University Museum, Michigan State University, East Lansing.

1979 The Archaeology and Physical Anthropology of 20LP98: A Woodland Burial Locale in Lapeer County, Michigan. *Michigan Archaeologist* 25(1-2).

1989 *Archaeological Investigations at the Weber I (20SA581) and Weber II (20SA582) Sites, Frankenmuth Township, Saginaw County, Michigan*. Michigan Cultural Resource Investigation Series, Vol. 1. Michigan Department of Transportation and Michigan Department of State, Lansing.

1993 *The Archaic, Woodland and Historic Period Occupations of the Liberty Bridge Locale, Bay City, Michigan*. Michigan Cultural Resource Investigation Series, Vol. 3. Michigan Department of Transportation and Michigan Department of State, Lansing.

2002 *A Bridge to the Past: The Post-Nipissing Archaeology of the Marquette Viaduct Replacement Project Sites 20BY28 and 20BY386*. Michigan State University Museum and Department of Anthropology, Michigan State University, East Lansing.

Lovis, W. A., K. Egan, G. W. Monaghan, B. A. Smith, and E. J. Prahl

1996 Environment and Subsistence at the Marquette Viaduct Locale of the Fletcher Site. In *Investigating the Archaeological Record of the Great Lakes State: Essays in Honor of Elizabeth Baldwin Garland,* edited by M. Holman, J. Brashler, and K. E. Parker, pp. 251–306. New Issues Press, Kalamazoo, Michigan.

Lovis, W. A., K. Egan, B. Smith, and G. W. Monaghan

1994 *Muskrat and Fish, Wild Rice and Goosefoot: Changing Subsistence Strategies and the Origins of Indigenous Horticulture at the Schultz Site.* Submitted to Committee for Research, National Geographic Society, Washington, D.C. Michigan State University Museum, Michigan State University, East Lansing.

2001 Wetlands and Emergent Horticultural Economies in the Upper Great Lakes: A New Perspective from the Schultz Site. *American Antiquity* 66:615–632.

Lovis, W. A., and M. Holman

1976 Subsistence Strategies and Population: A Hypothetical Model for the Development of Late Woodland in the Straits of Mackinac/Sault Ste. Marie Area. *Michigan Academician* 8(3):267–276.

Lovis, W. A., M. B. Holman, G. W. Monaghan, and R. K. Skowronek

1994 Archaeology, Geology, and Paleoecology: Perspectives on Regional Research Design in the Saginaw Bay Region of Michigan. In *Great Lakes Archaeology and Paleoecology: Exploring Interdisciplinary Initiatives for the Nineties,* edited by R. I. MacDonald, pp. 81–94. Quaternary Sciences Institute, University of Waterloo, Waterloo, Ontario.

Lovis, W. A., and R. I. MacDonald

1999 Archaeological Implications of Great Lakes Paleoecology at the Regional Scale. In *Taming the Taxonomy: Toward a New Understanding of Great Lakes Archaeology,* edited by R. F. Williamson and C. M. Watts, pp. 125–150. Eastend Books and the Ontario Archaeological Society, Toronto.

Lovis, W. A., R. C. Mainfort, and V. E. Noble

1976 *An Archaeological Inventory and Evaluation of the Sleeping Bear Dunes National Lakeshore, Leelanau and Benzie Counties, Michigan.* Archaeological Survey Report No. 5. Michigan State University Museum, Michigan State University, East Lansing.

Lovis, W. A., and J. O'Shea

1994 A Reconsideration of Archaeological Research Design in Michigan: 1993. *Michigan Archaeologist* 39:107–126.

Lovis, W. A., G. Rajnovich, and A. Bartley

1998 Exploratory Cluster Analysis, Temporal Change, and the Woodland Ceramics of the Portage Site at L'Arbre Croche. *Wisconsin Archeologist* 79:89–112.

Lovis, W. A., and J. A. Robertson

1989 Rethinking the Archaic Chronology of the Saginaw Valley of Michigan. *Midcontinental Journal of Archaeology* 14:226–260.

Luedtke, B.

1976 Lithic Material Distributions and Interaction Patterns during the Late Woodland Period in Michigan. Ph.D. dissertation, University of Michigan, East Lansing. University Microfilms, Ann Arbor.

Luxenberg, B.

1972 Faunal Remains. In *The Schultz Site at Green Point: A Stratified Occupation*

Area in the Saginaw Valley of Michigan, edited by J. E. Fitting, pp. 91–116. Memoirs No. 4. Museum of Anthropology, University of Michigan. Ann Arbor.

Mangold, W.
1981   Middle Woodland Ceramics of Northwestern Indiana and Western Michigan. Master's thesis, Department of Anthropology, Western Michigan University, Kalamazoo.

Martin, S. R.
1989   A Reconsideration of Aboriginal Fishing Strategies in the Northern Great Lakes Region. *American Antiquity* 54:594–604.

Martin, T., and J. C. Richmond
1993   Animal Remains from 20SA1034. In *20SA1034: A Late-Prehistoric Site on the Flint River in the Saginaw Valley, Michigan,* edited by C. A. Dobbs, C. Johnson, K. E. Parker, and T. Martin, pp. 119–135. Reports of Investigations No. 229. Institute for Minnesota Archaeology, Minneapolis.

Mason, R. J.
1958   *Late Pleistocene Geochronology and the Paleo Indian Penetration into the Lower Michigan Peninsula.* Anthropological Papers No. 11. Museum of Anthropology, University of Michigan, Ann Arbor.
1966   *Two Stratified Sites on the Door Peninsula of Wisconsin.* Anthropological Papers No. 26. Museum of Anthropology, University of Michigan, Ann Arbor.
1981   *Great Lakes Archaeology.* Academic Press, New York.

McHale Milner, C.
1998   Ceramic Style, Social Differentiation, and Resource Uncertainty in the Late Prehistoric Upper Great Lakes. Ph.D. dissertation, University of Michigan, Ann Arbor. University Microfilms International, Ann Arbor.

McHale Milner, C., and J. O'Shea
1998   The Socioeconomic Role of Late Woodland Enclosures in Northern Michigan. In *Ancient Earthen Enclosures of the Eastern Woodlands,* edited by R. Mainfort and L. Sullivan, pp. 181–201. University Press of Florida, Jacksonville.

McPherron, A.
1967   *The Juntunen Site and the Late Woodland Prehistory of the Upper Great Lakes Area.* Anthropological Papers No. 30. Museum of Anthropology, University of Michigan, Ann Arbor.

Mead, B.
1982   The SW 1/3 of Section 8, Taymouth Township, Saginaw County, Michigan. Manuscript on file, Office of the State Archaeologist, Michigan Historical Center, Department of State, Lansing.

Mead, B., and R. G. Kingsley
1985   20IS46, a Late Archaic Cemetery in Iosco County, Michigan. *Michigan Archaeologist* 31:67–81.

Meltzer, D., and B. Smith
1986   Paleoindian and Early Archaic Subsistence Strategies in Eastern North America. In *Foraging, Collecting, and Harvesting: Archaic Period Subsistence and Settlement in the Eastern Woodlands,* edited by S. Neusius, pp. 3–32. Occasional Paper No. 6. Center for Archaeological Investigations, Southern Illinois University at Carbondale, Carbondale.

Mickelson, D. M., L. Clayton, D. S. Fullerton, and H. W. Borns

1983   The Late Wisconsin Glacial Record of the Laurentide Ice Sheet in the United States. In *Late-Quaternary Environments of the United States.* Vol. 1, *The Late Pleistocene,* edited by H. E. Wright Jr., pp. 3–38. University of Minnesota Press, Minneapolis.

Miller, B. B., and R. Kott

1989   Molluscan Faunal Changes in the Lake Michigan Basin during the Past 11,000 Years. *National Geographic Research* 5(3):364–373.

Milner, C. M.

1998   Ceramic Style, Social Differentiation and Resource Uncertainty in the Late Prehistoric Upper Great Lakes. Unpublished Ph.D. dissertation, Department of Anthropology, University of Michigan, Ann Arbor.

Monaghan, G. W.

1985a   Stratigraphic Evidence for the Erie Interstade in the Lake Michigan Basin. *Geological Society of America Abstracts with Programs* 17(4):319.

1985b   *Deep Testing at a Bridge Replacement along Deer Creek, Saginaw County, Michigan.* Report submitted to Caminos Associates, Bay City, Michigan. Report on file with the Office of the State Archaeologist, Lansing, Michigan.

1990a   Survey Methodology. In *The Great Lakes Gas Transmission Company Natural Gas Pipeline Corridor (MP 562.6–972.9): A Preliminary Sensitivity Model and Testing Strategy,* edited by M. Branstner, pp. 25–34. Great Lakes Archaeological Research, Williamston, Michigan. Report on file with the Office of the State Archaeologist, Lansing, Michigan.

1990b   Systematic Variation in the Clay-Mineral Composition of Till Sheets: Evidence for the Erie Interstade in the Lake Michigan Basin. In *Late Quaternary History of the Lake Michigan Basin,* edited by A. F. Schneider and G. S. Fraser, pp. 43–49. Special Paper 251. Geological Society of America, Washington, D.C.

1991   Geology of the Third Street Bridge Right-of-Way, Bay City, Michigan. In *Archaeological Investigations at Sites 20BY77, 20BY78, and 20BY79 at the Third Street Bridge Replacement, Bay City, Michigan,* edited by W. A. Lovis. Submitted to Michigan Department of Transportation and Michigan Department of State, Lansing. Michigan State University, East Lansing.

1993   Geology of the Third Street Bridge Project Area, Bay City, Michigan. In *The Archaic, Woodland, and Historic Period Occupations of the Liberty Bridge Locale, Bay City, Michigan,* edited by W. A. Lovis, pp. 35–40. Michigan Cultural Resource Investigation Series, Vol. 3. Michigan Department of Transportation and Michigan Department of State, Lansing.

1994a   Geology and Geochemistry of the Study Area. In *1991 Great Lakes Gas Transmission Limited Partnership Pipeline Expansion Projects: Phase III Investigations at the Shiawassee River (20SA1033) and Bear Creek Sites (20SA1043), Saginaw County, Michigan,* edited by M. C. Branstner and M. J. Hambacher, pp. 5–32. Report No. 93–01. Submitted to Great Lakes Gas Transmission Company, Detroit, and Natural Resources Group, Minneapolis. Great Lakes Research Associates, Williamston, Michigan. Report on file with the Office of the State Archaeologist, Lansing, Michigan.

1994b   *Report of Deep Testing Along the West Bank of the Saginaw River, Bay City Michigan.* Report on file with the Michigan State University Museum, Michigan State University, East Lansing, Michigan.

1995a   Geomorphic and Physiographic Setting. In *1991 Great Lakes Gas Transmission Limited Partnership Pipeline Expansion Projects: Phase III Investigations at the Casassa Site (20SA1021), Saginaw County, Michigan (FERC Docket No. CP89-*

892-000), edited by M. C. Branstner and M. J. Hambacher, pp. 2–22. Report No. 95-01. Great Lakes Research Associates, Williamston, Michigan. Report on file with the Office of the State Archaeologist, Lansing, Michigan.

1995b Geomorphic and Physiographic Setting. In *1991 Great Lakes Gas Transmission Limited Partnership Pipeline Expansion Projects: Phase III Investigations at the Vogelaar Site (20SA1021), Saginaw County, Michigan (FERC Docket No. CP89-892-000)*, edited by M. C. Branstner and M. J. Hambacher, pp. 2–21. Report No. 95-02. Great Lakes Research Associates, Williamston, Michigan. Report on file with the Office of the State Archaeologist, Lansing, Michigan.

1995c Physiographic and Geologic Background. In *Cultural Resources Surveys: US-23 Corridor Alternates, Arenac and Iosco Counties, Michigan*, edited by S. B. Dunham, T. M. Branstner, and M. C. Branstner, pp. 8–19. Report submitted to the Michigan Department of Transportation, Lansing. Great Lakes Research Associates, Inc., Williamston, Michigan. Report on file with the Office of the State Archaeologist, Lansing, Michigan.

1999 Physiographic and Geologic Background. In *Cultural Resource Surveys: US-31 Corridor Alternates, Allegan, Ottawa and Muskegon Counties, Part 1: 1995 Alternate Corridor Surveys*, edited by S. B. Dunham, M. J. Hambacher, T. M. Branstner, and M. C. Branstner, pp. 8–25. Report submitted to the Michigan Department of Transportation, Lansing. Great Lakes Research Associates, Inc., Williamston, Michigan. Report on file with the Office of the State Archaeologist, Lansing, Michigan.

2002 Geoarchaeology of the Marquette Viaduct Relocation Project Sites 20BY28 and 20BY387, Bay City, Michigan. In *A Bridge to the Past: the Post-Nipissing Archaeology of the Marquette Viaduct Replacement Project Sites 20BY28 and 20BY386, Bay City, Michigan.* edited by W. A. Lovis, 2.1–2.38. Michigan State University Museum and Department of Anthropology, Michigan State University, East Lansing.

Monaghan, G. W., and J. Brashler
2002 *Deep Testing at a Proposed Addition to the Gerald R. Ford Museum, Grand Rapids, Kent County, Michigan.* Report on file with Commonwealth Cultural Resources Group, Jackson, Michigan. Report on file with the Office of the State Archaeologist, Lansing, Michigan.

Monaghan, G. W., and L. Fay
1989 Geology of the Weber Site I. In *Archaeological Investigations at the Weber I (20SA581) and Weber II (20SA582) Sites, Frankenmuth Township, Saginaw County, Michigan*, edited by W. A. Lovis, pp. 41–50. Michigan Cultural Resource Investigation Series, Vol. 1. Michigan Department of Transportation and Michigan Department of State, Lansing.

Monaghan, G. W., and A. K. Hansel
1990 Evidence for the Intra-Glenwood (Mackinaw) Low-Water Phase of Glacial Lake Chicago. *Canadian Journal of Earth Science* 27:1236–1241.

Monaghan, G. W., and D. H. Hayes
1994a Geoarchaeology. In *Stage III Archaeological Investigations at Whitney Creek No. 1 Site (ANR-39; A037-01-0024) Genesee County, New York*, edited by J. A. Robertson, K. C. Egan, and D. J. Weir, pp. 1–35. Commonwealth Cultural Resources Group, Jackson, Michigan. Report on file with the Office of the State Archaeologist, Lansing, Michigan.

1994b Geoarchaeology. In *Stage III Archaeological Investigations at Arc Site (ANR-29; A037-01-0004) Genesee County, New York*, edited by J. A. Robertson, K. C. Egan, and D. J. Weir, pp. 1–38. Commonwealth Cultural Resources Group,

Jackson, Michigan. Report on file with the Office of the State Archaeologist, Lansing, Michigan.

1994c Site Geomorphology and Geoarchaeology. In *Stage III Archaeological Investigations at Zinselmeier No. 1 Site (ANR-222; A069-15-0026) Ontario County, New York,* edited by D. J. Weir, pp. 1–36. Commonwealth Cultural Resources Group, Jackson, Michigan. Report on file with the Office of the State Archaeologist, Lansing, Michigan.

1994d Geoarchaeology. In *Stage III Archaeological Investigations at McVicker Site, Ontario County, New York,* edited by J. A. Robertson, K. C. Egan, and D. J. Weir, pp. 1–36. Commonwealth Cultural Resources Group, Jackson, Michigan. Report on file with the Office of the State Archaeologist, Lansing, Michigan.

1997 Archaeological Site Burial: A Model for Site Formation within the Middle-to-Late Holocene Alluvial Settings of the Great Lakes. Paper presented at Taming the Taxonomy: Towards a New Understanding of Great Lakes Prehistory, the Joint Symposium of the Ontario Archaeological Society and Midwest Archaeological Conference, North York, Ontario.

1998 Millennial-Scale Patterns to Middle-to-Late Holocene Alluviation in the Great Lakes and Mid Atlantic Regions, USA. Geological Society of America. *Programs with Abstracts* 30:7.

1999 *Geoarchaeology of the Vector Pipeline.* Submitted to Commonwealth Cultural Resources Group, Jackson, Michigan. Report on file with the Office of the State Archaeologist, Lansing, Michigan.

2001 Archaeological Site Burial: A Model for Site Formation within Middle-to-Late Holocene Alluvial Settings of the Great Lakes and Mid-Atlantic Regions, USA. Geological Society of America. *Programs with Abstracts.*

Monaghan, G. W., and G. J. Larson

1986 Drift Stratigraphy of the Saginaw Lobe, South-Central Michigan. *Geological Society of America Bulletin* 97:329–334.

Monaghan, G. W., G. J. Larson, and G. D. Gephart

1986 Late Wisconsinan Drift Stratigraphy of the Lake Michigan Lobe in Southwestern Michigan. *Geological Society of America Bulletin* 97:329–334.

Monaghan, G. W., W. A. Lovis, and L. Fay

1986 The Nipissing Transgression in the Thumb Area of Michigan. *Canadian Journal of Earth Sciences* 23:1851–1854.

Monaghan, G. W., and R. Schaetzl

1994 The Geology and Depositional History of the Bear Creek Site. In *1991 Great Lakes Gas Transmission Limited Partnership Pipeline Expansion Projects: Phase III Investigations at the Shiawassee River (20SA1033) and Bear Creek Sites (20SA1043), Saginaw County, Michigan,* edited by M. C. Branstner and M. J. Hambacher, pp. 5–33. Report No. 93-01. Great Lakes Research Associates, Williamston, Michigan. Report on file with the Office of the State Archaeologist, Lansing, Michigan.

Montet-White, A.

1968 *The Lithic Industries of the Illinois Valley in the Early and Middle Woodland Period.* Anthropological Papers No. 35. Museum of Anthropology, University of Michigan, Ann Arbor.

Morner, N-A., and A. Dreimanis

1973 The Erie Interstade. In *The Wisconsinan Stage,* edited by R. F. Black, R. P. Goldthwait, and H. B. Willman, pp. 107–134. Memoir 136. Geological Society of America, Washington, D.C.

Mueller, J.
1980   *Phase II Completion Report for Conference on Michigan Archaeology: Major Problem Orientations in Michigan Archaeology 1980–1984.* Report No. R-2134. Prepared for the Conference on Michigan Archaeology. Commonwealth Associates, Jackson, Michigan. Report on file with the Office of the State Archaeologist, Lansing, Michigan.

Muller, E. H., and V. K. Prest
1985   Glacial Lakes in the Ontario Basin, In *Quaternary Evolution of the Great Lakes,* edited by P. F. Karrow and P. E. Calkin, pp. 213-229. Special Paper 30. Geological Society of Canada, St. John's, Newfoundland.

O'Shea, J.
1988   Social Organization and Mortuary Behavior in the Late Woodland Period in Michigan. In *Interpretations of Culture Change in the Eastern Woodlands during the Late Woodland Period,* edited by R. Yerkes, pp. 68–85. Occasional Papers in Anthropology No. 3. Department of Anthropology, Ohio State University, Columbus.
2003   Inland Foragers and the Adoption of Maize Agriculture in the Upper Great Lakes of North America. *Before Farming* 1(3):1–21.

O'Shea, J., and M. Shott (editors)
1990   *The Bridgeport Township Site, Archaeological Investigation at 20SA620, Saginaw County, Michigan.* Anthropological Papers No. 81. Museum of Anthropology, University of Michigan, Ann Arbor.

Ozker, D. B.
1982   *An Early Woodland Community at the Schultz Site 20SA2 in the Saginaw Valley and the Nature of the Early Woodland Adaptation in the Great Lakes Region.* Anthropological Papers No. 70. Museum of Anthropology, University of Michigan, Ann Arbor.

Papworth, M. L.
1967   Cultural Traditions in the Lake Forest Region during the Late High-Water Stages of the Post-Glacial Great Lakes. Ph.D. dissertation, University of Michigan, Ann Arbor. University Microfilms, Ann Arbor.
N.D.   The Vogelaar Site, 20-SA-1033. Manuscript on file, Museum of Anthropology, University of Michigan, Ann Arbor.

Parachini, K. E.
1984   Botanical Remains from the Eidson Site. In *Archaeological Investigations in the Lower St. Joseph River Valley, Berrien County, Michigan,* edited by E. Garland, pp. 757–794. Submitted to Michigan Department of Transportation, Michigan Department of State, and United States Department of Transportation. Western Michigan University, Kalamazoo.

Parker, K. E.
1993   Plant Remains from 20SA1034. In *20SA1034: A Late Prehistoric Site on the Flint River in the Saginaw Valley, Michigan,* edited by C. A. Dobbs, C. Johnson, K. E. Parker, and T. Martin, pp. 137–180. Reports of Investigations No. 229. Institute for Minnesota Archaeology, Minneapolis.
1996   Three Corn Kernels and a Hill of Beans: The Evidence for Prehistoric Horticulture in Michigan. In *Investigating the Archaeological Record of the Great Lakes State: Essays in Honor of Elizabeth Baldwin Garland,* edited by M. Holman, J. Brashler, and K. E. Parker, pp. 307–340. New Issues Press. Kalamazoo, Michigan.

Payne, J. H.

    1995   *Archaeological Testing of a Proposed Ameritech Utility Trench at the Northwest Corner of M-29 and Sass Road, Macomb Co, Michigan.* Report No. R-950187. Commonwealth Cultural Resources Group, Jackson, Michigan. Report on file with the Office of the State Archaeologist, Lansing, Michigan.

Peebles, C. S.

    1978   Of Archaeology and Archaeologists in Saginaw County, Michigan. *Michigan Archaeologist* 24:83–129.

Peske, G. R.

    1963   Argillite of Michigan: A Preliminary Projectile Point Classification and Temporal Placement. *Papers of the Michigan Academy of Science, Arts, and Letters* 48:557–566.

Pleger, T. C.

    2000   Old Copper and Red Ocher Social Complexity. *Midcontinental Journal of Archaeology* 25(2):169–190.

Prahl, E. J.

    1970   The Middle Woodland Period of the Lower Muskegon River Valley and the Northern Hopewellian Frontier. Ph.D. dissertation, University of Michigan, Ann Arbor. University Microfilms, Ann Arbor.

    1987a   *A Phase I Archaeological Survey of a Boat Launching Ramp and Parking Area in Section 21 of Tittabawassee Township (T13N-R3E), Saginaw Co, Michigan.* Commonwealth Cultural Resources Group, Jackson, Michigan. Report on file with the Office of the State Archaeologist, Lansing, Michigan.

    1987b   *Archaeological Field Investigations to Determine the Original Bank of the Saginaw River, An Addendum to: Preliminary Land Use History, Fletcher Property, Bay City, Michigan, Section 21 T14N, R5E.* Report on file with the Office of the State Archaeologist.

    1991   The Mounds of the Muskegon. *Michigan Archaeologist* 37:59–125.

Quimby, G. I.

    1958   Fluted Points and Geochronology of the Lake Michigan Basin. *American Antiquity* 23:247–254.

    1960   *Indian Life in the Upper Great Lakes.* University of Chicago Press, Chicago.

    1963   A New Look at Geochronology in the Upper Great Lakes Region. *American Antiquity* 28:558–559.

    1966   The Dumaw Creek Site: A Seventeenth Century Prehistoric Indian Village and Cemetery in Oceana County, Michigan. *Fieldiana: Anthropology* 56(1).

Raber, P., and F. J. Vento

    1990   The Evidence for Buried Paleosols and Archaeological Sites in the Upper and Central Susquehanna and Juniata Drainage Basins. In *Genetic Stratigraphy, Paleosol Development and the Burial of Archaeological Sites in the Susquehanna, Delaware, and Upper Ohio Drainage Basins, Pennsylvania,* edited by F. J Vento and P. Raber, pp. 30–100. On file in Grants Office, William Penn Museum and Historical Commission, Bureau of Historical Preservation, Harrisburg, Pennsylvania.

Rapp, G., and J. Gifford (editors)

    1985   *Archaeological Geology.* Yale University Press, New Haven, Connecticut.

Richner, J. J.

    1973   Depositional History and Tool Industries at the Winter Site: A Lake Forest

Middle Woodland Cultural Adaptation. Unpublished Master's thesis, Department of Anthropology, Western Michigan University, Kalamazoo.

Robertson, J. A.
1987   Inter-assemblage Variability and Hunter-Gatherer Settlement Systems: A Perspective from the Saginaw Valley of Michigan. Unpublished Ph.D. dissertation, Department of Anthropology, Michigan State University, East Lansing.

Robertson, J. A., W. A. Lovis, and J. Halsey
1999   The Late Archaic: Hunters-Gatherers in an Uncertain Environment. In *Retrieving Michigan's Buried Past: The Archaeology of the Great Lakes State*, edited by J. Halsey, pp. 95–124. Bulletin 64. Cranbrook Institute of Science, Bloomfield Hills, Michigan.

Robertson, J. A., and G. W. Monaghan
1994   *Geomorphology at the St. Clair River Crossing for the Proposed ANR Link to the Intercoastal Pipeline, Columbus and St. Clair Townships, St. Clair Co, Michigan.* Report No. R-0171. Commonwealth Cultural Resources Group, Jackson, Michigan. Report on file with the Office of the State Archaeologist, Lansing, Michigan.

Robertson, J. A., K. C. Taylor, M. J. Hambacher, W. A. Lovis, and G. W. Monaghan
2000   *Overview Study of Archaeological and Cultural Values on Shiawassee, Michigan Islands, and Wyandotte National Wildlife Refuges in Saginaw, Charlevoix, Alpena, and Wayne Counties, Michigan.* 2 Vols. Report No. R-0309. Commonwealth Cultural Resources Group, Jackson. Report on file with the Office of the State Archaeologist, Lansing, Michigan.

Robinson, G. G., G. W. Monaghan, and M. L. Jeakle
1993   *Phase I Archaeological Survey, Deep Site Testing and Limited Phase II Testing of the Proposed Karn Plant Pipeline, Frankenlust Township, Bay County, Michigan.* Report No. R-0139. Commonwealth Cultural Resources Group, Jackson, Michigan. Report on file with the Office of the State Archaeologist, Lansing, Michigan.

Roper, D. C., J. Schuldenrein, D. R. Hayes, and D. J. Weir
1984   *Phase I Archaeological Investigation and Deep Site Testing along M-45, Ottawa Co, Michigan.* Report No. R-2588. Commonwealth Cultural Resources Group, Jackson, Michigan. Report on file with the Office of the State Archaeologist, Lansing, Michigan.

Ruggles, D. L.
2001   Mobility, Style, and Exchange among Upper Great Lakes PaleoIndians. Unpublished Ph.D. dissertation, Department of Anthropology, Michigan State University, East Lansing.

Saarnisto, M.
1975   Stratigraphic Studies on the Shoreline Displacement of Lake Superior. *Canadian Journal of Earth Sciences* 12:300–319.

Salzer, R. J.
1974   The Wisconsin North Lakes Project. In *Aspects of Upper Great Lakes Anthropology: Essays in Honor of Lloyd A. Wilford*, edited by E. Johnson, pp. 40–54. Minnesota Historical Society, St. Paul.

Sauer, N. J., and S. Dunlap
1979   *The Human Skeletal Material from the Paint Creek Site, Evidence for Spatial and Temporal Continuity of the Treatment of the Dead in the Lower Great Lakes*

Area. Report submitted to Oakland University. On file at the Department of Anthropology, Michigan State University, East Lansing.

Schneider, A. F., and M. Reshkin
1970   Age and Correlation of the Glenwood Stage of Glacial Lake Chicago. *Geological Society of America Abstracts with Programs* 2(6):404.

Schuldenrein, J.
1991   Coring and the Identity of Cultural Resources Environments. *American Antiquity* 56:131–137.

Schurr, M. R.
1997   Using the Concept of the Learning Curve to Increase the Productivity of Geophysical Surveys. *Archaeological Prospection* 4:69-83.

Sellinger, C. E.
1999   Discussion. In *Proceeding of the Great Lakes Paleo-Levels Workshop: The Last 4000 Years,* edited by C. E. Sellinger and F. H. Quinn, pp. 35–42. Technical Memorandum ERL GLERL-113. NOAA, Ann Arbor, Michigan.

Sellinger, C. E., and F. H. Quinn (editors)
1999   *Proceeding of the Great Lakes Paleo-Levels Workshop: The Last 4000 Years.* Technical Memorandum ERL GLERL-113. NOAA, Ann Arbor, Michigan.

Shannon, G. W.
1982   *An Archaeological Survey of the United States Naval/Marine Reserve Center in Saginaw, Michigan.* Archaeological Survey Report No. 54. Michigan State University Museum, Michigan State University, East Lansing. Report on file with the Office of the State Archaeologist, Lansing, Michigan.

Shoshani, J., H. Wright, and A. Pilling
1990   Ecological Context of Two Early Archaic Projectile Points from Michigan: A LeCroy and a Kessell Point Recovered at 20OK394. *Michigan Archaeologist* 36:1–20.

Shott, M. J.
1986   Settlement Mobility and Technological Organization among Great Lakes Paleo-Indian Foragers. Unpublished Ph.D. dissertation, Department of Anthropology, University of Michigan, Ann Arbor.
1993   *The Leavitt Site: A Parkhill Phase Paleo-Indian Occupation in Central Michigan.* Memoir No. 25. Museum of Anthropology, University of Michigan, Ann Arbor.
1999   The Early Archaic: Life after the Glaciers. In *Retrieving Michigan's Buried Past: The Archaeology of the Great Lakes State,* edited by J. Halsey, pp. 71–82. Bulletin 64. Cranbrook Institute of Science, Bloomfield Hills, Michigan.

Shott, M., and P. Welsh
1984   Archaeological Resources of the Thumb Area. *Michigan Archaeologist* 30:1–80.

Shott, M., and H. Wright
1999   The Paleo-Indians: Michigan's First People. In *Retrieving Michigan's Buried Past: The Archaeology of the Great Lakes State,* edited by J. Halsey, pp. 59–70. Bulletin 64. Cranbrook Institute of Science, Bloomfield Hills, Michigan.

Simons, D. B.
1972   Radiocarbon Date from a Satchell-type Site. *Michigan Archaeologist* 18:209–213.

1979 New Data on the Satchell Complex from the Pinegrove Cemetery Site (20-GS-28) in Genesee County, Michigan. Paper presented at the Eastern States Archaeological Federation meetings, Ann Arbor, Michigan.

1989 Michigan Meadowood/Pomranky Phase Lithic Types from Mortuary and Habitation Contexts. Paper presented at the 1989 Ontario Archaeological Society Annual Conference, London, Ontario.

Simons, D. B., M. Shott, and H. Wright
1984 The Gainey Site: Variability in a Great Lakes Paleo-Indian Assemblage. In *New Experiments Upon the Record of Eastern Paleo-Indian Cultures: Archaeology of Eastern North America,* edited by R. Gramly, 12:266–279.

Sly, P. G., and C. F. M. Lewis
1972 *The Great Lakes of Canada-Quaternary Geology and Limnology.* Guidebook for Field Excursions A43. Twenty-fourth International Geological Congress, Montreal.

Smith, B. A.
1990 Systems of Subsistence and Networks of Exchange in the Terminal Woodland and Early Historic Periods in the Upper Great Lakes. Ph.D. dissertation, Michigan State University, East Lansing. University Microfilms International, Ann Arbor.

1994 Faunal Remains (20SA1033). In *1991 Great Lakes Gas Transmission Limited Partnership Pipeline Expansion Projects: Phase III Investigations at the Shiawassee River (20SA1033) and Bear Creek Sites (20SA1043), Saginaw County, Michigan,* edited by M. C. Branstner and M. J. Hambacher, pp. 103–111. Report No. 93-01. Submitted to Great Lakes Gas Transmission Company, Detroit, and Natural Resources Group, Minneapolis. Great Lakes Research Associates, Williamston. Report on file with the Office of the State Archaeologist, Lansing, Michigan.

1996 Systems of Subsistence and Networks of Exchange in the Terminal Woodland and Early Historic Periods in the Upper Great Lakes. Ph.D. dissertation, Department of Anthropology, Michigan State University, East Lansing. University Microfilms International, Ann Arbor.

2004 The Gill Net's "Native Country": The Inland Shore Fishery in the Northern Lake Michigan Basin. In *An Upper Great Lakes Archaeological Odyssey: Essays in Honor of Charles E. Cleland,* edited by W. Lovis, pp. 64–84. Cranbrook Institute of Science, Bloomfield Hills, Michigan.

Spence, M. W., R. H. Pihl, and C. R. Murphy
1990 Cultural Complexes of the Early and Middle Woodland Periods. In *The Archaeology of Southern Ontario to A.D. 1650,* edited by C. J. Ellis and N. Ferris, pp. 125–169. Occasional Publications No. 5. London Chapter, Ontario Archaeological Society, London, Ontario.

Spencer, J. W.
1888 The St. Lawrence Basin and the Great Lakes. *Science* 11:99–100.

1891 High Level Shores in the Region of the Great Lakes, and Their Deformation. *American Journal of Science* 41:201–211.

Speth, J. D.
1972 Geology of the Schultz Site. In *The Schultz Site at Green Point: A Stratified Occupation Area in the Saginaw Valley of Michigan,* edited by J. E. Fitting, pp. 53–75. Memoir No. 4. Museum of Anthropology, University of Michigan, Ann Arbor.

References

Stanley, G. M.

1936   Lower Algonquin Beaches of Penetanguishene Peninsula. *Geological Society of America Bulletin* 47:1933–1960.

Stein, J. K.

1986   Coring Archaeological Sites. *American Antiquity* 51:505-527.

1991   Coring in CRM and Archaeology: A Reminder. *American Antiquity* 56:138– 142.

Stothers, D., and T. Abel

1993   Archaeological Reflections of the Late Archaic and Early Woodland Time Periods in the Western Lake Erie Region. *Archaeology of Eastern North America* 21:25–109.

Stothers, D., J. Graves, and S. Conway

1983   The Weiser Site: A Sandusky Village in Transition. *Michigan Archaeologist* 29(4):59–90.

Stothers, D., D. Pratt, and O. Shane

1979   The Western Basin Middle Woodland: Non-Hopewellians in a Hopewellian World. In *Hopewell Archaeology: The Chillicothe Conference,* edited by D. Brose and N. Greber, pp. 47–58. Kent State University Press, Kent, Ohio.

Taggart, D. W.

1967   Seasonal Patterns in Settlement, Subsistence and Industries in the Saginaw Late Archaic. *Michigan Archaeologist* 13:153–170.

Tanner, H.

1986   *Atlas of Great Lakes Indian History.* University of Oklahoma Press, Norman.

Taylor, F. B.

1894   A Reconnaissance of the Abandoned Shorelines of the South Coast of Lake Superior. *American Geologist* 13:365–383.

1897   The Nipissing-Mattawa River, the Outlet of the Nipissing Great Lakes. *American Geologist* 16:65–66.

Taylor, K. C., C. S. Demeter, and D. J. Weir

1992   *Phase II Archaeological Testing at the Emerson, Fitzhugh, Salt/Fraser and Webber CSO Facilities, City of Saginaw, Saginaw Co, Michigan.* Report No. R-0095. Commonwealth Cultural Resources Group, Jackson, Michigan. Report on file with the Office of the State Archaeologist, Lansing, Michigan.

Thompson T. A.

1992   Beach-Ridge Development and Lake-Level Variation in Southern Lake Michigan. *Sedimentary Geology* 80:305–318.

Thompson, T. A., and S. J. Baedke

1995   Beach-ridge Development in Lake Michigan: Shoreline Behavior in Response to Quasi-Periodic Lake-Level Events. *Marine Geology* 129:163–174.

1997   Strandplain Evidence for Late Holocene Lake-Level Variations in Lake Michigan. *Geological Society of America Bulletin* 109:666–682.

1999   Strandplain Evidence for Reconstructing Late Holocene Lake Level in the Lake Michigan Basin. In *Proceeding of the Great Lakes Paleo-Levels Workshop: The Last 4000 Years,* edited by C. E. Sellinger and F. H. Quinn, pp. 30–34. Technical Memorandum ERL GLERL-113. NOAA, Ann Arbor, Michigan.

Vento, F. J., and P. Raber (editors)

1990   *Genetic Stratigraphy, Paleosol Development and the Burial of Archaeological Sites in the Susquehanna, Delaware, and Upper Ohio Drainage Basins, Pennsylvania.*

On file with to Grants Office, William Penn Museum and Historical Commission, Bureau of Historical Preservation, Harrisburg, Pennsylvania.

Voss, J. A.
1977   The Barnes Site: Functional and Stylistic Variability in a Small Paleo Indian Assemblage. *Midcontinental Journal of Archaeology* 2:253–306.

Walcott, R. I.
1970   Isostatic Response to Loading of the Crust in Canada. *Canadian Journal of Earth Sciences* 7:716–727.

Weikel, K. M.
1985   *Cultural Resource Survey of the Shiawassee Flats Levee Project (Flint and Cass Rivers), in Saginaw Co, Michigan*. Report No. R-1558. Commonwealth Cultural Resources Group, Jackson, Michigan. Report on file with the Office of the State Archaeologist, Lansing, Michigan.

Weir, D. J.
1981   *A Cultural Resource Inventory—St. Vincent to St. Clair Gas and Sault Lateral Pipelines—Minnesota, Wisconsin and Michigan*. Submitted to Great Lakes Gas Transmission Company, Detroit. Commonwealth Associates, Jackson. Report on file with the Office of the State Archaeologist, Lansing, Michigan.

Weir, D. J., C. S. Demeter, J. R. Kern, W. E. Rutter, J. Schuldenrein
1983   *Archaeological and Geoarchaeological Phase II Evaluation for the I-94 Blue Water Bridge Plaza Revision*. Report No. R-2542. Commonwealth Cultural Resources Group, Jackson, Michigan. Report on file with the Office of the State Archaeologist, Lansing, Michigan.

Weir, D. J., J. Schuldenrein, and C. E. Cantley
1984   *Phase I Archaeological and Geoarchaeological Site Location Survey for the M-49 Bridge Replacement Project, Camden, Michigan*. Report No. R-2674. Commonwealth Cultural Resources Group, Jackson, Michigan. Report on file with the Office of the State Archaeologist, Lansing, Michigan.

Weir, D. J., J. Schuldenrein, G. W. Lantz, and C. A. Pierce
1992   *Stage I Archaeological Investigations for the Empire State Pipeline Project, New York State*. Submitted to ANR Pipeline Company. Commonwealth Cultural Resources Group, Jackson, Michigan. Report on file with the Office of the State Archaeologist, Lansing, Michigan.

Weir, D. J., J. Schuldenrein, C. A. Pierce, and B. K. Miller
1994   *Stage I Archaeological Investigations for the Empire State Pipeline Project, New York State*. Submitted to ANR Pipeline Company. Commonwealth Cultural Resources Group, Jackson, Michigan.

Wobst, H. M.
1968   The Butterfield Site, 20BY29, Bay County, Michigan. In *Contributions to Michigan Archaeology*, by J. E. Fitting, J. R. Halsey, and H. M. Wobst, pp. 173–275. Anthropological Papers No. 32. Museum of Anthropology, University of Michigan, Ann Arbor.

Workman, L. E.
1925   A Pleistocene Section in the Vicinity of the Thorton Reef. Master's thesis, Department of Geology, University of Chicago, Chicago.

Wright, G. A.
1972   Historic Flooding in the Saginaw Basin. In *The Schultz Site at Green Point: A*

Stratified Occupation Area in the Saginaw Valley of Michigan, edited by J. E. Fitting, pp. 43–52. Memoir No. 4. Museum of Anthropology, University of Michigan, Ann Arbor.

Wright G. F.
    1918   Explanation of the Abandoned Beaches about the South End of Lake Michigan. *Geological Society of America Bulletin* 29:235–244.

Wright, H. T.
    1964   A Transitional Archaic Campsite at Green Point (20SA1). *Michigan Archaeologist* 10:17–22.

Wright, H. T., and R. E. Morlan
    1964   The Hart Site: A Dustin Complex Fishing Camp on the Shiawassee Embayment. *Michigan Archaeologist* 10:49-53.

Wright, H. T., and W. B. Roosa
    1966   The Barnes Site: A Fluted Point Assemblage from the Great Lakes Region. *American Antiquity* 31:850–860.

Wynn, J. C.
    1986   Review of Geophysical Methods Used in Archaeology. *Geoarchaeology* 1:245–257.

Zurel, R.
    1999   Earthwork Enclosure Sites in Michigan. In *Retrieving Michigan's Buried Past: The Archaeology of the Great Lakes State,* edited by J. Halsey, pp. 244–248. Bulletin 64. Cranbrook Institute of Science, Bloomfield Hills, Michigan.

Index

Algoma beach, 59

Alluviation: and archaeological site burial, 11, 12–13, 14, 48, 101–2, 145, 150, 151, 157, 160–62, 166, 168, 199–200, 217, 219; and changes in surrounding uplands, 156, 158; climate effects on, 60, 103, 151, 152–55, 156, 158, 160, 161, 218–19; cyclical pattern of, 50, 151, 157–58, 160, 166, 167, 218–19; flooding and, 44, 54, 59–60, 64, 117, 158, 160–62, 164, 165, 166; and human settlement patterns, 13, 52, 150, 157, 158, 162; lake-level effects on, 13, 44–45, 47, 48, 50, 64, 155–56, 218; and land-use practices, 8, 48, 51, 52, 68; modern, 50, 68; regional pattern of, 157, 158; and soil formation, 13, 149, 150

Andrews site, 71, 76, 77, 78

Archaeological Site Potential Framework: applications of, 194–95, 199, 223; data collection and construction of, 173–74, 175–76, 177–81, 182–83, 189–96, 199–200, 223; goals of study, 175, 196, 199, 222; project study area, 174–75

Archaeological sites: Archaic Period, 8, 12, 52, 54, 58, 73–78, 121, 159, 166–67, 200, 217; burial mechanisms, 101; climate and burial of, 151, 168, 221; cyclical burial of, 166, 167; drainage patterns and location of, 83, 199–200; Early Woodland period, 77, 79–80, 159, 167; eolian deposition and burial of, 11, 12, 97, 100, 144–45, 217; ephemeral occupational horizons at, 165, 166; erosion of, 218; fishing base camps, 73, 90; flooding and burial of, 48, 51, 54, 144, 146, 164, 165, 166, 168, 220; glacial deposition and burial of, 11–12, 101; hunting camps, 73, 86; Initial Woodland period, 81–83; lake-level regression and burial of, 102; lake-level transgression and burial of, 7, 11–12, 13, 48, 51, 52, 54, 85, 100, 101, 102, 217; Late Woodland period, 8, 9, 87, 88, 89, 97–98, 110, 117; logistic procurement sites, 77; methods of locating, 203–8; Mid-Atlantic states, 150; "midden-like" sites, 162, 163, 164, 165, 166; Middle Woodland period, 77, 82–85, 97, 110; mobile/transient camps, 77; mortuary, 73,

77, 80, 83, 88; New York, 150; Paleo-Indian period, 70–72, 100, 101; repeat occupation of, 12, 73, 82, 83, 84, 88, 101, 150, 159, 163, 220; residential camps, 74, 77, 80, 83; ritual, 81, 86; Saginaw Bay region, 8, 13, 45, 58, 76–77, 84, 85, 100, 103; seasonal occupation of, 75, 76, 79, 81, 82, 85–86, 88, 89, 92, 119, 125–26, 127, 141; sediment types and prediction of, 146; settlement patterns and burial of, 9, 12, 151, 152, 163; shoreline processes and burial of, 101, 102, 144–45; stream alluviation and burial of, 11, 12–13, 14, 48, 101–2, 145, 150, 151, 157, 160–62, 166, 168, 197–98, 217, 219; transient, 77; types, 77; in urban environments, 97–98, 144–45; weathering of surfaces and burial of, 150, 151, 152, 162; Wisconsinan Period, 8. *See also:* Andrews site; Arrowhead Drive site; Arthurburg Hill site; Barnes site; Bear Creek site; Bergquist site; Birch Run Road site; Brandt site; Bridgeport Township site; Burnt Bluff Caves; Bussinger site; Campau House; Carrigan Mound, Casassa site; Center for Environmental Research Training site; Columbus Beach; Conservation Park site; Converse site; Croton Dam Mounds; Dehmel Road Bridge Replacement site; Dumaw Creek site; Ebenhoff Dune site; Eidson site; Ekdahl-Goodreau site; Elam site; Feeheley site; Fletcher site; Flint River site; Fort Brady site; Fort Michilimackinac site; Fort Wayne Mound; Gainey site; Green Point site; Gyftakis site; Hi-Lo site; Hodges site; Holcombe site; Johnson site; Juntunen site; Kantzler site; Kawkawlin River site; L'Arbre Croche/Portage site; Leach site; Leavitt site; Liberty Bridge Replacement Project site; Little Cedar River site MacGregor site; Marquette Viaduct; McNeal site; Moccasin Bluff site; Mushroom site; Naomikong Point site; Naugle site; Nelson site; O'Neil site; Pomranky site; Portage site; Prison Farm site; Riverside site; Riverside II site; Riviere au Vase site; Rock Hearth site; Sack Bay site; Samel's Field

Index

base, 74, 76; small point, 76; square, 79; stemmed, 73, 76, 77, 80; straight stemmed, 119; Thebes cluster, 135; triangular point, 123; Vogelaar site, 131; Zemaitis site, 141, 142

Radial mobility, model of, 78, 80, 84
Raisin River, 175
Resource-based locational model, 82
Reindle site, 71, 79
Rifle River, 14, 175
Riverside site, 30, 71, 73
Riverside II site, 71, 79
Riviere au Vase site, 71, 93
Riviere ware, 139, 140
Rock Hearth site, 71, 75, 79
Rose Hill Spit, 33
Rouge River, 175

Sack Bay site, 71, 73
Saginaw Bay region: archaeological significance of, 47, 104; archaeological sites in, 8, 13, 45, 58, 76–77, 84, 85, 100, 103; alluvial history of, 8, 45, 47, 50–54, 56, 59, 62–63, 64, 66; downcutting in, 51, 52, 53, 54, 62, 63, 66; flooding in, 164, 165; Nipissing transgression in, 50, 54–58, 181; premodern high phase, 67; premodern low phase, 66; settlement patterns in, 79, 90–92, 182; subsistence patterns in, 77, 91, 92; wetlands in, 55, 77, 181
Saginaw Formation, 15
Saginaw Ice Lobe, 17, 21, 26, 29, 31, 34, 216
Saginaw River, 50, 55, 56, 65, 104, 105, 107, 175
Saginaw Thin ceramics, 90, 91
St. Clair River, 19, 21, 25, 35, 36, 37, 216
St. Joseph River, 50, 63, 75, 79, 83, 175
St. Mary's River, 18, 21, 38, 39, 40
Samel's Field site, 71–72
Satchell Complex, 71, 72, 76
Sawdust Pile site, 71, 82
Schultz site: agriculture at, 91; alluviation at, 65, 215; archaeological significance of, 51, 106–7; artifacts at, 80; earthworks at, 85; flooding at, 48, 65, 110, 159, 163, 164, 165; location and background of, 46, 71, 98, 103–4; maize at, 91; midden at, 165; and Nipissing transgression, 159; and post-Algoma high, 65; and post-Algoma low, 64; repeat occupation of, 84; settlement patterns at, 84, 92, 137, 167; similarities to Bear Creek, Ebenhoff, and Zemaitis sites, 63, 137, 144; stratification of, 84, 90, 159; stratigraphy of, 63, 85, 104–6; as Woodland period site, 79, 84, 137
Schwerdt site, 71, 90
Screaming Loon site, 71, 74

Sedimentation, shoreline. See: Shoreline processes
Settlement patterns, human: and alluviation, 13, 48, 52, 150, 157, 158, 162; and archaeological site burial, 9, 151, 152, 163; and carbonate bedrock formations, 16; Chippewa model for, 82; and climate, 149, 152, 168, 219, 221–22; and flooding, 159, 164; and horticulture, 222; and lake level variation, 51, 73, 74, 75; models for, 82; repeated site use, 12, 159, 163; resource-based model for, 82
Sheguiandah phase (Lake Algonquin), 21, 38
Shiawassee Embayment, 52, 55, 56
Shiawassee Flats, 13, 45, 56, 59, 62, 64, 68, 104, 132
Shiawassee lowland, 81
Shiawassee River: alluvial history of, 45, 52, 53, 59, 63, 66, 67, 120, 121, 127; and Bear Creek, 53, 54, 66, 67, 120, 121, 127, 226; channel migration at, 66, 67, 127, 226; discharge outlets, 53, 56, 59, 175; downcutting at, 52, 53, 63; erosion-resistant bed at, 63; and Nipissing transgression, 56
Shiawassee River site: alluviation at, 67, 215; artifacts at, 117, 118, 119–20; location and background, 46, 56, 57, 98, 117–18; settlement patterns at, 118–19, 137; shallow burial of, 3; significance of, 118–20; stratigraphy of, 118, 141, 144; subsistence patterns at, 120
Shoreline processes: and archaeological site burial, 101, 102, 144–45, 217; effect of lake level fluctuations on, 102; types of, 11, 12, 102, 217
Simcoe delta, 30
Sissung site, 93
Skegemog Point site, 71, 89
Soil formation: and alluviation, 13, 149, 150, 162; climate effects on, 149, 150, 152, 162; cyclical pattern of, 14; and flooding, 156, 162, 166, 168
Spider Shelter site, 71, 81
Split-spoon sampling, 204, 205
Squirrel River, 70
Stoney Creek dolomite, 80
Storm deposits, 12, 102, 217
Stover site, 71, 75, 79
Stratigraphy: Bear Creek site, 124–26, 127; CERT site, 108–10; Ebenhoff site, 132–35; Flint River site, 138–39; Green Point site, 104–6; Marquette Viaduct site, 109; as record of site environmental and settlement history, 13, 150, 162; Schultz site, 63, 104–6; Shiawassee River site, 118; Vogelaar site, 128–30; Weber I site, 114–16
Sturgis morainal system, 16
Summer Island site, 71, 81